The POWER *of*
PITTSBURGH

URBAN
TAPESTRY
SERIES

TOWERY
PUBLISHING, INC

PHOTOGRAPHY EDITING BY TOM BELL ■ PROFILES IN EXCELLENCE BY JIM URBAN ■ CAPTIONS BY ABBY MENDELSON

The POWER of
PITTSBURGH

Art Direction by Brian Groppe ■ Sponsored by the Greater Pittsburgh Chamber of Commerce

LIBRARY OF CONGRESS CATALOGING-IN-PUBLICATION-DATA

The Power of Pittsburgh / photography editing by Tom Bell ; profiles
   in excellence by Jim Urban ; captions by Abby Mendelson.
      p. cm.
   Includes index.
   ISBN 1-881096-11-4 (alk. paper)
   1. Pittsburgh (Pa.)—Economic conditions—Pictorial works.
   2. Pittsburgh (Pa.)—Social conditions—Pictorial works..
   3. Industries—Pennsylvania—Pittsburgh—Pictorial works.   I. Bell,
   Thomas Kenneth, 1950-   . II. Urban, James Stephen, 1965-   .
   HC108.P7P75   1998
   330.9748'11043—dc21   98-12633
                                                  CIP

PUBLISHER: J. Robert Towery
EXECUTIVE PUBLISHER: Jenny McDowell
NATIONAL SALES MANAGER: Stephen Hung
MARKETING DIRECTOR: Carol Culpepper
PROJECT DIRECTORS: Aphrodite Corsi, Dawn Park-Donegan, Jim Tomlinson

EXECUTIVE EDITOR: David B. Dawson
MANAGING EDITOR: Michael C. James
SENIOR EDITORS: Lynn Conlee, Carlisle Hacker
EDITORS/PROJECT MANAGERS: Lori Bond, Jana Files
STAFF EDITORS: Mary Jane Adams, Susan Hesson, Brian Johnston
ASSISTANT EDITORS: Pat McRaven, Jennifer C. Pyron, Allison Ring
EDITORIAL CONTRIBUTORS: Cynthia Bent, Gretchen McKay, Jim Strader, Lydia Strohl
EDITORIAL CONSULTANT: Prentiss Orr

PROFILE DESIGNERS: Laurie Beck, Kelley Pratt, Ann Ward
DIGITAL COLOR SUPERVISOR: Brenda Pattat
DIGITAL COLOR TECHNICIANS: Jack Griffith, Darin Ipema, Jason Moak
PRODUCTION RESOURCES MANAGER: Dave Dunlap Jr.
PRODUCTION ASSISTANTS: Geoffrey Ellis, Enrique Espinosa, Robin McGehee
PRINT COORDINATORS: Tonda Thomas, Beverly Timmons

BY DENNIS YABLONSKY
President and CEO
Carnegie Group

THE EYES OF THE WORLD ARE FOCUSED ON PITTSBURGH AS A model for how an economy can make a successful transition from a manufacturing base to a technology powerhouse. The story is dramatic: A region that once produced as much as one-third of the primary metals in the world collapsed in the 1980s,

thrusting 157,000 residents into the unemployment lines. Just over a decade later, the Pittsburgh region is becoming a world-class center for software development, telecommunications, biomedical technology, environmental technology, robotics, and advanced manufacturing. In 1988, high-technology companies represented 3 percent of the firms in the area; today, that figure is 9 percent.

If you find that hard to believe, it's because Pittsburgh's image is still a bit rusty. But the compelling facts shine through. More than 3,600 high-technology businesses in the region employ 100,000 people, for a combined annual payroll of $4.25 billion. And in 1997, Pittsburgh ranked fifth in the nation in the employment of computer software professionals.

The information technology sector alone employs more than 25,000 people in more than 450 different firms, with a growing concentration of companies in the areas of the Internet, electronic commerce, data warehousing, and data mining.

The Pittsburgh area is home to nearly 850 firms directly or indirectly involved in environmental technologies.

Biomedical research and advanced technology in the area encompass more than 25,000 scientists, 170 research facilities, and 700 companies.

Pittsburgh still has a solid manufacturing base, which now includes 4,100 manufacturing firms that use advanced processes and new technology to provide diversified products to markets around the world.

The region's environmental products and services sector has a long history of aggressively tackling regional environmental challenges. There's a tremendous demand to reclaim and clean up

industrial sites right in our own backyard, which creates high interest locally in developing new solutions.

Pittsburgh is one of the nation's major health care centers and is the world's leading center for organ transplantation. We have a rich legacy of medical breakthroughs, including the polio vaccine and synthetic insulin. There are also extensive university and hospital research facilities exploring initiatives such as cancer therapies, tissue engineering, medical imaging, and molecular biology.

Pittsburgh continues to have a vibrant manufacturing base. Many of the region's manufacturers are using advanced practices to ensure continual improvement in their processes and products. The

manufacturing base has shifted from one dominated by large, traditional companies making traditional products to many smaller firms making diversified products for niche markets.

Carnegie Group, like many of the other technology companies in the area, has its roots in the brainpower and daunting technology resources of the area's universities. The Computer Science Department, Robotics Institute, and Software Engineering Institute at Carnegie Mellon University (CMU) attract students from around the globe. CMU recently was rated one of the top three institutions for software engineering by *Business Week*.

The University of Pittsburgh has a highly ranked medical school and medical center. The

One of countless free events that mark the civic calendar year-round, the annual Fourth of July fireworks display attracts celebrants to the West End Overlook, located just down the Ohio River from the Point (PAGES 8 AND 9).

ROBERT P. RUSCHAK

The Power of

university is renowned for its biological sciences and biotechnology research programs, whose innovations give Pittsburgh the potential to be a key center of biomedical commercialization.

The university community should provide a high-quality talent pool for technology companies in the area, but employers often aren't aggressive enough to keep bright graduates from flocking to Silicon Valley and other technology hot spots that lure students by the thousands. The challenge to local employers is to make students who benefit from the academic excellence and technology leadership at our cutting-edge universities aware of the opportunities locally. It *is* possible to thrive professionally right here in Western Pennsylvania. The opportunities for graduates abound—whether they choose to follow their own entrepreneurial dreams, work for one of the numerous and fast-growing technology start-ups, or join one of the large, well-established technology mainstays of the region's economy.

The high-technology community now has a critical mass necessary to sustain continued growth. Numerous venture capital firms are helping Western Pennsylvania's entrepreneurs obtain the financing they need to meet aggressive growth goals and seize market opportunities. Some 29 initial public offerings in the past several years raised $2 billion in capital. Regional development initiatives, such as the Working Together Consortium, are defining goals and charting the progress of economic development. With a rapidly growing presence in the local economy, technology companies work to capture the attention of government decision makers at the local, state, and national levels to ensure that the economic climate can help this burgeoning industry compete globally.

The focus of the new economy is a logical evolution, not a departure, from Pittsburgh's roots. After all, it was technological innovation that led to the area's industrial base of steelmaking, inland transportation, chemical processing, and plastics fabrication. That industrial base supported a commercial and cultural infrastructure that area residents continue to enjoy today. For example, technology companies doing business in Western Pennsylvania have ready access to a host of professional service firms in the financial services, legal, accounting, and marketing areas that have expertise in solving technology business challenges.

Doing business from Pittsburgh is also easy. The Pittsburgh International Airport is the third largest in the country, making domestic and global markets readily accessible. We're within a two-hour flight of nearly 70 percent of the nation's population.

Another advantage technology firms enjoy in the area is our enviable lifestyle. A 1996 *Fortune* magazine report ranked Pittsburgh ninth nationally in terms of factors that contribute to the quality of life and work. Our rich cultural and recreational amenities and Middle America quality of life, combined with a strong work ethic, often elude more publicized technology regions. Professional sports draw fans year-round, with the Steelers, Pirates, and Penguins all playing here. Affordable, good-quality housing of every vintage and size, and short commutes abound. Area school systems, including the Pittsburgh Public Schools, have received national acclaim for innovative programs.

Technology leadership and Pittsburgh: It's an ironic, but not surprising, combination, and it's on an upward growth curve. The spirit of innovation that built the nation's infrastructure and that was the envy of the industrial revolution is still vibrant and forward-looking, right here in its Pittsburgh home. Yesterday's blast furnaces may be silenced, but there's a quiet storm brewing in hundreds of high-tech ventures that dot the Western Pennsylvania landscape and reach to the next horizon. ☞

Just as Pittsburgh changed from an 18th-century trading post to a 19th-century manufacturing colossus, so has it raced into the post-industrial age. Although steel is still made here, the landscape, once dotted with mills like U.S. Steel's Carrie Furnace (OPPOSITE), has given way to cutting-edge technologies, developed at such facilities as the Pittsburgh Technology Center (LEFT).

By Frank V. Cahouet
Chairman, President, and CEO
Mellon Bank Corp.

PITTSBURGH'S FINANCIAL COMMUNITY IS A SOURCE OF TREMENdous energy. Those who focus on finance help move hardworking individuals toward many of their goals. They generate the resources to start small businesses—and keep fueling bigger ones. They have the collective leverage

to boost the nation's economy and the ingenuity to impact the way the world does business. With experience as the engine behind the industrial revolution, the financial community of Pittsburgh is positioned for greatness in the new millennium.

This is a region that won't stand still—not when the city is home to three major financial institutions. Many big U.S. cities don't host any. But Mellon Bank Corp., PNC Bank Corp., and mutual fund giant Federated Investors are all based in Pittsburgh. And Clevelandbased National City Bank has a major presence in the Pittsburgh region. Add to this an army of other financial institutions—community banks, savings and loans, credit unions, and others—and the result is a powerfully talented and committed team that works hard to help Pittsburgh's businesses and individuals succeed.

One of the most important characteristics of the city is the Pittsburgh Regional Alliance. This organization was established to coordinate the efforts of the Greater Pittsburgh Chamber of Commerce, Penn's Southwest Association, the Regional Industrial Development Corporation, and the World Trade Center of Pittsburgh.

Formed in 1995, the Alliance provides a single point of contact for businesses that are locating, expanding, or trading in the region. Guided by a charter to develop a regional international marketing plan and retention strategy, the organization works relentlessly toward the overall goal of helping to create more jobs.

All of these organizations are part of the community that helps regenerate and build the area's economy. Almost as plentiful as the region's hills, a large number of institutions and organizations have helped empower the people of Pittsburgh during its history.

In the late 1800s and early 1900s, Pittsburgh's bankers listened carefully to individuals who often walked in off the street with little more than ambitious dreams of success and high hopes to start their small businesses. The keen judgment of bankers helped identify those who held the spark of genius that would one day provide the foundation for the Aluminum Company of America (Alcoa), Westinghouse, Gulf Oil Corp., and the Koppers Company—just a few of the industrial leaders that received early financial backing from the banks of Pittsburgh.

Local community banks have withstood the test of time with intimate service to loyal customers in the region's more than 80 distinct neighborhoods, formed in part by the area's numerous rivers and hills. Many of Pittsburgh's savings and loans are strong survivors of a difficult period for such organizations across the nation, guided by smart managers who know how to run a profitable business in a highly competitive financial community. Although undergoing their own consolidation, the region's credit unions remain abundant and durable. And the area's larger regional

banks adeptly marshal the resources necessary to operate continuously in the interest of their many stakeholders, actively participating in ongoing industrywide bank consolidation as buyers or sellers, as appropriate.

The synergy among these local institutions enables them to keep up with the changing world. To broaden their business lines and extend the distribution of their products, they will sometimes buy or borrow these capabilities from one another. They'll also respond to customers with comprehensive, custom-tailored solutions that might include asset

▲ TOM BELL

One attribute that has sustained Pittsburgh's might for more than a century is its unwavering commitment to education. Located in the city's Oakland section, the neoclassical Mellon Institute is very much a part of this rich heritage, standing as a cornerstone of much of the region's progress (PAGES 12 AND 13).

The Power of

management services, such as mutual funds, as well as leasing, benefits consulting, and insurance. In fact, some of the most notable innovators in the financial services industry today are located right here in Pittsburgh.

Even from their inception, a number of Pittsburgh's innovative financial companies have demonstrated their value as astute risk managers who are willing to invest in good ideas. As a result, they have not only supported the region's growth and added to its list of achievements, but they've also helped finance a Northeast-based industrial revolution that has elevated the United States to its current position as the economic leader of the world.

As one of the largest employers in Pittsburgh today, the financial community continues to help stimulate the region. In the tradition of our founders, local financial companies have provided billions of dollars in loans to individuals, businesses, and neighborhoods to develop property, launch new enterprises, and realize big dreams.

With products and services that are in demand beyond state and national boundaries, financial institutions draw money into the city from outside of the state. Constantly striving to find technologies that move money and financial information quickly and safely, banks and other financial institutions form a powerful force that pulls technology breakthroughs and experts into town.

But what really brings people to a community is all of what the city offers—the quality of the jobs, schools, housing, cultural attractions, and sports—the special combination of factors that say this place could be the best spot in the world for an individual or a family to lead a full life of rewarding work and great fun.

Through human and financial resources, Pittsburgh's financial community supports the arts, promotes cultural diversity, and addresses health and human service needs, with particular emphasis on low- and moderate-income areas and residents.

With its proud history and ongoing efforts, Pittsburgh's prominent financial sector is a solid source of the energy and resources required to make the most of our place on Earth. ☞

Dressed for success: Although many of the city's top corporations and law firms now favor casual Fridays, well-tailored suits are still de rigueur. Marked by vibrant, upscale shopping, the city's Golden Triangle—as well as such outlying sections as the South Side and Shadyside—are great places for fine clothing, dining, and entertainment.

By Thomas J. Usher
Chairman and CEO
USX Corporation

T HAS BEEN SAID BEFORE, BUT IT BEARS REPEATING—THERE IS SOMEthing special about Pittsburgh. ■ Why Pittsburgh? Why do we live here, work here, rear our families here? What keeps us here in our retirement years when our counterparts in other cities have long since fled to the Sun Belt? What's magical about the region? ■ Well, simply put, Pitts-

Many have called Pittsburgh the biggest small town in America (PAGES 16 AND 17). Truly, it is a city of hills and valleys and more than five dozen distinct neighborhoods, each with its own history, ethnicity, and flavor. Around every corner, there are always new places to discover and fabulous foods to eat!

burgh is a great place to live. Our cost of living, for example, makes everybody's paycheck go a lot further than in other metropolitan areas. This is one instance where we're happy we're below the national average.

Homes cost less here. One recent study showed that a $150,000 house in Pittsburgh would cost $355,000 outside New York City, $405,000 in Chicago, and $525,000 in San Francisco.

Our crime rate, too, is well below that of other large cities in the United States. In fact, Pittsburgh has been listed as the safest of the 25 most populated metropolitan areas in the nation, according to a recent FBI Unified Crime Report of serious crimes.

We're perhaps the only city with a front door. Emerging from the Fort Pitt Tunnel, especially on Light Up Night, gives motorists a panorama of beauty and splendor that's truly spectacular.

Our location is perfect. We're within a 500-mile range of 51 percent of the U.S. population, 50 percent of the Canadian population, 63 percent of the national industrial output, 20 other metropolitan areas with populations of a million or more, and more than 73 million people in urban markets.

We're the transportation hub of the northeastern United States. Our new Greater Pittsburgh International Airport maintains nonstop flights to 120 cities worldwide, as well as connecting flights to hundreds of other destinations. Its operations are rarely closed due to weather conditions.

The Port of Pittsburgh, meanwhile, is the largest inland waterway port in the United States in terms of waterborne tonnage shipped, received, or moved. And our three rivers make this a great place for recreational boating.

We're crisscrossed by four interstate highways, including the Pennsylvania Turnpike; three main railroad lines serve the region; and more than 200 air and surface freight companies call Southwestern Pennsylvania home. No matter where you're going—on land, on water, or in the air—you can get there from here.

We've been consistently rated as one of the top 10 most livable cities in North America, and we've also received top 10 rankings for home business opportunities, relocation, city revitalization, overall business, working mothers, public school art programs, the local housing market, our airport, and our status as a tour destination. *Too Cool* magazine even called us Hip City USA. (Pittsburgh? Hip City? Andrew Carnegie is rolling over in his grave.)

Truth is, America is discovering that the smoky steel town image that Pittsburgh has long endured hasn't been accurate for decades.

It's not, however, that we didn't earn that reputation. For a long time, Pittsburgh was the industrial engine of North America. The first oil fields in the United States were discovered near here, and coal was and still is found in abundance; and because of this and our strategic location, we became a world center for steel, glass, electrical, and food products. Around the turn of the 20th

century, Pittsburgh produced half of the world's glass and iron, two-thirds of the country's crucible steel, and most of the world's supply of oil.

Times have changed, of course. All the industries that built the fortunes of Pittsburgh have gone through substantial restructurings and dislocations over the years—at considerable pain to the region—and to some extent have been supplanted as major employers by the region's medical, high-technology, financial, and academic endeavors.

But make no mistake: Pittsburgh is still an industrial city—

HERB FERGUSON

The   Power   of

a city that is corporate home to eight Fortune 500 companies, a city where companies and people still make things that make society better.

There are approximately 1 million jobs in the Pittsburgh area. About 17 percent of them are in goods-producing industries—well-paying jobs that enable hardworking people who are not college educated to buy homes, send their kids to college, and build a comfortable life. In fact, manufacturing remains the largest job producer in the Pittsburgh area, and is second only to retail in the amount of private sector employment.

Contrary to popular rumor, we still make steel in the Pittsburgh area—a lot of steel. USX-U.S. Steel Group, for example, has invested about $750,000 over the last decade in its steel operations in the Monongahela Valley. Andrew Carnegie's first mill still stands, though now it's part of a

world-class, modern complex that was recently named America's best plant. Not bad for an old-line company that's approaching its 100th birthday.

What the region has—and what it wishes to expand—is a sizable base of value-added manufacturers who need access to a skilled workforce and the support of advanced technology firms. Fortunately, Pittsburgh has plenty of both.

Incidentally, anyone who thinks that basic industry is low-tech hasn't been inside a plant recently. Today, there are probably more computer operators and technicians in a plant than there are laborers. There are no unskilled jobs and no unskilled workers in modern industry.

People, of course, are what make the difference, whether it's on the job or in the neighborhood. Pittsburgh people have deep roots and deep loyalties. Ethnic neighborhoods still abound, and true Pittsburghers still have friends they met in the first grade. It's a city where black-and-gold clothing is acceptable in any season for any occasion. We like tailgating at the football game, and we like going to the symphony. We like safe streets and old friends and good jobs and good schools and going to church. We like old sports rivalries. And new challenges. ☞

Pittsburgh's diverse outdoor activities include white-water rafting and woodland biking, nature walking and downhill skiing, power boating and hitting the links. For culture lovers, there's the annual Three Rivers Arts Festival, which literally paints the town in arts, crafts, and music, music, music (PAGES 20 AND 21).

By Sharon K. Williams
President and CEO
Minority Enterprise Corporation

PITTSBURGH IS KNOWN FOR ITS RICH AND DIVERSE CULTURE, advanced medical care facilities, academic institutions, and sports franchises. With all of this to be proud of, another element is emerging and is becoming the wellspring of economic vitality in our region: entrepreneurship. ■ Nationally,

entrepreneurs are the catalysts for the growth and energy of the American workforce. Entrepreneurs create two of every three new jobs, produce 39 percent of the gross national product, and invent more than half of the nation's technological innovations. Locally, entrepreneurs represent an important source of economic resources, employment, and vitality to the city. New business incorporations for the Pittsburgh metropolitan statistical area grew to 3,879 in 1996, up from 3,500 the year before. The rate of business formation and the success of newly formed businesses are important indications of the health of a region's economy. Business growth signals an attractive market, a strong economy, a

fertile business climate, and the ability to foster new ideas, products, and technologies.

Pittsburgh has many resources to draw upon. Civic and community resources, as well as the area's network of foundations, have always played a vital role in assisting the development of neighborhoods, education, the arts, and businesses.

One such resource is the Minority Enterprise Corporation, which is dedicated to providing technical assistance and business training, as well as enhancing economic opportunities for potential and experienced entrepreneurs. Other organizations—such as the U.S. Small Business Administration, the Center for Economic Development, the Small Business and Development Centers, and

the Enterprise Corporation—are also instrumental in entrepreneurial training and assistance.

The city's resources and support ensure that interested and experienced entrepreneurs have the opportunity to accomplish their goals and make valuable contributions to the city. For example, Ronald R. Davenport, dean of Pittsburgh's Duquesne University Law School from 1970 to 1981, decided to create his own destiny in broadcasting. He is the founder and owner of Sheridan Broadcasting Corporation, incorporated in 1972 as the first black-owned radio group.

Today, under Davenport's leadership, Sheridan Broadcasting Network is the nation's largest completely black-owned news,

A man's reach should exceed his grasp—a lesson well learned by this carefree toddler at Pittsburgh's hands-on Children's Museum (BELOW) and by these workmen as they painstakingly fit massive steel sections to forge the Veterans Bridge over the Allegheny River (OPPOSITE).

TOM BELL

sports, and entertainment network, reaching more than 9 million Americans weekly. Sheridan Broadcasting has come to contain five networks: American Urban Radio, STRZ Entertainment, SBN Sports, Urban Public Affairs, and SPM Urban.

There are many more pioneers who have paved the way for today's entrepreneurs, and because of their dedication to opening more doors to opportunity, the spirit of entrepreneurship is alive and well in the city. Pittsburgh has a number of successful entrepreneurial companies—such as the Antaire Corporation and Trilogic—that continue to keep the city's economic pulse beating.

The Antaire Corporation is a minority-owned data-processing firm that offers automated consulting to its clients in support of their human resources management function. Antaire predicts a high-profit potential, due to the company's high degree of technological sophistication, as well as the lack of direct competition in the area.

Trilogic's unique position as a multivendor company reduces the challenge of entering into the networking arena. The enterprisewide integration staff specializes in small to large local and wide area networks. With their vendor and application independence, a multivendor, multitechnology, and multiprotocol network can be implemented. Trilogic offers a complete service from a single-source company.

Keystone Minority Capital Fund and Minority Enterprise Corporation have recognized both Antaire and Trilogic for their commitment to quality, and have invested in these entrepreneurial companies in an attempt to help them continue the development of their products and services.

Other successful entrepreneurial companies in Pittsburgh include the Carnegie Group, Wise Wire Corporation, Allegheny Housing Rehabilitation Corporation, Redzone Robotics, and a

host of others. In order for our city to maintain its economic vitality, we need to nurture these companies, appreciate their contributions, and stimulate the growth and development of other such businesses.

In this way, entrepreneurial efforts will maintain their position as progenitors of local economic success. We must remind ourselves frequently that new businesses create new jobs, which, in turn, result in a stronger economic base, the development of new technologies and products, and healthy competition. With this role in mind, entrepreneurship will continue to be an important source for economic growth throughout the economy, and throughout the region. 🤝

There's often a pot of gold at the end of the rainbow (PAGES 24 AND 25). Hardships that might easily crush less-resilient regions are just opportunities for growth in Pittsburgh. Although mills departed and corporations downsized in the 1980s, the city rallied as it turned to high technology, software development, biomedicine, robotics, and finance.

YOU GOTTA REGATTA! AS STATELY Mount Washington looks on, with the brightly painted Duquesne Incline crawling up its face (OPPOSITE), the Pittsburgh Three Rivers Regatta unfolds (THIS PAGE). Begun in 1977, the annual event features such crowd-pleasin' high jinks as Formula One racing and hot-air balloons.

T h e   P o w e r   o f

MORE THAN A HALF-CENTURY AGO, Pittsburgh's first redevelopment project, propelled by private investment and a passel of new state laws, transformed a sooty industrial wasteland (OPPOSITE) into the beautiful Point State Park, which today makes an ideal backdrop for a picnic atop Mount Washington (ABOVE).

The Power of

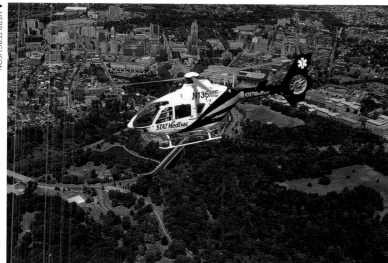

NOTHING BETTER SYMBOLIZES Pittsburgh's new skies, clean for a half-century or more, than their frequent use. Whether enjoying a bird's-eye view of Point Fountain (OPPOSITE), answering a medical emergency (TOP LEFT), buzzing the Three Rivers Regatta (BOTTOM LEFT), or reaching the scene of a breaking news story (RIGHT), Pittsburghers take to the friendly skies on just about any occasion.

T h e   P o w e r   o f

HILLY TERRAIN AND THICK FOLIAGE did not daunt the stalwart souls who built and settled Western Pennsylvania. To the contrary, the abundant houses along the Monongahela River in nearby Newell (OPPOSITE) and throughout the neighborhood of Morningside (ABOVE) aptly demonstrate Pittsburghers' mastery over seemingly intractable nature.

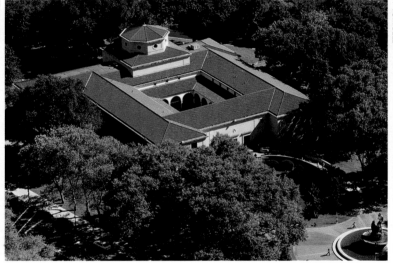

JUST THREE MILES FROM THE GOLDEN Triangle, tree-lined Oakland is home to many of the region's stellar cultural and educational institutions, notably (CLOCKWISE FROM TOP LEFT) the complex housing the Carnegie Museum of Art, Carnegie Museum of Natural History, and the Main Library of the Carnegie Library of Pittsburgh; the Board of Public Education; the University of Pittsburgh's Frick Fine Arts Building; and Carnegie Mellon University, renowned for its art, drama, computer, and engineering programs.

Back in downtown Pittsburgh, the fruits of university research and cultural activity enhance the fabric of civic life. The checkerboard pattern at PPG Place, home to one of the city's most successful global corporations, has become a popular setting for art exhibits (OPPOSITE).

IN 1945, PENNSYLVANIA'S LAND-mark smoke-control legislation helped clear the skies and paved the way for the nation's first rede-velopment projects. Though the amount of money invested in the Golden Triangle since that time cannot be calculated, the ongoing cooperation of labor and manage-ment has ensured Pittsburgh's continued climb up the economic ladder.

AS THE *New York Times* NOTED OF Pittsburgh in 1991, "The city is set in a ruggedly scenic landscape of wooded ridges and converging rivers. Ambitious rebuilding campaigns have added sleek new towers and revitalized the waterfronts. Skies are clear and the rivers run clean enough to support schools of game fish." We couldn't have said it better ourselves.

In the 1970s, landmark city-planning laws were passed that required all new buildings to earmark a percentage of their property for public spaces. Such vision helped re-create downtown Pittsburgh as a walkable, lunchable neighborhood. While one worker spends a solitary moment in all-weather PPG Place (PAGE 38), another grabs a quick bite across town in the CNG Tower's leafy pocket park (PAGE 39).

A FULL SPECTRUM OF SHOPPING opportunities embrace the Golden Triangle, from haute couture department stores like Saks Fifth Avenue to homegrown boutiques at Market Square. One of Market Square's favorite residents is Nicholas Coffee Co., where the home-roasted coffee and the hot-roasted peanuts are perennial—and irresistible—treats.

THANKS TO THE EFFORTS OF MANY concerned citizens, Pittsburgh has learned to cherish its grand architectural past. Evidence abounds, including the preservation of the Liberty Avenue warehouse-loft buildings (TOP), the adaptive reuse of the Pittsburgh and Lake Erie Railroad station as an entertainment complex (BOTTOM LEFT), and the designation of the Monongahela wharf area as the Firstside Historic District (BOTTOM RIGHT).

Similarly, 19th-century row houses have been lovingly restored along the famed Mexican War Streets, so called because they are named for battles and heroes of that conflict (OPPOSITE).

The area's revitalization marked the transformation of a blight-ridden piece of the city's Central North Side into a beautiful neighborhood and a prime piece of urban real estate.

The Power of

To SOLIDIFY ITS PLACE ON THE American architectural map, Allegheny County retained the services of master architect Henry Hobson Richardson to design its courthouse. The result was a late-19th-century, neomedieval masterpiece, featuring offices, courtrooms, a courtyard park and fountain, and a mazelike, multilayered staircase that must be experienced to be believed (ABOVE AND OPPOSITE LEFT).

The Power of

FOR WHOM THE BELL TOLLS: Although the First Lutheran Church (RIGHT) has been a visible landmark on Grant Street since it was completed in 1888, its tower was silent until October 1995, when three bells were recovered from the razed St. Paul's United Church of Christ and installed in the downtown cathedral.

MORE THAN JUST THE REGION'S largest employer, the University of Pittsburgh is also home to thousands of traditional and nontraditional students in a wide variety of places and programs. Piercing the Oakland sky, the school's omnipresent Cathedral of Learning reminds students of the valued place of education in the city firmament. Designed by Charles Z. Klauder, the 42-story structure, overlaid with Indiana limestone, was completed in 1936.

The Power of

FOR MORE THAN A CENTURY, THE renowned Mellon family has lent its influence and financial strength to virtually every local endeavor, from art to education to com- merce. Two well-known structures that bear the famous name include the Mellon Institute, whose library contains volumes dealing prima- rily with chemistry, biochemistry, biophysics, and the biological sci- ences (OPPOSITE), and the richly detailed Two Mellon Bank Center, formerly the Union Trust Build- ing (ABOVE).

IN THE GILDED AGE, LOCAL COMpanies often demonstrated their might to the world by creating a grand civic presence. These outward displays of wealth took on many forms, such as ornate entranceways, ferocious stone carvings, and elegantly molded metals.

The captains of industry demanded similar splendor in their homes, including grand stairways and immense spaces for fine dining and proper entertaining. Built circa 1870, the Gwinner-Harter house was rescued from demolition in 1995, when Ben and Joedda Sampson bought and began restoring the historic mansion (PAGES 52 AND 53).

EVERYTHING OLD IS NEW AGAIN IN
Pittsburgh, where architectural
treasures are being saved and reused in contemporary contexts. In
1997, the derelict and long-defunct
Bank Centre was reborn as the Library Center, a combined facility
for Point Park College and the
Carnegie Business Library. The
historic structure is ensconced in
marble—all magnificently restored
and adapted by gifted local architect Sylvester Damianos.

The Power of

PITTSBURGH GREW UP AS A BUSI-
ness town, where time was money
and every hand punched a clock.
These days, no matter where you
turn in the city, it appears that
time is still of the essence.

The Power of

For a city that got its start in the mills and mines, Pittsburgh sure does like crackin' the books. More than 100,000 students attend some 30 local colleges and universities, while thousands more are enrolled in one of the area's 70-plus technical and trade schools. The Joseph M. Katz Graduate School of Business, part of the University of Pittsburgh, is nationally recognized for its accelerated, 11-month MBA program.

HATS OFF! LINING THE SPIRAL staircase in historic Old Main, members of Washington and Jefferson College's class of '96 gleefully await commencement— and a fond farewell to college days.

The Power of

PITTSBURGH MAY NOT DISPLACE Paris as the City of Light, but a look around town reveals that we're definitely in the running. From the magnificent ceiling of Benedum Center, a refurbished Roaring Twenties movie house (OPPOSITE), to the brightened outdoor rotunda of the former Pennsylvania Railroad Station (TOP) to the holiday luminaria display at PPG Place (BOTTOM), Pittsburgh truly knows how to sparkle.

STATELY PLEASURE DOMES: ONE OF the city's most elegant restaurants, the Grand Concourse at Station Square (OPPOSITE) opened in 1979 in the old Pittsburgh and Lake Erie Railroad Station, whose magnificent arched ceiling, glass dome, and fan light are ideal accompaniments to fine dining and other diversions (RIGHT). No less awe-inspiring is the lobby of the City-County Building, a major presence in the Golden Triangle (LEFT).

OF THE CITY'S GRAND PERFORMING
arts venues, none are more popular than Heinz Hall (ABOVE) and
Benedum Center (OPPOSITE).
Pittsburgh's symphony, ballet,
and opera companies, along with
numerous concerts and plenty of
touring plays, draw patrons by
the thousands to these restored
Golden Triangle movie houses.

NEARLY 40 YEARS AGO, WHEN THE shabby Penn Theater was considered for the new home of the Pittsburgh Symphony, naysayers called for the wrecking ball. But an $11 million donation from the Howard Heinz Endowment turned the facility into a lavishly appointed concert hall and sparked a revitalization of the arts in downtown Pittsburgh. Today, after a second, $6.8 million renovation in 1995, Heinz Hall's opulence speaks for itself—and for the great resiliency of the Golden Triangle, which continues to be the region's economic and cultural hub (PAGES 66 AND 67).

A REVERENCE FOR BEAUTIFUL architecture pervades Pittsburgh, from an ornate detail on a church facade (BOTTOM) to the Carnegie Museum of Natural History's Hall of Architecture, which showcases replicas of buildings from ancient Egypt to the Renaissance (TOP). Dr. Franklin K. Toker, a University of Pittsburgh professor and past president of the Society of Architectural Historians, confronts his specialty head-on at St. Paul's Cathedral in Oakland (OPPOSITE).

SINCE MANY PITTSBURGHERS ARE, by tradition, a religious lot, local churches of all denominations run a seven-day-a-week business. Notable for the commitment of its parishioners is Polish Hill's Immaculate Heart of Mary, which the local citizenry literally built themselves a century ago (OPPOSITE TOP).

LOCAL HOUSES OF WORSHIP ARE no stranger to pomp and circumstance, whether it's a grand religious procession at St. Bernard Church (OPPOSITE) or a wedding at Heinz Chapel on the University of Pittsburgh campus (ABOVE). The nonsectarian chapel, with its faux-medieval setting and elongated, stained-glass windows, is also the atmospheric home of Pitt's justly famous organ and choir concerts.

In Pittsburgh, symbols of faith abound, including the picture-window patterns of the St. Thomas More Church (TOP), the stunning stained glass of Beth El Synagogue (BOTTOM), and the Gothic prowess of the enormous St. Bernard Church (OPPOSITE TOP). Sometimes, a simple shadow on the pavement is enough to inspire passersby (OPPOSITE BOTTOM).

The Power of

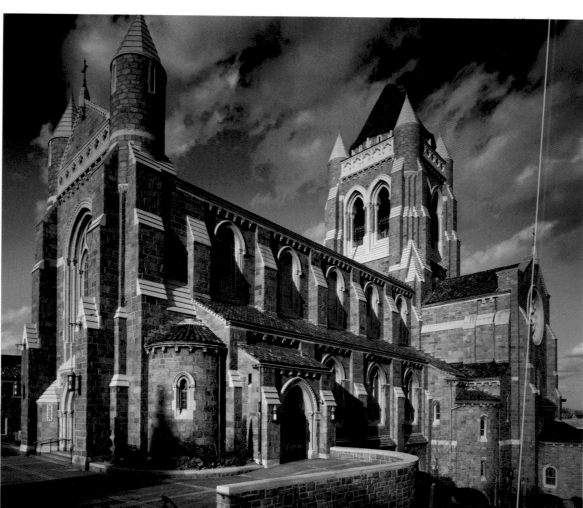

THERE'S A GRAVITY TO PITTS-burgh—a place where you often feel the weight of the past close at hand. From an old graveyard in Arlington Heights (OPPOSITE) to the historic cemetery at Trinity Cathedral (BOTTOM), there's an ongoing reverence for the times—and the people—that came before us. Those who want a preview of heaven can always slip the surly bonds of Earth and soar into the empyrean (TOP).

SPANNING THE DECADES: Pittsburgh's omnipresent suspension bridges reflect the important role the city's three major rivers have played in Steel Town's rise to the top.

WHETHER YOU'RE CHEERING ON the Stanley Cup champion Penguins beneath the retractable dome at the Civic Arena (TOP), or "scoping" things out in the observatory at Westminster College (BOTTOM), Pittsburgh is a great place to see the stars.

T h e   P o w e r   o f

WITH MULTIPLE WATERWAYS meandering throughout the urban landscape, Pittsburgh has more than a thousand river crossings.

Still, the city is so compact that most people feel they're never very far from home.

NOT FOR THE FAINT OF HEART: In a hilly metropolis like Pittsburgh, everything seems to exist on a vertical axis. Indeed, climbing the sheer pitch of St. John the Baptist Ukranian Catholic Church can only be an act of faith.

WHILE PITTSBURGH'S HARDWORK-
ing image has evolved over the
years, a colorful mural at the Federal Courthouse offers a glimpse
at the city's industrial beginnings
(PAGES 84 AND 85).

The Power of

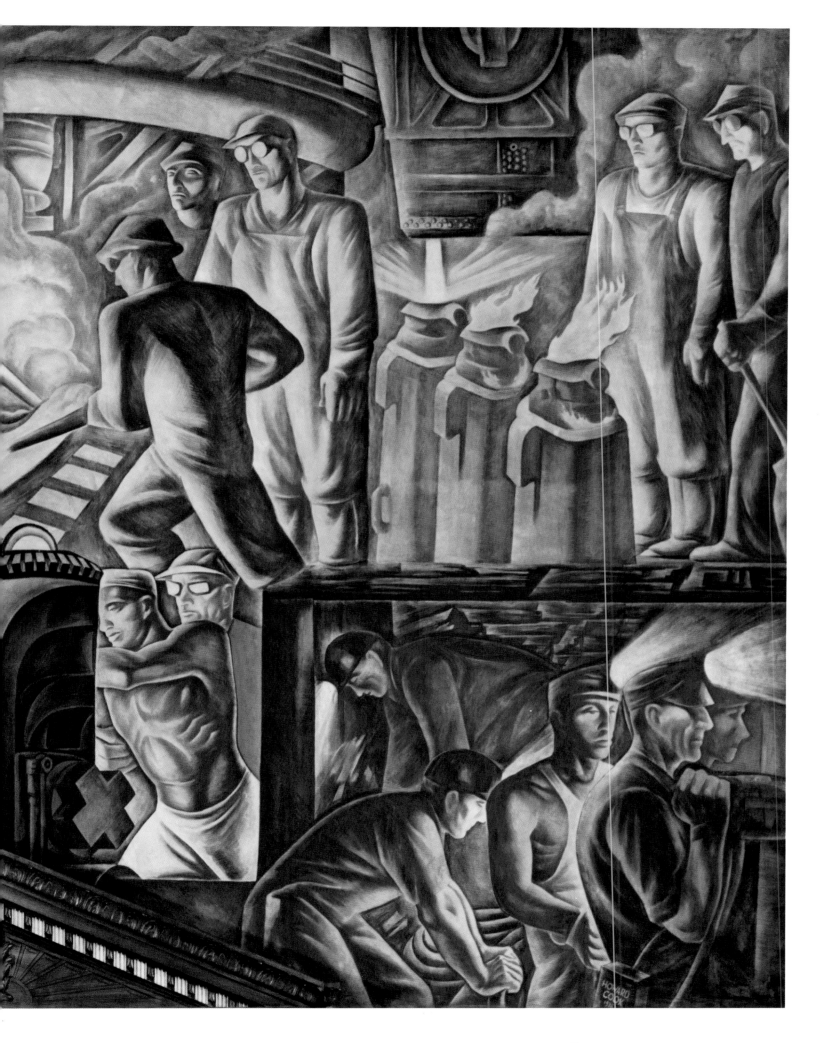

WHAT BEGAN AS AN ORE- AND OIL-rich region has emerged as one of the nation's great think tanks—a true movement from brawn to brains. As this display in the 300 Sixth Building reminds us (RIGHT), Pittsburgh produced half the world's glass and iron, two-thirds of the nation's crucible steel, and most of the world's oil in 1900. Today, the city is also one of the top technology sites in the nation, and the Carnegie Science Center showcases Pittsburgh's expertise in robotics and other sciences (OPPOSITE).

The Power of

FOR ALL THE CHANGES IN AND around Pittsburgh, the region still has the ready workforce and technical know-how to get the job done. With more than 4,000 manufacturing firms operating in the area, places like Homestead, where the massive USS Homestead Works once dominated, now host smaller, spin-off industries.

AT ONE TIME, THE MONONGAHELA River was a virtually unbroken U.S. Steel production line. Although the number and intensity of such efforts have certainly di- minished in the past 20 years, many active sites remain, includ- ing the famed Clairton Coke Works, which transforms the region's abundant coal supplies into the coke needed for remaking iron ore into raw and finished steel.

The Power of

IN THE 1980S, AS MILLS CLOSED and Pittsburgh lost 100,000 manufacturing jobs, the city added telecommunications, biomedical, high-tech, and service-sector jobs.

Documenting this transformation are views of downtown in August 1982 (TOP) and October 1988 (BOTTOM).

EVEN WHEN CHALLENGED BY OLD Man Winter, coal production helps maintain the Port of Pittsburgh as the nation's busiest inland waterway for waterborne tonnage (TOP). Still, the city's reputation for heavy manufacturing has not stopped other industries from coming to town; Pittsburgh ranks fifth nationally for computer software professionals, with more than 450 information technology firms employing some 25,000 people. It's a fact highly touted by Mayor Tom Murphy, pictured here at one of the city's many groundbreaking ceremonies (BOTTOM).

The Power of

ALTHOUGH GALILEO THE MAN would likely smile on Pittsburgh's technological strides, his likeness outside the Carnegie Museum of Natural History doesn't seem too pleased with the winter blanket Mother Nature has supplied.

A FORCE TO BE RECKONED WITH: On the street, on the picket line, or on parade, Pittsburghers have always been a strong, hardworking, and loyal lot. Even President Bill Clinton shows his admiration for the United Steelworkers of America during a 1994 rally in Greensburg (BOTTOM RIGHT).

WHETHER THEY'RE CARING FOR cars or nurturing natural-gas lines, women are an integral part of Pittsburgh's well-trained, highly skilled, and professional workforce. The national spokes- person for Jiffy Lube and a Penn Hills institution, Lucille Treganowan holds forth on her nationally syndicated TV show, *Lucille's Car Care Clinic* (OPPOSITE).

ROLL OUT THE BARREL: From industrial plastics to shiny beer kegs, quality is paramount in Pittsburgh. The city has survived and prospered, thanks to its renowned excellence in manpower and materials.

FROM THE TIME OF THE EARLIEST settlers, locally brewed beer has been a Pittsburgh specialty, popular among mill hands and the college crowd alike. Located on the former site of the Frauenheim and Vilsack Brewery, which opened in 1861, the Pittsburgh Brewing Company keeps this tradition alive with its popular Iron City brand (BOTTOM LEFT). A newcomer by comparison, Penn Brewery opened in 1989 as the state's first brew pub (TOP; BOTTOM RIGHT).

The Power of

THE SCION OF A 200-YEAR-OLD Pennsylvania beer-making family, Tom Pastorius studied time-honed brewing methods in Ger- many before opening his Penn Brewery in Troy Hill. Today, the popular establishment, which hosts the annual Microbrewer's Fest, combines the deep flavor of traditional German pilsners with the old-world sound of oompah bands.

FROM HOT ROCK TO COOL COMEDY, Pittsburgh has a rich and varied entertainment scene. Middle Eastern fare served in an exciting atmosphere draws fun-loving folks to Zythos, located on the South Side (TOP). In nearby Ross Township, the extensive selection of draft beers at Kangaroo's Outback Cafe attracts such nationally known stars as comedian Billy Elmer, a Pittsburgh native (BOTTOM).

The Power of

INDUSTRIAL-STRENGTH JAZZ: A former Strip District warehouse, Metropol, like its sister, Rosebud, is one of the hottest nightspots in town (TOP). But in Pittsburgh, fancy footwork isn't reserved for the dance floor. Strutting their stuff at Benedum Center is the Men's Project, a group organized by Kevin Maloney to knock down male stereotypes (BOTTOM).

DINING ALFRESCO IS NOT UNCOM-
mon in Pittsburgh, where cafés
like Shadyside's Thai Place, famous for its traditional pad thai
noodle stir-fry, often spill onto
the sidewalk (OPPOSITE). In the
nearby Strip District, Rosebud
(TOP) and Electra (BOTTOM) also
draw crowds.

Two hotbeds of not-quite-haute cuisine are the landmark Oakland Original, a favorite hot dog hangout for Pitt students (BOTTOM), and Primanti Bros., justly famous for its sandwich with french fries on the inside (TOP). The preferred dressing, of course, is Heinz ketchup, made across the river on the North Side (OPPOSITE).

PITTSBURGH TALENT HAS A WAY OF going national. From funnyman Mario Joyner, former host of MTV's *Half-Hour Comedy Hour* (OPPOSITE), to Houserocker frontman Joe Grushecky (ABOVE), legions of local performers have left the Steel Valley for a chance at fame.

LOCAL MUSIC THRIVES IN THIS CITY, where something's happening every night of the week. Donnie Iris, who hails from Beaver Falls and made his first record at age nine, is often credited with helping to put Pittsburgh on the national music map in the 1970s (OPPOSITE). Doing its part to keep us there, newcomer Brownie Mary released its first major-label album, *Naked*, in 1998 (ABOVE).

DESPITE THE DOMINANCE OF SUCH longtime corporate residents as USX, Alcoa, PPG, Mellon, PNC, and Federated Investors, the Golden Triangle can look stunningly futuristic after dark.

WEST MIFFLIN'S 100-YEAR-OLD Kennywood Park is the acknowledged roller-coaster capital of the world. Originally built in 1924, the Thunderbolt, with its breathtaking 90-foot drop, remains the nation's greatest wooden-scaffold coaster.

The Power of

SWING YOUR PARTNER: FROM performances by the world-class Pittsburgh Ballet Theatre (OPPOSITE) to square dancing at Chartiers-Houston High School (BOTTOM), Pittsburghers are always light on their feet. Of course, those who want to sit this one out can take a ride on Kennywood's classic Roaring Twenties carousel (TOP).

MEMBERS OF PITTSBURGH'S African-American community have made their mark on a local and national level, including Dr. Vernell A. Lillie, founder and director of the Kuntu Repertory Theatre (RIGHT), and novelist Albert French, whose acclaimed *Patches of Fire* documents his experience during and after the Vietnam War (OPPOSITE, TOP LEFT).

The city remembers its African-American heritage with myriad cultural events, such as the 1996 Gospel Convention (OPPOSITE, BOTTOM LEFT), and performances by African dance group Umoja (OPPOSITE, BOTTOM RIGHT). In 1997, Pittsburgh further established its link with history during a landmark visit from Rosa Parks, originator of the Montgomery bus boycott that fueled the civil rights movement (OPPOSITE, TOP RIGHT).

The Power of

WHILE PITTSBURGH HAS NEVER been known as a jazz town, it *has* nurtured many fledgling talents of the uniquely American art form, including pianist/songwriter Erroll Garner (OPPOSITE) and guitarist/singer George Benson (RIGHT). Welcoming musicians from just about every genre, the outdoor amphitheater at Hartwood Acres presents summertime concerts on the grounds of a beautiful estate, donated to Allegheny County by Mary Flinn Lawrence in 1969 (CENTER).

T h e   P o w e r   o f

TOOTING THEIR OWN HORNS ALL over town are sax man Kenny Blake (OPPOSITE), trombonist Harold Betters (TOP), and the euphonious River City Brass Band, who'll give you an earful for your money (BOTTOM).

An appreciation for music begins early in Pittsburgh, where ambitious students audition for the Youth Symphony Orchestra (OPPOSITE) in hopes of one day joining the world-renowned Pittsburgh Symphony, which celebrated its centennial season in 1995-1996 (THIS PAGE).

Cookin' up a storm: From
Polish kielbasa to Italian cannoli,
Pittsburghers take their culinary
exploits seriously. Just ask Justin
Miller, a Baden, Pennsylvania,

native who became the world's
youngest chef when his book,
Cooking with Justin, was published
in 1997 (OPPOSITE), or beloved en-
tertainer Don Brockett, whose

alter ego, Chef Brockett, has
shared delicious recipes on his
frequent visits to Mister Rogers'
neighborhood (ABOVE).

CLOWNING AROUND IS SERIOUS business in Pittsburgh, where mimes, fools, and spellbinders catch the eye—and spirit—of everyone they meet.

Setting sail: Each May, the Pittsburgh Children's Festival draws thousands of kids to West Park, where fanciful ships and unlikely pirates are the order of the day (LEFT). The nautical theme continues on a South Side facade, complete with its own "Yellow Submarine" (BOTTOM RIGHT). And for a look at the real thing, military buffs can visit the USS *Requin*. Though a bit less colorful, this World War II vessel still draws the crowds from its spot in the Ohio River outside the Carnegie Science Center (TOP RIGHT).

The Power of

WARNING! NO LIFEGUARD ON
duty: At the very tip of the Golden
Triangle, where Point State Park
pokes into the Ohio River, rests

Point Fountain. On a hot summer
day, it's required dunking for any
child under the age of, oh, 105.

Fʀᴏᴍ ɪᴛs ɪɴɪᴛɪᴀʟ ᴅᴀʏs ᴀs ᴀ ᴛʀᴀᴅ-ing post to its present-day incarnation as a corporate and technology center, Pittsburgh has been a true melting pot. The city's ethnic groups celebrate their diversity through a variety of religious events and festivals, including services at the Hindu-Jain Temple in Monroeville, which opened in 1984 (ᴛᴏᴘ ʟᴇꜰᴛ); the Highland Games in Ligonier, running since 1958 (ᴏᴘᴘᴏsɪᴛᴇ); and the annual Pittsburgh Folk Festival, begun in 1956 (ʙᴏᴛᴛᴏᴍ).

The Power of

IN PITTSBURGH, EVERYBODY GETS into the act. Memorable events like the 1986 Hands Across America gathering bring out a cross section of citizens, from comical clowns to former Steelers great and pro football Hall of Famer Franco Harris (TOP AND OPPOSITE TOP).

The Power of

THE FINE ART OF ENTERTAINING children is alive and well among locals, as evidenced by the award-winning productions at Point Park Playhouse (OPPOSITE BOT-TOM). Pausing during the Covered Bridge Festival, held in nearby Mingo Creek Park, are Sunshine and Wee Willie, a mother-and-son clowning team (BOTTOM). The dizzy duo really take their work to heart, er, mouth; Sunshine's teeth are made of inlaid enamel.

FARMER'S MARKETS SPRING UP LIKE toadstools in parking lots across Pittsburgh, as the region's fertile soil turns out bushels of fresh produce virtually year-round. For something sweeter, pay a visit to the famed Ice Ball Man in West Park (CENTER). Bet you never thought shaved ice and syrup could taste this good!

WHETHER THEY'RE TAKING DOLLY for a walk, making the most of a shady spot, or getting a kiss from grandpa, locals enjoy their share of quiet, tender moments. With our relaxed pace, and plenty of opportunities to enjoy it, it's no wonder that, in 1996, Pittsburgh made *Fortune*'s Top 10 for quality of life and work.

The Power of

PUTTIN' ON THE DOG: IN PITTS-
burgh, there are endless parks,
nature trails, mountain paths,
and river walks—plenty of places
to park your pooch, buss your
bowser, hug your hound, or just
plain cuddle your cur.

The Power of

Lions and tigers and bears, oh my! With a host of wildlife to look at and learn from, the Pittsburgh Zoo is a favorite attraction with children of all ages. Young animal lovers especially adore the Kids Kingdom, a 77-acre interactive exhibit that opened in 1995 (BOTTOM RIGHT). Showcasing birds from six different continents, the National Aviary in nearby West Park allows visitors to get up close and personal with some wondrous winged creatures (BOTTOM LEFT).

PERHAPS NO ONE HAS DONE MORE
to bolster Pittsburgh's cultural
scene than Andrew Carnegie, who,
in 1896, started the annual International Exhibition to educate the
public about art. He was also responsible for founding the Carnegie
Museum of Art, which features
American works from the late
19th century, French impressionist and postimpressionist paintings, and European and American
decorative arts from the late 17th
century.

FOR MORE THAN A CENTURY, THE Carnegie Museum of Natural History has worked tirelessly to capture, cull, and catalog the world's greatest treasures. The renowned Dinosaur Hall features 10 skeletons, including the type specimen of a *Tyrannosaurus rex*.

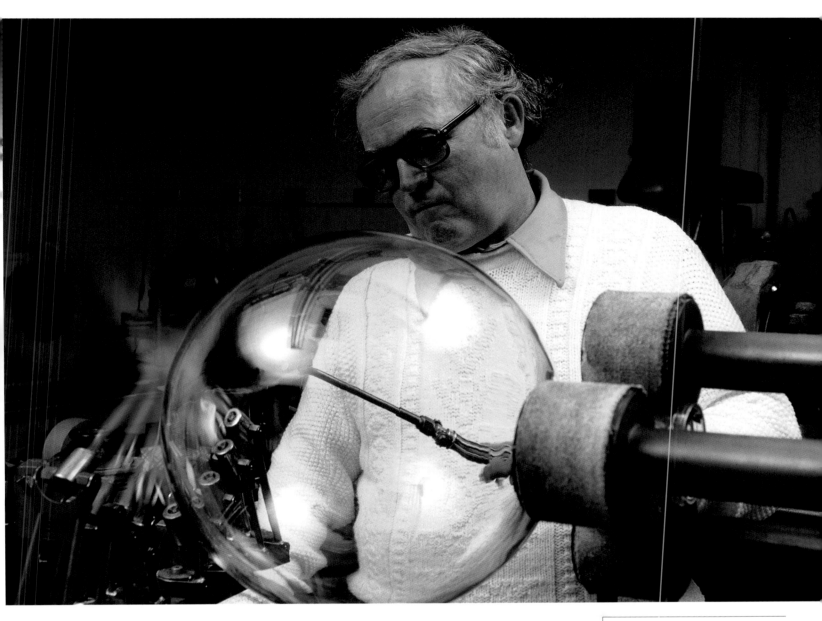

LIFE MAY INDEED IMITATE ART, BUT the mating display of a western chorus frog simply can't match the beauty of a perfect glass sphere fashioned by a University of Pittsburgh chemist.

The Power of

WITH PLENTY OF INSPIRATION from Western Pennsylvania's verdant hills and waterfalls, architect Frank Lloyd Wright created Fallingwater in the mid-1930s (ABOVE). By cantilevering the house over the falls at Bear Run, Wright beckoned nature indoors, making the sound of the water a part of every room in this architectural masterpiece.

The Power of

THE STEEP HILLS AND VALLEYS OF Western Pennsylvania have kept the region's urban areas fairly compact, while leaving hundreds of square miles of wilderness for year-round hiking and camping. In Ohiopyle, on the nearby Youghiogheny River, thousands of outdoor enthusiasts enjoy biking, fishing, white-water rafting, kayaking, canoeing, and countless other activities.

Y OU'RE NEVER TOO OLD—OR TOO young—to enjoy Western Pennsylvania's abundant, clean waterways, from Moraine to Kinzua, and from Brady's Bend to Chartiers Creek.

FOR ALL ITS FORMIDABLE INDUS-
trial development, Pittsburgh has
been smart enough to leave the
great natural bounty of Penn's
Woods relatively untouched. On
any given day, locals can fly-fish
at Oil Creek State Park, canoe
through Cook Forest, backpack
over Hickory Creek in the Allegheny National Forest, or simply soak
up a warm summer day by the river.

OVER THE PAST DECADE, PITTS-burgh has joined the Rails-to-Trails movement, transforming defunct railroad corridors into multipurpose public paths fit for recreation and nonmotorized transportation. One particularly good rail-trail is at Ohiopyle, where the scenery is simply spectacular and the ride offers a perfect after-noon workout. Sometimes, it's more fun to venture off the beaten path, pitch a tent, and rough it for a while.

ALTHOUGH NOT GENERALLY KNOWN for agriculture, Pennsylvania's vast heartland is home to count-less family-owned and -operated farms, some of them more than a century old (PAGES 158 AND 159).

NOT SO FAR FROM THE HURLY-burly of Pittsburgh, you'll see Western Pennsylvania's pastoral side, where plowed fields, small towns, and covered bridges are the norm, not the exception. In fact, Washington, Greene, and Fayette counties hold the annual Covered Bridge Festival to celebrate a method of fording streams that has never gone out of style.

The Power of

A VERITABLE WONDERLAND OF birds and butterflies exists in Western Pennsylvania's great outdoors, where Mother Nature provides the perfect inspiration to send a dandelion shower across a quiet meadow.

No matter where you turn, spring promises blossoms galore across Western Pennsylvania. But at Oakland's Phipps Conservatory, green is the color of choice year-round. Donated to the city by Henry Phipps in 1893, the 2.5-acre conservatory features 13 glass-enclosed display rooms filled with indigenous and exotic plants.

ONE OF THE FINEST FACILITIES OF its kind in the nation, the Phipps Conservatory is noted as much for its statuary as for its botanic displays. In addition to likenesses of Christopher Columbus, Robert Burns, and Edward Bigelow (one of the fathers of Pittsburgh's parks), the grounds are home to statues celebrating the water deity Triton (OPPOSITE) and the members of the Allegheny County Medical Society who served in World War I (ABOVE).

LOVE AND MARRIAGE: Enjoying
their newfound bond, a bride and
groom seal their commitment
with a kiss (PAGES 168 AND 169).

The Power of

FOR ALL ITS BIG-CITY WAYS, WEST-ern Pennsylvania is still a very rural place. In Endeavor, an old logging town on the Allegheny River, a Greek Revival building stands the test of time (OPPOSITE), not so far from the seemingly endless—and endlessly wild—Allegheny National Forest (ABOVE).

▶ JOHN BEALE

WORLDS AWAY FROM LIFE IN THE city, many of the state's Amish farmers make their home in Lawrence and Somerset counties. Often erroneously called Pennsylvania Dutch—stemming from a time when anyone of German origin was labeled Dutch— members of the intensely private sect still plow the fields with horse-drawn teams and live as their ancestors did 200 years ago (PAGES 172-175).

WHILE WINTER HAS ITS OWN STARK beauty, the region's prime season is autumn. As the days grow shorter, Western Pennsylvania's unique mix of climate and terrain sets the stage for spectacular displays, from flaming red maples and burnished yellow sycamores to sultry brown oaks and stalwart evergreens.

ALTHOUGH SOME MAY CONSIDER winter an interruption, the old-time farmers who still work the hills and valleys surrounding Pittsburgh know that it is a blessed time—a time to rest while the earth itself hibernates under a coating of ice.

WESTERN PENNSYLVANIA DOESN'T stop just because there's snow on the ground. The real fun begins when locals venture outdoors to try their hand at ice fishing, barrel downhill at record speed, or take part in the dogsled race in Kane.

WITH INNUMERABLE HILLS AND A healthy annual snowfall, Western Pennsylvania is one grand snow bowl. Although you can ski cross-country virtually anywhere there's open ground, downhillers consider nearby Boyce Park or the Laurel Highlands to have the best schussing in the state.

WHEN FRIGID TEMPERATURES descend on Pittsburgh, even the area's rivers begin to look like one big skating rink (PAGE 185). For a less adventurous turn on the ice, children and adults alike flock to Schenley Park, just three miles from the Golden Triangle, where spectacular sunsets and views of downtown are the major attractions (PAGE 184).

I N 1988, BRENDAN GILL NOTED IN the *New Yorker*, "If Pittsburgh were situated somewhere in the heart of Europe, tourists would eagerly journey hundreds of miles out of their way to visit it." Truly, the beauty of the Golden Triangle and the surrounding region is enough to lure even the most cynical of travelers.

The Power of

WHILE SNOW CAN SOFTEN THE harsh lines of Pittsburgh's cityscape, spreading a beautiful blanket of white, it can also bring danger. Fire is a frequent winter hazard—the fault of bad wiring, careless use of space heaters, and open flames. But never fear, local firefighters are always ready to brave icy roads and cold winter winds whenever duty calls.

WITH A PROUD TRADITION OF military service dating back to the French and Indian War, Pittsburgh is today home to the USS *Requin*, a restored navy submarine that has found new life as an educational resource for the Carnegie Science Center. Since coming to town in 1990, the historic vessel has welcomed countless visitors and inspired its share of pomp and circumstance.

DEDICATED IN 1996, A MEMORIAL in Roberto Clemente Park honors Allegheny County police officers who have lost their lives in the line of duty. This life-size bronze statue, sculpted by Susan Wagner as part of the moving tribute, stands as a reminder of the solitary dedication of Pittsburgh's finest.

PITTSBURGH HAS A SOLID SENSE OF the past, thanks to the people and places that preserve it, including Old Economy Village, the lovingly restored home of the 19th-century Harmonists (TOP); Pittsburgh native and Pulitzer Prize-winning historian David McCullough, who has spearheaded efforts for the Senator John Heinz Pittsburgh Regional History Center (BOTTOM LEFT); and the city's myriad memorials and plaques, here honoring the men who lost their lives on the USS *Maine* (BOTTOM RIGHT).

▲ COURTESY WILLIAM B. MCCULLOUGH

The Power of

THE WESTERN PENNSYLVANIA landscape offers endless opportunities to learn about local history, from the Frick Art & Historical Center in Point Breeze (TOP) to Fort Necessity National Battlefield, site of the opening battle of the French and Indian War (BOTTOM LEFT), to the town crier, who reads the *Pittsburgh Post-Gazette*'s headlines in Market Square every day (BOTTOM RIGHT).

▲ AUDREY GIBSON / THE IMAGE FINDERS

PITTSBURGH'S MILITARY HISTORY lives on in *Braddock's Defeat*, filmed in Raccoon State Park for the Learning Channel (OPPOSITE), and at Point State Park, where a blockhouse and the outlines of the city's original forts still stand (ABOVE).

In the tradition of Mary Flinn Lawrence, who stipulated in her will that her now-public estate be kept available for equestrian-related activities, Hartwood Acres has played host to the Family House Polo Match each year since 1983. The fund-raiser helps support local facilities that serve patients receiving treatment for long-term illnesses.

The Power of

DURING THE POPULAR FAMILY House Polo Match, horses aren't the only mode of transportation; the crowds also enjoy a vintage car show. All in all, the much-anticipated event at Hartwood Acres provides the perfect occasion to dress in your finery, indulge in elegant tailgating festivities, and generally see and be seen.

GENTLEMEN, START YOUR ENGINES! Winding its way through verdant Schenley Park, three miles east of the Golden Triangle, is the Pittsburgh Vintage Grand Prix, an annual fund-raiser that boasts impossibly gorgeous antique autos and the finest woodland setting Western Pennsylvania has to offer.

THERE WAS A TIME, NOT SO LONG ago, when Western Pennsylvania produced more professional athletes than any other region in the country. Still a fruitful breeding ground for football, Pittsburgh—and its aspiring athletes—can look to such gridiron greats as Johnny Unitas, Joe Namath, Joe Montana, and Dan Marino for inspiration.

CONSISTENTLY RATED AS ONE OF the top athletic programs in the country, the University of Pittsburgh offers a full spectrum of interscholastic and intramural programs for both men and women— a fact to which this Panthers cheerleader would no doubt attest!

WHETHER YOU'RE ON THE GRID-iron or *en pointe*, there are myriad opportunities to stretch your legs in Pittsburgh. When it comes to cheering on Pitt's noted football team, however, you may want to leave the acrobatics to the professionals.

PITTSBURGH MAY BE HOME TO THE ever popular Pirates and Penguins, but the town's heart is with the four-time Super Bowl champion Steelers. Playing at Three Rivers Stadium, just across the Allegheny River from the Golden Triangle, the team attracts fantastic—and fanatical—crowds.

The Power of

WE'RE NUMBER ONE! WHEN THE Penguins won the Stanley Cup twice in the early 1990s, hockey fans turned out by the thousands to celebrate.

SINCE 1933, THE ROONEY FAMILY has headed up the world-class Pittsburgh Steelers—from team founder Art to his son Dan, who currently serves as president (BOTTOM). Contributing to the club's popularity is announcer Myron Cope, whose insights, colorful nicknames, and screeching commentary make home games unforgettable (TOP RIGHT). For his part, Coach Bill Cowher has established a nearly unparalleled record of success, including a Super Bowl visit in 1996, just four years after he arrived in Pittsburgh (TOP LEFT). But throughout the Steelers' eventful history, perhaps no other player has so captured the fans' imagination as quarterback Kordell "Slash" Stewart, who came to town in 1995 and has helped lead his team into the play-offs every year since (OPPOSITE).

PITTSBURGH IS PROUD OF ITS sports legends, including Pirates right fielder and Hall of Fame inductee Roberto Clemente, whose tribute was unveiled at the 1994 All-Star Game (TOP); retired Dallas Cowboy and former Panthers running back Tony Dorsett, who led Pitt to a national championship in 1976 (BOTTOM LEFT); and two-time Olympic gold medalist Roger Kingdom, who holds the world record in hurdling (BOTTOM RIGHT).

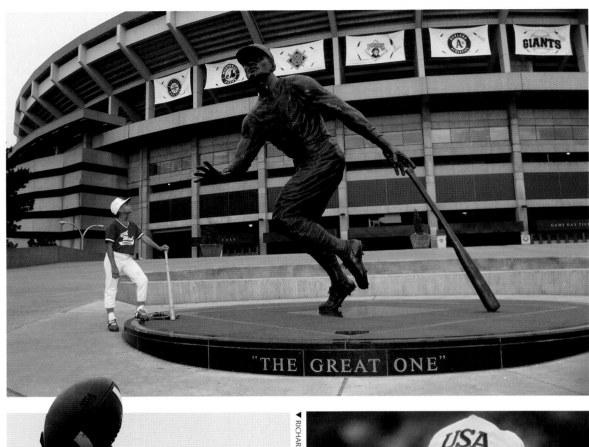

"THE GREAT ONE"

The Power of

CONSIDERED ONE OF THE MOST beautiful ballparks ever built, Forbes Field, which once stood adjacent to the University of Pittsburgh in Oakland, was home to the Pittsburgh Pirates from 1909 to 1970. Now, all that's left are a few markers and a piece of the center field wall (TOP). Half a dozen miles away, on the South Side, South High Stadium proudly hosts championship football games and track meets (BOTTOM).

A LOCAL INSTITUTION SINCE 1876, the Pirates, originally known as the Alleghenies, have been a summertime favorite for generations of Pittsburghers. Adept at developing new talent, the venerable ball club currently features such fine young stars as pitcher Francisco Cordova (BOTTOM LEFT), left fielder Al Martin (BOTTOM RIGHT), and budding right field superstar Jose Guillen (OPPOSITE), whose batting prowess and rifle arm remind many of Roberto Clemente—a comparison not made lightly in Pittsburgh.

The Power of

In Pittsburgh, nothing seems more appropriate than to celebrate Clemente, Mazeroski, Lambert, and company in a Golden Triangle mural, created by award-winning artist Judy Penzer (LEFT). Of our recently retired heroes, perhaps none has brought more honor than Hall of Famer Mario Lemieux, the city's greatest hockey player ever— and arguably the sport's all-time best (BOTTOM RIGHT). Also in the pantheon is 1996 Olympic gold medal wrestler Kurt Angle of Mt. Lebanon (TOP RIGHT).

The Power of

KEEPING UP A PROUD TRADITION, the Pitt Panthers basketball squad is a perennial Big East contender, filling the venerable Fitzgerald Field House with thousands of enthusiastic students and alumni.

T h e   P o w e r   o f

LOCALS FLOCK TO THE WATER, whether it's for the annual Three Rivers Regatta, which draws 250,000 spectators annually (OPPOSITE), major interscholastic swim meets at the University of Pittsburgh's Trees Pool (TOP), or a high-powered cruise down the Allegheny River (BOTTOM).

IT'S STRICTLY HIGH FLYING AT
Kennywood Park, where visitors can
choose from heart-stopping roller
coasters (TOP), fear-inducing water
slides (BOTTOM RIGHT), or a death-
defying swing ride (OPPOSITE TOP).

JOHN WEE

The   Power   of

THERE ARE PLENTY OF WAYS TO BEAT the heat in Pittsburgh. From its prime location on the Monongahela River, Sandcastle offers its share of wet and wild attractions, including a veritable maze of water slides (OPPOSITE, BOTTOM LEFT). And at Boyce Park, the teeth-rattling wave pool is all you need to cool off on a hot summer day (BOTTOM).

The Power of

GATEWAY CLIPPER FLEET

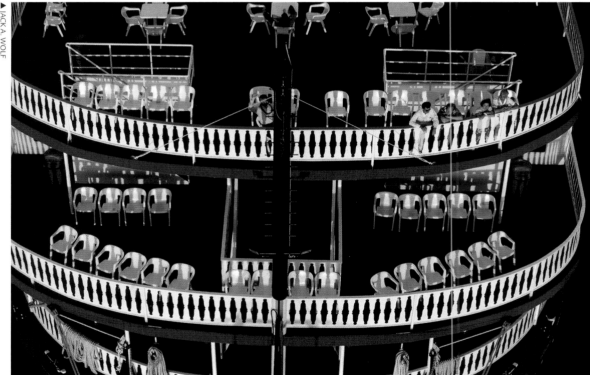

AS THE FINAL DESTINATION ON ITS run from New Orleans, the stern-wheeler *American Queen* makes an annual stop in Pittsburgh (OPPO-SITE). For a more homegrown ride, the Gateway Clipper Fleet—with its party boats, ferries, and the *Good Ship Lollipop*—runs along the Monongahela River from its dock at Station Square (RIGHT).

PITTSBURGHERS MAY NOT BE ABLE to walk on water, but we've found plenty of ways to get around on the wet stuff. Shuttle boats transport passengers from the South Side to Pirates and Steelers games at Three Rivers Stadium (OPPOSITE), while some locals choose to make their own waves (LEFT). Still others try their luck in the Anything That Floats contest during the annual Three Rivers Regatta (RIGHT). Needless to say, life jackets *are* required.

T h e   P o w e r   o f

WATER, WATER EVERYWHERE: While the lakes in and around Pittsburgh offer a dose of serenity for city dwellers, *some* opportunities for canoeing are not so welcome.

Back in 1972, as Hurricane Agnes swallowed Pittsburgh, floodwaters covered a good bit of the Golden Triangle and other low-lying areas.

GENERALLY SMOOTH AS GLASS, Pittsburgh's ubiquitous rivers provide an ideal venue for sculling, rowing, and kayaking. Within sight of the Golden Triangle, where the water was once choked with industrial waste and raw sewage, even the University of Pittsburgh rowing team gets in on the act (OPPOSITE BOTTOM).

EVEN WITHIN PITTSBURGH'S URBAN setting, the natural beauty of Western Pennsylvania abounds, and locals are quick to take advantage of an idyllic lakeside expanse or indulge in a sun-drenched paddleboat ride. For a serene, meditative spot, try the Westinghouse Memorial, erected in Schenley Park in 1930 to commemorate local inventor George Westinghouse (BOTTOM).

The Power of

T h e   P o w e r   o f

OUT OF NECESSITY OR CONVE-
nience, Pittsburgh is a city of
many bridges. Spanning the
Monongahela River between the
Golden Triangle and Station
Square, the 1883 Smithfield Street
Bridge is one of the world's few
remaining lenticular-truss structures (OPPOSITE). In Oakland, new
climate-controlled skywalks connect the neighborhood's hospitals
and help keep pedestrians safe
from the wind and cold (ABOVE).

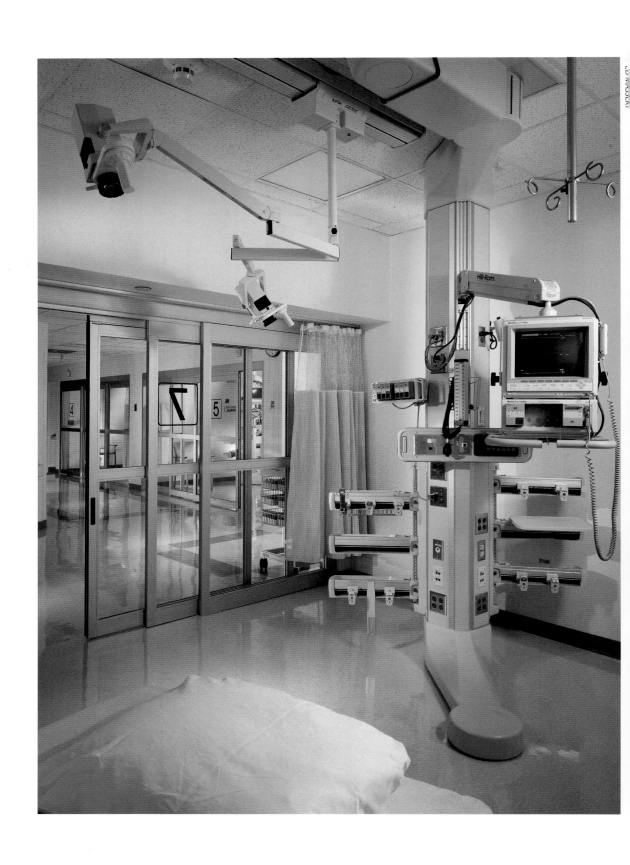

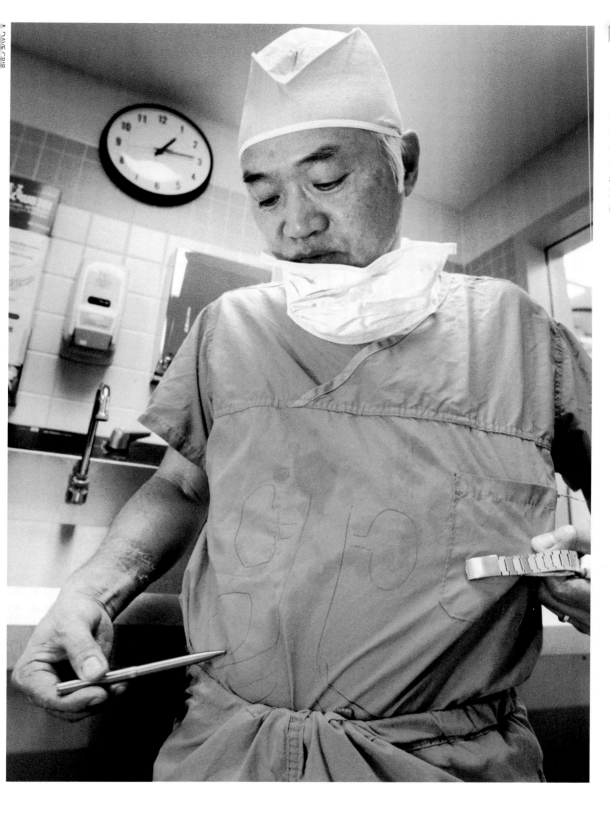

WITH A NUMBER OF RENOWNED hospitals—including major trauma centers, advanced burn units, and oncology research facilities—it's no surprise that Pittsburgh's medical community performs a transplant every 18 hours. At Allegheny General Hospital, the state-of-the-art trauma unit stands ready (OPPOSITE) and a surgeon maps out the logistics of a kidney transplant (LEFT).

The Power of

WHETHER IT'S EDUCATION, FINANCE, medicine, or high technology, Pittsburgh's nonmanufacturing businesses now account for more than 80 percent of the local economy. From robots built to walk on Mars to advanced molecular chemistry, institutions like the University of Pittsburgh are leading the way and securing the future.

In a town that pioneered such innovations as the air brake and the liver transplant, locals still take pride in working with their hands. Many Pittsburghers do their part to keep time-honored trades alive and well, including the city's cobblers, whose shops seem to dot virtually every neighborhood (RIGHT). In nearby Oakmont, Robert Hallet custom designs fine jewelry (OPPOSITE TOP), while craftsmen hone their skills at Pryor Furs, the city's only African-American-owned furrier (OPPOSITE BOTTOM).

LIKE ANY GOOD CONSERVATIVE, midwestern town, Pittsburgh reveres its past. In 1996, the boutique-sized Historical Society of Western Pennsylvania relocated to the mammoth Senator John Heinz Pittsburgh Regional History Center, a former warehouse in the Strip District (PAGE 234). Featuring mountains of historic documents and artifacts, the facility also showcases old trolley cars and landmark signage, including the giant lobster from the now-defunct Klein's seafood restaurant (PAGE 235).

IN PITTSBURGH, OLD SIGNS REVEAL a lot about a neighborhood. Oakland's family-owned Kunst Bakery has delighted discriminating palates with its delectable pastries since 1937.

The Power of

GONE BUT NOT FORGOTTEN: Although Scotty's Diner became Charlie's in 1993, the traditional railcar establishment in Point Breeze has been pleasing patrons with its greasy spoon fare for more than 50 years (TOP). Across town in Dormont, the old Fibber McKee's Tavern served up its share of sandwiches and spirits until the neighborhood saloon was replaced by a stop on the Port Authority's 10.5-mile subway line (BOTTOM).

FOR A RELATIVELY PRIVATE BUNCH, Pittsburghers can air their dirty laundry with the best of them. While Kay's calls all men to put it on and the North Side's Laundry Tyme tells 'em to take it off, some folks ignore those appeals and let it all hang out.

Balanced high above the entrance to the Carnegie Museum of Art is George Segal's *Tightrope Walker*, created in 1969 (ABOVE). An eye-catching addition to the facility's vast collection of sculpture, she is rivaled by *Athlete Pouring Oil into His Hand*, housed in the neighboring Museum of Natural History (OPPOSITE).

The Power of

IN PITTSBURGH, NOT ALL ART IS confined to museums. The region's most successful batik artist, Gambian immigrant Saihou Njie shows off his exquisite, hand-printed fabric (LEFT). Fueling the city's vibrant African-American culture, artist Dee Currin works actively on behalf of Women of Visions, Inc., promoters and conservators of African-American art (OPPOSITE).

ALL TIED UP: ONE OF PITTSBURGH'S
most visible successes of the past
decade has been the line of colorful ties designed by local artist
Burton Morris (OPPOSITE, TOP
LEFT). Favored by the Hollywood
crowd, including the cast of
Friends and *Relativity*'s David
Conrad (RIGHT), the distinctive
neckwear is always an eyeful, as
are Morris' ad designs for such
products as Absolut and Perrier.

Also on the national circuit is
political cartoonist Rob Rogers,
whose skewering of the pompous,
the pooh-bahs, and the just plain
preposterous appears regularly in the
Pittsburgh Post-Gazette (OPPOSITE
BOTTOM). Keeping track of such
cultural comings and goings is
Rogers' fellow journalist Robert
Jay Gangewere, the wise and witty
editor of *Carnegie Magazine*
(OPPOSITE, TOP RIGHT).

I'LL GET YOU, MY PRETTY! Pittsburghers know there's no place like home when the lights go down at Point Park Playhouse (TOP LEFT) or a familiar face delights an aspiring artist (TOP RIGHT). Displayed in the Silkscreen Printing Studio at the Pittsburgh Children's Museum, Andy Warhol's *The Wicked Witch of the West* may be just the inspiration visitors need as they learn the technique so favored by the pop art master (BOTTOM). At the nearby Andy Warhol Museum, Curator of Education Jessica Arcand helps locals embrace the creative experimentation that characterized Warhol's work (OPPOSITE).

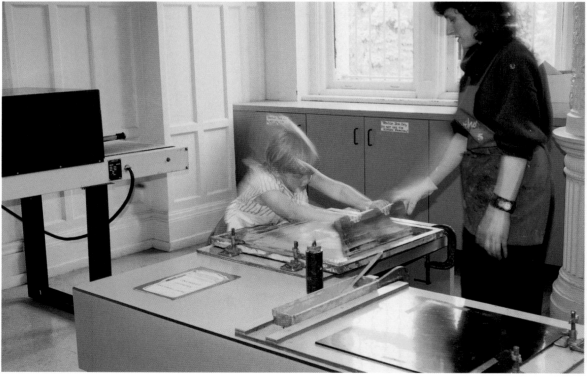

The Power of

During his own "15 minutes of fame," pop art purveyor Andy Warhol was one of Pittsburgh's most celebrated native sons (oppo-site). In the North Side museum that salutes Warhol's career hangs a tribute to his mother, featured here behind brother John Warhola, who stayed in town and kept the extra "a" in the family name (right).

PITTSBURGH

In PITTSBURGH, WE LINE UP OUR houses like soldiers and design them with respect for tradition. From the modern abodes on Washington's Landing (RIGHT) to a string of homes from the early 20th century (OPPOSITE TOP) to a virtual community of architecturally inspired mailboxes (OPPOSITE BOTTOM), Pittsburghers truly know how to get their ducks, er, houses in a row.

The Power of

The Power of

THE HILL DISTRICT, JUST EAST OF the Golden Triangle, was hit particularly hard by urban blight and racial unrest in the mid-1900s, and for many years, it was feared that the development boom that had fortified other neighborhoods would never materialize. Thanks to the enlightened political and community leadership of the 1990s, however, Crawford Square has risen from the ashes to take its rightful place as a viable Pittsburgh neighborhood (OPPOSITE RIGHT).

AN ENGAGING WALL MURAL ILLUS-
trates what those who live here
already know: Pittsburgh's neighborhoods are more than just
bricks and mortar—they're time-
less communities that are as vital
and breathtaking as the city's
high-tech hospitals and sparkling
skyscrapers.

ONE OF THE CITY'S FINER ADDRESSES only a century ago, the North Side became so wrecked by blight and flight that, by the 1970s, many had left it for dead. Hunkering down, Pittsburghers set about reinvesting and rebuilding, and today, the North Side is a safe, integrated neighborhood—home to numerous parks and museums, Three Rivers Stadium, and the Carnegie Science Center.

OME WOULD ARGUE THAT STEEL
Town is also "wheel town," where
bikes of the manual and motor-
ized sort are common both on
and off the job. But don't let the
Harleys lined up at Rosebud fool
you; it's one of the most popular all-purpose clubs in town
(OPPOSITE).

ONE WAY OR ANOTHER, LOCALS always seem to be in motion. The annual 10K Great Race, a smaller sibling to the Pittsburgh Marathon, draws thousands of runners who can't resist the typically gorgeous spring weather and the natural beauty of Schenley Park (BOTTOM). For the wheeled set, there is the grand-prix-style Thrift Drug Classic, a grueling cycling event that draws contestants from all over the world to challenge the city's alpine terrain (TOP AND OPPOSITE).

T h e   P o w e r   o f

NO, TRAFFIC DOESN'T USUALLY move this fast. It just seems that way. Strategically positioned at the intersection of numerous interstates (OPPOSITE), Pittsburgh is within a day's drive of most of the nation's major markets and 70 percent of the U.S. population. Within the city limits, the T's the thing. Built in 1980, Pittsburgh's light-rail transit system connects the South Hills with the Golden Triangle via such stations as Steel Plaza, located beneath the 64-story USX Tower (ABOVE).

IN THE DAYS BEFORE AUTOMOBILES choked the cities, people relied on other forms of transportation. Today, the T rumbles into town from hilly neighborhoods like Allentown and the South Hills (TOP AND OPPOSITE). For a relaxing jaunt out of town, Amtrak, which routes passengers through the renovated Pennsylvania Station, can still do the trick (BOTTOM).

The Power of

PITTSBURGH ALWAYS LOOKS FABU-
ous at night, from the glori-
ously lit Golden Triangle (TOP)
to the subtle glow of the Alle-
Stadium (OPPOSITE). Even the
new Greater Pittsburgh International Airport shimmers when
the sun goes down. Opened in
1992, the $700 million airport is
the third largest in the country,
offering direct flights to 120 cities worldwide (BOTTOM).

AS BOATS NESTLE IN THE OHIO
River west of the Point—in prime
position for a spectacular summer
fireworks display—the city's future
looks bright indeed (PAGES 270
AND 271).

T h e   P o w e r   o f

ONCE AN UGLY JUMBLE OF SMOKY warehouses, fiery factories, and tangled rail lines, the Strip District was burned to the ground in 1877 during the Pennsylvania Railroad strike, one of the bloodiest labor conflagrations in U.S. history. Today, the rebuilt Strip has become a leisure seeker's paradise, thanks to the scenic Boardwalk (OPPOSITE) and such popular waterside nightspots as Donzi's (ABOVE).

274

WHEN THE SUN COMES OUT, SO do the sunbathers. Although these folks have found their own warm spot, the best place to soak up the rays is Point State Park, where acres of riverside lawn are conducive to shedding shirts, showing skin, and snoozing.

The Power of

WHILE REGIONAL GROWTH HAS been neither sudden nor startling, locals know that it has been far healthier than the boom-or-bust cycles so many other cities endure. As a result, our town benefits from high-power corporations and a strong economy without losing the scenic public spaces—like Point State Park—that make Pittsburgh so beautiful.

The POWER of PITTSBURGH

PROFILES in EXCELLENCE

A look at the corporations, businesses, professional groups, and community service organizations that have made this book possible. Their stories—offering an informal chronicle of the local business community—are arranged according to the date they were established in Pittsburgh.

■ ABB Extrel ■ Aerial Communications, Inc. ■ Alcoa ■ Allegheny County Sanitary Authority (ALCOSAN) ■ Allegheny Financial Group, Ltd./Allegheny Investments, Ltd. ■ Allegheny Teledyne Incorporated ■ Ampco-Pittsburgh Corporation ■ Anchor Hocking Specialty Glass ■ The Andy Warhol Museum ■ ANSYS, Inc. ■ Aristech Chemical Corporation ■ Armco Inc. ■ Armstrong World Industries ■ The Art Institute of Pittsburgh® ■ Babcock Lumber Company ■ Bayer Corporation ■ Bohlin Cywinski Jackson ■ Buchanan Ingersoll ■ Calgon Carbon Corporation ■ Calgon Corporation ■ Carnegie Group, Inc. ■ Carnegie Library of Pittsburgh ■ Carnegie Museum of Art ■ Carnegie Museum of Natural History ■ Carnegie Science Center ■ Catholic Diocese of Pittsburgh ■ Center for Organ Recovery and Education (CORE) ■ Central Blood Bank ■ Chelsea Building Products, Inc. ■ Children's Hospital of Pittsburgh ■ The Chubb Group of Insurance Companies ■ Coldwell Banker ■ Columbia Gas of Pennsylvania ■ Compunetics, Inc. ■ Computerm Corporation ■ Consolidated Natural Gas Company ■ Contraves Brashear Systems, L.P. ■ Copperweld Corporation ■ Corporate Accommodations, Inc. ■ R. Davenport & Associates ■ David L. Lawrence Convention Center ■ Dietrich Industries ■ Dollar Bank ■ DQE/Duquesne Light Company ■ Eat'n Park ■ Equitable Resources, Inc. ■ Federated Investors ■ First Western Bancorp, Inc. ■ Fiserv ■ Frank B. Fuhrer Holdings, Inc. ■ G&G Investments Inc. ■ The Galbreath Company ■ General Motors Metal Fabricating Division—Pittsburgh Metal Center ■ Getting to the Point, Inc. ■ Giant Eagle, Inc. ■ Grafner Brothers Inc. ■ Grantmakers of Western Pennsylvania ■ Greater Pittsburgh Chamber of Commerce ■ Harbison-Walker Refractories Company ■ Highmark Blue Cross Blue Shield ■ H.J. Heinz Company ■ ICF Kaiser International ■ Industrial Scientific Corporation ■ International Technology Corporation ■ Interstate Hotels ■ J&H Marsh & McLennan ■ Joy Mining Machinery ■ Kaufmann's ■ KDKA-TV2 ■ Ketchum Public Relations ■ Kirkpatrick & Lockhart LLP ■ Koppers Industries, Inc. ■ Kvaerner Metals ■ La Roche College ■ L.D. Astorino & Associates, Ltd. ■ Le Mont ■ Magee-Womens Hospital ■ Management Science Associates, Inc. ■ Mannesmann Demag Corporation ■ MARC ■ MCI Telecommunications Corp. ■ Mellon Bank Corp. ■ Metplas Inc. ■ Meyer, Unkovic & Scott LLP ■ Michael Baker Corporation ■ Microbac Laboratories, Inc. ■ The Minority Enterprise Corporation ■ MotivePower Industries, Inc. ■ National City Bank of Pennsylvania ■ Oberg Industries ■ OMEGA SYSTEMS Inc. ■ The Pennsylvania State University ■ Pitt-Des Moines, Inc. ■ Pittsburgh Annealing Box Company ■ Pittsburgh Brewing Co. ■ Pittsburgh Business Consultants Inc. ■ Pittsburgh Mercy Health System ■ Pittsburgh Penguins ■ Pittsburgh Pirates ■ Pittsburgh Post-Gazette ■ Pittsburgh Zoo ■ PNC Bank Corp. ■ Port Authority of Allegheny County ■ Powerex, Inc. ■ Price Waterhouse LLP ■ Prudential Preferred Realty ■ Ramada Plaza Suites & Conference Center ■ Reed Smith Shaw & McClay LLP ■ Respironics ■ RPS, Inc. ■ Ryan Homes ■ St. Barnabas Health System ■ St. Francis Health System ■ Sargent Electric Company ■ Schiffman Jewelers, Inc. ■ Sewickley Academy ■ The Soffer Organization ■ Sony Technology Center-Pittsburgh ■ Source W ■ Sumitomo Corporation of America ■ Three Rivers Aluminum Company (TRACO) ■ Tube City, Inc. ■ Union Switch & Signal Inc. ■ The University of Pittsburgh ■ UPMC Health Systems ■ USX Corporation ■ WESCO Distribution, Inc. ■ The Western Pennsylvania Healthcare System, Inc. ■ Westinghouse Air Brake Company (WABCO) ■ Zambelli Fireworks Internationale ■ Zink Partners/Dorchester Towers Apartments

FOUNDED IN 1786, THE *Pittsburgh Post-Gazette* HAS BEEN proud to serve Western Pennsylvania for more than two centuries. And just as the United States has progressed since the days of the founding fathers, so has the *Post-Gazette*, which now stands as Western Pennsylvania's most complete

news and information package.

The newspaper was founded by John Scull, and was originally published as a weekly under the name *Pittsburgh Gazette*. In order to start his publication, Scull had the first hand-printing press delivered over the Allegheny Mountains; he was so determined to produce his newspaper, he would accept payment from his subscribers in the form of chickens, flour, or grain.

Over the next 50 years, the paper changed names several times, although it always kept Gazette in its title. In 1927, it merged with the *Post-Sun*. Paul Block Sr. served as the publisher of the newspaper, now delivered six days a week. This marked the dawn of the most successful era of the *Pittsburgh Post-Gazette*, still run today by the Block family. The Blocks have followed in the strong tradition of dedicated corporate families in Pittsburgh.

With the Block family's 1992 purchase of *The Pittsburgh Press*, the *Pittsburgh Post-Gazette* established the Sunday and daily editions that now stand as Western Pennsylvania's most widely read newspaper. By the late 1990s, the *Post-Gazette* had cemented itself as the Pittsburgh region's dominant newspaper, and it continues to grow circulation in

its Newspaper Designated Market and Retail Trading Zone, the two areas advertisers value most.

A COLORFUL EDITION

Today's award-winning newspaper has changed dramatically from Scull's first edition off the hand-printing press. The *Post-Gazette* utilizes the most modern reporting and printing processes, including a recent, multimillion-dollar investment in new color presses at its home on the Boulevard of the Allies, to publish a full-color edition filled with the most up-to-date news every morning.

The *Post-Gazette* has always delivered news from around the world, the nation, and the city. Its readers have followed conflicts from the Civil War to the Gulf War. The paper reported the rise and fall of the steel industry, and kept residents aware of the changes to the city during Renaissance I and II.

The editorial page of the *Post-Gazette* serves as a forum for the community, examining all of the key issues and how they impact its readers. More than 250 writers, photographers, and editors now form the news staff, which has captured every one of the industry's most renowned national and local awards, including the Pulitzer Prize and the national Freedom of the Press award.

Pittsburgh is also home to some of America's most enthusiastic sports fans, and the *Post-Gazette* provides a daily dose of news, notes, box scores, and more. The Sports section offers complete pre- and postgame coverage as well as features on the great outdoors. Readers turn to the *Post-Gazette* every day for the latest from professional, college, and high school sports.

Every week, the paper produces sections designed to inform read-

When the *Post-Gazette* occupied this building at Wood Street and Liberty Avenue (ca. 1930), the paper was at the dawn of its most successful era (top).

The *Post-Gazette*'s home at 34 Boulevard of the Allies has recently undergone a multimillion-dollar installation of the most advanced printing presses (bottom).

ers on specific topics of interest, including Your Health, Food, and Weekend Mag. Special inserts on area events and Pittsburgh's best-known people are also published regularly in the paper.

No one else can match the *Post-Gazette* as a marketplace. With a reach of more than 1.2 million consumers every week, the paper serves as a powerful center of commerce. People looking to buy meet people looking to sell in the pages of the *Post-Gazette* every day.

The *Post-Gazette* also offers zoned advertising so that small businesses can target specific areas of Western Pennsylvania. In addition, the classified section is filled with thousands of commercial and private party listings every day.

A Committed Company

The *Post-Gazette* is so committed to the community that it created PG Charities to oversee its four nonprofit organizations: Dapper Dan Charities, Free Care Fund, Goodfellows, and Corporate Giving Fund.

Thanks to Dapper Dan Charities, at-risk area children receive the help and guidance they need through sports-related programs. The Pittsburgh Pirates, Steelers, and Penguins often join Dapper Dan in its activities, such as the Youth Sports League program.

Through a long-standing partnership with Children's Hospital, the *Post-Gazette* created the Free Care Fund. It is designed to ensure that every child in the tristate area will receive necessary medical care, regardless of his or her parents' financial status. For 50 years, the Goodfellows holiday toy fund has provided new toys to needy children living in hospitals, institutions, orphanages, and poverty-stricken homes across Western Pennsylvania. In addition, the *Post-Gazette* recently introduced its own Corporate Giving Fund, created to provide endowments to various community organizations.

An Exciting Future

As Western Pennsylvania's oldest manufacturer, the *Post-Gazette* has established itself as more than a newspaper; it's a local tradition.

William Block Jr. (left), copublisher and president, and William Block Sr., chairman, are part of the city's strong corporate family tradition.

More than 1.2 million readers turn to Western Pennsylvania's number one source of news and information every week.

Just as Pittsburgh has been able to thrive through all of the economic and social changes it has undergone in recent years, so has the *Post-Gazette*.

Thanks to years of dedication and innovation, the *Post-Gazette* has become the area's most widely read newspaper. The paper looks forward to sharing the innovations that will shape Pittsburgh for years to come. It is this dedication to readers that will continue to guide the *Pittsburgh Post-Gazette* as Western Pennsylvania's indispensable source of news and information.

T

HE UNIVERSITY OF PITTSBURGH TRACES ITS ROOTS TO THE chartering of the Pittsburgh Academy in 1787, the year the United States Constitution was adopted. The academy's founder, Hugh Henry Brackenridge, hoped the school, then consisting of a single log cabin, would serve as a "candle

The central landmark of the University of Pittsburgh campus is the 42-story Cathedral of Learning, the tallest school building in the Western Hemisphere (left).

"The university's most prominent characteristic should be an unrelenting commitment to excellence, the successful pursuit of quality in everything we do," says Mark A. Nordenberg, 17th chancellor of the University of Pittsburgh (right).

lite in the forested wilderness." In the more than 200 years since, both the University of Pittsburgh and the City of Pittsburgh have evolved in extraordinary ways, their histories closely interconnected.

On the eve of the 21st century, the University of Pittsburgh is an internationally recognized center of learning and research, strong in the arts and sciences and the professions. Fondly known to students and alumni as Pitt, the university is a major provider of top-quality higher education in its region, one of the nation's largest producers of pioneering research, and a leading American institution creatively interacting with the rest of the world. The University of Pittsburgh Medical Center is now recognized among the top 10 in the country.

Mark A. Nordenberg, the university's 17th chancellor, oversees a Pittsburgh campus of 16 undergraduate, graduate, and professional schools, as well as regional campuses in Bradford, Greensburg, Johnstown, and Titusville, Pennsylvania. He is the former dean of Pitt's law school and a member of the university community since 1977. "We are building on a strong foundation," says Nordenberg, "the result of the talent and dedication of others. The university's most prominent characteristic should be an unrelenting commitment to excellence, the successful pursuit of quality in everything we do. This we owe to all who depend on us."

FAR-REACHING IMPACT

A private institution for most of its past, the University of Pittsburgh became state-related in 1966, establishing a relationship with the Commonwealth of Pennsylvania that has benefited both partners. Looking back over the three decades of Pitt's state-related status, Nordenberg sees an era characterized by accomplishment, growth, and a steady rise in intellectual stature for the university, with far-reaching effects for the citizens of Pennsylvania.

During the past three decades, Pittsburgh has conferred nearly 190,000 academic degrees, more than 40 percent of them reflecting the graduate-level learning experience so often essential for success in today's increasingly complex and competitive world. In recent years, University of Pittsburgh students have achieved high levels of attainment, including winning many Rhodes and Marshall scholarships.

The university has earned international recognition for the world-class quality of its programs in disciplines as diverse as transplantation surgery and philosophy. Ranked among the top 20 institutions nationally in attracting federal grants, Pitt annually imports $250 million in sponsored research. Funding to Pitt from the National Institutes of Health now amounts to more than 2.3 cents for every federal dollar awarded

by that agency, up from 1.3 cents in 1985, the largest increase in market share of any university in America.

Pitt has been elected to membership in the Association of American Universities, representing the top 60 research universities in North America. The university's research breakthroughs in just the past year include the discovery of a new planetary system within our galaxy, contributions by a team of engineers in developing a silver-sheathed superconducting wire, and the first applications of gene therapy techniques in the treatment of rheumatoid arthritis.

The university has also initiated an innovative strategy of outreach programs dealing with a broad range of economic, health, and social issues. A linchpin for invigorating the Western Pennsylvania economy, Pitt supports economic development through such initiatives as the Manufacturing Assistance Program and the Center for Biotechnology and Bioengineering. Pitt is among the largest employers in the six-county Pittsburgh region, and its employees return millions in tax revenue and purchasing power to the region.

A VISION FOR THE FUTURE

In 1996, Pitt's board of trustees, working closely with Nordenberg, put forward a five-point vision to guide the university to new levels of educational strength. This blueprint for entering the 21st century included aggressively pursuing excellence in undergraduate edu-

cation, ensuring operational efficiency and effectiveness, securing an adequate financial base, maintaining excellence in research, and partnering in community development. "We must become even stronger and more innovative in these challenging times—true to the work ethic of Western Pennsylvania, rich in intellectual rigor, and committed in every respect to effectively preparing students for life and careers in the 21st century," says Nordenberg. Institutional commitments also extend to the people and economy of the region. One example is an aggressive focus on technology transfer. These efforts have a dual goal: generating additional revenue, while spurring the creation of regional jobs. They involve a special focus on such fields as biomedicine, information science, new materials, and supercomputing.

Nordenberg affirms "that the strength of the university is directly dependent upon the strength of the region. It is also true, more than ever, that the strength of the region requires a strong University of Pittsburgh. We are a major economic force in the region. And by expanding the existing base of knowledge, we help people to lead fuller, healthier, more productive lives."

As Pitt defines its missions for the next century, it remains a place of enduring tradition. At the heart of the university complex stands a 42-story, Gothic tower, the Cathedral of Learning. It contains, among other treasures, 24

international classrooms, each the product of several years' work by artisans from the countries represented—and an international microcosm of the diverse cultures of the world that have converged in Pittsburgh, where the "candle lite" of the city's namesake university now shines brighter than ever before.

Clockwise from top:
The Pittsburgh Panthers bring the excitement of Big East athletics to the city of Pittsburgh. In addition to football, the university competes in 17 other athletic programs for men and women.

As one of the leading research universities in the country, Pitt excels in a broad range of research programs including the basic sciences, biomedical and bioengineering sciences, materials science, and supercomputing.

The University of Pittsburgh's William Pitt Union is housed in the former Hotel Schenley, restored to its turn-of-the-century grandeur and used for student organizations and activities.

EVERY CITY NEEDS A TOP EDUCATIONAL INSTITUTION THAT PLACES a high value on the merits of hard work, academic achievement, and moral and intellectual development. In Pittsburgh, Sewickley Academy is such an institution. The oldest independent school in the area, it has been preparing young people to be responsible citizens and contributing members of their communities since it first opened in 1838.

Nestled among the quiet, tree-lined streets of Edgeworth, a charming residential community located approximately 12 miles from downtown, Sewickley currently enrolls more than 750 boys and girls in prekindergarten through 12th grade. The 30-acre campus boasts numerous educational amenities, including 55 classrooms, two libraries with a total of 33,600 volumes, two gymnasiums, four computer labs, state-of-the art student publication centers, and several studios for music, dance, art, and drama.

The 30-acre campus provides a dynamic setting for teaching and learning, with state-of-the-art facilities, technology-capable classrooms and laboratories, and abundant areas for quiet contemplation.

ACADEMICS FIRST

Sewickley Academy is well known for its rigorous academic program (nearly one-third of all seniors are National Merit Scholars, Semifinalists, or Commendees), as well as its ability to cultivate the individual talents of students. Classes average just 16 students in elementary grades and 12 students per class in the high school. The student-teacher ratio is 9-to-1, allowing each child to receive the care and nurturing that promote success.

The academy also prides itself on its diverse student body, which draws from a wide socioeconomic background and reflects the rich cultural fabric of the Pittsburgh region. The school attracts students from more than 50 different school districts from Southwestern Pennsylvania, including the city of Pittsburgh, as well as from eastern Ohio and northern West Virginia. More than 20 percent receive some sort of need-based financial aid. Because the academy is able to handpick its enrollees—fewer than half of all who apply are actually admitted—students are surrounded by a group of very talented and motivated peers who constantly challenge one another to succeed.

BEYOND ACADEMICS

Sewickley Academy encourages its pupils to get involved in many extracurricular activities, which teach them the fine art of time management and help to create a more well rounded individual. To that end, the school boasts a surprising number of interscholastic and intramural sports, including soccer, cross-country, tennis, baseball, softball, golf, ice hockey, lacrosse, wrestling, field hockey, and swimming. On the Sewickley campus are four athletic fields, five tennis courts, and two playgrounds, not to mention a 635-seat auditorium.

Beginning with the youngest students, there are regular classes in art, music, dance, foreign languages, and computer skills. By the middle school grades, pupils can choose from electives in the arts, with foreign languages and computer science integrated into the academic program. The senior school curriculum offers courses in photography, studio art, theater, and music, as well as electives in English, science, math, foreign languages, and social sciences. Computers are used as learning tools in all disciplines and students master word processing, data analysis, and research via the Internet.

"We believe in providing a wide range of opportunities for our students," says Headmaster Hamilton Clark, "and in creating a community where everyone par-

ticipates and no one is left on the sidelines to simply spectate."

Much of the academy's success can be attributed to its instructors, who are dedicated to developing their students' intellectual curiosity, as well as their emotional and social growth. Teachers, the majority of whom hold advanced degrees and hail from cities across the nation, serve as mentors, counselors, athletic coaches, club sponsors, and academic advisers.

Likewise, parents play an important role in the Sewickley Academy experience, lending a hand in everything from manning the booths at athletic activities and helping backstage during performances to volunteering in the classroom, chipping in at a used book sale, and chaperoning on field trips.

In the Community

All Sewickley Academy students learn from an early age that they have an obligation to the world at large. They may choose from a variety of service work, from constructing valentines to send to a local nursing home, collecting and delivering food to a local shelter, and volunteering at a nearby hospital or rehabilitation center, to

helping build a house for Habitat for Humanity.

Completing 30 hours of community service during the junior and senior years is a graduation requirement. The reason is simple: "All children, no matter what age level, need to understand that the world is bigger than just this school or their own community, and that they have a responsibility to share their talents and gifts with others," says Clark.

Sewickley Academy is also unique in the fact that it is one of the few private schools in the Pittsburgh area to bring its entire student body together on one campus. Though separated by grade

among several buildings, students are able to interact and learn from one another on a daily basis. Middle school girls, for example, talk to the elementary girls about peer influences, while high schoolers routinely volunteer to read stories or teach songs in French to preschoolers. Older students, in particular, serve as positive role models to the younger children.

The result is that Sewickley Academy is a place where students not only learn to think independently, but also cooperatively, in a supportive and caring atmosphere. Says Clark, "We're dedicated to preparing young people for a lifetime of discovery and learning."

Clockwise from top:
Art classes teach students in all grades to think and express themselves visually. Studio electives in design, painting, crafts, printmaking, and other media challenge the most talented artists.

Athletics are an important component of the school's program, along with academics and the arts. In 1997, men's soccer and basketball teams both won state championships.

Small classes and a hands-on approach to learning create an environment where each student is challenged to achieve his or her fullest potential.

A S CHRISTIANITY ENTERS ITS THIRD MILLENNIUM, THE CATHOLic Diocese of Pittsburgh is confident in its ability to meet the challenges of extending God's kingdom on earth in today's complex society. It is a task for which the diocese has been preparing itself through a comprehensive program of revitalization and spiritual renewal, outlined in Bishop Donald W. Wuerl's pastoral letter, The Great Jubilee.

The effort has been complemented by Wuerl's call for a diocesan synod, aimed at organizing the local church for years to come in all aspects of ecclesial life. This multiple rekindling of spiritual fervor reinforces the belief that the Diocese of Pittsburgh will continue to be an influential force in the life of the Greater Pittsburgh area, as it has been since it was established by Pope Gregory XVI on August 8, 1843, with Michael O'Connor as its first bishop. He was followed by 10 others, including Wuerl, who has headed the diocese since 1988.

The diocese today embraces six counties—Allegheny, Beaver, Butler, Greene, Lawrence, and Washington. It has more than 200 parishes with more than 800,000 members, who represent approximately 40 percent of the six counties' total population.

A DIOCESE COMMITTED TO EDUCATION

Among the most visible of the diocese's multiple ministries are the Catholic schools, which make up the area's second-largest educational system, with the City of Pittsburgh schools being the largest. Approximately 36,000 students receive an academically excellent and values-enriched education at more than 120 elementary and secondary schools.

The educational excellence of the schools was recognized in 1990, when the Catholic school system was given accreditation of all of its elementary schools by the Middle States Association of Colleges and Schools, the first time that any major diocese had received such recognition. Students in both elementary and secondary schools regularly score well above national norms in standardized tests, with more than 100 secondary school students being named National Merit Scholarship finalists in the past 10 years.

The diocese also has committed itself to education in the inner city, demonstrated best perhaps by its alliance with the business community in the Extra Mile Education Foundation. This foundation, which supports three Catholic elementary schools in Pittsburgh, was established in 1990 when local corporate and philanthropic leaders responded to an invitation from Wuerl to combine their abilities and resources in maintaining educational opportunities for students in disadvantaged city neighborhoods.

EDUCATION BEYOND SCHOOLS

More than 55,000 young Catholics who attend public schools in the diocese receive firm grounding in their faith through parish-based religious education programs. Programs for all these students include thorough education on the Church's teaching.

This focus on total Catholic education is extended into a comprehensive program for adult education as well. One important aspect of this educational effort is the preparation of the laity for active ministry in the church. To accomplish this, the Institute for Ministries was founded to prepare laypersons for certified ministry.

The Diocese of Pittsburgh's efforts in education are well respected far beyond the confines of Southwestern Pennsylvania, with many teaching materials developed in the diocese being used across the United States. These include Wuerl's television program, The Teaching of Christ, shown on the Odyssey Channel

The Gothic spires of St. Paul Cathedral, the "heart" of the Catholic Diocese of Pittsburgh, are a familiar landmark in Pittsburgh's Oakland district (left).

Bishop Donald W. Wuerl has championed the cause of Catholic education at all levels, from the primary grades through adult classes (right).

DOUGLAS BOOTH

DOUGLAS KAUP

nationally, as well as other faith-focused instructional tapes featuring the bishop.

The diocese has also been a national leader for many years in the field of educational and spiritual ministries serving persons with disabilities. As evidence of this commitment, a religious education program for Catholic children and adults with mental retardation was prepared under the guidance of the diocesan Department for Persons with Disabilities and has been distributed nationwide.

Other Priorities

Beyond its pastoral and educational ministries, the Catholic Church is engaged in many initiatives vital to the well-being of the wider Southwestern Pennsylvania community. The Sisters of Mercy founded Pittsburgh's first hospital 150 years ago, followed by St. Francis Hospital two decades later. Today,

Catholic-sponsored health care has grown in the diocese to the point where there are now two health care systems with hundreds of thousands of patients treated annually. In addition, Catholic nursing homes provide an important source of care for elderly or frail persons. Realizing that health care today is undergoing rapid change, the diocese is encouraging communications between the church and the health care industry as well as the advancement of parish-based health services.

In these and other areas of social concern, the diocese concentrates on the role for which it is best qualified, that of bringing a moral dimension to community issues. The diocese, for example, has been an active participant in the Youth Crime Prevention Council, an effective program using prevention, intervention, and community mobilization in reducing juvenile crime. The

diocese has also taken a leadership role in the struggle against racism.

Helping the less fortunate is also a priority of the diocese. Under diocesan or other Catholic sponsorship, a wide variety of social services exist for the unemployed, persons with handicaps, single mothers, and the homeless. Catholic Charities of the Diocese of Pittsburgh, the church's agency for delivery of a wide range of these social services, is well respected for its work. With a focus on families and their members, Catholic Charities cares for and counsels more than 55,000 people annually, regardless of their religious background or ability to pay.

As the Catholic Diocese of Pittsburgh looks to the future, it is with the conviction that its tradition of faith, education, and service will help Pittsburgh grow as a community for generations to come.

Clockwise from top left:
The eucharistic liturgy is at the heart of spiritual life at parishes throughout the diocese.

The first mass within the present city of Pittsburgh was celebrated on April 17, 1754, by a French priest, Father Denys Baron, chaplain for a French army expedition into the area.

Students in more than 120 elementary and secondary Catholic schools of the diocese are offered an academically excellent education firmly rooted in moral values.

Educational enrichment is a key component of summer day camp at the Ozanam Cultural Center in Pittsburgh, a multiservice facility operated by Catholic Charities.

DOUGLAS BOOTH

DOUGLAS BOOTH

 N 1843, PITTSBURGH WAS A BUSTLING INDUSTRIAL CENTER WITH A population of 40,000. In that year, seven members of the Sisters of Mercy arrived from Carlow, Ireland, at the invitation of Bishop Michael O'Connor, the city's first Roman Catholic Bishop. In 1847, the Sisters established Mercy Hospital, beginning a long history of service to

the city of Pittsburgh.

Today, Pittsburgh Mercy Health System (PMHS) includes Mercy Hospital, Mercy Providence Hospital, St. Joseph Nursing and Health Care Center, St. Pius X Residence, Southwestern Nursing and Rehabilitation Center, Mercy Behavioral Health Services, the Institute for Health Communities, Mercy Primary Care, and the Pittsburgh Mercy Foundation.

Mercy is also a founding member of the Eastern Mercy Health System (EMHS), a regional, multi-institutional system for health care sponsored by nine communities of the Sisters of Mercy of the Americas. In 1997, EMHS announced the formation of one of the nation's largest not-for-profit health systems. Catholic Health East, a new, mission- and values-based, Catholic-sponsored health care system, is

the collaboration of EMHS, the Franciscan Sisters of Allegany Health System of Tampa, and the Sisters of Providence Health System based in Holyoke.

IN THE COMMUNITY

Today, Mercy Hospital of Pittsburgh is a 506-bed, licensed teaching and general referral hospital, offering medical and surgical services in a variety of specialties— including cardiology, oncology, obstetrics/gynecology, pediatrics, and burn trauma—and Centers for Excellence for psychiatry and rehabilitation.

The hospital has a rich tradition of public service and medical innovation. During the Civil War, for instance, Secretary of War Edwin M. Stanton called upon the Sisters of Mercy at Mercy Hospital to treat injured Union soldiers. In all, 27 sisters served at Stanton Military Hospital in Washington, D.C., and nine sisters took charge of a local hospital designated for the military.

As Pittsburgh faced smallpox, diphtheria, and typhoid epidemics during the 1870s, Mercy Hospital provided the isolation necessary to contain the spread of infectious diseases and provided dignified care for patients. It was also during this time that Mercy physicians organized to form Pittsburgh's first medical staff.

At the turn of the century, Mercy established the Pasteur Institute for the Treatment of Rabies. Using Dr. Louis Pasteur's revolutionary methods, Dr. Aimee Leteve, an associate of Pasteur's, saved hundreds of rabies victims from almost certain death. When the Great Depression arrived, it

Pittsburgh Mercy Health System continues to fulfill the mission established by the Sisters of Mercy more than 150 years ago: to minister to those in need by providing compassionate, affordable, quality health care.

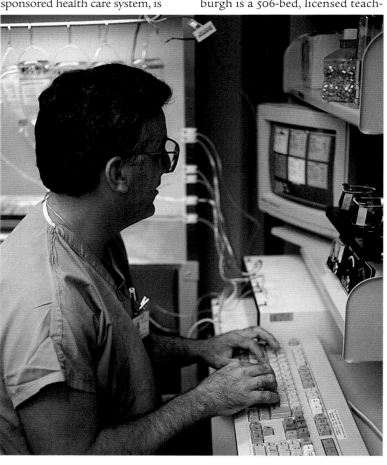

Throughout the years, Mercy has never failed to offer its patients the latest advancements in medicine.

The Power of

brought with it a great need for free medical care. In 1931, Mercy Hospital donated more than $600,000 in free health care to the people of Pittsburgh—and this during a time when one day in the hospital cost under $4. By the time the decade of economic depression ended, Mercy Hospital had established the first blood bank in the region.

Throughout the years, Mercy has never failed to offer its patients the latest advancements in medicine. Mercy opened diabetic and allergy clinics, as well as Western Pennsylvania's first bronchoscopy clinic, which drastically reduced the mortality rate among children who had swallowed foreign objects. The hospital formally organized a diet-planning program and an anesthesiology department, and Mercy physicians collaborated with scientists from the Mellon Institute to identify a cure for pneumonia.

As the Sisters piloted Mercy through the physician and nursing staff shortages of World War II, Mercy became one of the first hospitals in Western Pennsylvania approved for U.S. Cadet Nurse Corps Training. During the 1960s, the Hospital Planning Commission urged the Sisters of Mercy to relocate Mercy Hospital to the suburbs, but citing their commitment to the underserved in the city, the Sisters declined.

In 1893, Sister Magdalene Phelan opened the Mercy Hospital School of Nursing, one of the region's first diploma schools of nursing. Today, the hospital sponsors six residency programs, operates a diploma school of nursing, and offers fellowships in pediatrics, critical care medicine, and cardiovascular anesthesia, as well as head, neck, and microvascular surgery. Some of Mercy's current research projects include interventions to prevent falls in elderly populations, study of the cancer-preventing effects of certain foods, and pharmaceutical interventions that halt damage caused by strokes and heart attacks.

MODERN-DAY MERCY

In 1993, the Sisters of Mercy acquired the former Divine Providence Hospital, changing the name of the 146-bed, licensed community hospital on Pittsburgh's north side to Mercy Providence Hospital. Mercy Providence provides 24-hour treatment of medical, surgical, and psychiatric emergencies. The hospital offers free courtesy van service to patients with scheduled appointments on the hospital campus.

During the 1990s, Mercy has reaffirmed its commitment to making primary care accessible to the many communities it serves. The hospital's growing primary care network, Mercy Primary Care, offers family practice, pediatrics, obstetrics/gynecology, and internal medicine services through medical practices in both the city and its suburbs, and is expanding into surrounding counties.

The system also includes Mercy Behavioral Health Services, a community-based continuum of more than 50 specialized programs and services for individuals and families experiencing mental illness, mental retardation, or addiction to alcohol or other drugs.

Since a large part of Pittsburgh's population is elderly, Mercy founded the Mercy Life Center Corp. (MLCC) in 1988 to expand and promote the PMHS continuum of care, and to develop and manage the system's long-term care facilities and services. MLCC works in collaboration with Mercy Hospital's Skilled Nursing Facility and Center for Aging to provide a range of senior care services to patients of St. Joseph Nursing and Health Care Center, a 158-bed, licensed skilled nursing facility, and residents of St. Pius X Residence, a 26-bed, licensed personal care home. In addition, MLCC holds a management contract for Southwestern Nursing and Rehabilitation Center.

Through these and other services, Pittsburgh Mercy Health System continues to fulfill the mission established by the Sisters of Mercy more than 150 years ago: to minister to those in need by providing compassionate, affordable, quality health care.

During the 1990s, Mercy has reaffirmed its commitment to making primary care accessible to the many communities it serves. The hospital's growing primary care network, Mercy Primary Care, offers family practice, pediatrics, obstetrics/gynecology, and internal medicine services through medical practices in both the city and suburbs, and is expanding into surrounding counties.

HE VALUES AND MISSION OF THE WESTERN PENNSYLVANIA Healthcare System, Inc. (WPHS) were established in 1848 when civic leaders, recognizing that Pittsburgh lacked adequate institutional resources to meet the health care needs of its population, envisioned a hospital "worthy of

our city and vicinity and the age in which we live." In 1912, the expanding needs of patients and staff led The Western Pennsylvania Hospital to relocate from its first site near downtown to its present location on Friendship Avenue in the Bloomfield section of Pittsburgh. "The hospital built on friendship," as West Penn became affectionately known, is the flagship hospital of The Western Pennsylvania Healthcare System.

For 150 years, The Western Pennsylvania Hospital has taken care of the people of Pittsburgh, through floods and flu epidemics, through wars and depressions, and through this century's industrial

prosperity and spirit of renaissance. Growing and changing to meet the needs of the city and its people, West Penn Hospital was the first public hospital chartered in Pittsburgh; first in the area to serve as a veterans' hospital (1863); first in the area to sponsor a medical college (1883); first in Pittsburgh to open an intensive care unit (1959); first in the area to perform a bone marrow transplant (1967); first hospital in Pittsburgh to build a heliport (1971); first to open a center dedicated exclusively to breast diagnostic imaging (1985); and first hospital in Pittsburgh totally dedicated to patient-focused care (1995).

WPHS includes The Western Pennsylvania Hospital, Suburban General Hospital in the Pittsburgh suburb of Bellevue, The Western Pennsylvania Hospital Foundation, and West Penn Corporate Medical Services.

THE WESTERN PENNSYLVANIA HOSPITAL

The Western Pennsylvania Hospital has a rich history of leadership in providing the highest quality of care and service to people throughout the region, and has been ranked among the nation's top 40 hospitals according to *U.S. News & World Report*'s guide to America's Best Hospitals.

West Penn Hospital is particularly known for its state-of-the-art treatment programs for burns, cancer, cardiovascular diseases, and diabetes; its imaging programs; and health care services for women, infants, and children. West Penn Hospital has specialized centers for foot and ankle surgery, geriatric care, pain management, and sleep disorders. In addition, the hospital has a breast diagnostic imaging center, an infant apnea center, and an outpatient rehabilitation center.

BURN TRAUMA CENTER

Established in 1970, the Burn Trauma Center at The Western Pennsylvania Hospital is the largest burn care center in the tristate area, caring for approximately 1,000 patients annually from communities in Pennsylvania, Ohio, and West Virginia. The hospital's center was the first in the region to be verified as a burn center by the Committee on Trauma of the American College of Surgeons and by the American Burn Association.

COMPREHENSIVE CANCER SERVICES

Patients travel to The Western Pennsylvania Hospital from other states, as well as other countries, for specialized services of The Western Pennsylvania Cancer Institute. Founded in 1990 to broaden and extend oncology services for patients throughout the region, the institute provides the latest approaches for the treatment of all types of cancer, and has earned national recognition as a leader in bone marrow transplantation and the treatment of solid tumors, leukemia, and blood-related disorders. The Center for Neuro-Oncology at West Penn Hospital is one of seven national members of the Brain Tumor Cooperative Group, sponsored by the National Cancer Institute. The center is one of 12 sites in the nation, and the only site in Pennsylvania to treat patients using revolutionary radiation therapy technology that treats multiple brain tumors with pinpoint accuracy and without damaging surrounding tissue.

West Penn Hospital also participates in studies of the Gynecologic Oncology Group, a national organization funded by the National Cancer Institute. Current studies include the evaluation of treat-

The Western Pennsylvania Hospital celebrates 150 years of excellence and leadership in meeting the region's health care needs from 1848 to 1998.

The Power of

ments for ovarian cancer, tumors of the uterus (both endometrial carcinomas and uterine sarcomas), and cancer of the cervix and vulva.

HEART CARE

The Western Pennsylvania Hospital has been renowned for decades for its excellence in diagnosis and treatment of heart disease and cardiovascular disorders.

Each year, approximately 1,000 open-heart surgeries are performed at the Cardiovascular Institute, and more than 32,700 patients have echocardiograms. The Cardiac Catheterization Laboratory is now "cineless," with all images acquired, stored, and viewed without the use of film. In this state-of-the-art laboratory, more than 4,000 procedures are performed each year.

Research at the Cardiovascular Institute focuses on the trials of efficacy and safety of new drugs for hypertension; experimental agents for treating congestive heart failure and reducing the complications of angioplasty; new anticoagulant agents; and estrogen and progestin replacement in postmenopausal women with coronary heart disease.

In conjunction with the University of Pittsburgh, the Cardiovascular Institute is one of the 15 sites across the United States conducting the Heart and Estrogen Replacement Study (HERS).

HEALTH CARE FOR WOMEN, INFANTS, AND CHILDREN

The hospital's health care programs for women, infants, and children are directed by experienced teams of board-certified physicians, professional nurses, and support staff.

State-of-the-art facilities for obstetrical services at The Western Pennsylvania Hospital include 10 new labor, delivery, recovery, and postpartum suites in a beautifully designed setting that provides optimal comfort.

For families seeking a nontraditional birthing experience, the services of BirthPlace, the first freestanding midwifery birthing center in Western Pennsylvania, are available through the hospital. Low-risk deliveries take place in a

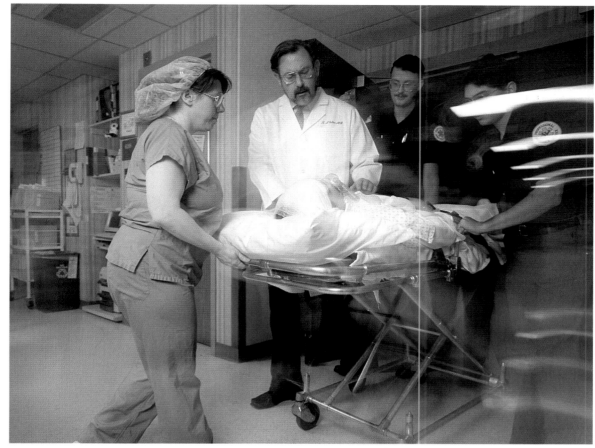

DAVID ASCHKENAS

restored Victorian home located close to West Penn Hospital.

West Penn Hospital is known throughout the region for its high-risk obstetrics and maternal-fetal medicine programs. Physicians have special expertise in preterm birth and premature ruptured membranes; diabetes and hypertension in pregnancy; fetal therapy, including fetal blood transfusions; targeted fetal ultrasound; and antepartum testing.

Other services include perinatal consultations, ultrasound evaluations (utilizing the latest ultrasound technology), fetal testing, and genetics services.

For pregnant women worried about the effects of exposure to medications, chemicals, or disease during pregnancy, the hospital's Pregnancy Safety Hotline provides them with information about such risks.

West Penn Hospital's Level III Neonatal Intensive Care Unit (NICU) provides the highest level of neonatal intensive care available, and is one of the region's largest referral sources for sick newborns.

In the Pediatric Unit at West Penn Hospital, infants, children, and adolescents are diagnosed and treated for a wide range of general pediatric conditions and complicated diseases.

The hospital's team of sub-specialists also provides tertiary gynecologic services that include the surgical, radiological, and chemotherapeutic treatment of advanced gynecological cancers, using nationally recognized and coordinated treatment protocols; the diagnosis and treatment of urinary incontinence, using sophisticated urodynamic testing techniques; the diagnosis and treatment of children with gynecologic disor-

The Western Pennsylvania Hospital's Burn Trauma Center is the largest burn center in the tristate area (top).

Patients of The Western Pennsylvania Cancer Institute benefit from state-of-the-art technology and the latest approaches to treatment (bottom).

The Western Pennsylvania Cardiovascular Institute offers comprehensive patient care, medical education, and research programs in cardiovascular disease (left).

West Penn Hospital neonatologists and other specialists in the care of high-risk infants work closely with babies' families to provide essential nurturing, as well as the most innovative and advanced treatments available (right).

ders; and the care and treatment of couples who experience infertility.

The Breast Diagnostic Imaging Center (BDIC) was established in 1985 as the first facility in Pittsburgh dedicated exclusively to conditions of the breast.

The BDIC is part of West Penn's Division of Diagnostic Radiology and Imaging, which has some of the most advanced instrumentation in the nation, and which offers virtually all diagnostic and interventional radiologic procedures.

West Penn Hospital was also the first health care facility in the region to acquire the Acuson Sequoia 512 Ultrasound System, which enables radiologists to view anatomy and physiology never before seen with ultrasound.

DIABETES CARE

The Joslin Center for Diabetes at West Penn Hospital is one of 12 affiliates in the United States of the world-renowned Joslin Diabetes Center in Boston, and demonstrates the hospital's commitment to en-

hancing the quality of diabetes care and management in the tristate area.

Patients of the Joslin Center for Diabetes at West Penn Hospital have access to a team of diabetologists who are board-certified in endocrinology, plus specially trained nurses, dietitians, nurse educators, and exercise therapists.

At the Joslin satellite office in Westmoreland patients receive multidisciplinary care in comprehensive outpatient clinic facilities.

NEW CONCEPTS IN PATIENT CARE

The Western Pennsylvania Hospital was one of the first in the region to have a dedicated Patient-Focused Care Unit, and in July 1995, opened the hospital's nine-story Patient Care Tower, specially designed around the patient-focused care concept.

The hospital's new, 30-bed Subacute Care Unit opened in 1996 to help patients make a smooth transition from the acute care hospital setting to home.

West Penn Hospital has also been at the forefront of meeting the growing needs for home health care in the communities it serves. West Penn Hospital's Home Health Agency is a Medicare-certified home health agency that provides skilled nursing and other therapies in patients' homes throughout Allegheny and all contiguous counties.

GRADUATE MEDICAL EDUCATION PROGRAMS

In 1883, Western Pennsylvania Hospital sponsored the first medical college in Western Pennsylvania, later to become the University of Pittsburgh School of Medicine. Continuing in its tradition of strong programs for the education of graduate physicians, West Penn Hospital today offers residency programs in anesthesiology, emergency medicine, family practice, internal medicine, obstetrics and gynecology, plastic surgery, podiatric surgery, diagnostic radiology, and general surgery. Also offered are an osteopathic medicine internship in affiliation with Lake Erie

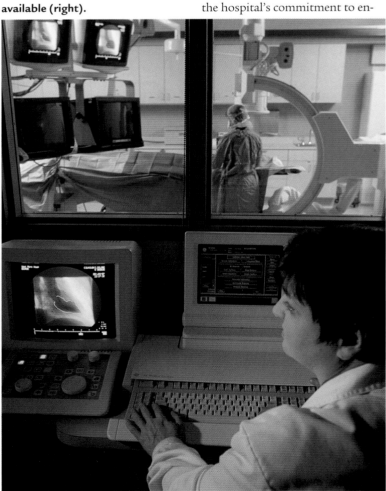

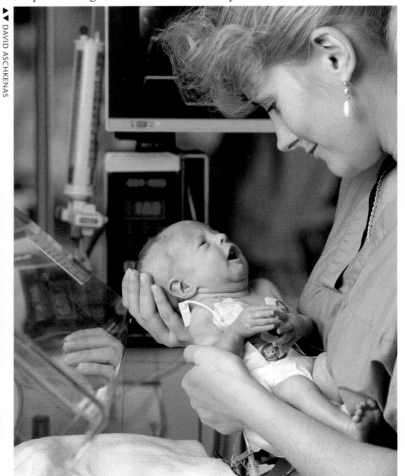

DAVID ASCHKENAS

The Power of

College of Osteopathic Medicine and six fellowship programs.

SUBURBAN GENERAL HOSPITAL

Suburban General Hospital, an affiliate of The Western Pennsylvania Healthcare System, Inc., is a modern, 195-bed community hospital located in the town of Bellevue, just a seven-minute drive from Pittsburgh's Golden Triangle. With a tradition of caring and a commitment to excellence, the employees and medical staff of Suburban General Hospital offer general medical and surgical services, as well as outpatient, emergency, cardiac, and intensive care services. In addition, Suburban General Hospital provides care to patients through a highly specialized rehabilitation unit and a skilled nursing unit.

THE WESTERN PENNSYLVANIA HOSPITAL FOUNDATION

The Western Pennsylvania Hospital Foundation raises, manages, and invests money to enable The Western Pennsylvania Hospital to further its mission of providing quality health care, community service, education, and research.

The foundation operates a state-of-the-art medical research facility to support basic biochemical and physiological research.

WEST PENN CORPORATE MEDICAL SERVICES

West Penn Corporate Medical Services (WPCMS) is a management services organization that provides a broad spectrum of services to physician practices, including clinical support, staffing support, billing services, lease and property management, and administrative leadership.

WPCMS provides support services to primary care practices located throughout the area.

COMMUNITY OUTREACH

Since its founding, West Penn Hospital has been committed to improving the health of the communities it serves.

The Western Pennsylvania Hospital-Vintage Community Care for Seniors program is a satellite ambulatory care program at Vintage,

a comprehensive geriatric service center located in the East Liberty area of Pittsburgh. The program encourages health awareness, healthy lifestyle changes, and early identification of disease in adults 55 and older.

West Penn Hospital operates Penn Circle Medical Associates, a health care center in the East Liberty area of Pittsburgh, which has been designated by the federal government as underserved by primary health care facilities. The center provides internal medicine, family medicine, and geriatric and pediatric care.

West Penn Hospital formed a partnership with the Pittsburgh Public School District to create an on-site Health and Wellness Center at Peabody High School in East Liberty. Services provided by the Center include physical examinations, treatment of medical problems that occur during the school day, screenings, follow-up care or referral for all students identified with health problems, and immunizations.

The Western Pennsylvania Hospital provides meaningful and rewarding opportunities to those

in the communities it serves through the hospital's Adult and Junior Volunteer programs. The Junior Volunteer Program is recognized as the largest such program in the area.

Building upon its 150-year history as a regional and national leader in health care, The Western Pennsylvania Healthcare System is proud of its past achievements, and is focused on continuing to provide the highest quality of health care and service into the next millennium.

The Western Pennsylvania Hospital sponsored the first medical college in Western Pennsylvania in 1883, and continues today to provide strong programs for the education of graduate physicians (top).

Suburban General Hospital offers general medical and surgical services, as well as outpatient, emergency, cardiac, intensive care, and rehabilitation services (bottom).

SINCE 1992, BUCHANAN INGERSOLL HAS SET NEW GROWTH records, reached all-time levels for business volume, and expanded its presence as a major eastern regional law firm. Buchanan Ingersoll has also become more visible as a business advocate and problem solver, and has been entrusted

with major, headline assignments. Each year, the firm represents clients in hundreds of business and financial transactions, together valued in the billions of dollars. *The National Law Journal*, in its survey of the nation's 250 largest firms, consistently ranks Buchanan Ingersoll among the top 100 firms in the nation.

From the boards of some of America's largest corporations to entrepreneurs of small start-ups, clients increasingly turn to Buchanan Ingersoll lawyers for combined business, financial, and legal advice. The firm's lawyers believe it is because they use their skills to achieve clients' business

objectives consistent with the degree of risk clients should take to reach bottom-line success—based on the strength of their individual businesses, obstacles, and personalities.

"Buchanan Ingersoll has never been stronger," says William R. Newlin, president and chief executive officer since 1980. "While the demands on the legal profession continue to increase, the firm continues to flourish. I think this is a testament to the hard work and commitment of our lawyers and the kind of value-added services they provide."

DIVERSITY AND COMPLEXITY

In recent years, Buchanan Ingersoll has been assigned projects "of as high a magnitude and complexity as I can recall," says Newlin. Among hundreds of examples, the firm has negotiated the sale of the Pittsburgh Pirates baseball team to the Kevin McClatchy investor group; performed boardroom and courtroom work in Conrail Inc.'s antitakeover defense against hostile bidders; and represented the attorney general of Pennsylvania in complex litigation against the major tobacco companies.

Buchanan Ingersoll's clients range from individuals and start-up companies to private and publicly held institutions and multinational conglomerates, including more than 50 of the Fortune 500 corporations.

Buchanan Ingersoll utilizes technologically sophisticated information and accounting systems to improve the way its lawyers serve clients. Every lawyer, legal assistant, and legal secretary has a desktop PC to access information and resources from a centralized system as well as from external databases.

Buchanan Ingersoll CEO William Newlin (left) represented Mayor Tom Murphy (right) and the City of Pittsburgh in the sale of the Pittsburgh Pirates to Kevin McClatchy (center) to keep the team in the city. Each year, the firm represents clients in hundreds of major business and financial transactions, collectively valued in the billions of dollars (top).

One floor of Buchanan Ingersoll's offices at One Oxford Centre in Pittsburgh is devoted to client service, and features this colorful reception area and 16 conference and meeting rooms in a unique configuration (bottom).

The Power of

Highlights of these technologies focus on accounting, billing, project analysis, videoconferencing, timekeeping, time management, local area networks, utilization of intellectual property, information management, and electronic document delivery.

Buchanan Ingersoll has been recognized by major publications for its commitment to women. Though the firm does not focus on totals or percentages of lawyers based on gender, there is no question that a major strength comes from its diversity and the leadership roles and performance of its women lawyers. Since 1992, women have served on the firm's management committee.

Buchanan Ingersoll has helped build the support structure for technology companies in Pennsylvania and New Jersey. The firm was directly involved in establishing the Pittsburgh High Technology Council, the New Jersey Technology Council, the New Jersey Private Investor's Network, the Central Penn Technology Council, and the Pittsburgh Biomedical Development Corporation.

THE FIRM'S HISTORY

Buchanan Ingersoll was founded in 1850 by Judge Moses Hampton, and is the oldest commercial law firm in continuous practice in Pittsburgh. The firm changed from a partnership to a professional corporation in 1980, one of the first Pittsburgh law firms to do so. Since that time, Buchanan Ingersoll's level of business has grown eightfold, its number of lawyers has more than tripled, and the number of its regional offices has tripled. Buchanan Ingersoll continues to be one of the strongest major firms in the eastern region.

The firm has offices in five states and the District of Columbia, with its headquarters in Pittsburgh. This regional office system provides clients with cost-effective access to more than 300 lawyers through an integrated network. Buchanan Ingersoll has opened seven new offices since 1992, and now has 11 overall—in Pittsburgh, Harrisburg, Philadelphia, and Bryn Mawr, Pennsylvania; Miami, Tampa, and Aventura, Florida; Lexington, Kentucky; Princeton, New Jersey; Buffalo, New York; and Washington, D.C., with affiliate offices in England and Belgium.

The firm's clients expect and receive excellence in advocacy, work product, service, and cost-effective representation. They count on access to the best legal talent. Clients anticipate prompt return of telephone calls and timely replies to inquiries. They expect to be part of the decision-making process, and they demand successful results. The firm strives to satisfy its clients' legal expectations in a highly competent, cost-effective, and successful manner.

In addition to traditional areas of practice, Buchanan Ingersoll has kept pace with the region's changing economy by expanding into developing areas such as energy and health care restructurings, trade secret protection, and the Internet and security alarm industries. The firm handles hundreds of client matters each year and is noted for facilitating, not impeding, their consummation. Practical business judgment and innovative thinking enable Buchanan Ingersoll to help clients get the deal done.

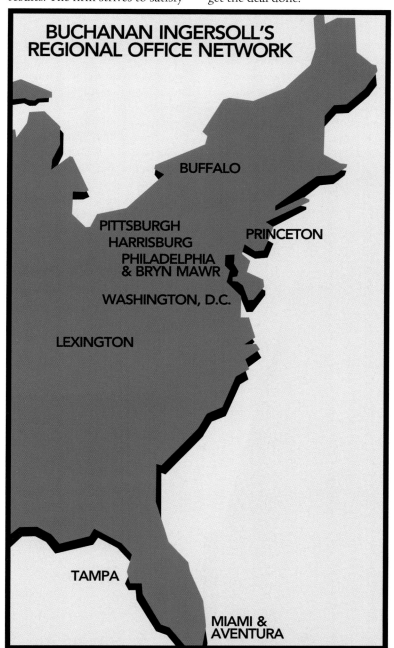

BUCHANAN INGERSOLL'S REGIONAL OFFICE NETWORK

BUFFALO

PITTSBURGH
HARRISBURG
PHILADELPHIA
& BRYN MAWR

PRINCETON

WASHINGTON, D.C.

LEXINGTON

TAMPA

MIAMI &
AVENTURA

Buchanan Ingersoll is one of the largest law firms in the eastern United States, and its regional office network provides clients with access to hundreds of the firm's lawyers.

AS EMPLOYEES AND CUSTOMERS HURRY TO BOARD ELEVATORS in the lobby of PNC Bank Corp.'s headquarters building in downtown Pittsburgh, they pass two bronze, sculptured doors, the kind you might expect to find gracing the entrance to a 15th-century Italian Renaissance palace.

PNC Bank's headquarters building stands at the corner of Fifth Avenue and Wood Street, where the company has been conducting business since 1858 (left).

PNC Bank's Regional Community Bank serves more than 3.3 million households and 135,000 small businesses in six states (right).

At first glance, these ornate doors seem out of place in a 1970s granite building recognized for its simple, understated architecture. The massive structures—mounted on the walls at each end of the lobby—are approximately 12 feet tall, weighing one ton each.

Originally placed in the bank's lobby as a reminder of the company's long history, the doors once stood at the entrance to one of PNC Bank's proud predecessors, whose office building was fashioned after a palace in Siena. Today, the mighty doors serve an additional purpose—as symbols of PNC Bank's enduring strength

and stability. Since its beginnings as a Pittsburgh-based bank in the mid-1800s, PNC Bank Corp. has grown to become one of the largest diversified financial services organizations in the United States, with more than $70 billion in assets and 25,000 employees in 30 states.

A LONG HISTORY

Pittsburgh's oldest bank was established in January 1852 under the name of Pittsburgh Trust and Savings. Within months, it had moved its offices to Wood Street, one door from the corner of Fifth Avenue, and in 1858, the corner lot was acquired. PNC Bank has been doing business at the corner of Fifth Avenue and Wood Street ever since.

The expansion of the iron, steel, glass, and coal industries after the Civil War provided the foundation for PNC Bank's profitable growth. The opportunity to grow beyond Greater Pittsburgh, however, came in 1982, when Pennsylvania changed its laws to permit statewide banking. Pittsburgh National, a descendant of the original Pittsburgh Trust and Savings, and Provident National in Philadelphia were the first two institutions

to take advantage of the new legislation, engaging in the nation's largest bank merger at that time. Later they adopted the name PNC Bank, which took the shared initials of their holding companies. Ever since, PNC Bank has merged with banks inside and outside the state, and acquired financial services companies, enabling it to provide a broad array of financial products and services delivered through seven lines of business.

The Regional Community Bank provides lending, deposit, credit card, and investment services to more than 3.3 million households and 135,000 small businesses throughout Pennsylvania, New Jersey, Delaware, Ohio, Kentucky, and Indiana.

The National Consumer Bank delivers a full range of financial products and services to more than 2.6 million customers nationwide. Innovative affinity relationships, including an alliance with the American Automobile Association, give PNC Bank exclusive marketing access to more than 32 million club members.

Corporate Banking serves businesses and government entities with annual revenues of $10 million a

The Power of

PNC Bank is one of the largest bank money managers in the nation, with discretionary authority over more than $138 billion.

The ornate, sculptured doors in the headquarters lobby are a reminder of PNC Bank's proud and elegant past.

year or more, including specialized industries such as health care, financial institutions, communications, high technology, energy, metals, and mining.

Private Banking offers investment management, brokerage, personal trust, estate planning, and traditional banking services to affluent clients in its six-state region, as well as in Massachusetts and Florida.

Secured Lending incorporates PNC Bank's activities in its Real Estate, Business Finance, and Leasing divisions. Real Estate, with annual loan originations of more than $3 billion, works with a broad base of clients nationwide, ranging from smaller regional groups to national and institutional market shapers.

PNC Mortgage originates, acquires, and services residential mortgage loans, as well as holding them in portfolio. PNC Mortgage, with more than 100 offices nationwide, funded $6.14 billion in residential mortgages in 1997, servicing in excess of 460,000 loans with outstanding principal balances totaling about $41 billion.

PNC Bank has built one of the nation's premier integrated investment organizations, and is now ranked among the 25 largest U.S. asset managers; is the sixth-largest U.S. bank money manager; and one of the largest U.S. providers of mutual fund services. PNC has expanded the scope of BlackRock Financial Management—a recog-

nized, world-class fixed-income investment advisor—to include liquidity and equity management and a $14.4 billion mutual fund family.

COMMITMENT TO COMMUNITY

Although PNC Bank has grown well beyond Southwestern Pennsylvania, it hasn't forgotten its roots. PNC Bank has consistently received the highest rating from the Office of the Comptroller of the Currency in recognition of efforts to fulfill the credit needs of all of Pittsburgh's communities, including low- and moderate-income neighborhoods and households. In fact, PNC Bank has received the same lofty rating in all the major markets where it operates. Furthermore, the PNC Bank Foundation contributes millions each year to enrich and

grow the communities it serves. And the more than 7,000 employees in Pittsburgh play active roles in a variety of community development efforts.

Much like the ornate, massive doors that have assumed a prominent location in its lobby, PNC Bank has taken its place among the leadership ranks in Pittsburgh. From its days as a one-office bank at the corner of Fifth Avenue and Wood Street to one of the nation's largest diversified financial services providers, PNC Bank has built an organization recognized for its strength and stability. And PNC Bank's pride in its Pittsburgh heritage is reflected in its growing operations in Southwestern Pennsylvania and its continuing commitment to improving the quality of life for everyone in the region.

BACK IN 1855, CHARLES A. COLTON HAD A NOVEL IDEA. HE wanted to create a bank that would cater to the common man—miners, foundry workers, mechanics, farmers, and blacksmiths—not just to the wealthy. Colton wanted to serve the people whose life savings were found tucked under

their mattresses or packed in old mason jars or cigar boxes.

"The object in view," Colton declared, "is to induce persons who have never saved a penny to lay by and deposit a portion of their earnings, and when so deposited, invest it where it will be safe as the hills of Allegheny County." Today, more than 140 years later, thousands of hardworking people in Western Pennsylvania and northeastern Ohio do their banking at Dollar Bank, the oldest bank in the Pittsburgh region. Beginning with initial deposits totaling $53, the bank's assets now exceed $2.6 billion. And though still serving its original market, Dollar has evolved into a respected corporate bank as well.

PROSPERITY OVER THE YEARS

Dollar Bank's history spans the Civil War, the Great Depression, two world wars, the Cuban missile crisis, and several recessions. Interest rates have climbed and fallen, and all along, Dollar Bank has prospered, which is something few other banks can say.

The main reason for its prosperity is innovation. In 1976, for example, Dollar Bank was the second bank in the nation, and the first in the Pittsburgh region, to offer a telephone bill-paying service. Dollar also was the first bank in the Pittsburgh region to pay interest on NOW accounts.

Behind these innovations is a strong desire to respond quickly to customer needs. "At Dollar Bank, we have chosen to be driven by the needs of our customers," says Stephen C. Hansen, president and CEO of Dollar Bank. "For example, we realize everyone has different uses for a checking account. That's why we offer three different types of checking accounts. And, when

changes occur in the economy or the marketplace that affect the financial needs of our customers, we are ready to address those needs. Being driven by the needs of our customers means that we must constantly be aware of what they need and want. Every action and every decision is made to reassure our customers that they chose well in choosing Dollar Bank."

INNOVATION TODAY

The innovation continues today with Dollar Bank operating as a full-service bank with more than 50 facilities in Cleveland and Pittsburgh, two of the mid-Atlantic region's most thriving metropolitan areas. At these facilities, the activity stretches well beyond the typical consumer banking to a host of services, including private banking that enables wealthier individuals to build and protect their estates with the help of their personal Dollar Bank professional.

The bank stresses personal service on the corporate side as well, offering fixed-rate and floating-rate term loans with a variety of amortization schedules, lines of credit, business checking accounts, automatic investment services, and equipment leasing. Dollar Bank's cash management services include funds concentration, balance reporting, account reconcilement, and direct deposit. Corporate customers can manage their cash flow with the easy-to-use, PC-based cash management system called Cash Analyzer®.

A respected commercial real estate lender, Dollar provides construction and permanent financing for hotels, motels, office and apartment buildings, residential developments, and shopping centers. Its Commercial Real Estate Department has evolved into a leading lender for major real estate

Twenty-four branches and five Dollar Bank Loan Centers are located in the Pittsburgh region. Over the past few years, extensive renovations have occurred in the branches to increase customer convenience by upgrading ATMs and adding drive-thru facilities.

The Power of

projects throughout the United States. This wide array of services has helped diversify Dollar's customer base, which now includes low- and high-tech manufacturing companies, professional corporations, retail operations, and specialty service firms.

A more recent addition to the Dollar Bank repertoire is Net-Banking, which was rated one of the Top Ten Banks in Cyberspace by *The Money Page*, the Net's comprehensive guide to banking finance. NetBanking is accessible with any computer using Netscape Navigator or Microsoft Explorer. Without needing to purchase additional software, customers can view account activity, check account balances, transfer money between accounts, and pay bills all from their home or office. Employing the latest firewall technologies, Dollar Bank has taken every precaution to ensure that this site is completely secure. Now customers are in touch with Dollar Bank 24 hours a day and can start banking on-line, not in line.

THE FUTURE

What makes Dollar Bank unique is that it is a mutual bank, with no stock to offer. Mutuality preserves the bank's independence and insulates it from the fast-paced merger and acquisition activity that has become rampant in the banking industry. Strongly capitalized, Dollar Bank has no reason to sell and will continue to be managed by a hometown banker, not by a bank whose headquarters and primary interests may be hundreds of miles away. As a result, the community benefits as a whole, since Dollar Bank invests heavily in the Pittsburgh area.

Dollar Bank's financial position has remained strong throughout the years. Today, and in the future, customers will continue to reap the benefits of the qualities that have always been paramount at Dollar Bank: experience and innovation. "You will continue to see many positives here at Dollar Bank," Hansen says. "Our long-range plan is to serve the customer better than any other bank." After all, concludes Hansen, "We never forget whose money it is®."

In 1855, the first Dollar Bank office opened on Fourth Avenue in downtown Pittsburgh. It is still in operation today and has received recognition on the National Register of Historic Places.

WE NEVER FORGET WHOSE MONEY IT IS®

First Time Visitor? | Our Community | Calculators

Serving the Pittsburgh And Cleveland Areas

At www.dollarbank.com, individuals can find a wealth of banking services and information, from customizing the perfect checking and savings accounts to educational material on loans. Customers can also access NetBanking, from Dollar Bank—voted one of the Top Ten Banks in Cyberspace.

ATIONAL CITY BANK OF PENNSYLVANIA WAS FORMED IN 1996, as a result of the merger of parent company National City Corporation, based in Cleveland, and Integra Bank, a longtime Western Pennsylvania financial institution. ■ The merger gave the bank new capabilities, moving from a predominantly retail emphasis into a full-service financial institution. National City Bank of Pennsylvania specializes in small-business banking and offers commercial, retail, and private client lines of business. The bank has been the premier SBA lender in the Pittsburgh District for the past six years.

Today, National City Bank of Pennsylvania is one of the largest banks within National City Corporation and employs approximately 4,000 people throughout Western Pennsylvania. The bank believes that each employee's focus must be on the customer. "Banks aren't banks, anymore," says Thomas Golonski, president and chief executive officer of the bank. "They're broad-based financial services companies. Our bankers must be rela-

The senior management team for National City Bank of Pennsylvania (from left): Stephen G. Hartle, executive vice president, Private Client Group; John C. Williams Jr., executive vice president, Corporate Banking; Thomas W. Golonski, president and chief executive officer; David L. Tiemann, executive vice president, Credit Administration; and Paul Clark, executive vice president, Retail Banking

tionship managers, seeing people face-to-face, listening to their needs, and providing the products and services that answer those needs at every stage of their business and personal lives. We have $53 billion in resources to make that happen."

National City's Corporate Banking Group is a large business segment at the bank and provides a complete and sophisticated range of financial services for major businesses in this region. In addition to its core lending strengths, the Group helps to coordinate the delivery of depository and treasury management services, leasing products, institutional trust and investment services, investment banking products and expertise, venture capital, international services, and employee benefit products. Corporate Banking's emphasis is on providing superior customer service by maintaining local control of customer relationships and lending authorities. The Corporate Banking Group's professional staff is committed to utilizing the entire array of National City Corporation resources in order to provide creative, thoughtful, and timely responses to the financial needs and challenges of its customers.

National City Bank of Pennsylvania's Private Client Group provides access to a team of experts through one primary contact—a relationship manager—who coordinates all the resources necessary to meet financial planning and management needs. Clients benefit from total balance sheet management based on an in-depth understanding of their financial position and objectives.

Investment management, trust services, financial consulting, private banking, and brokerage services are available at National City and its affiliates. The result is coordinated credit and investment strategies to help clients achieve their goals. The Private Client Group oversees billions of dollars in assets under management with a proven commitment to performance and growth.

The bottom line is that National City provides a broad array of retail and commercial products. In each line of business, the bank is a relationship manager that customizes and personalizes the bank's capabilities for each customer—"a market of one."

A MEMBER OF THE COMMUNITY
Community involvement is the cornerstone of National City's philosophy. In 1996, National City consolidated its Pennsylvania

headquarters into one flagship location in Pittsburgh. With the enthusiastic support of Mayor Tom Murphy, National City Center at 20 Stanwix Street became the bank's home.

The bank believes that community investment is an ongoing process, not a project. The bank is not only committed to providing the highest-quality products and services, but it is also committed to improving the quality of life in the communities it serves. In 1982, National City Corporation formed one of the first bank community development corporations in the country. Since that time, various affiliates in National City's four-state marketplace of Pennsylvania, Ohio, Indiana, and Kentucky have invested $82.3 million in local community development projects.

Pittsburgh's Washington's Landing, an underutilized site along the Allegheny River, is a shining example of National City Bank of Pennsylvania's commitment to such projects. Working closely with the Urban Redevelopment Authority of Pittsburgh and a team of developers, National City provided financing and assistance that transformed

TOM FITZPATRICK, VISUAL PERCEPTIONS, INC.

this location from a contaminated eyesore into one of the most innovative and dynamic neighborhoods in the region.

Another landmark lending project for the bank was the conversion of the old Hornes Department Store into a new retail and office complex. Additionally, the bank is financing the continuing development of the Pittsburgh Technology Center near Second Avenue. Through the Pittsburgh Economic and Industrial Development Corporation, National City is financing a single tenant office building for a multinational medical supply company.

National City's commitment to the region also extends to its workforce. The bank is an active corporate citizen with its management and employees taking leadership role in events such as the United Way Day of Caring, Family House Polo, and the March of Dimes Teamwalk.

Looking to the next century, National City Bank of Pennsylvania is poised to build on its heritage of excellence. The result will be a performance culture and a sales environment dedicated to excellence in community commitment, financial performance, and customer service.

Clockwise from top left: Customers enjoy streamlined service at National City's Bank Express office, where the platform and teller areas are combined into a semicircular counter. Each financial services representative can handle any customer banking transaction.

National City is the primary lender in the conversion of an underutilized river site into a dynamic residential-commercial development in Pittsburgh—Washington's Landing. Examining blueprints are (from left) Karyn Rubinoff, vice president, The Rubinoff Company; Mark Schneider, vice president, The Rubinoff Company; Robert B. Powderly, vice president, National City; Pittsburgh Mayor Tom Murphy; and Dick Rubinoff, president, The Rubinoff Company.

Since the program originated in 1990, more than 10,000 area students have submitted essays in the bank's African-American history essay contest. Area President Richard L. Lewis and Vice President Stephanie Cipriani present commendations to recent winners Eboni Wilson (left) and Tomorrow Snyder.

N 1860, WHEN THOMAS MORTON ARMSTRONG BEGAN WHAT IS NOW Armstrong World Industries as a tiny, two-man cork-cutting shop in Pittsburgh, the national frontier barely reached beyond the western mountain ranges of Pennsylvania. Today, five generations later, Armstrong is a worldwide family of 10,500 employees in 49 locations,

including a plant in Beaver Falls, Pennsylvania.

The company manufactures and markets hundreds of products worldwide, including floor covering and installation products, acoustical ceiling and grid systems, insulation for heating and cooling systems, and high-performance gasket materials for the automotive industry. In 1996, total sales reached $2.1 billion, with net earnings of $156 million. Armstrong's Building Products Operations (BPO), which runs the Beaver Falls plant about 25 miles northwest of downtown Pittsburgh, is the world's largest manufacturer of the acoustical ceiling systems used in buildings and homes. Its 1996 sales totaled nearly $700 million.

Armstrong World Industries is a worldwide family of 10,500 employees. The Beaver Falls Plant outside of Pittsburgh is run by Armstrong's Building Products Operations, the world's largest manufacturer of acoustical ceiling systems.

THE EARLY YEARS IN PITTSBURGH

Soon after starting his own company, Armstrong became one of the first American entrepreneurs to discard the old business maxim "Let the buyer beware," and replace it by practicing the principle of "Let the buyer have faith." He was also a brand-name pioneer, stamping Armstrong on each cork as early as 1864, and including a written guarantee in each bag of corks.

As buyer confidence in the Armstrong brand grew, so did sales. The Pittsburgh shop soon moved to larger quarters on Third Avenue, and constructed an even larger factory on 24th Street in 1878. The Armstrong Cork Company was eventually incorporated

in 1895 and emerged as the world's largest cork company.

By the 1890s, the Pittsburgh plant had large amounts of scrap cork that resulted from cutting round corks from square sheets. Rather than discarding it, company officials decided to take advantage of cork's natural insulating properties and use the scrap to manufacture insulating corkboard. However, a new facility was needed to produce the product. A site search committee was formed, with requirements that the location be near Pittsburgh and have an industrious population, good transportation, availability of high-grade fuels, and easy access to the clay required in the manufacturing process. The committee selected a site along 27th Street in Beaver Falls, and by 1904, the new

plant was in full operation. To handle increasing demand, the company purchased an additional facility on 13th Street in 1936 and expanded it twice during the years that followed.

CONVERTING FROM CORKBOARD TO CEILINGS

World War II drastically curtailed the importation of cork, and as a result, the company was forced to seek a substitute for raw cork in its insulation. Mineral wool—a scrap by-product of steel production from nearby mills—was used, and this development, in turn, led to the production of Travertone, an incombustible acoustical ceiling made largely from mineral wool. Initially manufactured in 1947, Travertone ceilings are still produced at the plant today.

Once the flagship of Armstrong's insulation products, corkboard eventually became obsolete with the advent of fiberglass insulation, and in 1959, the company stopped production of this product at Beaver Falls to concentrate on the growing market for acoustical ceilings. By 1974, all Beaver Falls operations were consolidated at the 13th Street plant, and the original nine-acre site on 27th Street was donated to Geneva College.

In 1983, Armstrong introduced a new line of acoustical ceilings called Cirrus. Produced at the Beaver Falls plant, these panels feature a fine textured appearance that instantly became popular in the interior design world. Today, Cirrus ceilings include a number of multipanel systems with carved or sculpted designs that can be combined to create a variety of custom looks.

The Travertone and Cirrus ceilings produced at Beaver Falls are only part of a much wider product line that provides beauty, noise reduction, and fire resistance to offices, health care facilities, schools, stores, restaurants, hotels, and other commercial spaces worldwide.

A LEGACY OF REUSE

Armstrong makes great efforts to protect the environment and use resources intelligently. Much as

Thomas Armstrong did in the 1890s, the company today bases a large part of its manufacturing process on the reuse of scrap materials. For example, up to 79 percent of the raw materials used to manufacture Armstrong ceilings are waste materials from other industries: newsprint, paper, and mineral wool. Approximately 60 percent of the recycled paper is postconsumer, usually in the form of old newspapers and telephone books. Each year, Armstrong's Building Products Operations rescues more than 340 million pounds of waste materials from going to landfills.

BPO also recovers more than 90 percent of the scrap generated during its own manufacturing and reuses it in the production process to prevent further landfill use. In nearly all cases, the scrap results from visual defects, not technical flaws, so scrap is reused without compromising product performance. Environmental efforts such as these helped Armstrong Building Products Operations, in 1995, become the only building materials organization to ever win

the Malcolm Baldrige National Quality Award.

The award resulted from the efforts of what Armstrong always believed to be his company's greatest asset: its people. The employees at Beaver Falls play a key role in everything from new product development to improvements in the production process. Each day, they meet the challenge to manufacture ceilings better and faster, so customers can continue to believe in the operating principle Armstrong set more than a century ago: Let the buyer have faith.

The employees at Beaver Falls play a key role in everything from new product development to improvements in the production process.

N THE 1940S, WHEN THE MILLS OF PITTSBURGH PUMPED OUT THE steel used to build the Allied war machine, workers at the end of their shift would cross the street to a pub, and order an Iron City beer. When the Pittsburgh Steelers won four Super Bowls in six years during the 1970s, fans at Three Rivers Stadium celebrated

with Iron City. And in the 1990s, Pittsburgh's young professionals crack open Original Twists as they jam Market Square on Friday afternoons. Every step of the way, from a steel-based economy to today's technology-based economy, Pittsburgh Brewing Company has been a Pittsburgh mainstay.

A Long History

The history of Pittsburgh Brewing Company can be traced back to 1861, when Edward Frauenheim and Leopold Vilsack founded the Frauenheim and Vilsack Brewery, later called Iron City Brewing. Brewing was a popular industry in Pittsburgh's early years, and dozens of small neighborhood breweries competed for the favor of the Steel City's blue-collar workers. Throughout the 1800s, tight competition, consolidations, and plant closings thinned the ranks of Pittsburgh brewers, but Iron City survived, merging with 20 other local brewing companies

Pittsburgh Brewing Company has been brewing quality beers for more than 135 years.

Pittsburgh Brewing Company has 600-barrel brew kettles, where the wort is boiled and hops are added for flavor and aroma.

in 1899 to become the Pittsburgh Brewing Company. This merger created the largest brewery in Pennsylvania and the third largest in the country.

Today's Brews

Iron City Beer, the flagship brew of Pittsburgh Brewing Company, has been the mainstay of the company since 1861. Recognized as one of the first true lager beers brewed in the United States, Iron City continues to outsell all national and local brands in the regular beer category regionally. In taverns and restaurants, at parties and athletic fields, Iron City and its slogans have been a rallying cry for loyal Pittsburghers. Further cementing its ties with the city, Pittsburgh Brewing produces specialty beer cans for Iron City Beer centering around Pittsburgh professional sports teams, including the Steelers, Pirates, and Penguins.

But Pittsburgh Brewing is not willing to rest on its laurels, creating several new brews that are popular with the locals. I.C. Light has grown to be a Pittsburgh favorite, becoming even

more popular when Pittsburgh Brewing added two variations known as the Original Twist, flavored with either Rio Cherry or Acapulco Lime. The initial demand for the new flavors was so overwhelming that wholesalers began taking orders for both flavors well before Pittsburgh Brewing began its second run of the premium light beer.

Perhaps the best-known Pittsburgh Brewing creation is one for which it gets little credit. In 1984, Pittsburgh Brewing Company partnered with Boston Beer Company to develop the recipe for the first 700 barrels of the award-winning Samuel Adams Boston Lager, which was brewed in Pittsburgh. As the original brewers for the Boston Beer Company, Pittsburgh Brewing at one point brewed more than 70 percent of the different flavors of Samuel Adams. More than 90 percent of the beers that earned medals under the Samuel Adams name were produced at Pittsburgh Brewing, and this quality alliance continues today, testament to the dedication to quality that Pittsburgh Brewing Company has held for more than 135 years.

THE PITTSBURGH PIRATES HAVE BEEN PLAYING BASEBALL FOR well over a century, and boast a history filled with world championships, legendary athletes, and some of baseball's most memorable plays. The Pirates competed in the first-ever World Series game in Boston, winning 7-3 over the then

Boston Pilgrims. The team also participated in arguably the most dramatic moment in baseball history, when Pirates second baseman Bill Mazeroski hit a home run in the bottom of the ninth inning to win Game 7 of the 1960 World Series.

Today's team is continuing in that tradition, building a nucleus of young and talented players who are making some history of their own. For instance, during the 1997 season, even though pundits picked the Pirates to lose 100 games, the team sat in first place at the All-Star break and took the division race with the Houston Astros to the final week. Before it was over, the Pirates would win 79 games under Manager Gene Lamont and finish in second place in the National League Central division.

THE MODERN PIRATES

Professional baseball was first played in Pittsburgh in 1876, and the early Pirates won world titles in 1909 and 1925. Under the Galbreath family, who purchased the team in 1946 and owned it for nearly four decades, the Pirates won three World Series—in 1960, 1971, and 1979.

Each of those title teams holds a special place in the history of Major League Baseball. The 1960 team clinched its title with the famous Mazeroski home run; the 1971 team featured Hall of Famer Roberto Clemente, who batted .414 against the Baltimore Orioles in the World Series and was voted MVP; and the 1979 Pirates championship team, led by Willie Stargell, became known nationally as the "Family," having come back from a three-games-to-one deficit to win the title from the Orioles.

The Galbreaths sold the team in 1985 to Pittsburgh Associates, a group consisting of Mellon Bank,

PNC Bank, PPG Industries, USX Corporation, Westinghouse Electric Co., Alcoa, Carnegie Mellon University, and three individuals. During this era, the Jim Leyland-coached Pirates won National League East titles in 1990, 1991, and 1992, and began developing a minor-league system that could set the stage for the championship teams of the future.

TODAY AND THE FUTURE

The latest chapter of this storied baseball franchise began on February 14, 1996, when a group of investors led by Kevin McClatchy purchased the Pirates from Pittsburgh Associates. The current ownership group is committed to staying in Pittsburgh, and hopes to build a baseball-only ballpark along the north shore, not far from the team's current home at Three Rivers Stadium.

Meanwhile, the group has further developed the Pirates' minor-league system, now considered one of the most talent-laden in Major League Baseball. With a history of excellence and a future that promises even more exciting baseball, the Pirates are more than just a team in Pittsburgh—they're an institution.

Clockwise from top: Hall of Famer Willie Stargell established many records during his remarkable 21-year career with the Pirates, and he was also a member of two World Championship teams.

Veteran outfielder Al Martin has provided consistent leadership, on and off the field, during seven full seasons with the Pirates.

Pirates fans, young and old, cherish the memory of the legendary Roberto Clemente as they stand by the statue dedicated in his honor at Gate A of Three Rivers Stadium.

Catcher Jason Kendall is one of many talented young players who contribute to the Pirates' bright future in Pittsburgh.

ARBISON-WALKER REFRACTORIES COMPANY WAS FOUNDED as the Star Fire Brick Co. in 1865, when post-Civil War rebuilding created a booming market for refractory products—raw mineral products that are refined into heat- and chemical-resistant ceramics used as linings for

Headquartered in Pittsburgh, Harbison-Walker Refractories Company is a world leader in the refractory industry, providing raw minerals, refractory products, and technology licensing to more than 1,000 customers in some 70 countries. Harbison-Walker also spans the globe with affiliates in Canada, Mexico, Chile, and Germany, and has entered joint ventures in China and Thailand (top).

Harbison-Walker manufacturing plants in the United States and Canada produce more than 300 refractory ceramic products in a wide variety of shapes and sizes used to line high-temperature furnaces and vessels in the steel, copper, aluminum, glass, cement, and petrochemical industries (bottom left).

Harbison-Walker refractory monolithics can be sprayed on the inside walls of furnaces and still maintain brick-like qualities (bottom right).

industrial furnaces, kilns, incinerators, and other high-temperature process vessels. The company took its current name in 1875, when Samuel Harbison, the company's ambitious accountant, and Hay Walker, a major stockholder, partnered as the company's owners. At that time, the competition within the so-called high-temperature industries was fierce, with many companies vying for the business of building the rails and tools the United States needed for its voracious westward expansion. Harbison and Walker sought to help their customers achieve market dominance by delivering a consistently high-quality refractory product.

So along with the name change came an emphasis on research and development that led to a thorough knowledge and understanding of the chemistry of refractory clay, as well as rigorous dedication to matching the raw material to its intended purpose. This devotion to research has kept Harbison-Walker on the leading edge for more than a century.

Today, Harbison-Walker is a subsidiary of Global Industrial

Technologies Inc. in Dallas. But proof that the company's philosophy of research and development still holds manifests itself in the bottom line: More than 25 percent of Harbison-Walker's sales are derived from products developed within the past five years. Total sales in 1996 were $370 million, and this growth comes despite huge downturns in the industry, concurrent with downturns in the steel industry in the 1980s.

MODERN-DAY HARBISON-WALKER

Key to Harbison-Walker's success is the location of its plants, which

are near major producing sites throughout the country. The company has also acquired reserves of the raw minerals needed to produce high-quality refractory products, allowing it to control the entire process from the mining of raw materials through the manufacturing, transportation, and distribution of the finished product. Harbison-Walker mines or produces more than 25 percent of the raw minerals it uses, and has long-term contracts for the remainder. Supply and pricing are thus less vulnerable to fluctuating world supply, and stringent internal sourcing and external purchase specifications can ensure uniform quality of the materials, which then ensures quality in the final product. Harbison-Walker, through its Minerals Group, supplies raw materials to its own U.S. and Canadian operations, as well as to other refractory and nonrefractory producers worldwide.

With this firm grasp in the industry, Harbison-Walker is a global producer, supplying more than 1,000 customers in more than 70 countries with raw materials, refractory products, services, and technology. With its Canadian affiliate, the company operates 12 plants in North America. In keeping with

the strategy of being close to the customer, the past five years have seen the company's global reach expanding with the acquisition of leading refractory companies, including Refractarios Mexicanos (REFMEX) in Mexico, Harbison–Walker Magnesitwerk Aken in Germany, and two refractory operations in Chile—Refractarios Chilenos (RECSA) and RESCA-LOTA.

Harbison-Walker has also entered into a joint venture to manufacture refractories for use in China's burgeoning coal gasification business, as well as a partnership with Thailand's Siam Cement Group to build refractory plants throughout Southeast Asia. These foreign markets are all on the brink of growth—China and Southeast Asia lead all other regions of the world for sustained, rapid growth—so the company is uniquely positioned to share in unparalleled investment opportunities.

A CENTURY OF GROWTH AND RESEARCH

Harbison-Walker has been able to survive and consistently grow when many of its competitors have faltered. In order to do so, the company has maintained continuous product development and engineering with an eye to producing the longest lasting, most consistent, and most cost-effective refrac-

tory products on the market. To fulfill this goal, the company operates the Harbison-Walker Garber Research Center, one of the largest and most sophisticated research and development capabilities in the industry. The tradition Harbison and Walker launched more than a century ago—that of careful attention to research and development—manifests itself here still. Continual feedback from customers, attention to individual issues, and relentless advancement of engineering techniques have resulted in proprietary advances and patents.

But Harbison-Walker's role in the industry goes far beyond the research, development, and man-

ufacturing of the products. The company's technical partnerships with customers provide them with refractory engineering systems, as well as financial, management, and business expertise that may not be readily accessible through local sources. In many countries, Harbison-Walker partners with others in the industry, providing technical licensing agreements and joint ventures to aid these companies in developing their industry locally.

Harbison-Walker's ability to provide comprehensive or tailored services and products that span the needs of the entire refractory industry, as well as its dedication to continually looking ahead, leaves it well positioned for future growth.

Clockwise from top left: Heat- and chemical-resistant Harbison-Walker refractories are used to line steel ladles and furnaces.

Harbison-Walker is a world leader in refractory research and technology. At its Garber Research Center, near Pittsburgh, hundreds of new refractory products have been developed and introduced. Research engineers use state-of-the-art microprobe equipment to study microstructural features of refractories.

Workmen inspect a rotary cement kiln lined with Harbison-Walker refractories.

TO HEAL THE BODY, MIND, AND SPIRIT. THAT'S THE MISSION the Sisters of St. Francis set out to fulfill in 1865, when they opened a hospital in a small frame house on 37th Street in the Lawrenceville section of Pittsburgh. Since the founding of that first, 15-bed hospital, St. Francis

has expanded to a regional health system with three hospitals, more than 1,300 beds, three skilled nursing facilities, numerous satellite centers, and a staff of more than 3,600 dedicated to meeting the needs of communities throughout Western Pennsylvania, northern West Virginia, and eastern Ohio.

The tertiary hospital of St. Francis Health System is St. Francis Medical Center, located at 44th Street in Lawrenceville on the spot where the enterprising sisters opened a second hospital in 1866. Located about four miles from

downtown Pittsburgh, the referral teaching facility offers services from cardiac care to addiction treatment.

CENTERS OF EXCELLENCE

Giving St. Francis Medical Center a regionwide reputation for quality care are several service lines, including cardiothoracic surgery and cardiology, addiction and psychiatric care, physical rehabilitation, critical care medicine, and laser and advanced surgery. "Although the Medical Center still serves the surrounding neighborhoods, the service lines attract patients from all over the tristate area," says Sister Florence Brandt, chief executive officer of St. Francis Medical Center.

At the Center for Cardiac Care, nearly 100 cardiologists and cardiothoracic surgeons are trained in today's most efficient, comprehensive, and up-to-date medical and surgical procedures. The Food and Drug Administration (FDA) selected St. Francis Medical Center as one of the first to study the effectiveness of the excimer laser, and, as a result, the FDA recommended the approval of the technology for opening blocked blood

vessels as an alternative to more invasive surgery.

The Division of Psychiatric and Addiction Services is believed to be one of the first to submit a medical diagnosis of alcoholism as a primary disorder, and today treats more than 7,000 people each year with a wide range of prevention, education, research, and treatment services for all forms of substance abuse. St. Francis has been a leader in mental health care, treating patients suffering from mental illness since 1873. When other institutions were treating psychiatric disorders with isolation, St. Francis realized the importance of treatment using therapeutic activities such as sewing, gardening, and arts and crafts.

HIGH TECH, HIGH TOUCH

St. Francis' services include the fields of oncology, neurosciences, orthopedics, ophthalmology, oral and maxillofacial surgery, and pulmonary medicine. Physicians, professional and practical nurses, respiratory care practitioners, and nurse anesthetists are trained through a wide array of high-tech educational programs available right at St. Francis. In fact, through-

Clockwise from top:
St. Francis Central Hospital is a community hospital located across from the Civic Arena in downtown Pittsburgh.

St. Francis Hospital of New Castle is an acute care community hospital located an hour northwest of Pittsburgh in New Castle, Lawrence County.

St. Francis Medical Center, the flagship of St. Francis Health System, is a regional referral, tertiary care hospital located in the Lawrenceville section of Pittsburgh.

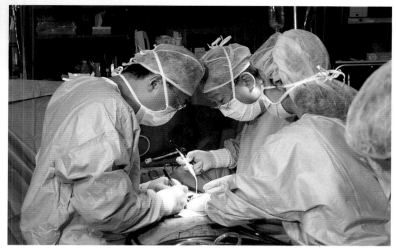

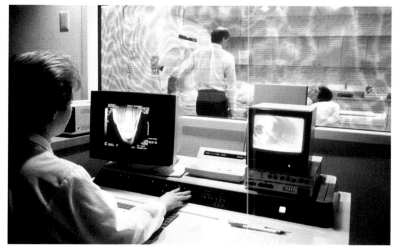

out St. Francis Health System, the care is described as combining "high tech with high touch."

St. Francis' state-of-the-art technologies include lithotripsy, critical care helicopter and ground transport, positron-emission tomography (PET) scanning, magnetic resonance imaging (MRI), hyperbaric medicine, and the Greater Pittsburgh Sleep Center. St. Francis has 11 surgical suites, and five new maternity suites that incorporate labor, delivery, and recovery, giving mothers the chance to have their babies in a homelike atmosphere, but with all the security of high-tech equipment.

St. Francis also offers treatment to the community with services at St. Francis Central Hospital, a 202-bed, acute care teaching hospital across from the Civic Arena in downtown Pittsburgh. Like the Medical Center, its strengths lie in cardiothoracic surgery and advanced interventional cardiology. St. Francis Central provides primary care to the community in five Family Health Centers, located in downtown Pittsburgh, Brookline, Mount Washington, Pleasant Hills, and Trafford. These centers allow the hospital to reach out into area neighborhoods with health and prevention education.

WIDENING GEOGRAPHIC REACH

In 1991, St. Francis Hospital of New Castle, a 193-bed hospital that has served the community since 1908, joined St. Francis Health System. The hospital offers comprehensive services, including the Lawrence

County Chest Pain Center, Lawrence County Diabetes Center, and Family Birth Center, as well as the Wellness in Neighborhoods (WIN) program, which offers area residents health screenings and educational programs at more than 15 community-based locations. Comprehensive mental health services are provided through the Lawrence County Behavioral Health Center at St. Francis. Like the Medical Center, St. Francis Hospital of New Castle also specializes in cardiac care, physical rehabilitation, and laser and advanced surgery. Continued care is offered through the home health and hospice care services.

The health system also offers care at St. Francis Cranberry, a community hospital built to serve the burgeoning suburban population of Cranberry Township. The hospital incorporates a 24-hour emergency department and a same-day surgery center, as well as St. Francis Regional Cancer Center and a skilled nursing facility.

Throughout the system, the practice of medicine is grounded in the belief of holistic treatment of body, mind, and spirit. What was once just humanitarian instinct has now been scientifically documented: The mind cannot be separated from the body when it comes to medical care. Serious mental illness will affect a patient's physical health, and physical ailments can affect mental health by inducing anxiety or depression.

This philosophy plays out in everyday treatment at all St. Francis health care facilities. Medical care is not overlooked for patients suffering from mental illnesses, and psychological and spiritual support is provided to allay the fears that accompany physical ailments. Add to that the finest in technology, caring staff and physicians, and a desire to make medical care as convenient and painless as possible, and it is evident that St. Francis Health System is fulfilling the mission envisioned by its founders more than a century ago.

Clockwise from top left: Cardiothoracic surgeons Chong S. Park, M.D. (left), and his father, Sang B. Park, M.D., perform open-heart surgery together. The elder Park has the reputation as one of the best cardiac surgeons in Pittsburgh.

The field of diagnostic radiology has made leaps and bounds in recent years, allowing patients and physicians more accurate diagnoses that save time and effort when deciding appropriate treatment.

The Division of Psychiatric and Addiction Services at St. Francis is nationally recognized for its expertise in the treatment of behavioral health. St. Francis' models of addiction treatment set the standard for treatment in Allegheny County.

I N ADDITION TO BEING THE REGION'S LARGEST NETWORK OF tertiary, specialty, and community hospitals, UPMC Health System is an integrated health care delivery system that serves the comprehensive health needs of the citizens of Western Pennsylvania. UPMC Health System includes physician practices, insurance products, and

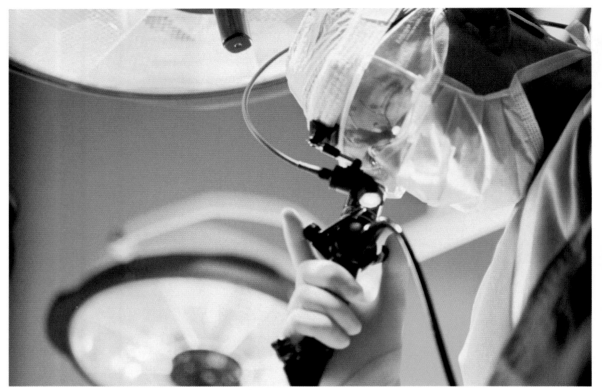

UPMC Health System's surgeons have led the region in performing operations through ever smaller "keyhole" incisions, allowing faster recovery, less pain, and more relief. The health system's tertiary care hospitals have introduced more types of minimally invasive surgery than any other hospital in the tristate region—including outpatient procedures through incisions so small that the scars are nearly invisible.

a broad spectrum of other health-related services.

With more than 21,000 employees, UPMC Health System has become the largest nongovernmental employer in the region. It also is one of the largest not-for-profit integrated health care systems in the country.

A FOCUS ON THE FINEST CARE

At the heart of UPMC Health System is the region's finest academic medical center. Through its affiliation with the University of Pittsburgh School of Medicine and other schools of the health sciences, UPMC offers more advanced treatments, educates more medical professionals, and carries out more research than any other hospital in the tristate area. The health system's focus on offering the latest diagnostic and treatment technologies has not only made it unnecessary for Pittsburghers to leave the region for treatment for any disorder, it has drawn patients

to UPMC Health System from around the world.

The health system's tertiary care hospitals, UPMC Presbyterian and UPMC Shadyside, provide advanced care for all human illnesses, no matter how complex, as well as the opportunity to participate in clinical trials of the latest treatments. UPMC medical and surgical programs include the University of Pittsburgh Cancer Institute and the Thomas E. Starzl Transplantation Institute, as well as comprehensive services in cardiology, cardiothoracic surgery, geriatrics, occupational and environmental medicine, AIDS and immunology, trauma, otolaryngology, neurosurgery, critical care medicine, and orthopedic and sports medicine. Specialized services are provided at Eye & Ear and at Western Psychiatric Institute and Clinic.

In addition to its academic core, UPMC Health System includes a growing number of community

Consistently over the years, UPMC Health System and its hospitals have been cited by leading local and national publications for excellence in health care, includung *Good Housekeeping, Men's Journal, U.S. News & World Report, American Health, The Best Doctors in America,* and *Pittsburgh* magazine.

The Power of

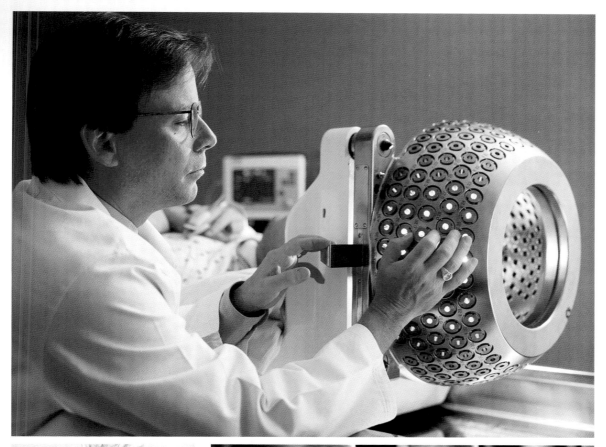

Clockwise from top:
The Gamma Knife radiosurgery device precisely focuses 201 beams of therapeutic radiation on inoperable brain tumors or blood vessel malformations in a way that spares surrounding healthy tissues—all without a surgical incision. UPMC Health System introduced the first clinical Gamma Knife in North America, and today has the only two in the Pittsburgh region.

When people see a primary care physician who's affiliated with UPMC Health System, they're not only in excellent hands—they're in the hands of an entire network of care, with doctors' offices throughout the region.

UPMC Health System scientists are enlisting the body's own defenses in the war against cancer. White blood cells like the dendritic cells (far left) have the ability to attack tumor cells as if they were invading microbes; UPMC researchers have uncovered some of the chemical signals that turn on these defenses, and are now using them in preliminary trials against a variety of human cancers.

hospitals as well. UPMC Beaver Valley, UPMC Braddock, UPMC McKeesport, UPMC Passavant, UPMC South Side, UPMC St. Margaret, and others provide medical and surgical services in convenient locations throughout the region.

A FOCUS ON COMPREHENSIVE CARE

UPMC Health System encompasses a broad spectrum of health-related services that go far beyond in-hospital care. Through UPMC's Physician Division, the health system manages same-day surgery centers, satellite physicians' offices, and practices consisting of more

than 3,000 primary care and specialist physicians—the region's top academic "teaching" doctors and its finest community practitioners.

Through its Diversified Services Division, UPMC offers long-term care, staffing, and management of emergency departments for a number of hospitals in the region, in-home services, retirement living options, a mail-order pharmacy, a regional reference laboratory, durable medical devices, rehabilitation and occupational

medicine services, technology transfer ventures, and international health care initiatives.

UPMC Health System's Insurance Division offers a number of new managed care programs to serve the needs of the citizens of the region.

A FOCUS ON RESEARCH

Research has fueled much of UPMC Health System's growth: Not only does UPMC offer a full range of the latest treatments for every type of human illness, but also, in many cases, UPMC physicians and researchers helped to develop these treatments. Time and again, UPMC's research has been recognized by the ultimate vote of confidence: funding from the National Institutes of Health, private foundations, and high-tech corporations. In fact, UPMC Health System receives much more extra-mural funding than any other medical institution in the region.

UPMC researchers continue to shape the medicine of tomorrow. UPMC trials of gene therapy have produced some of the first, preliminary successes in a revolutionary new approach to treating diseases as diverse as arthritis, cancer, and inherited genetic defects. UPMC Health System has introduced more types of minimally invasive surgery than any other hospital in the region. The physicians at UPMC are developing a computerized system that will enable surgeons to operate with much finer precision than is possible with the human hand.

UPMC researchers are pioneering new imaging technologies to better understand neurological and psychiatric problems; these technologies also allow investigators to see which parts of the

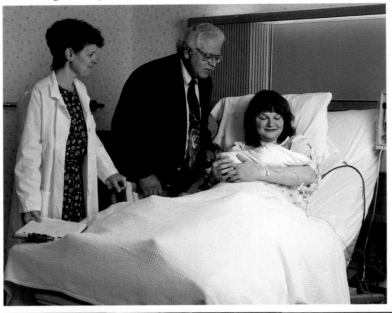

A number of UPMC Health System facilities offer quality prenatal and maternity services, including single-room maternity care, in which mothers labor, deliver, and receive follow-up care in one specially equipped room. In addition, neonatal intensive care facilities are available for newborns who require special attention.

UPMC scientists have revealed a graphically stunning universe of vital life processes using innovative molecular and microscopic tools. With a new generation of transmission electron microscopes and other instruments, they are probing ever smaller causes of human illness.

The Power of

brain become active when people think. Clinicians and bioengineers are working together at UPMC to develop revolutionary new artificial hearts, lungs, kidneys, pancreases, livers, and blood substitutes that promise to deliver thousands from untimely death sentences.

But this focus on research would mean little if it weren't harnessed to UPMC Health System's central goal: providing the region's best care for patients. By offering the latest technologies for medical care, the health system helps people in the region and around the world live healthier, more productive lives; by educating the next generation of health care professionals, it helps to maintain standards of excellence in the medical profession; and by generating new knowledge, it helps to create new tools to alleviate human suffering. Clinicians and researchers at UPMC Health System aren't merely at the forefront of medical discovery—they are pushing far beyond.

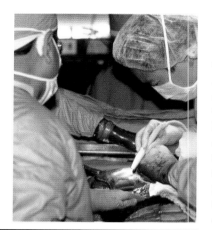

As the world's leading organ transplant center, UPMC Health System performs more transplants and more types of transplant procedures than any other medical center. UPMC clinicians and researchers continue to lead the transplant field, spearheading the use of the new, more effective antirejection drugs; pioneering multiorgan and intestinal transplants; exploring the rejection process with the goal of getting patients' bodies to accept transplanted organs as if they were the body's own; and developing permanent artificial organs that may someday make some transplants unnecessary (top).

UPMC Health System doctors' efforts to keep patients alive while awaiting organ transplants have produced an unexpected dividend: lessons that may enable the creation of the world's first permanent artificial organs. Here, successive computer-designed improvements in the Streamliner artificial heart pump show progressively more efficient blood flow (yellow) (middle).

UPMC Health System scientists are at the forefront of the quest to unlock the secrets of the gene. Their discoveries are already producing the first preliminary successes in gene therapy for disorders as different as arthritis, cancer, and inherited defects (bottom).

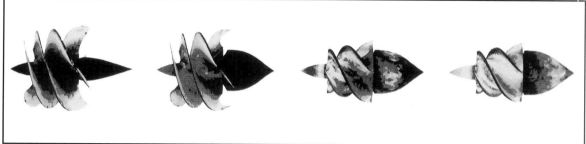

H.J. HEINZ COMPANY

THROUGHOUT THE WORLD, PITTSBURGH-BASED H.J. HEINZ Company and its products are synonymous with quality, purity, and wholesome nutrition. The commitment to quality started in 1869 when founder Henry John Heinz, then 25, began a business that sold horseradish to grocers in

the Pittsburgh area. The young entrepreneur set himself apart from competitors by packaging his product in clear glass bottles to show consumers that no fillers were added to extend the horse-radish, while rivals used green glass jars to obscure the ingredients in their products. The genius of Heinz was to make quality the hallmark of his company from the first day he began operating the business at his family's farmhouse in Sharpsburg, a town on the north shore of the Allegheny River, near Pittsburgh.

Henry John Heinz began his business in 1869. The H.J. Heinz Company was growing into a food industry giant by the turn of the century.

A GLOBAL ENTERPRISE

Today, quality remains the driving principle at the H.J. Heinz Company, which has grown into one of the world's premier food processors. The company's annual sales exceeded $9.3 billion in 1997, double its sales a decade earlier and about 10 times its sales in the early 1970s. To be sure, Heinz is best known for its flagship product, Heinz Ketchup, introduced in 1876. More than a century later, Heinz Ketchup is the indisputable market leader, stocked in more than 90 percent of U.S. households.

But Heinz products extend far beyond condiments and the famous

"57 Varieties" slogan coined by Henry Heinz in 1896. Today, Heinz is a global company that offers more than 4,000 products and markets its brands on every inhabited continent. Its six core global businesses are food service, which supplies products to restaurants and institutions; retail ketchup and condiments; infant feeding; pet food; tuna; and weight control. The company's branded products include Heinz Ketchup; StarKist tuna; Ore-Ida retail frozen potatoes; 9-Lives cat food; powerful market leaders The Budget Gourmet and Weight

Watchers brand frozen entrées; Earth's Best baby food; and Ken-L-Ration and Kibbles 'n Bits dog foods, to name just a few.

AN ENDURING LEGACY

Heinz and Pittsburgh have shared a strong bond since Heinz and his friend L. Clarence Noble formed Heinz & Noble in Sharpsburg. After early success selling horseradish, pickles, sauerkraut, and vinegar, the enterprise was forced into bankruptcy during the banking panic of 1875. A year later, Heinz formed a new company, F & J Heinz Company, with his brother John and cousin Frederick. In 1888, the company's name was changed to H.J. Heinz Company after Heinz bought out his partners. In the decades that followed, Heinz would grow into a food industry giant with more than 40,000 employees at more than 200 locations worldwide, while maintaining its roots in Pittsburgh.

Today, Heinz's world headquarters is in the USX Tower on Grant Street, in the heart of downtown Pittsburgh. Across the Allegheny River, Heinz U.S.A.'s venerable North Side factory (built in 1892) produces jarred

Heinz built its Pittsburgh North Side factory in 1892. Today, the company has more than 40,000 employees at more than 200 locations worldwide.

baby food, condensed and ready-to-serve soups, pureed foods, single-serve ketchup, and other condiments.

Overall, about 1,600 people work at the Pittsburgh factory and Heinz U.S.A.'s adjacent headquarters. Heinz U.S.A. markets retail and food service products primarily under the Heinz label in the United States, including ketchup, Heinz 57 Steak Sauce, pickles, gravy, relish, baby foods, vinegar, and sauces. In addition to providing jobs, Heinz supports Pittsburgh and other communities through the H.J. Heinz Company Foundation, which awards more than $6 million annually to hundreds of organizations and matches employee contributions.

A HISTORY OF STRONG LEADERSHIP

The Heinz name first gained international renown when the founder introduced his products to England in the late 1800s and the company opened facilities in the United Kingdom in 1905. Heinz led the company until he died of pneumonia in 1919 at the age of 75. The baton of leadership was passed to his son Howard Heinz, who guided the company's continuing growth until he died in 1941.

Henry John "Jack" Heinz II, the founder's grandson, became president of the company in 1941 at the age of 33. Just five years later, Heinz became a public company through its first public stock offer-

▶ BILL EXLER

ing. Jack Heinz steered the company's growth in the 1950s and 1960s before retiring as chief executive officer in 1966.

The company's fourth leader was R. Burt Gookin, whose 13-year stint as chief executive was marked by acquisitions, growth, and restructuring. Under Gookin, annual sales at Heinz topped $1 billion for the first time in 1972. They reached $2 billion by 1979, the year he retired. It was Gookin who brought Dr. Anthony J.F. O'Reilly to the company. O'Reilly, a native of Ireland, became president and CEO in 1979, launching an era of impressive international growth at Heinz. Under O'Reilly, Heinz created production bases in Spain, Portugal, and New Zealand; acquired Weight Watchers; developed thousands of new products; and penetrated emerging markets such as South Africa, Russia, China, India, Korea, Zimbabwe, Botswana, Thailand, and Eastern Europe.

A FUTURE OF GROWTH

Heinz hasn't been content to relish its past success; it continues to strive for sustained growth in an ever changing global marketplace. In 1997, Heinz embarked on Project Millennia, an ambitious growth initiative and the largest reorganization in its history. Under the leadership of President and Chief Operating Officer William R. Johnson, Project Millennia will help the company to achieve double-digit earnings growth into the 21st century and significantly strengthen Heinz's global businesses.

"As we approach the new millennium, our goal at Heinz is nothing less than world leadership in our six core categories," says O'Reilly. "Quality is the way forward for Heinz, just as it was in 1869, when a young man who sold horseradish in clear glass bottles created what would become one of America's great companies."

Clockwise from top left: The Heinz Ketchup line is the company's flagship product.

Heinz has a worldwide line of products that include many of the most famous names in the industry.

The company's U.S. headquarters and factory complex, along the Allegheny River, is responsible for producing a variety of Heinz products, including ketchup, baby food, and private-label soup.

L

IKE THE CITY IN WHICH IT IS HEADQUARTERED, MELLON BANK Corporation has met each challenge that has come its way and emerged stronger and more competitive. Through a balanced strategy and growth, Mellon is positioned very well for the changes likely to dominate the financial services industry into the 21st century.

Mellon is proud to have played a significant role in shaping Pittsburgh's past and looks forward to helping to define the city's future. Established locally as T. Mellon & Sons' Bank in 1869, Mellon financed the birth of the steel, coke, and aluminum industries in this region and throughout the East Coast. The bank has influenced the development and growth of companies across the country and around the world. This business heritage is also linked to the success of a highly respected family whose members have been leaders in economic progress, education, and philanthropy.

Mellon Bank Corporation continues to strengthen its position in the financial services industry through strategic acquisitions, reconfiguring consumer businesses and delivery systems, continuing its commitment to expanding trust and investment management services, and establishing specialized products and building relationships to better serve customers (top).

Mellon's constant pursuit of improvement and innovation is founded in the belief that it can always make things better. To solidify relationships, increase its responsiveness, and expand its value to clients, Mellon fosters teamwork and cooperation among the business lines of the organization. Since 1869, the Mellon name has defined strength, innovation, and integrity. Today, Mellon remains determined to transcend the boundaries of traditional banking in anticipation of—and in response to—its customers' changing needs (bottom).

MELLON TODAY

The decade of the 1980s was a period of rapid expansion for Mellon, as changes in state law enabled it and other Pennsylvania banks and bank holding companies to acquire bank holding companies in other regions of the state for the first time. During this decade, Mellon capitalized on expansion opportunities throughout the state—from Erie and State College to Harrisburg and the highly competitive Philadelphia market—as well as in Delaware and Maryland.

In the late 1980s, Mellon overcame asset quality problems of the type that were affecting virtually every major U.S. banking company.

Under the direction of Chairman, President, and Chief Executive Officer Frank V. Cahouet, the corporation rebounded from its loss in 1987, partly by undertaking the revolutionary "good bank/bad

The Power of

bank" transaction, through which it shed nearly $1 billion of lower-quality domestic assets and raised new equity capital to move the company forward. This action, along with significant restructuring of Mellon's businesses, enabled the corporation to embark upon its strategy of being a broad-based financial services company with a bank at its core.

Mellon's tradition of innovative strategy continued into the 1990s, when it introduced supermarket banking to Western Pennsylvania. The program, which has since expanded to central and eastern Pennsylvania, Delaware, and New Jersey markets, is just one component of a long-term strategic initiative to reconfigure Mellon's retail delivery system. The goal is to provide customers with more convenience, service, information, and choices by striking a balance between high tech and high touch; achieving the right mix of electronic services—telephone, PC, and video banking; and face-to-face interaction.

As one of the nation's major players in the asset management and trust and custody businesses, Mellon boasts a long history of providing investment services to consumers, corporations, state and local governments, and other large institutions. Its presence increased considerably in 1993, following the acquisition of the highly regarded Boston Company, which added substantially to Mellon's institutional trust, investment, and private client businesses.

A little more than a year later, Mellon furthered its thrust into the investment business with its

JOHN WEE

purchase of The Dreyfus Corporation—the largest combination of a banking firm and a mutual fund company in the history of the financial services industry. The merger added a valuable brand name to Mellon's investment services. It also helped create a trust and money management powerhouse with a position of sustainable leadership.

ON TOP OF THE INDUSTRY

Competition, consolidation, and new products and services are constantly reshaping the financial services industry. To survive and prosper in this dynamic environment, Mellon follows a business strategy of providing sound and effective solutions for customers in an ever changing marketplace. Mellon has organized its businesses into four sectors—consumer fee services, consumer banking, business fee services, and business banking—with a strong focus on establishing multiple-product relationships with customers and

developing market segments that offer significant growth and return potential.

Driven by the needs of its customers, Mellon has expanded its geographic reach and its range of financial services, businesses, and products, thereby distinguishing itself as a leader in redefining the needs, solutions, and direction of the financial services industry. As a result, Mellon today is a diversified, broad-based financial services company with a bank at its core. With a foundation of integrity, hard work, and vision, Mellon employees have successfully proved their ability to maintain a strategic balance that controls risk, and to provide the flexibility necessary to respond effectively and quickly to an ever changing business environment. Mellon is well prepared to handle the profound responsibility of meeting the financial services needs of each generation, both in its headquarters city of Pittsburgh and around the globe.

Mellon's industry-leading financial performance is a benefit the company has gained from being driven by customer solutions. Today's customers are increasingly demanding three things from financial services providers: a complete, sophisticated array of products; responsive service from knowledgeable professionals they trust; and access to products and services at convenient times and places. As a company with unmatched breadth and depth across both investment and banking services, Mellon has done its best to anticipate and meet customers' needs with the right solutions for today and tomorrow.

THE YEAR 1869 WAS A SIGNIFICANT ONE FOR THE RAILROAD industry: The driving of the golden spike at Promontory Summit in Utah marked the completion of the first transcontinental railroad, making cross-country travel a reality. Back in Pittsburgh, George Westinghouse was making a

WABCO ARCHIVES

Clockwise from top:
Westinghouse Air Brake Company equipped the first passenger train with automatic air brakes in 1872.

WABCO's headquarters is located in Wilmerding, Pennsylvania.

In 1869, George Westinghouse successfully demonstrated the latest of his many inventions—the straight air brake—on a Pennsylvania Railroad passenger train. Since then, WABCO has engineered nearly every major development in railroad braking equipment.

little history of his own by successfully demonstrating the latest of his many inventions—the straight air brake—on a Pennsylvania Railroad passenger train. Since then, nearly every major development in railroad braking equipment has been engineered by Westinghouse Air Brake Company.

Today, WABCO is North America's largest manufacturer of air brakes and related equipment for locomotives, railway freight cars, and passenger transit rail vehicles. The company has significant operations in the Pittsburgh region, with its corporate headquarters and Locomotive Products Division situated in Wilmerding,

a quiet community about 10 miles east of downtown. Additionally, WABCO's Rubber Products Division is located in nearby Greensburg.

After more than 125 years, the company remains a market leader, maintaining a market share for railway braking components in excess of 50 percent in North America and a significant market share for its other principal products.

DURABLE AND INNOVATIVE PRODUCTS

The reasons for WABCO's continued success are quality and durability, two characteristics common throughout the company's product lines. In fact, many of the loco-

motive brake valves and freight brake control valves manufactured by WABCO in the 1930s and 1940s are still in service today, providing a fitting testimony to their reliability.

The same quality is expected from the products WABCO turns out today. To this end, the company is aggressively pursuing technology-driven new product development and product line expansion. In addition to internal research and development, WABCO continually evaluates licensing, joint venture, and acquisition opportunities that permit the company to offer a wider range of products to both new and existing customers.

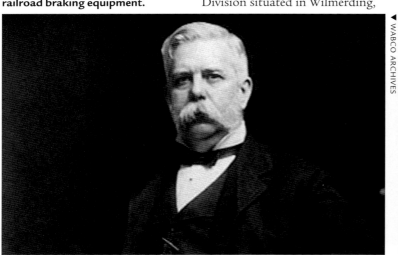

WABCO ARCHIVES

ED ROMBOUT

One example of WABCO's technology-driven innovation is the new Automated Single-Car Tester (ASCT). Federal regulations mandate that every freight car must undergo a series of safety checks periodically to ensure that all pneumatic and mechanical brake-related devices are in proper working order. The average time needed to conduct these tests using the current standards procedure is about 45 minutes. WABCO's computerized ASCT performs the same tests with much more accuracy in less than half the time. This type of innovation is crucial in rail yards today, where railroads are constantly seeking new and better means of monitoring their equipment and reducing downtime.

Almost 50 percent of WABCO sales are made directly to manufacturers of locomotives, freight cars, and passenger transit vehicles. WABCO products for locomotives include electronic and pneumatic air brake equipment, brake shoes, compressors, air dryers, and monitoring and control equipment. The product line broadened during the mid-1990s, following WABCO's acquisition of Pulse Electronics, to include end-of-train telemetry, black box event recorders, and computers for onboard locomotive systems. For freight cars, WABCO produces air brake components, brake shoes, draft gears, hand brakes, slack adjusters, and slackless connectors. For passenger transit, it produces electronic brake control equipment, compressors, disc and tread brake units, couplers, electronic wheel slip control equipment, third-rail connectors, electronic door openers, access ramps, and climate control systems.

WABCO's Rubber Products Division in Greensburg produces a vast array of gaskets, diaphragms, and check valves for railway pneumatic devices, along with a wide range of industrial rubber components, such as heavy-duty diaphragms used in pumping equipment.

SERVICING THE AFTERMARKET

WABCO's commitment to customers does not end with the sale of equipment to manufacturers. In fact, it's merely the beginning of a long relationship. In most cases, the end users—fleet owners, private car companies, and transit authorities—rely on WABCO's expertise to service equipment and train personnel when new products hit the market. The company offers a variety of training seminars, technical pamphlets, and instructional videos geared toward educating its customers on the basics of air brake fundamentals.

In addition to continuing education, WABCO offers a complete line of replacement parts, as well as proprietary remanufacturing and upgrade processes that transform older brake components into like-new, technologically advanced equipment. WABCO operates its aftermarket services from nine regional service facilities located near major railroad centers, thereby reducing repair times and travel distances.

COMMITMENT TO INNOVATION

Technological advances will continue to drive WABCO ahead of its competitors, both domestically and overseas. The technological advances are driven by the company's commitment to success. "A key component is our corporate culture," says WABCO Chairman and Chief Executive Officer William E. Kassling. "Our culture is defined in various ways. In terms of products, it is characterized by the commitment to innovative, high-quality, reliable products that meet the needs of our customers. In terms of organization, it can be viewed as action oriented, entrepreneurial, and fast moving, with the minimum number of reporting levels. Operationally, it is best defined by our commitment to continuous improvement efforts. This disciplined approach has produced a responsive, profitable company that will continue to thrive."

With a history of quality and innovation and a dedication to advancing technology, WABCO looks poised to continue its role as an industry leader. And while no one can predict the future, one thing is certain: WABCO will continue to keep pace with the needs of the changing railroad industry, just as it has for more than a century.

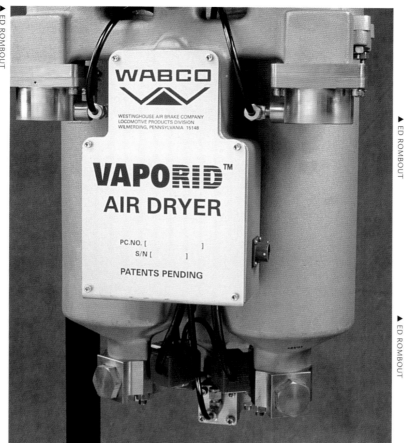

Clockwise from left:
Among the company's products for locomotives is the WABCO VAPORID Air Dryer.

William E. Kassling, WABCO's chairman and chief executive officer

One example of WABCO's technological innovation is the new Automated Single-Car Tester.

FROM THE OUTSIDE, THE KAUFMANN'S FLAGSHIP DEPARTMENT STORE in downtown Pittsburgh gives off an air of tradition and old-world grace. Comprising an entire city block, the 13-story, brick-and-stone building at the corner of Smithfield Street and Fifth Avenue, in the core of the city's shopping

district, features intricately carved stonework and rows of elaborately laid-out window displays.

It's the kind of store many Pittsburgh residents remember from Christmas shopping with their parents. One step inside, however, and customers of all ages are transported to the 21st century. The shopper is surrounded immediately by an infusion of brightness and color, and greeted by friendly, service-conscious sales associates. The merchandise is up-to-the-minute, with the latest designs and floor displays right out of a fashion magazine. It is this marriage of old and new that shoppers have come to know, love, and expect from Kaufmann's, Pittsburgh's premier, full-service department stores for the past 126 years. And today's shoppers show their sup-

port of Kaufmann's to the tune of $1.4 billion a year in sales.

A LONG HISTORY

Though the Kaufmann's of today boasts 47 stores in four states, the company was born in 1871 to much humbler beginnings. It started as the merchant tailoring business of two German immi-

grant brothers, Jacob and Isaac Kaufmann, who were soon joined by two younger brothers, Morris and Henry. In those days, Morris, the youngest, pulled guard duty at the store on Carson Street in the South Side of Pittsburgh, sleeping on the second floor with a long string tied to his big toe. Were a fire or other emergency to strike, a passerby could alert the young retailer by pulling on the other end of the string, which was dangling over the front door.

The store, which moved to its current quarters on Smithfield Street in 1877, initially offered only men's clothing, but the brothers' emphasis on quality and fair dealing attracted a larger and larger customer base. Kaufmann's remained a men's store until 1886, when the brothers added a wide range of

Though the Kaufmann's of today boasts 47 stores in four states, the company was born in 1871 to much humbler beginnings. It started as the merchant tailoring business of two German immigrant brothers, Isaac and Jacob Kaufmann (top).

In 1880, Kaufmann's accommodated its customers by offering a delivery and distribution service (bottom).

The Power of

items, such as women's clothing, shoes, yard goods, and housewares.

From its start, Kaufmann's has been a retail leader in Pittsburgh, always looking to the future with an innovative eye. At the turn of the century, for instance, noting the huge influx of immigrant workers in the area, Kaufmann's employed translators to make the new arrivals feel at home in its store. The store was also one of the first to hire women salesclerks, to ease multifloor shopping by installing electric escalators and hydraulic elevators, and to offer shopping under the glow of electric lights.

The second generation took over in 1910, when 33-year-old Edgar Jonas Kaufmann, known as E.J., took the reins. Under E.J.'s leadership, the store began to grow into the institution it is today, with an emphasis on high-quality fashion and service. In 1946, on its 75th anniversary, the store merged with the May Company; in 1961, Kaufmann's opened its first suburban store, in Monroeville, and then continued its regional expansion, adding stores in Ohio, New York, and West Virginia. Even today, when many retailers have been forced to close their doors, the Kaufmann's Division of May Stores continues to grow, with six more stores, including three in the Pittsburgh area, scheduled to open in the next six years.

KAUFMANN'S TODAY

Kaufmann's today resembles a series of stores all sharing one roof. The latest fashions and consumer electronics are offered alongside quality furniture, carpets, and housewares, and customers enjoy a wide selection of merchandise in all price ranges. Yet each department retains its own personality. The junior areas might have music videos running for atmosphere, while around the corner, shoppers can lose themselves in the earthy, classic world of Ralph Lauren.

At the downtown store, with 1 million square feet of space, shopping isn't the only attraction—there are also seven eating spots, three hair salons, a bakery, an eye-glass shop, a post office, and a dentist's office.

Kaufmann's now employs 14,500 workers throughout the Mid-Atlantic states, but its heart is still in Pittsburgh, the home of seven Kaufmann's stores. The store remains a place where customers are known by name—and where many Pittsburghers who have moved on to other cities retain their Kaufmann's cards and continue to shop there when visiting. As Jerry Eccher, senior vice president of sales promotion, explains, "Our customers know that they will see quality merchandise when they come in our store. But they also know that they're shopping in a place that is part of Pittsburgh, part of our local history."

Kaufmann's is investing in the future by spending $150 million on remodeling and new stores, says Eccher. But the downtown store is still the "heart," where all the merchandising, sales support, and store management are based. Company managers know they are never far from the merchandise, and from the customers that are essential to the future of Kaufmann's.

And that is why, as Eccher notes, Pittsburghers feel like they're "going to a friend each time they visit Kaufmann's."

"Meet me under the clock" is a familiar phrase in Pittsburgh. The Kaufmann's clock has been at the corner of Fifth and Smithfield since 1913 (left).

The merchandise and presentation at all Kaufmann's stores is up-to-the-minute (right).

**T**O LOOK AT SOURCE W TODAY, YOU'D NEVER KNOW THAT IT BEGAN in 1872 as a company that typeset promotional literature for Westinghouse Electric Corp., one of the nation's manufacturing giants. Now, more than 125 years later, the Pittsburgh-based corporation is setting much more than

type—it's setting the standard for digital communications.

Pulling from a spectrum of industries that define traditional and interactive media, Source W's 130-plus-member staff brings decades of experience in production, engineering, planning, marketing, and management to every communications project. Source W offers state-of-the-art media productions, including traditional graphic communication products and services; electronic publishing of new media, including CD-ROM, Internet, and electronic catalogs; on-line publishing; distributing; and printing services. The company is widely known for its creativity, innovative technology, and superior customer service.

Source W, which tallies nearly $17.5 million in annual sales, is headquartered in 6 Gateway Center in downtown Pittsburgh. It also operates a major production facility in Trafford, located approximately 15 miles east of the city, as well as several other satellite operations. In the 1990s, Source W has extended its national presence by opening

offices in New York City and Washington, D.C.

HARNESSING TECHNOLOGY VIA PARTNERSHIPS

Source W recognizes that no single firm can understand every emerging technology or process, especially in a rapidly changing industry such as multimedia communications. Long ago, the company recognized that to assemble

an agile internal team, it had to equip that team with equally powerful external resources. As a result, Source W established partnerships with leaders in software development, hardware manufacturing, Internet hosting and access services, and translation services, as well as with others who provide critical capabilities to the development and deployment of communication solutions. These partnerships dramatically extend Source W's ability to fulfill clients' needs.

Source W selects quality partners whose standards of reliability and service match its own. In 1997, for example, Source W forged an alliance with Pittsburgh-based Multilingual Communications Corp. (MCC). Bridging the gap between business communications and foreign markets, the partnership combines the talents of quality media professionals from Source W with MCC's highly experienced multilingual professionals. MCC provides and coordinates text translation of Source W's technically designed Web pages, thereby enhancing the global competitiveness of Source W's clients.

Source W offers state-of-the-art media productions, including traditional graphic communication products and services; electronic publishing of new media, including CD-ROM, Internet, and electronic catalogs; on-line publishing; distributing; and printing services.

Source W established partnerships with leaders in software development, hardware manufacturing, Internet hosting and access services, and translation services, as well as with others who provide critical capabilities to the development and deployment of communication solutions.

HELPING BUSINESSES COMMUNICATE

Source W's graphic designers are adept at communicating highly complex technical information using a wide variety of traditional and electronic media. Because of those capabilities, Source W has developed a reputation for helping major businesses utilize technology to reach customers in a broad spectrum of markets. For instance, when mutual fund giant Federated Investors was looking to quickly distribute accurate information to its clients and prospective investors, it turned to Source W, which produced comprehensive data on Federated's many mutual funds and trusts in digital form on compact discs. As a result, investment houses on and off Wall Street can access crucial information with the simple click of a mouse. Since then, other companies across a broad spectrum of industries have tapped into the speed and economy of digital publishing.

Source W has also produced interactive electronic presentations for Federated Investors for marketing its products and services. And because live presentations are still an essential marketing tool in the investment field, Source W works closely with Federated managers to develop more effective communications vehicles for use by the company's field representatives.

VOLUMES OF INFORMATION

Another Source W client is the Cutler-Hammer Division of Eaton Corporation, which is one of the world's largest suppliers of electrical control systems and components. Cutler-Hammer, like most large manufacturers, faces the constant problem of communicating effectively with its customers and employees. To address this problem, Cutler-Hammer tapped into Source W's expertise to develop both traditional and state-of-the-art marketing communications techniques.

The relationship between the two companies actually began

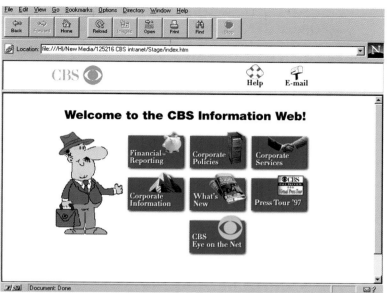

many years ago, when Source W started printing and distributing all of Cutler-Hammer's product literature. Although it still provides that service to Cutler-Hammer, Source W also puts together thousands of pages of product literature on compact discs in the form of electronic catalogs. Through data compression and graphic display software, Cutler-Hammer customers can hold virtually every piece of the company's product literature, specifications, and other technical data in one hand.

Source W is also working to distribute information on Cutler-Hammer's new products by refining the company's World Wide Web site, which enables customers to access new product and application data before the information is printed.

THE FUTURE

In the late 1990s, the longtime Source W parent, Westinghouse Electric, was split into CBS Inc. and Westinghouse Electric Co. (WELCO). Source W has remained under the WELCO umbrella, but continues to do work for operations for both companies, as well as its many clients that were independent of the former Westinghouse.

Today, although its services have expanded into multimedia communications, Source W remains among the Pittsburgh region's five largest printing operations. In the future, the company will continue serving its clients with a growing array of services as new media opportunities come on-line.

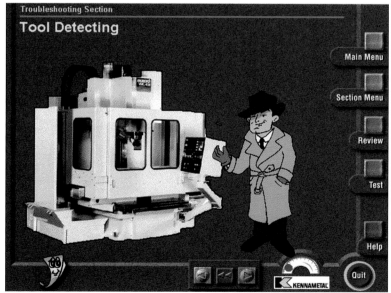

Source W's graphic designers are adept at communicating highly complex technical information using a wide variety of traditional and electronic media.

S INCE 1876, WHEN PITTSBURGH'S CHAMBER OF COMMERCE was founded to serve the needs of the city's business community, the Chamber's mission has changed little. However, with every new generation, every new technology, and every new market, the range of services necessary to meet

the demands of today's business community has spiraled ever higher. Starting in 1998, the Chamber took a step forward, and assumed the lead role in addressing the demands of a region poised for major growth.

"We are taking the most proactive approach in our history towards the retention and growth of regional businesses," says Barbara Bateman McNees, executive director of the Chamber. "We have positioned ourselves to be the 'front door' to the region. We are now a clearinghouse of information and resources for any business, anywhere, seeking to relocate or grow in the Pittsburgh region."

THE PRA

In 1995, the Greater Pittsburgh Chamber of Commerce served as the anchor organization in the formation of a unified economic development delivery system. The result, the Pittsburgh Regional Alliance (PRA), represents a strategic federation of six key business and economic development organizations. In addition to the Chamber, the PRA includes Penn's Southwest Association, Pittsburgh High Technology Council, Southwestern Pennsylvania Industrial Resource Center, Regional Indus-

trial Development Corporation of Southwestern Pennsylvania, and the World Trade Center Pittsburgh.

At the heart of PRA's strategy is giving its customers—both existing and prospective Pittsburgh businesses—what they want. Foremost, that means improving the availability of early stage capital resources, accelerating university technology transfer, creating business incubators, and retaining entrepreneurial talent. The PRA also launched its regional customer calling program, established a regional advocacy coalition, instituted a regional business financing system, created a regional marketing coalition, and initiated an internal marketing volunteer program. Most important, all of this is happening as a collaborative effort by the various PRA member agencies, each of which brings unique expertise to the PRA.

Penn's Southwest Association is the region's principal marketing and business attraction agency. The Pittsburgh High Technology Council provides technical, administrative, and economic assistance to advanced technology companies

in both the manufacturing and service sectors. The Southwestern Pennsylvania Industrial Resource Center (SPIRC) provides management and technical support services to small and medium-sized manufacturing companies. The Regional Industrial Development Corporation of Southwestern Pennsylvania (RIDC) provides land and planning services to assist new business and growth industries locate real estate in the region. The World Trade Center Pittsburgh helps companies develop international business.

"We have a superb foundation upon which to build our new Pittsburgh regional economy," says Timothy Parks, president and CEO of the PRA. "Our region's future lies not with Harrisburg, nor with Washington, nor with winning some form of economic development super lottery. Our future rests squarely with each of us and our willingness to work together."

CHAMBER PROGRAMS

While becoming a more proactive chamber, the Greater Pittsburgh Chamber of Commerce has also maintained many of its traditional

The diversity within Pittsburgh's landscape parallels the diversity of Chamber members, who enjoy a close relationship with both the African-American and Hispanic Chambers of Commerce.

Perhaps the greatest benefit of a membership in the Chamber is supporting the economic growth of its 10-county region.

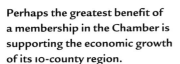

The Power of

programs that have served the region well over many decades.

One such program is Leadership Pittsburgh, which seeks to cultivate and broaden leadership resources within the regional community. Every year, 50 diverse and highly motivated community leaders are selected through a competitive application process to participate in a 10-month, tuition-based program that is designed to develop leadership skills and expose participants to a wide range of issues challenging the Pittsburgh region. A similar program, the Leadership Development Initiative, is geared toward young professionals, who are sponsored by their employer or a community organization.

DINAMO, the Association for the Development of Inland Navigation in America's Ohio Valley, represents a nearly $5 billion investment in the region's waterways and economic future. Since 1981, DINAMO has assisted in the authorization, funding, and/or construction of 15 locks and dams.

The British-American Business Council Pittsburgh Region serves as the region's link to the city's most accessible European markets. Annual trade missions, seminars, and forums serve as vital means of informing the Pittsburgh business community of new and emerging markets in the United Kingdom and overseas.

The Greater Pittsburgh Chamber of Commerce also employs the services of a government affairs advocate, who regularly communicates the initiatives and objectives of the Pittsburgh Regional Alliance to state representatives in Harrisburg and to congressional and senate staffers in Washington, D.C. The Government Affairs office also hosts four legislative or public affairs meetings throughout the year, offering every Chamber member the opportunity to meet and speak with his or her elected officials.

Other equally important programs of the Chamber are the weekly seminars, trade shows, public forums, and roundtable discussions that the Chamber staff plans, organizes, and markets on

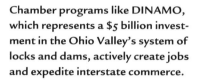

behalf of the many subcommittees, comprised solely of members, who seek to make the region a better and better-informed community in which to do business. On a monthly basis, the Chamber also produces a newsletter, a mailing of members' literature, and a very popular business-to-business exchange where members may network socially or in the presence of guest speakers.

THE FUTURE

In early 1998, the Chamber moved into new and larger offices, where all the member agencies of the PRA will be located, creating a one-stop shop for business retention and attraction.

"It's an exciting and promising time for the Chamber, as we move ahead guided by an enhanced mission," says McNees. "The Greater Pittsburgh Chamber of Commerce has effected a number of fundamental and far-reaching changes. We have new staff, new strategies, and a renewed commitment to delivering membership benefits and programming. This will support the most proactive agenda in the Chamber's long history."

Chamber programs like DINAMO, which represents a $5 billion investment in the Ohio Valley's system of locks and dams, actively create jobs and expedite interstate commerce.

From mom-and-pop shops to Fortune 500 corporations, the Greater Pittsburgh Chamber of Commerce serves the interests of every sector of the economy.

REED SMITH SHAW & McCLAY LLP IS A DYNAMIC LAW FIRM WITH 400 attorneys located in eight mid-Atlantic cities. The firm's largest office is in the heart of Pittsburgh's central business district, where Reed Smith attorneys are supported by scores of other professionals—paralegals, agents, clerks, legal

secretaries, and other administrators—each of whom is an integral part of the firm.

Founded in Pittsburgh in 1877 as Knox & Reed by Philander C. Knox and James Hay Reed, the firm grew along with the industries and financial institutions of the Pittsburgh area. Virtually from its inception, the firm served as legal counsel to some of the world's largest manufacturing concerns, and to such prominent individuals as Andrew Carnegie, Henry Clay Frick, and the Mellon family, among others. The firm played a significant role in the formation of United States Steel Corporation, in the establishment of the National Gallery

of Art in Washington, D.C. and in the litigation of the famous 1952 Steel Seizure Case.

More recently, Reed Smith has been counsel in some of the largest corporate acquisitions; played a principal role on behalf of the asbestos industry in developing the unprecedented Asbestos Claims Facility; assisted a major financial institution in developing a state-of-the-art mechanism for disposing of a large portfolio of troubled loans; and is currently advising a major player in the health care insurance business with respect to the paradigm shift under way in the health care arena. The firm continues to counsel a wide

array of Fortune 500 corporations, in addition to leading privately held companies and emerging businesses. Reed Smith also played a key role in the 1996 deal that kept the Pirates and professional baseball in Pittsburgh.

The firm has successfully represented the interests of clients, both large and small, across a broad spectrum of legal concerns. "Our long-range planning annually defines dozens of specific action items to improve our client service and our internal operations," says Daniel I. Booker, managing partner. "But the plan every year is based on the same two imperatives: Number one, never let a client

A dramatic two-story atrium greets visitors to Reed Smith Shaw & McClay LLP.

down; and number two, always improve."

Reed Smith is able to offer services to any client out of any of its offices, thanks to a state-of-the-art computer network. All offices and their attorneys are linked, enabling the instantaneous transmission of resources and information to geographically disparate locations. When needed, the expertise of an attorney in one office can be tapped to enhance the capacity of professionals at other locations.

THE PRACTICE AREAS

Reed Smith's practice areas are organized on a firmwide basis, and consist of business and finance law; employment law and benefits; litigation; and regulatory and government affairs.

The offices outside Pittsburgh are located in Philadelphia; Harrisburg; Washington, D.C.; New York City; McLean, Virginia; and Newark and Princeton, New Jersey. From these locations, Reed

Smith lawyers counsel banks and financial institutions; colleges; health care providers; foundations and other nonprofit organizations; industrial corporations; family businesses; governmental bodies; and individuals in the United States and in other countries.

"Reed Smith competes aggressively in quality, service, and price as it grows its legal practice," Booker says. "The core clients are businesses—regardless of size—that demand responsive, sophisticated, and aggressive legal services." The work Reed Smith does for these clients includes corporate finance and securities, mergers and acquisitions, intellectual property, employee relations, government relations, litigation, bankruptcy, environmental, and all other business law disciplines.

For more than 120 years, Reed Smith Shaw & McClay LLP has proved its ability to evolve with the changing marketplace and adapt to the changing needs of its

varied clients. The firm's philosophy of continuous improvement and service to the client guarantees that Reed Smith will continue this tradition of success in its second century of practice.

Reed Smith has 400 attorneys located in eight mid-Atlantic cities. The firm's largest office is in the heart of downtown Pittsburgh in the James H. Reed Building, which features a rooftop deck (shown at left). Pictured above is a conference room in the firm's Pittsburgh office.

A WALK THROUGH THE MODERN ANCHOR HOCKING SPECIALTY Glass plant in Monaca, Pennsylvania, evokes a wide range of impressions. Railcar loads of raw materials are mixed together at 2,700 degrees Fahrenheit to form molten glass. Giant, flame-spewing machines run at breakneck speed,

Anchor Hocking Specialty Glass' modern plant is located in Monaca, Pennsylvania.

forming and blowing glass of all shapes and sizes. Thousands of glass pieces travel through long annealing ovens that slowly heat, and then cool, the pieces to make them stronger. Ordinary glass pieces are made extraordinary by adding color, texture, and design.

It's a long way from the handblown kerosene lamp chimneys made at The Phoenix Glass Company when it started in 1880. That evolution is the real story of the company, which was acquired by Anchor Hocking Corporation in 1970, then by Newell Company in 1987. By changing its line of specialty glass products in order to adapt to new market opportunities, the company became the industry leader. Now known as Anchor Hocking Specialty Glass, its line of lighting products has evolved from kerosene lamps to enclosed gaslight fixtures, and then to globes and domes with the advent of electric lighting.

In response to marketplace demand, the company recently developed a much broader product line in addition to its core lighting products. Secondary producers now use Anchor Hocking Specialty Glass for proprietary and stock items in

other industries, such as small appliance, floral, premium, and utility metering.

KEEPING CUSTOMERS SATISFIED

"Our philosophy is pretty simple, but it takes a lot of work to live by it," says President George Hamilton. "We provide our customers with a quality product and optimum customer service, at the best price/value relationship."

The approximately 700 employees at the Monaca facility and the roughly 50 decorators at the company's Bremen, Ohio, operation work closely with customers to produce a quality product that meets the customers' need for de-

sign, fashion, and function. Keeping a close eye on the market helps Anchor Hocking Specialty Glass to deliver the best value.

Recent company growth is a result of this philosophy. Anchor Hocking Specialty Glass is moving into rapidly growing markets. A recent, $7 million plant expansion added sales capacity, increased the company's flexibility among different production methods, lowered costs, and added jobs.

Anchor Hocking Specialty Glass is a member of Newell Company, a family of consumer products companies in the housewares, home furnishings, hardware, and office products markets. With the backing of a $3 billion corporation, Anchor Hocking Specialty Glass can take advantage of growth opportunities as they arise. Newell's decentralized approach to the manufacturing and marketing side of the business allows the employees of Anchor Hocking Specialty Glass to control their work environment, while the disciplines of financial control ensure the company's continued success.

The future will demand new and better ways of making specialty glass items for many markets. Anchor Hocking Specialty Glass is helping develop those markets, while maintaining its commitment to serving its customers with excellence.

The company's history dates back to 1880, when The Phoenix Glass Company began manufacturing kerosene lamp chimneys (left).

In response to marketplace demand, the company recently developed a much broader product line in addition to its core lighting products. Secondary producers now use Anchor Hocking Specialty Glass for proprietary and stock items in other industries, such as small appliance, floral, premium, and utility metering (right).

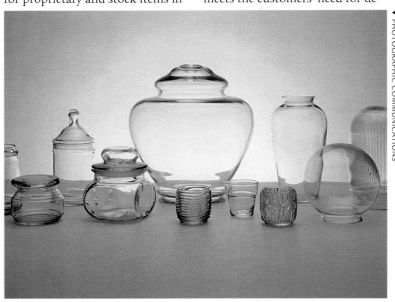

PHOTOGRAPHIC COMMUNICATIONS

The Power of

N TODAY'S DEREGULATED ENERGY MARKETS, BUSINESSES AND consumers have the opportunity to choose the company that will supply the power that drives their machinery and heats their homes. It's a completely different energy market from the monopoly-driven system that dominated Pennsylvania for decades. Perhaps

no company pushed harder for deregulation and the economic benefits it brings than Equitable Resources, Inc. (ERI), a fully integrated energy exploration, distribution, and marketing company that offers customized energy solutions to wholesale and retail customers.

ERI started more than a century ago as a company seeking to procure and sell natural gas. Today, the corporation founded as Equitable Gas Company in 1888 serves a broad base of customers throughout the United States through its primary business segments: ERI Utilities, ERI Supply & Logistics, and ERI Services.

COMPLETE ENERGY SOLUTIONS

Equitable Gas Company remains perhaps the best-known entity within the ERI Utilities business segment. It provides natural gas distribution services to more than 260,000 residential, commercial, and industrial customers located primarily in the city of Pittsburgh, the surrounding seven counties in Southwestern Pennsylvania, and municipalities in northern West Virginia.

Also under the ERI Utilities umbrella is Equitrans L.P., a pipeline company established by ERI in response to the changing marketplace that is driven by competition. Through Equitrans, ERI services industrial customers and markets that it had previously been unable to reach. Other ERI Utilities pipeline operations include Kentucky West Virginia Gas, Nora, and Three Rivers Pipeline Corp.

With its strategic focus on the Appalachian and Gulf Coast regions, Houston-based ERI Supply & Logistics is the company's exploration and production business that develops, supplies, and transports all forms of energy. ERI Supply & Logistics is responsible for mon-

itoring the supply, storage, and distribution of resources for ERI and its subsidiaries, as well as other customers.

As competition spawns new opportunities in deregulated markets, ERI's newest business segment, ERI Services, creates and delivers customized energy solutions to businesses seeking to improve their total energy efficiency. ERI Services offers commodity brokering of all forms of energy and provides resource management, energy consulting, and engineering services, including financing and facility management.

ERI Services has offices and customers throughout the United States. A prominent example of an ERI Service project is in the heart of Pittsburgh at Duquesne University. Under an energy services performance contract, ERI Services installed energy-saving technologies and equipment at no up-front cost to Duquesne. Duquesne pays ERI Services and other project expenses entirely from the savings in energy costs. Duquesne reaps the benefits of long-term savings and of the physical plant improvements. ERI provides the energy that lights

classrooms and powers computers on the campus. ERI Services acts as the university's total energy manager, with on-site staff managing day-to-day operations. The project is typical of ERI, providing intelligent energy solutions for its customers.

Through its ongoing efforts to find better ways of serving the needs of consumers, who previously never had a choice in their energy providers, ERI will continue to offer new and improved methods of delivering energy solutions to its customers in the region and across the United States.

▶ ED MASSERY

Built in 1925, Equitable Resources' headquarters in downtown Pittsburgh, a former pharmaceutical warehouse, has been designated a historic landmark by the Pittsburgh History and Landmarks Foundation (top).

The gas control center at Equitrans, the pipeline subsidiary of ERI Utilities, monitors 2,000 miles of pipeline on the company's system in Pennsylvania and West Virginia (bottom).

▶ TOBY SEGER

N INDUSTRY AFTER INDUSTRY, GOVERNMENT REGULATORS HAVE STEPPED aside, and new competitors have stepped in. These changes have been seen in the airlines industry, then the communications industry, followed by trucking, railroads, petroleum, natural gas, and financial services. With deregulation has come an often bewildering array of

choices, but also the advantages of competitive pricing. Consumer response has run the gamut from overjoyed to overwhelmed.

Now it's the electric power industry's turn. Recent legislation in Pennsylvania mandates full retail competition, beginning January 1, 1999. Pittsburgh-based energy services company DQE is strategically positioning itself to meet the needs of the expanding marketplace. Regionally, Duquesne Light Co., a core business of DQE, has been the primary source of power for Greater Pittsburgh for decades. Duquesne Light, which is engaged in the production, transmission, distribution, and sale of electric energy, has traditionally covered approximately 800 square miles in Southwestern Pennsylvania. In addition to serving more than 580,000 direct customers, the company sells electricity to other utilities.

"Electricity is a fundamental service, essential to the quality of life for everyone," says DQE President and Chief Executive Officer David Marshall. "Duquesne Light

strongly supports this move toward customer choice in electric power. We believe that, as in other industries, choice will bring with it greater innovation, tailored service, and market-driven prices.

"A wise Pennsylvanian, Benjamin Franklin, once wrote that government should go 'no further with trade than to protect it, and let it take its course.' We heartily subscribe to that sentiment," Marshall adds. "With the coming of consumer choice, a new era has dawned for electric power in Pennsylvania. And we welcome it. In the next few years, customers will enjoy the freedom to decide who generates their power. It will mean new relationships between consumers and electricity suppliers. By better understanding these relationships and the issues surrounding them, we will all help to make the future of competition bright."

BEYOND DUQUESNE LIGHT

While Duquesne Light is a mainstay of Pittsburgh, parent DQE is an evolving energy services company

that is much more. Other DQE business units include Duquesne Enterprises, which makes strategic investments beneficial to DQE's core energy business. These investments enhance DQE's capabilities as an energy provider, increase asset utilization, and act as a hedge against changing business conditions. Another business unit, Montauk, is a financial services company that makes long-term investments and provides financing for DQE's other market-driven businesses.

DQE Energy Services provides energy solutions for customers in domestic and international markets. Included are energy facility development and operation, independent power production, gas and electric energy/fuel management, and utility management services. Finally, DQEnergy Partners aligns DQE with strategic partners to capitalize on opportunities in the dynamic energy services industry. "These alliances enhance the utilization and value of DQE's strategic investments and capabilities,

Supervisors at Duquesne Light Co.'s Distribution Operations Center constantly monitor the entire service area for trouble spots, using the latest in computer technology. From their location in Manchester, these supervisors can ponpoint disruptions to electrical circuits, and reroute power and/or dispatch repair crews to minimize outages and return customers' power as quickly as possible.

while establishing DQE as a total energy provider," Marshall says.

TOP PERFORMANCE AND SERVICE

During the past 10 years, DQE has provided investors with one of the top total returns in the electric utility industry. For instance, the 1996 earnings per share of $2.32 reflected a 5.5 percent increase from the 1995 level and was the 10th consecutive annual earnings increase for DQE. The five-year compound growth rate in earnings per share through 1996 for DQE was 6.8 percent. Meanwhile, DQE has been one of only three electric utilities industrywide to increase dividends by 5 percent or more each year during the 1990s, and net cash flow from operations is among the strongest in the industry.

Duquesne Light has always provided top service to customers in Western Pennsylvania, as evidenced by its ability to maintain power supplies through devastating natural disasters, such as the 1993 blizzard that crippled the Northeast and the winter floods of 1996 that ravaged much of Western Pennsylvania.

Additionally, Duquesne Light has been a strong supporter of the community. Many of its executives serve on nonprofit boards, and the company contributes financial support to various community programs. Duquesne Light invests about $2 million annually in the community, targeting the four priority areas of education, health and human services, civic and community development, and arts and culture.

Additionally, Duquesne Light Co. annually sponsors the Three Rivers Environmental Awards, together with the Pennsylvania Environmental Council. The program honors local individuals and organizations for their demonstrated commitment to environmental excellence, leadership, and accomplishment. For years, Duquesne Light has been a leader among power utilities in preserving the environment, and was the first utility in the country to implement an emission-reducing, dual-fired system using coal and natural gas. Duquesne was also the first to treat drainage from a coal mine, developing technology that remains the industry standard today.

"We are committed to providing value to the people we serve," says Marshall. "That commitment is reflected in the safe and reliable electric energy we deliver to our customers. It can also be seen in our leadership in protecting the environment and our participation in public-private efforts to help rebuild the local economy."

The commitment of DQE/ Duquesne Light Co. is evident in the scope and quality of its service, as well as its community involvement, which provides added value to its customers and the communities in which it operates.

Members of Duquesne Light Co.'s Employee Community Action Committee and their families pose before taking part in the Juvenile Diabetes Walk for the Cure. This fund-raiser is just one of many charitable activities initiated by the energetic group of volunteers.

Duquesne Light Co. has served the Golden Triangle since 1880. From the city's early years as an industrial powerhouse in steel and manufacturing to its current world-renowned status as a medical hub, Duquesne Light has helped power Pittsburgh's growth.

ITH A HERITAGE THAT DATES BACK TO THE 1880S, Contraves Brashear Systems, L.P. produces some of the world's finest precision optical tracking and instrumentation systems. ■ Optics industry pioneer John Brashear established the company in Pittsburgh

in 1881. The John Brashear Company, as it was then called, and its successor, J.W. Fecker Systems, developed some of the largest telescopes in the world. After World War II, the company evolved from a producer of telescopes into a broader-based instrumentation company that could provide advanced engineering and manufacturing of optics, mechanical, and electronic systems. It was the knowledge and experience in these areas that gave Contraves Brashear the strong market position it continues to hold today.

Contraves Brashear Systems, L.P. is one of the world's premier manufacturers of optical systems and has built some of the largest telescopes in the world at the time of their manufacture.

OPTICAL EXCELLENCE
For decades, the U.S. Air Force (USAF) has been tracking objects in space, identifying and classifying everything from satellites to space junk. This ability comes largely from telescope technology developed by Contraves Brashear. The company is one of the world's premier manufacturers of optical systems and has built some of the largest telescopes in the world at the

time of their manufacture. In the 1880s, for example, the John Brashear Company polished the 30-inch Thaw Refractor for the Allegheny Observatory in Pittsburgh. This lens was one of the largest and finest of its time.

This leading-edge technology continues today with the Contraves Brashear-produced Advanced Electro-Optical System (AEOS) telescope. Much of the USAF's space monitoring will be con-

ducted by the AEOS telescope, located on the top of Haleakala, a 10,000-foot mountain in Maui. Contraves Brashear Systems produces about two or three similar telescopes annually, and is currently polishing an 8.3-meter mirror for a next-generation telescope that will be used for astronomical research in the 21st century.

PRECISION POINTING AND TRACKING
The company is known worldwide for high-quality precision instruments and optics technology. Contraves Brashear produces surveillance and fire control tracking systems for naval vessels, test range precision optical instrumentation, high-energy laser beam directors, and small arms fire control systems.

When the U.S. Navy sought to upgrade its close-in-weapons system that defeats incoming anti-ship missiles, it selected Contraves Brashear Systems to develop the Electro-Optical Stabilization Sys-

tem (EOSS). As a result of the EOSS capability, the improved PHALANX close-in-weapons system is more effective against sea-skimming, low-cross-section targets—an important consideration in the post-cold war era, when the navy's primary threats are terrorist groups using smaller vessels. Beyond the navy, Contraves Brashear products are used by personnel in all branches of the armed forces.

Contraves in Pittsburgh

Contraves Brashear is owned today by Optics Acquisition Co., whose owners are William E. Conway Jr. and his wife, Joanne Barkett Conway, a native of the area. On any workday, Contraves Brashear employees are working on multiple programs at the company's facility at the RIDC North industrial park in O'Hara Township, located about six miles northeast of downtown Pittsburgh. The company's large optics polishing facility is located in Wampum, Pennsylvania, about 50 miles northwest of Pittsburgh. In all, a total of 150 people work at both facilities. The company employs an engineering staff consisting of software, optics, mechanical, electrical, and design disciplines. Also critical to

the company's core technology are the precision optical personnel and the mechanical manufacturing, assembly, quality, and test personnel located at both locations.

Whether designing state-of-the-art technical solutions for deep

The U.S. Air Force's (USAF) ability to track, identify, and classify objects in space comes largely from telescope technology developed by Contraves Brashear. Much of the USAF's space monitoring will be conducted by the AEOS telescope (top right), located on the top of Haleakala, a 10,000-foot mountain in Maui.

space exploration or precision pointing and tracking systems for the armed forces of the world, Contraves Brashear Systems will continue its more than a century of service to national defense and the exploration of the universe well into the next millennium.

EVERY MORNING, IN CITIES AROUND THE WORLD, MILLIONS OF commuters ride rail rapid transit systems for a trip to work that is quick, inexpensive, and safe. Union Switch & Signal Inc. (US&S), a Pittsburgh company founded by George Westinghouse, is responsible for much of the technology that keeps these

transit systems safe and efficient. For more than a century, US&S has been a global leader in the design and manufacture of railway signaling and control systems and equipment.

Beyond the transit systems that touch the lives of people every day, the technology offered by US&S also keeps the nation's freight rail systems, the network of track on which massive amounts

of freight move each day, safe and efficient. These networks are monitored daily from such places as the CSX Kenneth C. Dufford Transportation Center in Jacksonville, Florida, and Union Pacific Railroad's Harriman Control Center in Omaha, Nebraska.

"Our range of products and capabilities extends from the latest electromechanical and microprocessor-based hardware to com-

plex, software-intensive command and control systems," says Gary E. Ryker, who was named president and chief executive officer of Union Switch & Signal in mid-1997. "We continue to set standards for safety, quality, and performance for railway control systems and equipment. Our products are used by every major railroad in the United States, Canada, and Mexico, as well as in many countries around the world."

HELPING TO KEEP RAILS SAFE

The work performed by air traffic controllers, who monitor airspace to make sure planes have a clear path to their destination, is well known. But similar work goes on in the railroad industry, thanks to technology developed by Union Switch & Signal. In the 1960s, US&S installed the railroad industry's first computerized, centralized traffic control system for the Union Railroad in Duquesne, a suburb

Nearly all of the CSX railroad, more than 19,000 miles of territory, is controlled by dispatchers at the Kenneth C. Dufford Transportation Center in Jacksonville, Florida. Union Switch & Signal (US&S), a Pittsburgh company founded by George Westinghouse, is responsible for much of the technology that helps to keep rail systems safe and efficient.

US&S is headquartered in a modern, 175,000-square-foot facility located in the new Pittsburgh Technology Center on the north bank of the Monongahela River.

The Power of

of Pittsburgh. More than two decades later, the company delivered comprehensive, multifunctional control systems that utilize video projection of the monitored territory for the CSX Dufford Control Center in Jacksonville and the Massachusetts Bay Transportation Authority's Operations Control Center in Boston. Traffic control centers such as these are the heart of today's automated rail systems.

Automatic train control, as the concept is known in the industry, relies on technology applied via the rails and in the trains that use them. So while there may be an engineer sitting in the locomotive of a freight train or a driver in the cab of a heavy or light-rail transit train, much of the control is governed by the high-tech components developed by US&S. For instance, the company's audio frequency track circuits detect trains on the rails and can, in conjunction with onboard vehicle control systems from US&S, regulate speed, automatically separate cars from one another, or cause a train to stop at certain stations. Some trains are driverless, thanks to the company's AF-900 digital track circuit system, which transmits bits of data to a train's onboard control system.

In all, more than one-third of the freight railroad territory in the United States is controlled by US&S computerized command and control systems. On the rail rapid transit end, the company's technology regulates rail transit operations in Boston, Pittsburgh, Los Angeles, Miami, Seoul, Taipei, and Dublin, Ireland.

THE WESTINGHOUSE LEGACY
The impact Westinghouse had on today's railroad industry is felt in many ways. He first invented the air brake and founded another Pittsburgh company, Westinghouse Air Brake, in 1869. Twelve years later, Westinghouse established US&S by consolidating the interests of Union Electric Signal Co. of Boston and the Harrisburg Interlocking Switch & Signal Co. Union Electric Signal was founded by Dr. William Robinson, who developed and held the patent for

the electric closed track circuit, while Harrisburg Interlocking Switch & Signal manufactured mechanical apparatuses that interlocked the operation of railroad track switches and signals. As Westinghouse brought these two companies together, the nation's railroad system was rapidly growing. Thus, there was great demand for improved signaling and control products.

Westinghouse died in 1914, and US&S became a subsidiary of Westinghouse Air Brake within three years. The entire operation was acquired by American Standard in 1968, and soon after, US&S became a division of American Standard. In 1989, American Standard sold the division to Ansaldo Trasporti, a Genoa-based company that is one of the world's oldest suppliers of signal and control products for the railroad industry. Today, US&S is one of several companies held by Ansaldo Signal, a global leader in rail transportation control that is traded publicly on the Nasdaq exchange under the symbol ASIGF.

US&S IN PITTSBURGH
After decades of growth and progress, US&S remains headquartered

in Pittsburgh. The company operates out of a 175,000-square-foot facility at the Pittsburgh Technology Center along the Monongahela River, where more than 450 employees work in three major business segments: signaling and train control systems, computerized command and control systems, and research and product development.

The systems and products designed in Pittsburgh range from electromechanical relays and microprocessor-based programmable controllers to integrated computerized traffic management systems that can control 20,000 miles of railroad. US&S also maintains a factory in Batesburg, South Carolina, where approximately 350 employees manufacture the company's product lines.

In the coming years, US&S will continue to aggressively pursue its current direction within the global railroad industry. Says Ryker, "The quest to identify and develop technological control applications for the rail transportation industry has been, and will continue to be, the core of Union Switch & Signal's mission of improving the efficiency and productivity of the world's railways."

The control system supplied by US&S for the Massachuseets Bay Transportation Authority's (MBTA) Operations Control Center in Boston integrates control and supervision of all of the MBTA's transit operations.

FOR MORE THAN A CENTURY, COLUMBIA GAS OF PENNSYLVANIA HAS played a major role in the development of the Pittsburgh region, delivering innovative solutions to energy problems, along with the service its customers have come to expect. From fueling the steel mills' blast furnaces during World War I to meeting the

unprecedented demand for gas heat following World War II, Columbia's goal has been to maximize the potential of natural gas. Today, the company looks to the future with great expectation as the utility industry enters a new phase of deregulation and increased competition.

THROUGH THE YEARS

Columbia Gas of Pennsylvania traces its roots to the Manufacturers Natural Gas Company, which was chartered in 1885. By 1915, industrialization had spurred mergers that extended Manufacturers' service to eastern Ohio and northern West Virginia. The utility's customer base grew by huge strides through both world wars and during the Great Depression.

Manufacturers Natural Gas Company evolved into the Columbia Gas System, Inc., which began to acquire and consolidate companies in hundreds of markets. Under its umbrella came regional providers

in five adjoining states, with delivery via the Gulf Interstate line reaching as far south as Louisiana. Today, Columbia Gas System serves a remarkable 2 million customers, with Columbia Gas of Pennsylvania serving 377,000 customers in 452 communities and 26 counties.

DELIVERING THE FUTURE

As natural gas has become the energy resource of choice for most modern homes and competitive businesses, Columbia is poised to meet the demands of an ever-changing marketplace. Columbia Gas advises its residential customers on how best to equip their homes and stretch their energy dollars, and offers businesses a wealth of efficient energy options. The company also works with state and city officials and chambers of commerce to help attract new businesses and further economic development.

As industry deregulation grows more comprehensive and the util-

ity industry opens to competition, Columbia will benefit from its solid foundation and preeminent service. With deregulation giving increased supplier choice, Columbia Gas has moved aggressively to educate residents of Western Pennsylvania on the new system. In 1996, Columbia initiated Pennsylvania's first energy choice pilot program in Washington County, followed by a program in Allegheny County.

The Washington County program was the first and largest energy pilot of its kind in the state, giving 37,000 customers a choice of suppliers. Depending on which gas supplier was selected, customers enjoyed monthly savings of up to 10 percent off their monthly bill. "Industrial and commercial gas users have been able to choose their gas suppliers for many years," says Gary J. Robinson, president and chief executive officer of Columbia Gas. "We are offering our residential and specific small commercial customers the same opportunity."

Columbia Gas' history of community involvement is as old as the company. President and CEO Gary J. Robinson greets children at the West Penn Recreation League in Lawrenceville as part of the United Way Day of Caring.

When it comes to cooking up a fluffy omelette, most experts agree that gas is the fuel of choice.

To further help customers make a supplier choice, Columbia Gas undertook an intensive community education campaign, mailing information directly to customers with their gas bills, and holding dozens of community meetings in the region to explain the program and answer customer questions.

RESPECTING RESOURCES

Making the most of the Earth's resources is a top priority at Columbia Gas, and finding new ways to power the world is a priority assignment for Columbia Gas engineers. The company developed and built experimental vehicles now in place in State College, where prospective Penn State students tour in a natural-gas-powered bus. In York, the transit authority uses an even more advanced bus to transport commuters every day. At Gettysburg, the nation's historic battlefields are maintained by caretakers using Columbia natural gas vehicles. While they find ways to maximize the resources available today, Columbia engineers are searching for the alternative fuels of tomorrow.

Columbia Gas also maintains a strong commitment to respect the Earth and its natural resources.

MISSION OF SERVICE

Over the past 100 years, the region's economic base has fluctuated

Columbia teams with customers like Cameron Coca-Cola to develop clean, natural-gas-powered vehicles that put the environment in the driver's seat.

between highs and lows in its transition from industrial to technological. Throughout, Columbia Gas has continued to provide dependable service, even in eras of uncertainty.

The utility considers its customers the backbone of Columbia Gas of Pennsylvania. Each one is a benchmark by which the company measures its success. Swift response to customer inquiries, coupled with dependable, efficient service, is a standard of the company. Columbia Gas of Pennsylvania knows its customers are doing more than just conducting business—they're investing in the Columbia

philosophy. While leading the way to the competitive energy marketplace of the future, Columbia Gas will continue to deliver unparalleled service and maintain its commitment to quality.

The customer's needs are as important today as they were at the turn of the century, when Columbia Gas employees used handheld lanterns to make their rounds. Clearly, the region and the world have changed remarkably in a century of turbulence, definition, and advancement. Columbia Gas has changed with the times, and will continue to adapt to meet the challenges of the future.

B

ABCOCK LUMBER COMPANY'S ROOTS IN WESTERN PENNSYLVANIA date back to 1887 when founder E.V. Babcock saw the demand for lumber and purchased his first sawmill and tract of timber in Ashtola, Pennsylvania. ■ Today, Babcock Lumber Company spans six states with manufacturing and wholesale distribution

During its first 110 years of operation, Babcock Lumber Company had only two CEOs: Edward Vose Babcock served from the time he founded the company in 1887 until 1948, and his son, Fred Courtney Babcock (foreground), served from 1948 until his death in 1997 (top).

In 1895, E.V. Babcock & Company was located at 416 Seventh Avenue in downtown Pittsburgh. Selling telephones by horse and buggy was a sign of the times (bottom).

CPS PHOTOGRAPHY

operations serving the retail trade. Producing lumber from the same Western Pennsylvania area, Babcock's Hardwood Division is located in Champion, Pennsylvania, just 40 miles southeast of Pittsburgh and 50 miles west of where operations began in Ashtola. Babcock is situated in one of the best hardwood areas of North America, producing cherry, oak, poplar, and other species that are highly valued by the hardwood industry. Babcock distribution centers provide rough-sawn lumber, manufactured millwork items, softwood lumber, kitchen and bath products, plywood, entrance doors, roof trusses, engineered wood products, and more. Combined facilities have more than 250,000 square feet of manufacturing capacity, nearly 1 million square feet of warehouse distribution space, and more than 2 million board feet of dry kiln capacity. Building materials are distributed within specific regional markets, and hardwood products are shipped throughout the United States, Canada, Europe, and Asia.

During the early part of the 20th century, E.V. Babcock purchased land and timber from Pennsylvania to Florida. Remote lumber camps in Tennessee, West Virginia,

Georgia, North Carolina, and Florida became self-sufficient towns that developed their own housing, commissaries, churches, schools, and medical facilities. Special narrow gauge railroads constructed by the company moved logs to the Babcock sawmills.

At the time, Babcock Lumber was the largest hardwood lumber company in the world, cutting more than 400,000 board feet per day. Most of the land was subsequently donated to federal and state governments under the condition that it be left in its natural state. Some of the more significant land contributions are the Babcock Division of the Gallitzin State Forest in Pennsylvania; the Babcock State Park in West Virginia; the Cherokee National Park in North Carolina; and a portion of the Great Smoky Mountains National Park in Tennessee.

A FAMILY LEGACY

The Babcock name and family roots have been woven deeply into the fabric of the city of Pittsburgh and Western Pennsylvania. The company moved from the original Seventh Avenue offices to become the first tenant of the Frick Building in 1903. In 1911, Governor John K. Tener appointed E.V. to a nine-member council in the City of Pittsburgh. He was mayor from 1918 to 1922 and Allegheny County commissioner from 1925 to 1931. During those years, his public service led to the construction of much of the infrastructure that is still in place today, including the expansion of the city water and sewage system; the establishment of new parks and recreational facilities; construction of many of the city's boulevards, including Allegheny River, Ohio River, Saw Mill Run, McKeesport, and Babcock boulevards. The Westinghouse,

Liberty, Sixth, Seventh, and Ninth Street bridges and the County Municipal Airport were also built during his time of service.

Perhaps E.V.'s proudest achievement was his purchase of more than 4,000 acres of land that now comprises North and South parks. An excerpt from the April 16, 1970, resolution by the Board of Allegheny County Commissioners reads as follows: "WHEREAS, this foresight was demonstrated by the late Edward Vose Babcock . . . through the early purchase of land tracts which in 1927 were transferred at cost to the County and became the beginnings of our splendid park system; and . . . NOW, THEREFORE, BE IT RESOLVED that this Board of County Commissioners on this date express the gratitude of the County and its people for the vision of E.V. Babcock who was willing to make great financial sacrifice for the perpetual enjoyment of his fellow citizens . . . " For this he became known as the Father of Allegheny County Parks.

Elected to the board of trustees of the University of Pittsburgh in 1909, E.V. and his wife, Mary, were instrumental in establishing the School of Nursing, as well as the construction of the Cathedral of Learning. After many years of support, E.V. was made a life member of the Pitt Band in 1940. At the beginning of each football game, the band played "Beautiful Dreamer" because it was his favorite song. At the age of 84, E.V. died quietly at his home on September 2, 1948.

Fred Babcock began working in his father's lumber mills at age 11 and was well schooled to take over the business in 1948. Recognizing the changes in both the use and supply of lumber products after World War II, the company began distributing softwood lumber and building materials, while continu-

ing to manufacture and distribute hardwoods. In 1959, the oldest tenant of the Frick Building moved its corporate headquarters to its current location in Swissvale, from which distribution and manufacturing operations continue to expand today.

Fred chose to maintain a more private life, but his legacy of charitable giving quietly touched many lives. Fred was a strong financial supporter of Grove City College and he served on the board of trustees for many years. He also established the Babcock Library at the Ellis School in Pittsburgh. Financial support was also given to many area hospitals, including the Shadyside Hospital Department of Education and Research for the Cooper Chair in Medicine. Youth programs through the Girl Scouts and Boy Scouts of America were also important to the Babcock family. The acreage and original buildings of Camp Redwing, in Renfrew, Butler County, were given to the Girl Scouts by the family in 1920. The Mary Lodge and Program Center was built in 1928 and named in honor of Mary Babcock, who founded the Girl Scouts of Allegheny County and was president of the organization from 1922 to 1930.

ENVIRONMENTAL CONCERN

Good land stewardship was always important to Fred Babcock, and his philosophy was always to "put more into the land than we take

out." Fred and the company have been honored in many ways for this attention to stewardship over the years. In 1987, Fred received the Florida Tree Farmer of the Year Award; in 1992, the Florida and the National Cattlemen's Association's Stewardship Awards; in 1993, the Florida Environmental Stewardship Award; and in 1992, the company was honored by the North American Wholesale Lumber Association as its Company of the Century for its long-standing history and excellence in commerce. The company has also been a member of the National Hardwood Lumber Association since 1906. Babcock Lumber continues to support the Temperate Forest Foundation for research and education within the industry.

As an example of Fred's desire to maintain a low profile, it was not until 48 years later that Florida Governor Lawton Chiles recognized him in 1996 for his substantial gift of 56,000 acres for use as a wildlife preserve. Today, this preserve is known as the Fred C. Babcock-Cecil M. Webb Wildlife Management Area. Adjacent to this sanctuary is the 90,000-acre Babcock Ranch, a cattle and farming operation. A unique guided wilderness tour on the ranch takes 50,000 people annually through the natural beauty of the Florida cypress swamp.

The Babcock Lumber Company continues to grow, employing approximately 600 and producing

annual revenues of $170 million. Property near Bloomington, Illinois, was purchased in 1997 to increase distribution capabilities, while additional hardwood manufacturing facilities are scheduled to be operational in early 1998 near Birmingham, Alabama. Fred's death in May 1997 ended a period of 110 years in which the company had only two CEOs. The vision of the future that this formidable father and son team provided during their two generations of leadership has left a legacy to the City of Pittsburgh and Babcock Lumber Company. Guided by the principles and high standards of this unique pair, the family and current management, led by President Carl P. Stillitano, who has 40 years of experience with the company, will strive to continue to build and serve the industry in the years ahead.

Clockwise from top left:
In honor of the family's personal and financial commitment to the University of Pittsburgh, Fred Babcock and his mother, Mary, dedicated the Babcock Tower Room at the top of the Cathedral of Learning to E.V. Babcock in 1958.

The Hardwood Division produces kiln-dried lumber, finished boards, stair parts, molding, furniture parts, and other custom millwork.

Computerization allows automation and optimization of the hardwood production facility at Champion, Pennsylvania.

T WOULD BE DIFFICULT FOR THE AVERAGE PERSON TO GET THROUGH A day without aluminum. From airplanes, automobiles, and beverage cans to bicycles, computer disks, and power cable, aluminum is a vital component. It is lightweight, highly resistant to corrosion, an excellent conductor of heat and electricity, naturally good looking,

and highly recyclable. Aluminum is the most valuable material in the waste stream, paying its own way through the recycling process.

Aluminum's popularity today, and the existence of Pittsburgh-based Alcoa, stems from an occurrence in the mid-1880s. Charles Martin Hall, who had experimented with metals since the age of 12, learned how to make aluminum oxide—or alumina. This white, powdery material is the crucial, intermediate step in the production of aluminum, and Hall used it to inexpensively fashion a mass of pure aluminum.

Hall later teamed up with six Pittsburgh industrialists, led by Captain Alfred E. Hunt, to form what is known today as Alcoa.

A WORLDWIDE PRESENCE
Today, Alcoa is the world's leading producer of aluminum and

Opening in mid-1998 on the north shore of the Allegheny River, Alcoa's new Corporate Center is designed with an open office system that emphasizes information sharing and teaming.

alumina, and a major participant in all segments of the industry: mining, refining, smelting, fabricating, and recycling. Alcoa serves customers worldwide in the packaging, automotive, aerospace, construction, and other markets with a great variety of fabricated and finished products. The com-

pany has 187 operating locations in 28 countries. Becoming part of the Dow Jones 30 Industrials in 1959, today Alcoa is the only Pittsburgh company still part of that list.

As the uses for aluminum continue to expand, such as in construction and automobiles, so does Alcoa. In 1997, sales surpassed $13.3 billion,

Americans use 100 billion aluminum beverage cans per year—and recycle most of them. This trend is now growing in markets around the world.

The Power of

The celebrated Audi A8 is designed around an aluminum spaceframe jointly developed by Alcoa and Audi. Alcoa makes subassemblies for the spaceframe in Soest, Germany.

up 71 percent from $7.8 billion in 1987. And while the United States remains aluminum's largest market, the Pacific Rim, China, Asia, Latin America, and Europe all present opportunities for substantial growth. Alcoa has formed joint ventures and strategic alliances, and has made major investments in key regional markets, to take advantage of these opportunities.

Hall would be proud of some of the company's other accomplishments. Around the world, Alcoa is at the forefront of safety, quality, and environmental preservation. Employee safety is the first internal priority, and Alcoa has improved its safety performance in each of the last 10 years. Not satisfied with being the aluminum industry's safety leader, the company continues to strive for its goal of zero injuries. Quality improvement initiatives are another constant throughout the company. In 1996, the Poços de Caldas plant of Alcoa Aluminio was honored with the Brazilian National Quality Award, that nation's highest for industry. And, also in 1996, the World Environment Center awarded Alcoa its Gold Medal for International Corporate Environmental Achievement, in recognition of the corporation's outstanding and well implemented environmental policy.

Aerospace is one of Alcoa's global growth markets. Every structural aluminum alloy flying today was developed by Alcoa.

The result of Alcoa's success is exemplified by the value added for its investors. The total market value of Alcoa shares has grown from $4.1 billion in 1987 to $11.8 billion in 1997.

ALCOA IN PITTSBURGH

In April 1994, Alcoa announced that it would build a new corporate center on the north shore of the Allegheny River, just across from downtown Pittsburgh. This brought good news to the city, as the project's timing coincided with the city's revitalization efforts in that area. The new building—which has more than 340,000 square feet of office

and meeting space—is six stories high and will be occupied in the summer of 1998. In creating the facility, Alcoa employed advanced concepts in workplace design, including an open office system, aimed at achieving superior levels of employee comfort and work flow efficiency.

Chairman Paul H. O'Neill has also helped transform the company's existing Alcoa Building into an economic development hub. Sitting on Mellon Square downtown, the 31-story tower, built in 1953, is in the process of becoming home to government, private, and academic agencies involved in regional economic planning and development.

ITH A SHOPPING MALL WITHIN A MERE STONE'S THROW of most suburban communities, Pittsburgh residents have many choices when it comes to buying gems, gold, pearls, and other fine jewelry. But when it comes to diamonds—one of the largest, and often most

important, jewelry investments most people ever make—many families will only go to Grafner Brothers in downtown Pittsburgh. Located on Liberty Avenue in the heart of the city's cultural district, the shop is barely noticeable from street level. But Grafner Brothers' second-floor showroom boasts counter after counter of the finest in precious stones, gold, sterling silver, clocks, and other exquisite gifts.

The store, founded in 1888 by Emanuel Grafner and his two older brothers, has called Liberty Avenue home for more than 110 years. James Lloyd, Grafner Brothers' current president, started working at the store in 1937, when he was hired as a delivery boy. A business-man and accomplished salesman at heart, Lloyd worked his way up in the company, and in 1954, pur-chased the store with four other partners. In 1980, he became Grafner Brothers' sole owner. Today, his three sons, David, Richard, and

John, join him in serving Pittsburgh's jewelry needs.

QUALITY JEWELRY, FAMILY ATMOSPHERE

Though Grafner Brothers now has 12 employees—many of whom have been with the company for more than 20 years—and attracts customers from the entire tristate area, the store looks much as it did in decades past when the cap-tains of Pittsburgh's steel indus-try shopped there. This sense of tradition adds to the company's reputation as one of the city's finest jewelry stores.

"In this business, reputation is everything," explains Richard Lloyd, who serves as vice president of Grafner Brothers. "People want to deal with someone they trust when shopping for diamonds, some-one who has been in the business for a long time. At Grafner Brothers, customers enjoy a certain comfort level." This is borne out by the fact

that customers often relate that their parents or grandparents shopped at Grafner Brothers. To maintain this customer satisfac-tion—an important factor in the jewelry business—Grafner Brothers prides itself on providing the best-quality merchandise at the lowest possible price.

The company has one of the largest selections of loose diamonds in the city, and many of the store's rings are shown to customers sim-ply as settings, so the customer may choose the size, quality, and shape of the stone. With a regis-tered gemologist on the premises, and decades of experience in pur-chasing only the best diamonds from Belgium, Grafner Brothers also ensures that customers receive good value.

"After so many years of ser-vice, we know how to buy," says Lloyd. Prices are lower than in many of the chain jewelry stores, which pass the costs of higher

Grafner Brothers still works today to fulfill the promise made in its 1932 calendar: "Every article we stock is representative of our entire store. Nothing is described or shown that does not fully measure up to our usual high standards of excellence."

overhead and larger profit margins directly on to the consumer. Additionally, Grafner Brothers does little advertising beyond sending out seasonal and special catalogs to 6,000 area customers each year.

RETAIL AND WHOLESALE

In addition to serving retail customers, Grafner Brothers is also a wholesale diamond merchant. For many years, it has supplied more than 200 area department and retail stores with jewelry, silver, clocks, watches, and other gift items.

Recently, the store has added a corporate gifts division, offering custom jewelry, Waterford crystal, fine pens, watches, picture frames, and clocks to businesses around the city. Many of Grafner Brothers' professional clients are directed there by friends and colleagues.

Grafner Brothers operates an insurance replacement division, as well, and through a network of replacement specialists, is able to replace almost any item with comparable merchandise. Company staff work with more than 40 insurance companies and their clients to provide expert appraisal of jewelry so that replacement in the event of loss or theft can be made as quickly as possible.

Years of experience have given the staff expertise in handling a variety of insurance claims. Whether it is a custom-designed piece or an antique family heirloom, Grafner Brothers can satisfy the insured while efficiently processing claims for insurance companies.

Grafner Brothers still works today to fulfill the promise made in its 1932 catalog: "Every article we stock is representative of our entire store. Nothing is described or shown that does not fully measure up to our usual high standards of excellence." It is this dedication that continues to draw thousands of area residents, in an age of fast food, catalogs, and large shopping malls, to a second-story showroom where their parents and grandparents shopped for fine jewelry.

Grafner Brothers has one of the area's largest selections of certified diamonds.

(From left) Richard, John, James, and David Lloyd serve Pittsburgh's jewelry needs.

CHILDREN'S HOSPITAL OF PITTSBURGH STARTED WHEN THE young son of a local pediatrician raised the money to endow a single cot to be used only for infants and children at a hospital. By 1890, enough funds were raised to open a 15-bed, dedicated children's hospital in the Oakland

section of Pittsburgh that would "meet the needs of the community in present day pediatrics and prevention."

Since that time, Children's Hospital of Pittsburgh has been committed to its three-part mission of providing the highest-quality patient care, biomedical research, and medical education, and its contributions have been recognized locally and around the world. The hospital's milestones include the development and introduction of the polio vaccine by Dr. Jonas Salk in the 1950s; the development of the Mr. Yuk poison prevention campaign in 1971, which has since saved countless lives; and the development of the world's largest and most advanced pediatric transplantation center, which began in collaboration with the University of

Pittsburgh School of Medicine and its newly recruited transplant pioneer, Thomas E. Starzl, M.D., Ph.D., in 1981.

Currently, Children's is the only hospital in Western Pennsylvania dedicated solely to the care of infants, children, and young adults. The hospital is a 235-bed, regional referral center, serving 5.5 million children throughout eastern Ohio, northern West Virginia, and Western Pennsylvania, with a staff of approximately 600 active physicians and more than 2,000 referring physicians. Children's is named consistently to several respected lists of pediatric health care facilities, including ranking among the top 10 children's hospitals in *U.S. News & World Report* magazine's annual listing of Best Hospitals in America.

Children's Hospital is recognized nationally and internationally for its centers of excellence in cardiology, cardiothoracic surgery, critical care medicine, diabetes, hematology/oncology, molecular biology, neurosurgery, organ and tissue transplantation, orthopaedics, otolaryngology, pediatric surgery, and pulmonology. The hospital maintains the only Level 1 Pediatric Regional Resource Trauma Center in Western Pennsylvania and the only dedicated pediatric emergency department in the region, treating more than 150 children each day.

Children's Hospital ranks among the top 10 centers in the nation for National Institutes of Health research funding, which contributes to the $12 million spent annually on pediatric research at

Since 1890, Children's Hospital of Pittsburgh has been committed to its three-part mission of providing the highest-quality patient care, biomedical research, and medical education (left).

In 1955, Jonas Salk (seated), a young investigator, developed the vaccine that would put an end to the ravages of polio that had plagued children for centuries. Dr. Salk conducted tests of his vaccine at Children's Hospital (right).

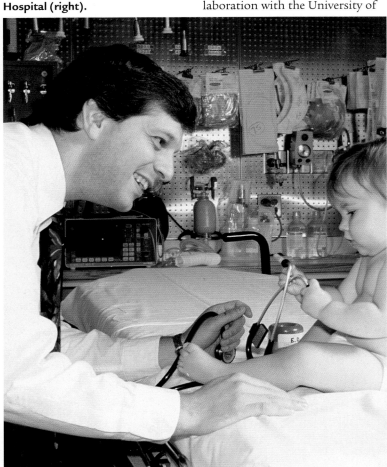

The Power of

the hospital. Among the significant clinical advances supported by this vital research is Children's juvenile diabetes program, which was initiated more than 50 years ago and is now one of the largest in the country, with an international reputation for diabetes care and research. The Otitis Media Research Center at Children's also has an international reputation as the center that has contributed the most to the current understanding of the cause and treatment of otitis media (middle ear disease) in infants and children.

Children's Hospital continues to pursue the highest levels of achievement that will help children live healthier and happier lives. This mission involves medical and surgical procedures as well as innovations in the social and educational arenas. For example, Children's established the first hospital-based child abuse investigation unit, and, with a grant from the Robert Wood Johnson Foundation, the hospital established the first program to provide foster children with consistent health care. Other examples of Children's unique services include summer camping programs that focus on quality of life after transplantation and heart disease; Positive Parenting classes, presented to more than 12,000 parents in 200 community venues, which aim to reduce parents' physical discipline of children; and Safe & Smart, the hospital's trauma prevention curriculum, which has been teaching school-age children how to prevent childhood injuries and abuse through education.

SERVING THE REGION

Children's Hospital offers comprehensive inpatient and outpatient services at its main campus in Oakland and provides outpatient and surgical services in key regional locations north, south, and east of Pittsburgh. Specialty services are also available through satellite physician offices throughout Western Pennsylvania. Through Children's Community Care, a hospital subsidiary, Children's offers a network of primary care pediatricians who have direct access to Children's Hospital's standard of care. Telemedicine links

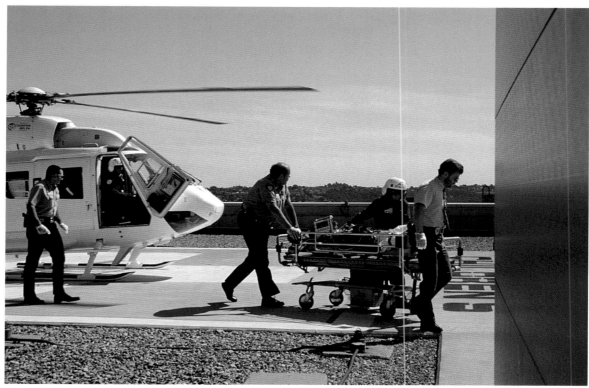

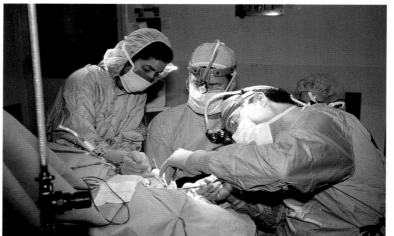

The hospital maintains the only Level 1 Pediatric Regional Resource Trauma Center in Western Pennsylvania and the only dedicated pediatric emergency department in the region, treating more than 150 children each day (top).

Children's Hospital is nationally and internationally recognized for its expertise in the areas of pediatric surgical care, trauma, and intestinal dysfunction (bottom).

Children's with outlying hospitals and provides access to the expertise of select hospital staff on a 24-hour basis. Pediatric consultations can be made without the discomfort and expense of transporting patients.

Children's pediatric residency training program, in conjunction with the University of Pittsburgh School of Medicine, is one of the finest in the country and attracts physicians who go on to practice in many local communities and hospitals.

The hospital also helps children by reaching out to parents and families through educational programs. Children's annually provides classes and workshops—many at no cost—for more than 8,500 adults and children in the region.

PLANNING FOR THE FUTURE

As managed care continues to permeate the region, Children's Hospital remains committed to providing a wide array of world-class health services and will continue its policy of not excluding any child from care. Children's is actively pursuing its goal of being the preferred pediatric provider for all insurers and networks, so that all children and families, regardless of insurance carrier, will have access to its preeminent health care services.

In its second century of service, Children's renewed commitment to cost-effective patient care, education, and research will advance health care for future generations of children in the area and throughout the world.

PITTSBURGH IS A CITY THAT HAS BECOME FAMOUS FOR reinventing itself to meet the challenges of the global economy. This description also fits Pittsburgh Annealing Box Company (PABCO), a manufacturer of annealing furnace components for the steel industry for more than a century.

Known worldwide for its durable, dependable annealing equipment, throughout the years PABCO has strategically sought out other markets where its expertise in metallurgy can be applied.

Over the years, PABCO has diversified to include a variety of products from cookware to bomb disposal units to financial services. It reaches these new markets through a group of subsidiaries—PABCO Specialty Products Division, NABCO, Clad Metals, All-Clad Metalcrafters, and Capital Resource Group—each of which has been successful in its own right.

"We're a group of small companies, but each is a leader and a specialist in its field, primarily because of high-quality products and service," says Sam Michaels, chairman of PABCO and its subsidiaries. "Yet at the same time, each company can use the resources of the others, which is unique to small companies."

Pittsburgh Annealing Box Company, headquartered in the North Side, was founded in 1893. Annealing, one of many steps involved in producing flat-rolled steel, restores the formability of the metal after it has been rolled flat for use in auto bodies, appliances, office furniture and a variety of other products.

PABCO has introduced more innovations in annealing equipment than any other manufacturer and is the supplier of most of the annealing covers in use in the steel industry today. The quality and design of its products are the international benchmark.

THE PABCO UNITS

PABCO's Specialty Products Division carries on one of the company's more traditional activities. From its base in McKees Rocks, five miles west of downtown Pittsburgh, the division produces industrial cylinders and heavy-wall pipe for special applications in the chemical, steel, and nuclear power industries.

This division welds and press-forms pipe from carbon and stainless steels, aluminum, copper, and nickel alloys, in wall thicknesses up to three inches, meeting specifications that are impossible to achieve in conventional rolled pipe.

Other PABCO companies are also market leaders in their respective industries. One of the company's fastest-growing and most exciting divisions is NABCO, manufacturer of a total-containment bomb disposal unit and worldwide leader in supplying customized bomb containment vessels. First used by the U.S. government during the 1984 Summer Olympics in Los Angeles, NABCO containment vessels are crafted from high-strength, high-impact steel, and allow law enforcement officials to safely detonate bombs on-site rather than undertaking the dangerous task of transporting a bomb to a remote location.

The company, which also produces all-terrain hydraulic transporters to carry the containment vessels, has recently expanded its line to include larger vessels, which

Pittsburgh Annealing Box Company (PABCO), a manufacturer of annealing furnace components for the steel industry since 1893, has diversified to include a variety of products from cookware to bomb disposal units to financial services. Shown is a barge shipment of large hydrogen anneal inner covers for a wire mill.

NABCO's containment vessels are used across the country by both federal government agencies and local governments, and are also sold to foreign governments around the world, including Germany, Argentina, Mexico, China, South Korea, and Israel.

The Power of

One of the company's fastest-growing divisions is NABCO, manufacturer of a total-containment bomb disposal unit and worldwide leader in supplying customized bomb containment vessels. This containment vessel, mounted on an all-terrain hydraulic transporter, is being shipped to the Philadelphia police department.

can handle suitcase-sized packages at the site of discovery.

NABCO's containment vessels are used across the country by both federal government agencies and local governments, including the FBI, U.S. Army and Navy, and police departments of most major cities. They are also sold to foreign governments around the world, including Germany, Argentina, Mexico, China, South Korea, and Israel.

Another subsidiary, Clad Metals, Inc. of Canonsburg, 25 miles south of Pittsburgh, was acquired by PABCO in 1988. It is one of the world's leading suppliers of specialty bonded metals. The company produces a variety of combinations of stainless steel, aluminum, and copper.

Clad Metals employs proprietary processes for bonding stainless steel and its highly stable, nonreactive properties, to other metals with entirely different properties. The development of the bonding processes contributed to an era of dramatic progress in the specialty metals industry. These bonded metals are used in applications for the aerospace, pharmaceutical, automotive, and cookware industries.

A division of Clad Metals, All-Clad Metalcrafters, Inc., pro-

duces fine cookware. Utilizing the bonded metals developed by Clad, All-Clad produces a unique and superior product, and is recognized as the maker of the world's finest cookware. Its lines of cookware are sold in upscale department and specialty stores across the United States.

FINANCIAL SERVICES

PABCO entered the financial services industry by acquiring Capital Resources Group (CRG) in 1985. In keeping with the tradition of the PABCO group of companies, CRG has established itself as a premier provider of financial services in Western Pennsylvania. CRG specializes in providing equipment lease/finance for vendors and end

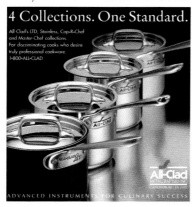

users in the industrial, technology, and tax-exempt markets. Transactions are structured with consideration given to cash flow, equipment obsolescence, tax benefits, and equipment residual values.

CRG also finances transactions for customers who are selling equipment outside the United States. By utilizing the proper financial and insurance tools, the company is able to mitigate the political and credit risks of doing global business. In addition, CRG has been very successful in assisting privately held companies that are seeking acquisitions or contemplating a divestiture. Extensive experience in negotiating, structuring, and financing acquisitions and divestitures allows CRG to consummate any transaction, regardless of its size.

Bonded together by a commitment to quality and customer service, PABCO and its subsidiaries have succeeded by taking advantage of changing trends and technologies to provide products and services for today's market. As it ushers in the new millennium, Pittsburgh Annealing Box Company is poised—like the city it calls home—for continued growth and success.

Another subsidiary of PABCO, Clad Metals, produces fine cookware through its All-Clad Metalcrafters, Inc. division. Its lines of cookware are sold in the finest department and specialty stores across the United States.

WHEN ANTONIO ZAMBELLI LEFT HIS NATIVE NAPLES and headed across the Atlantic Ocean to America a little over a century ago, among his possessions was a little black book. The information that filled that book has delighted and enriched the lives of millions of people for decades. The book contained Zambelli's secret formulas for the manufacture of fireworks; today, that book remains stored in a safe at Zambelli Fireworks Internationale headquarters in New Castle, about 50 miles northwest of Pittsburgh.

Zambelli is one of the country's oldest and largest fireworks companies. More than 1 million shells designed and manufactured by Zambelli are shot off every Independence Day, from more than 1,800 different sites across the country. "We maintain our reputation as the best in the business through a mix of family tradition and constant innovation. Whether it is a huge extravaganza or a small celebration, we perform each show with top craftsmanship," says George R. Zambelli Sr., president and general manager of Zambelli Fireworks Internationale, and one of seven children born to Antonio Zambelli.

A BIG BANG IN NEW CASTLE

Antonio Zambelli chose New Castle as the site for his company because the climate of Western Pennsylvania was similar to that of Naples.

By the early part of the 20th century, other Italian families had followed his example, and there were seven fireworks companies based in New Castle. Between them, they produced 25 percent of the nation's fireworks. Zambelli outlasted the competition to become one of the remaining manufacturers in the area.

Zambelli produces its fireworks at two isolated plants in the New Castle area. Aerial shell components are made at a 600-acre facility in New Castle, while ground shell manufacturing, assembly, and shipping are done at a plant in Nashua Harbor. Zambelli produces about 95 percent of all its fireworks components, and both plants operate year-round.

George Zambelli Sr. began working at his father's fireworks plant at the age of seven. Initially, he spent his days rolling firecracker tubes, but by age 16, he had graduated to setting off pyrotechnic displays as a fireworks shooter. Zambelli left the firm briefly to earn an accounting degree from Pittsburgh's Duquesne University, but eventually returned to the family business. He became president in 1957 and has guided Zambelli Fireworks Internationale ever since.

Zambelli Firworks Internationale remains a family business today. George Zambelli's wife, three of his five children, and a son-in-law are all involved with the family business, which has regional offices in Boca Raton, Florida, and in Shafter, California. The company employs about 50 full-time, year-round workers, and hires hundreds of others for the Fourth of July season, which accounts for two-thirds of the firm's annual business.

FIREWORKS' COLORFUL HISTORY

While several cultures take credit for inventing fireworks, most his-

Founded by Antonio Zambelli in 1893, Zambelli Fireworks Internationale today employs about 50 full-time, year-round workers, and hires hundreds of seasonal workers for the Fourth of July season.

torians point to the Chinese for their primitive fireworks of some 2,000 years ago. By packing saltpeter, sulfur, and charcoal into bamboo shoots, the Chinese created loud booms believed to drive away evil spirits. In the 1300s, Italian explorer Marco Polo traveled to China and was introduced to fireworks by his hosts. He wrote in his journal that fireworks made "such a dreadful noise that it can be heard for 10 miles at night, and anyone who is not used to it could easily go into a swoon and even die." Polo brought fireworks back to Italy, which became the leading European center for the new "art."

When the Continental Congress of the original 13 colonies approved the Declaration of Independence on July 4, 1776, severing its ties with England, patriot John Adams felt fireworks would be an excellent way to celebrate. With that, the American tradition of setting off fireworks on the Fourth of July took root. Since then, the Zambelli family has elevated Independence Day fireworks to a new level. The company was the first to use electronic firings, to synchronize fireworks with music, to create blazing displays of emblems and corporate logos, and to accentuate fireworks displays with laser-light shows. Today, residents annually crowd Point State Park in downtown Pittsburgh to watch Zambelli Fireworks Internationale shows on Independence Day, and during the Three Rivers Regatta and the Pittsburgh Pirates Fireworks Nights.

To date, Zambelli Fireworks Internationale has received a congressional citation for excellence, and holds world recognition for launching fireworks at the highest altitude, off USX Tower in downtown Pittsburgh. One of Zambelli's best-known displays is Thunder Over Louisville, the largest pyrotechnic display in the United States, which kicks off Kentucky Derby week each May. Other high-profile Zambelli displays include the Operation Desert Storm National Victory Celebration in 1991; the inaugurations and festivities for all of the presidents from President

The Pittsburgh Pirates Fireworks Nights (top) are among Zambelli Fireworks Internationale's displays. Other famous displays are Thunder Over Louisville, which opens Kentucky Derby week each May; the inauguration displays for all of the presidents from President John F. Kennedy to President Bill Clinton; and numerous Super Bowl displays.

Residents annually crowd Point State Park in downtown Pittsburgh to watch Zambelli Fireworks Internationale shows on Independence Day and during the Three Rivers Regatta (bottom).

John F. Kennedy to President Bill Clinton; and numerous Super Bowls and college football bowl games.

George Zambelli's personal favorite display was at the Statue of Liberty Anniversary Celebration on July 4, 1986. Zambelli illuminated the entire Manhattan skyline by launching more than 26,400 shells from New York Harbor. "I'm in

the fireworks business to give joy," Zambelli says today. "It doesn't matter whether someone is rich and extravagant, or on a limited budget. My reward is seeing the surprised faces, and hearing all the oohs and aahs of awed spectators. I try to treat people, to free them of daily worries through noise, bright colors, special effects, and style."

N 1895, WHEN LEGENDARY PHILANTHROPIST ANDREW CARNEGIE presented what is known today as the Carnegie Library of Pittsburgh to the region, his vision for it was clear: Carnegie wanted the library to offer to the people of Pittsburgh the same benefits he had reaped from the libraries he visited as a young boy and later as a young

entrepreneur. "The mission of the Carnegie Library of Pittsburgh is to be a force for education, information, recreation, and inspiration in the community it serves," says Robert Croneberger, library director.

THE MODERN-DAY CARNEGIE LIBRARY OF PITTSBURGH

Part of the mission of any library is to stay in touch with the needs of users. Today, the library strives to meet these needs by providing users with information via an efficient on-line information service. In 1996, the $10.5 million Electronic Information Network (EIN), a project spearheaded by the Carnegie Library, connected most public libraries in the Pittsburgh region to the World Wide Web and a wealth of other information resources. With more than 1,000 computer workstations in place at libraries throughout the region, those who might not otherwise have Internet access now have the ability to go on-line. Modern-day users can tap into the EIN to research employment opportunities and read the latest editions of popular periodicals. Others may just want to know what is going on in Pittsburgh's Cultural District, or need information about a recent medical diagnosis.

"In today's information-based society, it's crucial for citizens to have equal access to information that significantly affects the way we live, work, and learn," Croneberger says. "Since the EIN offers that access at no charge, we look at it as being public transportation on the information superhighway."

NUMEROUS FACILITIES

The Carnegie Library, through its various branches, reaches people throughout the Pittsburgh region. The library's main branch is located in the city's Oakland neighborhood, but it also has a significant

presence in downtown Pittsburgh at the Library Center, which opened in 1996. The 60,000-square-foot Library Center—a joint effort with Point Park College—combined the college's 124,000-volume Helen-Jean Moore Library with the Carnegie Library's Downtown Business Information Center's 30,000 volumes. Additionally, the facility includes more than 100 computer terminals that carry access to on-line databases and CD-ROMs.

The Library Center gives the downtown business community broad access to materials needed to make everyday business decisions—

from investing to hiring. The Carnegie Library also operates 18 branch libraries and three bookmobiles, as well as the Library for the Blind and Physically Handicapped.

Says Croneberger, "The library provides communities ready access to a wide range of resources to support formal and informal lifelong learning, to help users meet personal and professional needs for information, and to provide them with opportunities to explore contemporary and classic culture." And in so doing, the library continues to fulfill the mission set by its founder more than a century ago.

"The mission of the Carnegie Library of Pittsburgh is to be a force for education, information, recreation, and inspiration in the community it serves," says Robert Croneberger, library director.

WHEN THE WEALTHY INDUSTRIALIST AND PHILANTHROPIST Andrew Carnegie gave away his money, he rarely asked for anything in return. But when Carnegie funded the construction of the Carnegie Museum of Art in 1895, he added one condition: the museum

should acquire works by—as Carnegie put it—the "old masters of tomorrow."

It was Carnegie's way of making sure the museum would be a forum for the art of its times. Thus, the Carnegie Museum of Art is arguably the first in America to be devoted to modern art, while also being home to the work of Pittsburgh's top artists.

"Overall, what began in 1896 as a collection of art contemporary to that time has become a powerful historical representation, while also featuring the region in which this wonderful museum is located," says Richard Armstrong, director of the museum. "The arts have long flourished in Western Pennsylvania, and the museum's collection of local and regional art is the largest of its kind. Virtually every significant artist in the history of the Pittsburgh region is represented."

The Museum of Art is one of the four Carnegie Museums of Pittsburgh, which operate under the umbrella of Carnegie Institute. The Museum of Art is located in the city's Oakland neighborhood, across the street from the University of Pittsburgh's Cathedral of Learning.

THE INTERNATIONAL AND BEYOND

When Carnegie donated the money for the museum, he called for an annual exhibition of contemporary art, now known as the Carnegie International. The earliest Internationals led to the acquisition of such notable works as Winslow Homer's *The Wreck* in 1896 and Childe Hassam's *Fifth Avenue in Winter* in 1899. Today, the International is a triennial event that is America's most important forum for the presentation of new international art. This survey continues to serve as a primary source for the collection.

The Museum of Art has also developed its collection outside

▶ JOANNE DEVEREAUX

the International. During the 1960s and 1970s, works by old masters such as Perugino and Frans Hals were added to the collection. The museum also acquired important impressionist and post-impressionist works, including Claude Monet's *Water Lilies* and Pierre Bonnard's *Nude in Bathtub*.

A full century removed from the opening of its doors, diversification of the museum's collection continues, while honoring Carnegie's wishes. In 1993, the museum opened the Heinz Architectural Center, one of the most extensive facilities in an American art museum devoted to architectural expression. Focusing mostly on drawings, prints, and models, the greater part of the Heinz Center's collection is from the 19th and 20th centuries. Also on permanent display in the center is the office designed and used by Frank Lloyd Wright in San Francisco from 1951 until his death in 1959.

What began as one philanthropist's dream has become the premier art museum in the region. With a strong sense of history and an eye for the artists of tomorrow, Carnegie Museum of Art continues to blaze trails in the world of art.

Clockwise from top:
In 1993, the Carnegie Museum of Art opened the Heinz Architectural Center, one of the most extensive facilities in an American art museum devoted to architectural expression.

When Andrew Carnegie donated the money for the museum, he called for an annual exhibition of contemporary art, now known as the Carnegie International.

Today, the Carnegie is the premier art museum in the region.

▶ PETER HARHOLDT

N 1895, FOUR MEN CONTRIBUTED $600 APIECE TO START THE Glenshaw Glass Co. in a small, 30- by 60-foot facility located approximately 10 miles northwest of downtown Pittsburgh. Today, the century-old Glenshaw Glass Co. is a key holding of Pittsburgh-based G&G Investments, which is also the majority shareholder of

Canada-based Consumers Packaging Inc. and controls Anchor Glass Container Corporation.

John J. Ghaznavi, chairman and chief executive officer of G&G Investments, rescued Glenshaw Glass from near demise in 1988, when the company was mired in a severe business downturn. Through G&G, Ghaznavi built a management team with combined experience exceeding 100 years in the glass container industry. He also realigned the company's product mix to manage seasonality in sales via efficient manufacturing. Finally, Ghaznavi and the new

management team negotiated critical changes in the company's primary labor contract, extending its terms beyond the industry standard.

Since Ghaznavi took over, the company has tripled its production sales. "Today, Glenshaw Glass is well respected in the industry by customers and competitors alike," Ghaznavi says. "Our employees' dedication and commitment to quality has allowed Glenshaw Glass to grow and prosper in an industry that has seen many competitors fail and many plants close."

John J. Ghaznavi is chairman and chief executive officer of G&G Investments, which is the majority shareholder of Canada-based Consumers Packaging Inc. and controls Anchor Glass Container Corporation, as well as the century-old, Pittsburgh-based Glenshaw Glass Co.

CONSUMERS PACKAGING

In the early 1990s, with Glenshaw Glass stabilized and profitable, G&G Investments began to broaden its position within the glass container industry. In 1993, it acquired a controlling interest in Consumers Packaging, Canada's largest glass company and only producer of glass containers. The combination of Glenshaw Glass and Consumers Packaging created the fifth-largest glass container manufacturer in North America, with combined annual sales exceeding $500 million.

Under the guidance of G&G's management team, Consumers Packaging also underwent a business turnaround that culminated in the fourth quarter of 1994, when the company posted a profit in that traditionally slow period for the first time since 1987. "That was a true indicator of the extent of our turnaround," says Ghaznavi. "While our business is seasonal, with the second and third quarters being the strongest, our goal was to be profitable in every quarter."

Today, as the only ISO 9001-certified glass container company in North America, Consumers Packaging maintains manufacturing facilities and business interests in the United States, Canada, Mexico, Ukraine, Belarus, Italy, and Israel, as well as pursuing other opportunities in Europe and Asia. The company, which is traded publicly on the Toronto Stock Exchange under the symbol CGC, commands more than 85 percent of the Canadian glass-packaging market and distributes its products in key markets around the world.

ANCHOR GLASS CONTAINER CORPORATION

When G&G turned Consumers Packaging's profitability around, it set the company up for another acquisition within the glass container industry. In early 1997, Consumers Packaging acquired out of bankruptcy nearly all the assets of Tampa-based Anchor Glass Container Corporation. Anchor realized net profits from operations within months of the acquisition—the first since September 1995—and today, Anchor is the nation's third-largest manufacturer of glass containers.

Following their lead at Glenshaw Glass and Consumers Packaging, Ghaznavi and his team have cut Anchor's expenses, closed excess facilities, and begun a program of capital expenditures to increase productivity and improve quality. As a result, the combined companies have annual revenues in excess of $1.3 billion and control approximately one-third of the U.S. glass container market.

Anchor, which employs 4,000 people at nine plants nationwide,

supplies containers to producers of beer, juice, tea, wine, liquor, soda, and mineral water. Consumers Packaging employs 2,800 at six facilities throughout Canada and produces approximately 90 percent of that country's glass containers. Custom manufacturer Glenshaw Glass has 500 employees at its single location along the William Flinn Highway in suburban Pittsburgh, and operates around the clock, seven days a week. The corporate headquarters of G&G Investments is a few miles north along the same highway.

AIMING TO BE THE BEST

G&G is exploiting the synergies that exist between its three glass container producers. For instance, it is lowering costs for raw materials by combining the companies' purchases of soda ash, sand, and packaging materials. It is also shifting some Anchor production to

certain Consumers Packaging plants that are located closer to the customer, thereby reducing freight costs. The company is strengthening its customer base by marketing Glenshaw Glass, Consumers Packaging, and Anchor Glass as a trio of sister companies.

As a result of these strategic moves, G&G has attracted and retained as customers many high-profile producers of consumer drinks. Glenshaw Glass produces the colorful bottles that contain the popular Arizona Iced Tea and the bottles for Samuel Adams beer, as well as containers for Anheuser-Busch, which in 1997 recommitted itself to Anchor by tendering a purchase order.

Meanwhile, Ghaznavi is, as ever, positioning G&G Investments as a leader in the glass container industry. "We don't aim to be the biggest," he says. "But we do aim to be the best."

Custom manufacturer Glenshaw Glass has 500 employees at its single location along the William Flinn Highway in suburban Pittsburgh, and operates around the clock, seven days a week. The corporate headquarters of G&G Investments is a few miles north along the same highway.

ALLEGHENY TELEDYNE INCORPORATED MAY BE A NEW NAME in Pittsburgh, but one of its predecessors has called the city home for years. Until its August 15, 1996, combination with Teledyne, Inc., Pittsburghers knew that predecessor as Allegheny Ludlum Corporation, one of the world's leading producers of specialty steels, a major employer in the area, and for years one of the driving forces behind many of Pittsburgh's cultural and civic institutions.

Now, Allegheny Teledyne is the newest Pittsburgh-based business to be ranked among the 500 largest American companies. The combination transformed the new company into what *New Steel* called "a global specialty metals power . . . [whose] broad range of high-value products and financial strength are matched by few, if any, steelmakers."

A GLOBAL SPECIALTY METALS LEADER

Allegheny Teledyne is an operating company composed of more than a dozen operating units. Allegheny Ludlum is the largest of these units, and employs more than 5,000 people in Pittsburgh and the Kiski Valley. It offers specialty steels in about 150,000 combinations of properties, chemistries, finishes, forms, sizes, and other characteristics to customers that range from automobile makers and kitchen appliance manufacturers to high-technology aerospace companies. The company's reputation for quality and technical capability is confirmed by its ISO 9001 certification.

Allegheny Ludlum, along with other Allegheny Teledyne metals companies, is a leader in the global specialty metals market. In addition to the specialty metals from Allegheny Ludlum, these companies produce nickel-based superalloys, titanium, zirconium, hafnium, niobium, and vanadium, metals that are critical to a broad variety of specialized industries. A common characteristic is that they require advanced technology to produce the metallurgical characteristics demanded by their applications.

Superalloys and titanium are used to make critical components of jet engines for the world's commercial aerospace industry. Hafnium also is an alloying agent for metals used in jet engines. Zirconium, one of the most corrosion-resistant materials known, is used by the chemical processing industry in vessels and piping to contain highly corrosive substances. Niobium is in demand because of its superconducting properties, while vanadium is an alloying metal for steel products, and is also used in fusion and other leading-edge technologies.

Allegheny Teledyne's significant concentration in specialty metals is complemented by other technology-based manufacturing companies in the aerospace and electronics, industrial, and consumer segments. These companies serve a wide range of industries with hundreds of products for the industrial, consumer, medical, and government markets.

A PART OF PITTSBURGH FOR 100 YEARS

Allegheny Teledyne, Allegheny Ludlum, and their forerunners have been an integral part of Pittsburgh for more than a century. The family tree took root in Pittsburgh in 1897 with the establishment of the West Leechburg Steel and Tin

Allegheny Ludlum refines specialty steel in a basic oxygen furnace, one of several processes that removes carbon.

The Power of

Plate Co. Within a few years, an open-hearth furnace and five mills were in operation on the same Brackenridge site that today boasts Allegheny Ludlum's largest melt shop.

Through the years, the entity that was to become Allegheny Ludlum evolved into a pioneer in stainless steel. In 1922, it and General Electric produced the first melt of low-carbon, 12 percent chromium stainless steel. Then, as the Great Depression ravaged America's industrial landscape, the company's direct descendant, Allegheny Steel, merged with Ludlum Steel to form Allegheny Ludlum Steel Corporation. Ludlum brought an equally impressive history to the merger; its earliest incarnation, Pompton Furnace, furnished cannonballs to George Washington's Continental army and manufactured the great iron chain that Washington used to blockade the Hudson River.

Today, the company's facilities dot the Western Pennsylvania landscape. In addition to Brackenridge and Natrona Heights, the company's plants contribute to the economies of Vandergrift, Leechburg, Washington, and Latrobe. Allegheny Ludlum also has major facilities in Connecticut, New York, and Indiana.

CORPORATE AND COMMUNITY LEADERSHIP

Allegheny Teledyne is headed by Richard P. Simmons, its chairman, president, and chief executive officer. In 1980, Simmons, then president of Allegheny Ludlum Steel, led the $195 million leveraged buyout (LBO) that made the company independent of its parent, Allegheny Ludlum Industries. At the time, it was the second-largest LBO ever. After taking Allegheny Ludlum public in 1987, Simmons gained a reputation for generating superior returns for investors. Over the last 10 years, the return on average capital employed for Allegheny Ludlum and later Allegheny Teledyne has averaged 18 percent.

Led by Simmons, Allegheny Ludlum's civic, philanthropic, and cultural activism and leadership have helped Pittsburgh achieve a modern-day renaissance. The company has been a longtime major supporter of numerous community activities, including the Pittsburgh Symphony and WQED-TV public television. Simmons personally has created a venture capital fund dedicated to helping small and midsize companies grow and prosper in the Pittsburgh area; headed the Allegheny Conference on Community Development; and chaired the symphony and the United Way.

Allegheny Teledyne's vice chairman of the board, Robert P. Bozzone, also is a longtime civic and business leader in the Pittsburgh area. Former president and CEO of Allegheny Ludlum, Bozzone is involved in leadership activities for the Salvation Army and Boy Scouts of America, among other volunteer organizations. He also is a director of DQE and former chairman of the Pittsburgh branch of the Federal Reserve Bank of Cleveland.

Allegheny Teledyne's aerospace and electronics businesses are headed by another familiar Pittsburgh leader, Dr. Robert Mehrabian, president of Carnegie Mellon University from 1990 to June 1997, who was named an Allegheny Teledyne senior vice president in July 1997. While at Carnegie Mellon, Mehrabian led the development of a vision and plans for Pittsburgh's economic development strategies for the 1990s.

The Teledyne part of Allegheny Teledyne also has a close association with Pittsburgh. Its former chairman, CEO, and president, Dr. George A. Roberts, was educated at Carnegie Mellon University and has donated $8 million to the university for a major addition to its engineering school named Roberts Hall.

A vital factor in the Pittsburgh area economy for more than a century, Allegheny Teledyne looks forward to fulfilling that role in the years to come.

Stainless steel is cold rolled as part of the finishing process.

C

ONSUMERS TAKE IT FOR GRANTED THAT THEY SHOULD SHOP around for the best deal on a new home appliance or heating system. Now, a growing number of people also have the same opportunity to choose when it comes to buying the energy needed to power those appliances or heat their

homes. This new freedom is the result of the emergence of a competitive energy marketplace.

At the forefront of that changing industry is Consolidated Natural Gas Company (CNG). CNG is one of the nation's largest and strongest providers, not only of natural gas, but of electricity and energy-related products and services.

CNG is among the industry leaders in offering its longtime utility customers the freedom to select among different natural gas suppliers. Its Pittsburgh-based natural gas utility, The Peoples Natural Gas Company, was the first in the nation to voluntarily open its entire service territory to full competition. That means some 345,000 customers, including home owners, now can choose an energy supplier other than Peoples to heat their homes and fuel their appliances.

CNG also has set up a non-utility energy marketing subsidiary of its own. This subsidiary, known in Pennsylvania as Peoples Plus, competes vigorously against other independent energy suppliers to

CAMERON DAVIDSON

CNG Producing Company, Consolidated Natural Gas Company's exploration and production subsidiary, is one of the nation's largest independent producers of oil and natural gas.

serve retail customers—customers who formerly were served by other utility companies, as well as by CNG's own utility companies.

These radical changes in the marketplace do not mean, however, that CNG is no longer in the utility business. Its four local gas utilities, including Peoples Gas, still sell natural gas to any home owner who wants it, and transport gas to home owners no matter who the supplier is. In one way or another, CNG's utilities serve nearly

2 million customers in Pennsylvania, Ohio, Virginia, and West Virginia.

The changing marketplace offers many opportunities to serve customers in new ways. For instance, CNG will replace gas lines on customers' properties whenever necessary, in exchange for a small monthly fee. The company also offers a program that provides customers with services by pre-qualified contractors who repair appliances.

DAVID WELLS

Consolidated Natural Gas' (CNG) interstate pipeline carries natural gas to customers throughout the mid-Atlantic and Northeast.

A STRONG, DIVERSE ENERGY COMPANY

While it has a strong presence in Pittsburgh, CNG has subsidiaries in many parts of the nation and is involved in virtually every phase of the energy industry. CNG Producing Company, its exploration and production subsidiary, is one of the largest independent producers of oil and natural gas in the United States.

CNG Transmission Corporation carries natural gas to wholesale customers throughout the Northeast and mid-Atlantic via a 7,400-mile interstate pipeline system. CNG Transmission also operates North America's largest underground storage system for natural gas. CNG Energy Services Corporation, the firm's energy marketing subsidiary, is one of the nation's largest sellers of electricity at the wholesale level. The company also has stepped up its activities overseas; CNG International Corporation, a recently established international subsidiary, is building up business in Australia and South America.

Financial strength has long been a hallmark for CNG. The company has assets of some $6 billion, and consistently receives high ratings from New York rating agencies, such as Moody's and Standard & Poor's. CNG employs about 6,400 people.

While the company maintains strict cost controls, it stresses growth, not cost cutting, as the best means to building shareholder value. CNG is targeting its exploration and production, energy marketing, and international operations for growth, while the local gas utilities and interstate pipeline continue to provide a strong, steady earnings base.

CNG's ROOTS: A SHORT HISTORY

Consolidated Natural Gas began operating as an independent company in 1943, but its history dates back more than a century to the Standard Oil Company of John D. Rockefeller and the origins of the natural gas industry.

Standard Oil grew its integrated natural gas business from exploration to distribution by creating companies and acquiring others throughout the Appalachian region. Among those companies were several utilities that still are part of CNG today: The Peoples Natural Gas Company, The East Ohio Gas Company, and Hope Gas, Inc.

In assembling the system, Standard Oil also helped develop commercial markets for natural gas and developed the first pipelines—no easy task 100 years ago, especially in a terrain of rivers, forests, and mountains.

When the federal government ordered Rockefeller to break up his Standard Oil monopoly, the gas operations became the dominion of Standard Oil (New Jersey), Rockefeller's flagship company. There they remained until new laws regarding public utilities required Standard to spin off its gas companies unless it wanted to come under the control of government regulators. Thus, Consolidated Natural Gas was created as a completely independent entity in 1943.

EXPLORING FOR NATURAL GAS AND OIL

CNG runs one of the most successful and lowest-cost exploration and production companies in the nation: CNG Producing Company, based in New Orleans. CNG Producing's particular area of focus is in and around the Gulf of Mexico. It has recently had great success in the gulf's new frontier—the deep water beyond the continental shelf, where water depths can be thousands, rather than hundreds, of feet.

The company has part ownership of two deepwater projects, Popeye and Neptune, both of which involved some technological firsts. Popeye was the first project in the Gulf of Mexico to make extensive use of robots to assemble well equipment on the gulf floor. And Neptune was the first project anywhere to use a spar—a massive, floating cylinder—to support a production platform.

CAMILLE VICKERS

CNG Transmission Corporation operates the largest underground storage system for natural gas in North America.

PEOPLES GAS: AN INDUSTRY LEADER

More than 100 years ago, Peoples Gas became the first company chartered to provide natural gas service in Pennsylvania. Today, it delivers natural gas to more than 345,000 customers in 16 Southwestern Pennsylvania counties. Although the new competitive environment provides many new challenges and opportunities for Peoples Gas, its primary mission is the same: to provide a safe, reliable supply of natural gas to customers. The company has a long history of investing not only in its own infrastructure, but also in new and better natural gas products and in the communities it serves.

Home owners in the company's service area have long chosen natural gas for home heating, water heating, cooking, and clothes drying. Recently, new products, such as natural gas fireplaces, have become popular. Home builders and remodelers are incorporating many unique design ideas for zero-clearance and even unvented types of natural gas fireplaces that can be located almost anywhere.

Another recent product advancement is the York Triathlon natural gas heating and cooling system. The Triathlon is a natural gas heat pump system that produces both heat and air-conditioning from one energy-efficient, natural-gas-fueled engine. It is an example of the many research and development investments Peoples Gas has made over the years to improve natural gas product efficiency, lower operating costs, and increase customer benefits.

Recognizing that business growth is essential to a healthy economy, Peoples Gas works hard to encourage new business development in its service area. Through its direct giving program, Peoples Gas makes grants to local community developers. These grants are investments that help bring about promising economic development projects that, in turn, build businesses, create jobs, and improve the long-term economic health of the region.

In addition, Peoples Gas employs a staff of economic development specialists who can help companies expand or relocate. These staff experts offer information and services including site recommendations, financing assistance, energy/utility services, transportation facilities, labor analysis, and tax structures/incentives. Using a turnkey approach, Peoples Gas will help a company find a location that best suits its business needs.

Peoples Gas also has invested in many community outreach programs to enhance the lifestyle of its diverse customer base. The company and its employees have long supported the United Way and its agencies through both direct contributions and the Peoples Gas Volunteer Activities Committee. Peoples Gas' corporate direct giving program has focused on education and youth intervention. Peoples Gas also backs the Dollar Energy Fund, a fuel fund that assists people who cannot afford to pay their utility bills.

CNG has more than a thousand natural-gas-powered vehicles, or NGVs, of its own and provides the fuel for customer NGVs, including school buses, municipal buses, ferryboats, and forklifts (right).

CNG's five natural gas utilities deliver natural gas to homes, businesses, and factories, serving a total of nearly 2 million customers (left).

The Power of

T STARTED IN 1896 AS A MODEST COLLECTION OF ITEMS ON LOAN from scientific societies in the Pittsburgh region. From these simple beginnings, Carnegie Museum of Natural History has grown to holdings that today exceed 22 million artifacts and specimens, with some 16,000 on display, and the remainder used for research.

To many visitors, it's the Home of the Dinosaurs, since the museum is one of the largest repositories of dinosaur fossils in the world. The collection includes 20 complete skeletons, 10 of which are displayed in famous Dinosaur Hall. To others, the Museum of Natural History is a vehicle through which people young and old trace the evolution of our planet. The museum's programs touch more than 300,000 people annually.

"I like to view a museum as a door through which we can step into other worlds," says Dr. Jay Apt, a former astronaut who became director of the museum in 1997. "The fantastic creatures that lived on Earth in the past, separated from our world only by time, stretch the imagination. This museum has the resources to let people experience the breathtaking history of how Earth formed, how it and its creatures have changed, how we came to be, and how we have lived in our short time here."

REFLECTING CARNEGIE'S INTERESTS

The Museum of Natural History is one of the four Carnegie Museums of Pittsburgh, and was founded by legendary industrialist and philanthropist Andrew Carnegie. The Museum of Natural History sits on Forbes Avenue in the city's Oakland neighborhood, the same quarters it has occupied since

Carnegie financed a $5 million expansion in 1907.

Carnegie himself is responsible for the museum's dinosaur collection. His curiosity about prehistoric life led him to finance paleontological digs in Wyoming, Utah, and several other western states for more than 20 years. As a result, more than 700,000 pounds of fossils were shipped to Pittsburgh.

Later in the 20th century, the museum rounded out its exhibits by opening the Hillman Hall of Minerals and Gems, where visitors can view or touch more than 1,100 mineral and gem specimens. In the Benedum Hall of Geology, interactive technology and videos explain complicated geological theories regarding fossilization and other topics. The museum also houses displays on African and North American wildlife, Arctic life, and ancient Egypt. The newest exhibit,

on American Indians, opened in June 1997.

About 25 scientists maintain collections and actively conduct research in the areas of anthropology, amphibians and reptiles, birds, botany, entomology, invertebrate paleontology, mammals, minerals, and vertebrate paleontology. These activities take them to about 23 countries on five continents to collect specimens and study Earth, its life, and its cultures. As a result of this work, the Museum of Natural History is an important resource for researchers and educators around the globe.

"It is our job to give people the thrill of stepping into a world different from the present one," says Apt, "and to give our visitors a very clear concept of the evolution of our world and its life—where we have been, how life and Earth work, and where we might go."

Top left and right: Children and adults enjoy hands-on exploration of the natural sciences and anthropology in the Discovery Room at Carnegie Museum of Natural History.

A Carnegie botanist collects the flowers of a giant tropical aroid in the forest of Dominica.

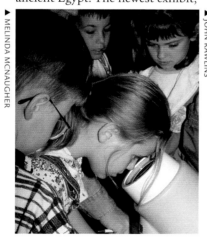

MELINDA MCNAUGHER

JOHN RAWLINS

Andrew Carnegie himself is responsible for the museum's dinosaur collection. His curiosity about prehistoric life led him to finance paleontological digs in several western states for more than 20 years. As a result, more than 700,000 pounds of fossils were shipped to Pittsburgh.

M

ORE THAN A CENTURY AGO, PHILANTHROPIST CHRISTOPHER Lyman Magee donated $125,000 for the construction of a zoological garden in Pittsburgh. The opening of the Zoo in 1898 gave Pittsburgh residents the opportunity to view exotic animals and flora they had never

seen before; today, the Zoo's more than 77 acres of beautifully landscaped walkways immerse the visitor into the habitats of the animals, encouraging an increased understanding of the natural world.

Home to more than 4,000 animals, from Siberian tigers to western lowland gorillas to sharks, the modern-day Pittsburgh Zoo features naturalistic habitats. Zebras, giraffes, elephants, and other animals graze in the African Savanna. One of the largest gorilla troops in the country, along with other primates, occupies the Tropical Forest. The Zoo is also only one of five zoos in the country to feature a major aquarium. And Kids Kingdom, the children's zoo, is ranked as one of the best children's zoos in the country.

But the Pittsburgh Zoo is much more than wildlife on display. The role of the Zoo has evolved, with the emphasis shifting from solely entertainment to education and conservation. To that end, the Zoo is active in worldwide research and wildlife conservation efforts. A strong education program, which includes community outreach, serves more than 100,000 participants annually.

The Pittsburgh Zoo participates in more than 30 Species Survival Plans©, a program founded by the American Zoo and Aquarium Association to ensure the survival of selected endangered species. Through breeding programs, research, the reintroduction of captive-bred wildlife into restored habitats, and increasing public awareness, the Zoo may help ensure the survival of such animals as the snow leopard, African elephant, and black rhinoceros.

Allen W. Nyhuis, the seven-acre facility combines animal exhibits and interactive areas that encourage children of all ages to learn more about animal behavior. Hands-on animal encounters include walk-through white-tailed deer and gray kangaroo yards. A fabulous sea lion pool with an underwater viewing area is a popular feature.

The 7,000-square-foot, air-conditioned Discovery Pavilion in Kids Kingdom features year-round exhibits. Special interactive displays include the Walk-through Aquarium, Bat Flyway, meerkat community, and a 15-foot baobab tree slide. Also featured are live presentations in the Bayer Science Education Amphitheater and a variety of traveling exhibits.

The public support attracted by these exhibits, as well as the Zoo's conservation efforts and educational programs, helps to secure the future for many threatened and endangered species at the Zoo. Celebrating its centennial in 1998, the Pittsburgh Zoo continues to provide an enjoyable family experience year-round, while making a significant contribution to conserving wildlife for the next century.

SPECIAL ATTRACTIONS

Hundreds of thousands of visitors flock to the Pittsburgh Zoo each year, making it the most visited cultural attraction in the region. Kids Kingdom, the new children's zoo, is one of the most popular attractions.

Kids Kingdom opened to rave reviews in May 1995. Rated as one of the top three children's zoos in the country by noted zoo critic

The Pittsburgh Zoo's Kids Kingdom, ranked as one of the top three children's zoos in the country, is one of the facility's most popular attractions, with a 7,000-square-foot Discovery Pavilion that features year-round exhibits.

In the Zoo's Tropical Forest, a western lowland gorilla cares for her infant, which was born September 13, 1997.

PAUL A. SELVAGGIO

PAUL A. SELVAGGIO

SARGENT ELECTRIC COMPANY IS A FAMILY-OWNED, INDUSTRIAL and commercial electrical contracting and service company that helps utilities efficiently generate power, and ensures that customers are able to put that power to use. Founded in 1907, the company is headquartered on Liberty Avenue in Pittsburgh and maintains offices nationwide.

Sargent has been a member of the Federated Electrical Contractors since 1983 and a member of the Engineers' Society of Western Pennsylvania since 1980. In addition, the company employs International Brotherhood of Electrical Workers (IBEW) employees on all projects and has been a signatory to labor agreements with the IBEW for more than 80 years.

COMMERCIAL, INDUSTRIAL, UTILITY, AND RESIDENTIAL GROUPS

Sargent tallies annual revenues of more than $80 million, a significant portion of which comes from its Commercial Group, which handles the wiring for new construction and renovation projects at schools, hospitals, office buildings, flex-space buildings, and government facilities ranging in size from 2,000 square feet to more than 1 million square feet. These projects have included power distribution systems with monitoring and backup subsystems and lighting and lighting control systems, as well as sophisticated data, communication, security, fire detection, emergency call, access control, and many other electricity-based systems. Oftentimes, Sargent will stay on as the facility's electrical maintenance contractor after a project is completed. A separate department in the commercial division dedicated exclusively to electrical testing offers both normal maintenance and emergency services.

Sargent's Industrial Group installs high-voltage cable for clients from heavy industries, such as steel, aluminum, coal, petrochemical, and automotive. And for those organizations that generate their own power, Sargent can maintain or retrofit a nuclear- or fossil-power-generating facility.

Sargent's Utility Group has built electricity-generating stations ranging from relatively small cogeneration facilities to two-unit nuclear power plants, and has constructed high-voltage switchyards, substations, and transmission and distribution lines.

Sargent's Residential Services Division offers a 24-hour emergency hot line and same-day service. Service calls are scheduled by date and time, and customers are guaranteed total satisfaction or their money will be refunded.

TEGG SERVICE

Sargent is the cofounder and primary developer of TEGG Corp., an organization that offers a unique business franchise opportunity to electrical contractors. Developed by a leading international industry team that sought to apply a new and better approach to providing preventive maintenance for electrical distribution systems, TEGG Service is the best and most cost-effective protection for minimizing both unexpected power outages and potential electrical fire hazards. TEGG Service enhances its customers' productivity and profitability by reducing business and facility downtime as well as the cost of owning and operating facilities.

CARING ABOUT PEOPLE

No matter what the task, worker safety is a top priority on every Sargent project. The company operates under a We Prize Safety® philosophy, awarding prizes to craftsmen and foremen who maintain safety on the project.

Sargent also works within the local community, annually assembling the giant Christmas tree that spans the corner of Penn Avenue Place and hanging lights along the landmark Smithfield Street Bridge.

Concern for its employees and its community truly distinguishes Sargent Electric Company, an industry leader both in Pittsburgh and nationwide.

In response to the nationwide race to construct cellular and PCS telephone networks, Sargent Electric has responded with a team focused on providing construction and maintenance services for wireless carriers. Up-to-date information on this and other subjects can be found at the company's Web site, located at www.sargent.com.

▲ WILLIAM J. BOYD

N 1900, THE DREAM OF ST. BARNABAS' FOUNDER BROTHER GOUVERNEUR Provoost Hance was to create a home for men and boys to supply their need for nourishment and Christian guidance, and to provide them with a warm and safe dwelling. With just a few dollars in hand, a conviction that "God is able," and the persistence to beg for

donations, Hance laid the foundation for what is now St. Barnabas Health System, Pennsylvania's largest health care concern of its kind.

St. Barnabas' original site was located on Third Avenue in downtown Pittsburgh. Its three-room operation included only four beds, a table, and some chairs. This humble offering of medical care and room and board—called St. Barnabas Free Home for Men and Boys—moved from downtown Pittsburgh to Carrick and then to McKeesport, before moving to its present location in Gibsonia, just 18 miles north of Pittsburgh. The campus occupies 303 acres of lush Richland Township countryside.

Representative of the growing and shifting needs of today's health care market, St. Barnabas now encompasses two skilled nursing care facilities, a retirement community, a charitable foundation, an outpatient medical center, and an assisted living center. Two of its facilities are located three miles from Gibsonia in Valencia.

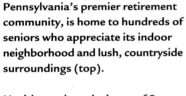

The Village at St. Barnabas, Western Pennsylvania's premier retirement community, is home to hundreds of seniors who appreciate its indoor neighborhood and lush, countryside surroundings (top).

Health care is at the heart of St. Barnabas' offerings. Outpatients of all ages receive general medical care, specialty treatment, and lab services at St. Barnabas Medical Center (bottom).

After Hance died, his mission for St. Barnabas was carried forward by Paul O.W. Hopkinson, who in turn passed the torch to William V. Day in the late 1960s. Since then, Day—who was originally hired as a consultant to see what future, if any, existed for the 63-bed nursing home—has undertaken nearly two dozen expansion projects and raised nearly $200 million in charitable contributions, as some 500,000 outpa-

tients and inpatients have been cared for regardless of their ability to pay.

More than 100,000 people each year can attest to being touched by St. Barnabas in some way or another. The Village at St. Barnabas is home to more than 300 retirees. St. Barnabas Nursing Home, the founding organization, and its sister, Valencia Woods Nursing Center, provide skilled nursing and rehabilitation to more than 500 patients annually.

Through St. Barnabas Charitable Foundation's Free Care Fund, these patients receive more than $4 million in free care and rehabilitation each year. The Charitable Foundation and its famous Presents for Patients program provide more than 16,000 holiday gifts and visits each Christmas season for men, women, and teenagers in Pennsylvania, New York, Ohio, and West Virginia care centers.

St. Barnabas Medical Center's general medicine, specialty treatment, dentistry, and home health agency treat 21,000 outpatients annually. The Arbors Assisted Living at Valencia, the most recent addition under the St. Barnabas umbrella, daily provides 24-hour supervision to 33 persons.

And, anyone who is anyone takes in at least one special

event at St. Barnabas, whether it's Founder's Day honoring outstanding people such as Charlton Heston, Barbara Bush, or Dr. Norman Vincent Peale, or a community-wide Independence Day celebration that draws tens of thousands to its campus.

SERVING SENIOR CITIZENS

St. Barnabas may be most widely known by Pittsburghers and Western Pennsylvanians by its retirement community. The Village at St. Barnabas is a virtual neighborhood within itself. The Village features 252 one-, two-, and three-bedroom homes connected by a one-third-mile shopping mall. Persons 65 and older live at the Village without customary worries. Weather, enjoyed by Villagers on their balconies, patios, or at the many parks and garden spots, isn't a concern. The interconnecting structure allows seniors to visit the Village Restaurant, entertain guests, attend a concert, collect their mail, have their hair styled, and attend chapel services—all without stepping outdoors.

The Village, completed in 1980, was the first retirement community of its kind in Western Pennsylvania. A financially sound organization, the Village doesn't require large up-front or endowment fees. Residents enter into an annual plan, with a onetime application fee that includes a spectrum of amenities: meals served by a wait staff, housekeeping, security, use of all the Village art and activity studios, events, and even "benefit days" at the two St. Barnabas nursing homes.

Often noted as a "second retirement," a Village lifestyle caters to individual needs of people who are active and independent. Although many of the benefits of retirement living at the Village are evident—the mingling of sociable seniors, a recreation calendar sporting more than 120 events each month, spacious and fully equipped homes, a bubbling waterfall in the Village park—the main attraction isn't as visible. Residents move to the Village because the right form of care and attention is on campus and in place when they need it.

St. Barnabas Medical Center, located just a few hundred yards from the Village, makes visiting physicians, dentists, specialists, and technicians very convenient. And it is this same medical staff that is able to follow residents to the hospital when necessary. The Medical Center's home health agency promotes independence by making nurse and companion visits available from two to 24 hours per day.

While St. Barnabas Health System moves into the 21st century as one of the country's leading health care providers, some of what Hance created at the turn of the 20th century still exists. The mission, to provide care for those in need, not only remains, but is strengthened daily with each Village resident, with each nursing home patient, and with each dollar raised.

St. Barnabas is, in the words of former President Gerald R. Ford, who visited the facility in 1983, truly "an outstanding, outstanding place."

Clockwise from top: Two patients in the early days of St. Barnabas Nursing Home in Gibsonia spend time with Brother Gouverneur Provoost Hance, the organization's founder.

Village residents, like Alverda Milligan, come from across the country and from several foreign countries to call the Village at St. Barnabas their home. Social activities are among the top benefits at the Village, and include the annual hoedown.

William V. Day, one of only three CEOs since St. Barnabas Health System's founding in 1900, has brought about tremendous progress for the charitable concern—more than two dozen expansion projects, raising nearly $200 million in donations and treating some 500,000 outpatients and inpatients.

PITTSBURGH-BASED USX CORPORATION CAN TRACE ITS ROOTS to two of the nation's premier companies: Marathon Oil, founded in 1887 as The Ohio Oil Company, and U.S. Steel, which, when founded in 1901 with an authorized capitalization of $1.4 billion, was the largest business enterprise

ever launched up to that time.

From its origin as strictly a steel producer, USX has responded over the years to changing economic conditions and new market opportunities through diversification and periodic restructuring. Today, it is primarily an energy company, involved in worldwide crude oil and natural gas exploration, production, and transportation; and domestic petroleum refining, marketing, and transportation. However, USX remains the largest integrated steel producer in the United States and has other operations in mineral resource management, engineering, and consulting services, as well as other businesses.

Marathon used one of the heaviest crane lifts ever in the Gulf of Mexico to install a recycled platform topsides at South Pass 89-D.

THE BEGINNING

USX Corporation began as U.S. Steel, a company that had its origins in the dealings of some of America's most legendary businessmen, including Andrew Carnegie, J.P. Morgan, and Charles Schwab. However, the company's principal architect was Elbert H. Gary, who also became U.S. Steel's first chairman. At the turn of the century, a group headed by Gary and Morgan bought out Carnegie's steel company and combined it with their holdings in the Federal Steel

Company. These two companies became the nucleus of U.S. Steel, which also included American Steel & Wire Co., National Tube Company, American Tin Plate Co., American Steel Hoop Co., and American Sheet Steel Co. In its first full year of operation, U.S. Steel made 67 percent of all the steel produced in the United States.

In the decades that followed, the corporation consolidated its various steelmaking and raw material subsidiaries and divisions through a series of reorganizations. Many of the corporation's divisions were related to or grew out of the company's original steel operations.

Significant diversification and restructuring actions occurred in the 1980s. In 1982, the corporation acquired Marathon Oil, one of the nation's 10 largest oil companies. In 1986, U.S. Steel expanded its energy business with the acquisition of Texas Oil & Gas Corp. (TXO), a firm primarily engaged in the domestic production, gathering, processing, and transportation of natural gas. During 1990, a substantial portion of the exploration and production assets of TXO was sold, and those remaining were integrated into Marathon. Today, Marathon remains one of the largest integrated oil companies in the United States.

Also in 1986, in recognition of the fact that it had become a vastly different corporation, U.S. Steel Corporation became USX Corporation, with principal operating units involved in energy, steel, and diversified businesses.

The decade of the 1980s also brought significant changes to the corporation's steel operations. Since 1980, in response to economic changes in the steel industry, the corporation has reduced its raw steel production capability by nearly two-thirds through a number of restructurings. In addition, the corporation entered into several

Responsible for spearheading Marathon's initial deepwater production project are members of the Ewing Bank 873 team at the Gulf Coast Production Region in Lafayette, Louisiana. Team members are (from left, seated) Geoff Crawford, Chris Hill, John Ebert, Tom Laylock, (from left, standing) Dave Petro, Mitch Burk, Mary Richard, Pat Sincox, Mike Hafner, Mark Heatherly, and Ray Brickey.

The Power of

steel joint ventures with both U.S. and foreign partners. At the same time, many of the units among the corporation's diversified businesses were sold or combined into joint venture enterprises. These included chemicals and agrochemicals businesses, an oil field supply business, and domestic transportation subsidiaries, as well as raw materials properties worldwide.

In 1991, shareholders approved both a proposal to change the capitalization of the corporation and the issuance of a new class of common stock called USX-U.S. Steel Group Common Stock, which was intended to reflect the performance of the corporation's steel and diversified businesses. USX Corporation common stock was changed into USX-Marathon Group Common Stock, which was intended to reflect the performance of the corporation's energy business.

Today, USX Corporation is essentially two separate businesses—the U.S. Steel Group and the Marathon Group—each with its own management, yet operating under the USX board of directors.

Delineation wells drilled by Marathon at the Green Canyon 244 unit in the deepwater Gulf of Mexico confirmed gross reserves of more than 200 million barrels of oil equivalent.

U.S. STEEL

U.S. Steel, with executive offices in Pittsburgh, manufactures and sells a wide variety of steel mill products, coke, and taconite pellets. Primary steel operations include the Gary Works in Indiana; the Fairfield Works near Birmingham, Alabama; and the Mon Valley Works, which includes the Edgar Thomson steelmaking and Irvin finishing operations on the Monongahela River near Pittsburgh. In addition, U.S. Steel operates a sheet and tin finishing plant at the Fairless Works near Philadelphia. U.S. Steel's coke production takes place at the Clairton Works—also on the Monongahela River outside Pittsburgh—and at the Gary Works. At Minntac, on northern Minnesota's Mesabi Range, iron ore mining and taconite pellet operations support the steelmaking effort.

Heavy investment in advanced technology has kept the steel company in the forefront among Ameri-

Marathon's ongoing, selective expansion of the Speedway station network helped to spur record retail sales.

can integrated steelmakers. U.S. Steel now produces 100 percent of its steel via continuous casters, and has reduced man-hours per ton of output to historically low levels that place the company in a leading position worldwide.

U.S. Steel's steep capital investment reflects a strong commitment to environmental enhancement. State-of-the-art technology con-

trols more than 95 percent of emissions from company production facilities. While U.S. Steel continues to improve its control technology, it increasingly is focusing on outright prevention of pollution at the source. At Clairton—the most environmentally advanced coke plant in the country—an internally developed program trains all employees on the efficient and

Clockwise from left:
Kristin Camilli, Marathon human resources representative, provides some on-site employee development consultation to Ronnie Winters (left) and Kenny Spriggs.

USX employees of the pickle lines at Irvin Plant of the Mon Valley Works include (from left) Marcie Omasta, laborer; Rich "Monty" Montgomery, utility man; Paul Tomcanin, millwright; Joe Bradley, APEX representative; and Pete Janicki, ironworker.

Marathon Pipe Line (MPL) Company's new, state-of-the-art SCADA control center helps operator Sara McDaniel exercise tight monitoring and control of her assigned part of MPL's 5,300-mile system.

effective operation of their facilities and their responsibility to the environment. The program has proved so successful that U.S. Steel has expanded it to other plants.

In addition to primary steel mill operations, U.S. Steel participates in several steel joint ventures, including USS-POSCO Industries in Pittsburg, California, and USS/Kobe Steel Co. in Lorain, Ohio. U.S. Steel is also involved in a number of other businesses, among them coal mining, mineral resources management, real estate development, engineering and consulting services, technology licensing, and leasing and financial services.

MARATHON OIL

Marathon Oil Company, with headquarters in Houston, is involved in global crude oil and natural gas exploration, production, and transportation; and in the domestic refining, marketing, and transportation of crude oil and petroleum products. Marathon also has formed a subsidiary to pursue power generation opportunities.

Internationally, Marathon's exploration and production activities extend to five continents, with production flowing from such varied locations as the United Kingdom, Ireland, and Egypt. The centerpiece of Marathon's international operations is the Brae Field complex in the North Sea off the northeast coast of Scotland. Here, Marathon has been producing liquid hydrocarbons on a major scale since the mid-1980s, and continues to develop substantial reserves.

On the domestic front, Marathon holds a 49.4 percent interest in and operates the Yates Field in West Texas. The field, which Marathon discovered in 1926, is one of the most prolific oil fields in U.S. history, and is still among the nation's leading fields in production and reserves.

Marathon is also active in the Gulf of Mexico. It holds working interests in 13 fields, producing from 34 platforms, 21 of which Marathon operates. Another company product is liquefied natural gas. Through a joint venture, Marathon operates two cryogenic tankers that take gas liquefied at a plant on Alaska's Kenai Peninsula and transport it, under U.S. export license, to two large utilities in Japan. Marathon continues to pursue attractive opportunities to find and produce oil and gas worldwide. Many of today's best prospects are in the international sphere, and a major area of focus for future activity is Russia, where Marathon is participating in a plan to develop offshore oil and gas fields near Sakhalin Island.

In 1998, Marathon Oil and Ashland, Inc. formed a new company called Marathon Ashland Petroleum LLC, a combination of the major elements of the two

The Power of

firms' downstream operations. The new company has seven refineries: Garyville, Lousiana; Catlettsburg, Kentucky; Robinson, Illinois; St. Paul Park, Minnesota; Texas City, Texas; Detroit, Michigan; and Canton, Ohio, with an in-use refining capacity of 935,000 barrels of oil per day. The company operates 84 light products and asphalt terminals in the midwestern and southeastern United States and has significant pipeline holdings. It conducts wholesale operations that market gasoline, diesel fuel and fuel oil, asphalt, heavy fuel oil, and commercial jet fuel. The company markets gasoline through approximately 5,400 retail outlets in 20 states: Alabama, Florida, Georgia, Illinois, Indiana, Kentucky, Louisiana, Michigan, Minnesota, Mississippi, North Carolina, North Dakota, Ohio, Pennsylvania, South Carolina, South Dakota, Tennessee, Virginia, West Virginia, and Wisconsin.

Retail outlets operate under Marathon and Ashland names, as well as SuperAmerica, Speedway, Bonded, Cheker, Starvin' Marvin, United, Gastown, Wake Up, Kwik Sak, and Rich Oil.

USX IN THE COMMUNITY

Over the years, USX has been one of the Pittsburgh region's strongest community benefactors. The company annually lends active support to the United Way, Junior Achievement, and many other groups. Moreover, as Pittsburgh enters the 21st century, USX Chairman Thomas Usher has been the point man for regional economic development efforts.

The company financially supports community groups via USX Foundation Inc., a non-profit membership corporation founded in Delaware in 1953 as the U.S. Steel Foundation. The purpose of the foundation is to provide support in a planned and balanced manner for educational, scientific, charitable, civic, cultural, and health needs, and to assist in meeting those and other major needs through support of selected organizations and projects. Priority is given to organizations and projects that serve the major operating areas of USX Corporation. During 1996, USX Foundation authorized more than $6.3 million for new and ongoing programs.

With roots stretching back for more than 100 years, USX Corporation has played a major role in the long history of Pittsburgh. The company's ability to respond to changing economic conditions and new market opportunities through diversification and restructuring, demonstrated by its continued growth and success, ensures that USX Corporation will remain an active and contributing member of the Pittsburgh community for many years to come.

Clockwise from top left:
On a recent visit to the Harley-Davidson motorcycle assembly plant in York, Pennsylvania, U.S. Steel Mon Valley Works employees (from left, front) Bob Zolock, Pam Lees, Byron Morant, (from left, back) Shirley Holmes, Bob Pendro, and Rege Gavalik learn how their steel is transformed into an American legend.

Bruce Reoli, door coordinator at Clairton Works, inspects oven No. B23's door sealing surface on the coke side.

At South Taylor Environmental Park (STEP), U.S. Steel's Jacqueline Gabel (left) and Susan Kapusta monitor elementary students collecting core samples from STEP's wetland area for use in science and environmental studies.

PON ENTERING THE MODERN OFFICES OF PRICE WATERHOUSE on the 28th floor of the USX Tower, it is difficult for the average visitor to visualize the firm's humble local beginnings more than 90 years ago. At that time, Price Waterhouse opened its office in the People's Savings

"We are committed to be the leading global consultant to the top-tier and rapidly emerging companies that reside in this region, and will continually improve the quality and range of services provided to them," says Jim Stalder, Price Waterhouse managing partner (left).

Price Waterhouse professionals are committed to providing their clients with outstanding business advisory and consulting services (right).

Bank Building with a staff of only four and began serving its first Pittsburgh-based client, United States Steel Corporation (now USX). Today, the firm's Pittsburgh office employs more than 190 staff members, and provides auditing, tax, consulting, and outsourcing services to major companies in the tristate area—from well-established manufacturers to leading-edge technology companies.

The Pittsburgh office is part of the Price Waterhouse worldwide organization, which, for nearly 150 years, has been helping the world's leading companies solve complex business problems. Through a worldwide network comprising 60,000 professionals in 119 countries and territories, Price Waterhouse assists clients in effecting organizational and structural change, using information technology for competitive advantage, complying with statutory audit and tax requirements, and implementing strategies to improve business performance and increase shareholder value.

IMPROVED CLIENT SERVICE

The firm believes a strong local presence is essential to better serving its clients' day-to-day needs. Specialization allows Price Waterhouse professionals to work efficiently and effectively to provide clients with superior business advisory services, based on industry knowledge and best practices.

Because of today's changing business environment, the Pittsburgh office is designed for "hoteling." This term refers to situations in which, for example, staff members might require a specific office to accommodate their work or project demands. The staff members can make reservations with the office concierge, and at the start of the business day, their requests are met, and an office is arranged just for them with their files, supplies, and even personal belongings all in place.

"In today's environment, we are focused on the clients and the industries we are committed to serve, which, in turn, mandates a more fluid assignment of people and office hoteling," says Managing Partner Jim Stalder. Today, Price Waterhouse professionals can plug a laptop computer into any office, project workroom, or conference room and log into the company's worldwide network. A quick flip of the switch and their phone lines are automatically routed.

COMMITMENT TO QUALITY

While the offices have changed, the commitment to quality and to client satisfaction have not. According to Stalder, today's executives want more than just the numbers—they want business advisers who will be there for them. "Clients want to work with professionals who will bring the right resources at the right time, make business recommendations for improved bottom-line results, develop innovative ideas, share industry knowledge, and, in short, contribute to

CARL P. STILLITANO / CPS PHOTOGRAPHY, INC.

CARL P. STILLITANO / CPS PHOTOGRAPHY, INC.

CARL P. STILLITANO / CPS PHOTOGRAPHY, INC.

the company's success. That's exactly the kind of service Price Waterhouse is known for—client service that translates into client satisfaction, the cornerstone of the firm's service approach," says Stalder.

When it comes to client satisfaction among America's powerhouse companies, Price Waterhouse stands alone, according to the most recent independent study conducted by the Emerson Company, a top market research firm and publisher of the prestigious *Emerson's Professional Services Review*. The study measured client satisfaction with the accounting profession's Big Six firms in a random sample drawn from 585 of the largest U.S.-based multinationals. In head-to-head competition with the other firms, Price Waterhouse came out on top or tied for leadership in the overall satisfaction category, and in seven of the 10 other satisfaction categories.

In addition to serving clients with a commitment to quality and excellence, the firm contributes to the community and the region through its participation in office-sponsored charity events, such as the United Way Day of Caring, March of Dimes Walkathon, MS Walk, and many others. The firm also is one of the highest contributors to the local United Way campaign and boasts 100 percent participation by its employees.

Many of the firm's staff members are active in civic, cultural, and charitable organizations. "We attract not only high-quality professionals,

but high-quality individuals who are committed to improving their communities and the region," says Stalder. The partners of the firm set the standard, serving on numerous boards, including such cultural organizations as the Pittsburgh Ballet Theatre, Pittsburgh Opera, Pittsburgh Public Theater, Pittsburgh Symphony, and non-profit organizations such as Three Rivers Youth, the Western Area YMCA, United Way of Southwestern Pennsylvania, the Pittsburgh Zoo, and American Red Cross.

The firm is committed to the future of the Greater Pittsburgh area, as well as to the Commonwealth of Pennsylvania, and has provided leadership and assistance with prominent initiatives that will benefit the region now and into the next century. Some of these efforts include the Regional Economic Revitalization Initiative, Pennsylvania Tax Blueprint Project, Regional Renaissance Partnership,

and Governor Tom Ridge's proposal to privatize the Pennsylvania Wine and Spirits industry.

Prospects for the future continue to look bright, with the pending merger of Price Waterhouse and Coopers & Lybrand. The merged firm will be able to provide clients with greater global coverage, more fully integrated expertise, faster deployment of resources, and accelerated access to new products, services, and methodologies.

"Price Waterhouse and its people have played a significant role in the development of the Greater Pittsburgh community since 1902, and we will continue to fulfill this role into the new millennium," says Stalder. "We are committed to be the leading global consultant to the top-tier and rapidly emerging companies that reside in this region, and will continually improve the quality and range of services provided to them."

Clockwise from top left:
Price Waterhouse helps its clients develop and execute integrated solutions to build value, manage risk, and improve global performance.

Price Waterhouse professionals can plug a laptop computer into any office, project workroom, or conference room and log into the company's worldwide network.

The firm provides publications about a wide range of topics to help clients anticipate trends and plan for opportunities.

Stalder and Tim Donnelly, partner

When Pitt-Des Moines, Inc. (PDM) opened in 1892 as Jackson and Moss, Engineers and Contractors, the firm was known for constructing municipal water systems and water distribution systems. The company was originally located in Des Moines, but in the early

Clockwise from left:
While Pitt-Des Moines has been involved in several high-profile projects, it is most proud of the St. Louis Arch, which stands 630 feet above the Mississippi River.

Among Pitt-Des Moines' projects is the unique Crystal Cathedral in Garden Grove, California.

In 1996, Pitt-Des Moines fabricated its first metric bridge project, the Blue Water Bridge spanning the St. Clair River between Port Huron, Michigan, and Sarnia, Ontario.

1900s, founders William H. Jackson and Berkley N. Moss, along with a new business partner, Edward Crellin, were looking east, to Pittsburgh, which was the center of the steel industry.

To really compete, the trio knew they needed a presence in Pittsburgh, where the steel so critical to their water and bridge projects was priced the cheapest. Land was purchased in 1907, and construction of a plant commenced at the new site in Pittsburgh—Neville Island. During 1910, the company decided to move its headquarters

to downtown Pittsburgh, then to Neville Island in 1927, where it continues to stand today.

THE EARLY YEARS

Within a decade of PDM's establishment of the Neville Island facility in Pittsburgh, the United States entered World War I. The firm was part of the war effort, and a landmark project during that period was the construction of a series of radio towers in France, eight of them standing 800 feet high. Located in Bordeaux, the towers were designed to improve

communications among Allied commanders.

The Great Depression followed soon after, but PDM weathered the storm as the federal government attempted to stimulate the economy by pumping money into public works projects. For Pitt-Des Moines, Inc., that meant water tank construction, one of its core businesses from the start. Soon after the depression ended, the company would work on additions to a well-known Pennsylvania landmark originally constructed in 1934—Beaver Stadium at Penn State University. The addi-

tions increased the stadium's seating capacity of 2,400 to more than 50,000.

When the United States became involved in World War II, PDM again played its part in the war effort. Pitt-Des Moines, Inc. took its expertise in building bridges, towers, and stadiums, and translated it into shipbuilding and other tasks crucial to the nation's success. The company also built several floating dry docks that were used to repair warships damaged in combat. The dry docks proved crucial to the war effort, quickly returning battleships, aircraft carriers, and cruisers back to the Pacific theater. At its peak, the company's shipyard and plant in Pittsburgh employed about 2,100 people.

Also, following World War II, PDM was very helpful to the National Advisory Committee for Aeronautics (NACA) and NASA by helping to design and build most of the wind tunnels and space chambers used to research and develop supersonic airplanes and space vehicles.

THE MODERN ERA

Today, the once-tiny company has grown into a diversified engineering and construction firm that also processes and distributes a broad range of carbon steel products. PDM now has more than 2,000 employees, and in 1996 reported earned revenues of $468 million. PDM lists among its projects such landmarks as the Jefferson National Memorial Monument, commonly known as the St. Louis Arch; the

Biosphere project in the Arizona desert; and the Crystal Cathedral in Garden Grove, California. Pitt-Des Moines, Inc.'s work on these projects has earned it a worldwide reputation. "PDM has become a recognized leader and pioneer in the field," says William W. McKee, president and CEO of PDM. "Hardly any project has been too difficult for the company to tackle, including complex conceptual design efforts, which have led us into many fields of endeavor."

While PDM has been involved in several high-profile projects, it is most proud of the St. Louis Arch, which stands 630 feet above the Mississippi River. The first sections of the arch were set in place in December 1962, and the final keystone was lowered into place in October 1965. "The St. Louis Arch is a fine example of one of those difficult projects, perfectly planned and executed," says W.R. Jackson,

president at the time of the project. "PDM is proud to have played a part in the construction of the tallest monument in the United States."

Today, the company remains involved in other complex projects. In 1996, for instance, PDM fabricated its first metric bridge project, the Blue Water Bridge spanning the St. Clair River between Port Huron, Michigan, and Sarnia, Ontario. PDM supplied 3,900 tons of structural components for the U.S. portion of the project. Meanwhile, the PDM Steel Service Centers continue to cut and shape steel plate to customer needs.

With more than a century of experience behind it, PDM looks forward to a bright future. "Pitt-Des Moines continues as a dominant force in engineering design, steel fabrication, and construction," says McKee. "We are pioneering in new fields, building upon our historical success."

The Pitt-Des Moines Steel Service Centers cut and shape steel plate to customer needs. The once-tiny company has grown into a diversified engineering and construction firm that also processes and distributes a broad range of carbon steel products.

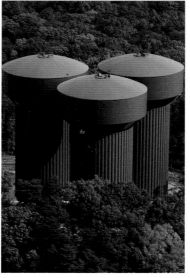

Pitt-Des Moines, a dominant force in engineering design, steel fabrication, and construction, demonstrates its talent in the three Hydropillars located in Bowie, Maryland—each able to hold 1.5 million gallons (right)—and the two 50,000-barrel spheres used to store butane and isobutane in Bakersfield, California (left).

FROM THE EARLY 1800S AS THE DAVY BROTHERS, THROUGH MANY changes in name, size, and mission, Kvaerner Metals has grown into an international force among metals industry service providers while remaining a corporate icon in the Pittsburgh region. Now, with a new parent company and an aggressive plan

for business development around the globe, Kvaerner Metals looks forward to its next century in Southwestern Pennsylvania, where the company has deep roots.

Kvaerner Metals provides engineering and construction services for the metals, mining, and minerals industries, and equipment for ferrous and nonferrous metals industries. The firm was founded in Sheffield in 1830, where the Davy Brothers specialized in equipment supply and engineering services for foundries, mills, and the railroads. By 1890, Davy Brothers Limited had secured its first forging press order in the United States from Andrew Carnegie. Carnegie's company, then known as Carnegie, Phipps and Company Limited, and the Davy Brothers began a partnership that would continue servicing the burgeoning steel industry for more than a century, playing a major role in making Pittsburgh an industrial giant and ruler of the steel industry. Back then, when steelmakers geared up to produce the steel used in building modern America's infrastructure, or to build the boats, planes, and tanks

Clockwise from top:
Kvaerner Metals, along with its sister company Kvaerner Songer, completed the No. 2 coke oven battery for Bethlehem Steel several months ahead of schedule. This $200 million project meets today's stringent national emissions standards and produces approximately 900,000 tons of coke annually.

The unique design of these hydraulic loopers at Gulf States Steel incorporate shearbeam load cells in the side frames for more direct strip tension measurement.

Kvaerner Metals recently completed this 3.5 million-ton pellet plant to allow IMEXSA, located in Mexico, to be more competitive in its growing international steel market.

that helped win two world wars, it was this equipment that added capacity to the steel plants, keeping them running full tilt so the steelmakers could meet their demand.

Over the decades, Kvaerner Metals grew in size and focus through acquisitions of other engineering and construction firms, gaining status as an international player serving the metals industry in both engineering and manu-

facturing products. By the early 1990s, Davy had acquired another Pittsburgh mainstay, Dravo Engineers, as well as the Clecim and Comstock companies, solidifying its role in global markets and expanding the broad range of services it could offer.

NEW NAME, SAME INGENUITY
Beginning in the early 1990s, various mergers resulted in Davy's new name and new affiliation

▲ MICKEY PRIM

TOM BARR

with its parent company, Kvaerner ASA, a Norwegian-owned, global organization based in London. With annual revenues of more than $10 billion, Kvaerner ASA is a leading engineering and construction firm known worldwide in a variety of industries. With the resources of Kvaerner ASA behind it, Kvaerner Metals now possesses the strength, the inventiveness, and the resources to lead the market in providing the metals industry with cutting-edge tools and technology for the 21st century.

Innovation is Kvaerner's trademark. The company rides the cutting edge in all its industries, from metals to construction to shipbuilding. For instance, Kvaerner built an ultra-high-tech sailing yacht, the *Innovation*, to compete in the Whitbread around-the-world race. Some of Kvaerner's other efforts worldwide include technology for the chemicals, oil and gas, pulp and paper, and construction industries. Kvaerner-designed plants generate about 45 percent of the world's methanol supply.

KVAERNER METALS' NICHE

Kvaerner Metals' experience in sophisticated technology for the metals industry is almost boundless. The company is a turnkey engineering and construction firm and an equipment supplier, meaning its engineers can provide one-stop shopping for mammoth plant construction projects. Kvaerner Metals engineers will take a project from beginning to end with no need to subcontract elsewhere for the minor details of a job. The integrated delivery of services often allows the company to build cost efficiencies into a project. Kvaerner Metals can provide a complete line of products from the ground up, from direct reduction plants to complex cold rolling facilities to blast furnace rebuilds.

The consolidation of all aspects of plant construction, from design through to installation and even financing, under one roof can provide tremendous savings in both time and money for the client. Operations mesh fluidly as efficient communication provides a better understanding of a project's end

goals, no matter how large or small. That means getting the product to market sooner and cheaper.

A leader in process control systems, Kvaerner Metals can provide automation equipment for comprehensive, plantwide functionality, including software packages for order management, product tracking, dynamic scheduling, and quality control for projects of all sizes. Computer modeling systems provide previously unimagined forecasting abilities, saving time and allowing creative optimization of facility layout. All these products can be tied together with fully integrated process control systems—all made possible by Kvaerner Metals' trademark project management teams.

SOLVING PROBLEMS

Problem solving through forward thinking is one of Kvaerner Metals' strengths. On a project for Dofasco Inc. in Ontario, Canada, for instance, Kvaerner Metals generated new efficiencies by employing novel piping systems, saving the client money and time. Dofasco, a leading producer of flat-rolled steel in Canada, needed to cut costs by producing its own steel

slabs, and it needed to start producing within an 18-month time window to avoid having to enter into new, external contracts for the slabs. Through team building among the engineers, Kvaerner Metals was able to meet the time and cost goals and complete the project one month ahead of schedule.

Kvaerner Metals employs its own intranet to allow video teleconferencing and instant communication with offices all over the world, maximizing communications and limiting project breakdowns. For example, during design, procurement, and construction of the Hadeed Direct Reduction Plant in Al-Jubail, Saudi Arabia, the individual project teams set up electronic communications links to maximize use of time zones among their partners in Mexico, India, Europe, England, Saudi Arabia, and the United States. Since project execution efficiency was a key factor, Kvaerner Metals staff ensured work around the clock. As work was ending in India and Saudi Arabia, it was beginning in Europe, then the United States and Mexico; the sun never set on the Hadeed project.

Kvaerner Metals built a completely new control pulpit with operator's stations for Gulf States Steel's 54-inch-wide hot strip mill upgrade.

The scope of Kvaerner Metals' activities doesn't stop at plant installation. It is one of the few firms that specializes in plant outage planning and handling emergency outage situations for integrated plants or minimills. Projects span the globe, from a reversing hot mill for Aluminum of Korea Ltd. in South Korea, to pelletizing plants in India, Brazil, and Mexico, to a U.S. Steel casting complex in Braddock, just south of Pittsburgh. For planned outages, Kvaerner Metals is adept at helping the steelmaker complete any maintenance work or upgrades on time so manufacturing can begin anew as scheduled.

Perhaps Kvaerner Metals' services are even more crucial when the outage is not planned and comes as a surprise. All steelmakers must be adept at managing such a plant outage crisis, since downtime at a plant quickly translates into lost profits for the steelmaker. Kvaerner Metals develops crisis management plans for steel producers, preparing them for the outage when it occurs and helping them get the plant back on-line in a short period of time. Over the years, quick, Kvaerner Metals-guided response to an unexpected outage has helped many steelmakers

minimize losses during an emergency outage.

A key to Kvaerner Metals' effectiveness, whether in construction or in managing a plant outage, is the team approach to managing

a task. With the complexities of today's industrial challenges, it takes more than just the hardware to create communication. Every aspect of a project requires cooperation between designers and

▼ TOM FITZPATRICK

The U.S. Steel Group of USX Corporation chose Kvaerner Metals to build the dual-slab caster at the Edgar Thomson plant in Braddock, Pennsylvania. One of the key facilities at the Mon Valley Works, selected by *IndustryWeek* magazine as one of America's Best Plants, the caster continues to perform to the highest standard of reliability and quality (top).

In the early 1990s, Kvaerner Metals signed a turnkey contract for the design and construction of ProTec's Hot Dip Galvanizing Facility, producing automotive-quality product. Recently, ProTec awarded a second equipment order to Kvaerner Metals for a similar line (bottom).

The Power of

doers. Kvaerner Metals' philosophy makes team building work by creating real rapport between the customer and its own project employees. One project even had the players on the project sit down together and tackle exercises, like solving brainteasers, while blindfolded. That kind of belief in communication results in comfortable relationships—and productivity.

Kvaerner Metals focuses on winning contracts in which the company handles a project from concept to completion. On these turnkey projects, the company does all the design, procurement, and construction for a facility, right through start-up. Or, as Jim McGrath, president of Kvaerner Metals Pittsburgh, puts it, "It's starting with a project that's a blank sheet and taking it to an operating facility." Kvaerner Metals Pittsburgh, along with its sister company, Kvaerner Songer, also located in the Pittsburgh area, billed more than $445 million in 1996, which was an increase from 1995. McGrath is expecting additional annual growth into the 21st century.

KVAERNER IN PITTSBURGH

Worldwide, Kvaerner Metals does almost $1.5 billion a year in business. The company employs about 900 in the city of Pittsburgh and 4,800 globally. Kvaerner Metals has offices in 35 countries and works in almost every country in the world. Kvaerner Metals made a commitment to stay in Pittsburgh with the signing of a long-term lease at the Strip District's Penn Liberty Plaza 1, where the company converted an abandoned warehouse into attractive new offices.

"By choosing this location, we made a long-term commitment to our employees and to the city of Pittsburgh," says McGrath. "We genuinely appreciate the interest and cooperation shown by the city government, who has worked hard to help keep us here."

The new office's three-floor location reflects the company's forward-thinking attitude with an open central atrium and modular furniture systems creating an office with few walls, and electronically linked workstations. The approximately 170,000-square-foot space is designed to promote the open exchange of information, encouraging employees to see more of each other as they pass through the open floor plan or congregate in the common meeting areas.

McGrath says the firm's location in Western Pennsylvania is an advantage because, in the field of metals technology, Pittsburgh is where the action is. "Pittsburgh is still seen as the center of the steel industry and is a real source of engineering talent because of its excellent universities. Carnegie Mellon University, the University of Pittsburgh, and others provide a pool of resources from which to draw."

And being in the Strip District is an important part of Kvaerner Metals' plan for the next century. "With developments such as a planned expansion of the convention center, the new history museum, and planned new parking facilities, the Strip is quickly becoming a vital area of the central business district," says McGrath.

It is Pittsburgh's talent pool and resources that will push Kvaerner Metals even further in the next century—and will help to maintain the Pittsburgh region's reputation as an industrial giant. Where once it was steel itself that rolled out of Pittsburgh, now the city will supply the world with the technology and know-how that make the industry prosper as Kvaerner Metals maintains its strength in the traditional core businesses of technology supply, project management, basic engineering design, and construction.

In the early 1890s, Davy Brothers Limited received its first forging press order from Andrew Carnegie's company, Carnegie, Phipps and Company Limited (top).

Back in 1943, these men were pouring a line of ingot moulds using the latest furnace technology available. Today, Kvaerner Metals continues to remain on the cutting edge of steelmaking technology (bottom).

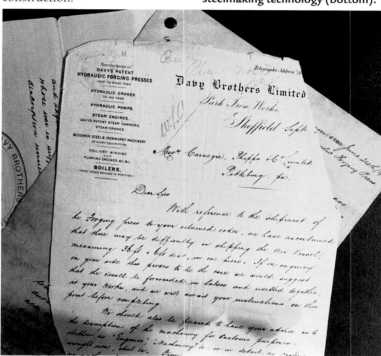

LONG BEFORE IT BECAME POPULAR TO PROMOTE WOMEN'S HEALTH, taking care of women was Magee-Womens Hospital's sole occupation. ■ The tradition continues today at Magee-Womens, an acute care, research, and teaching center that is one of the few specialty hospitals in the United States devoted

to the care of women and newborns. With this focus, it's no surprise that many women in the Pittsburgh area utilize the hospital's services—in fact, nearly 9,000 babies are born each year at Magee-Womens.

But the care doesn't end at delivering babies. Of the females born at Magee-Womens, many return throughout their lives for complete health care management. "Our philosophy starts with the young woman," says Irma Goertzen, president and chief executive officer of Magee-Womens. "We stay with her through her childbearing years, menopause, and later life. We treat a woman with dignity and empower her with education."

A HISTORY OF SERVICE

Founded in 1911, the earliest Magee-Womens Hospital was the home of Christopher Lyman Magee, a prominent 19th-century businessman, politician, and benefactor. In his will, Magee wrote that his estate should be used to build and endow a hospital that would be "open to the sick and

injured of all classes without respect to their religion, creed, color, or previous condition," and that women "be admitted without any question as to their lives and names." Following this mandate, Elizabeth Steel Magee Hospital, as it was known then, enacted a policy of free care to the indigent, and humane and dignified care for the unwed mother, a practice uncommon at that time.

Today, the hospital campus—now located in the Oakland section of Pittsburgh—has 263 adult beds, 80 bassinets, and 63 neo-natal intensive care unit beds. Magee-Womens has also become a teaching hospital, with medical and nursing students from the University of Pittsburgh learning about obstetrics and gynecology.

In addition, Magee-Womens operates a network of six Womancare Centers and four Neighborhood Health Centers for Women. The Womancare Centers offer a continuum of services ranging from standard gynecology and diagnostics to high-risk obstetrics. The Neighborhood Centers pro-

vide the community with a total spectrum of women's health care.

TOP CARE

The care provided by Magee-Womens, particularly in the fields of breast and gynecological cancer diagnosis and treatment, ranks among the best in the nation, due in large part to the skill of the providers and its state-of-the-art technology. Magee-Womens' infertility programs have also proved successful, boasting fertilization rates ranging from 28 to 30 percent, near the top in the nation.

Five of the top administrators at Magee-Womens are female, along with approximately 40 percent of the attending physicians, 68 percent of the resident physicians, and 90 percent of the nursing staff. The care is shaped daily for women, by women.

After nearly a century, Magee-Womens Hospital continues to fulfill its mission and more: The hospital that began as one man's goal to improve health care has now become an innovator in improving the health of women in Pittsburgh and the nation.

A brand-new mother receives assistance from a nurse as she prepares to go home with her newborn (right).

Magee-Womens Hospital's campus is located in the Oakland section of Pittsburgh, and has 263 adult beds, 80 bassinets, and 63 neonatal intensive care unit beds (left).

▲▼ JOHN MCCAULLEY

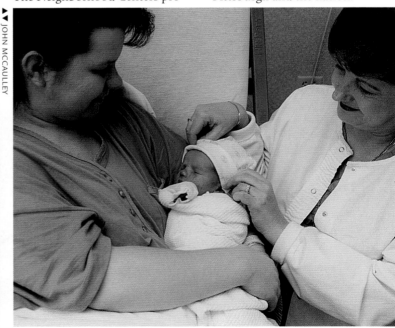

The Power of

OPPERWELD CORPORATION IS NORTH AMERICA'S LEADING manufacturer of steel tubing and the world's largest producer of bimetallic wire. The company's success in these mature markets is based on a market-driven, customer-oriented management philosophy and a willingness to invest in

leading-edge technology and facilities.

Copperweld was founded in 1915 in Rankin, near Pittsburgh, as the Copper Clad Steel Company. Today, Pittsburgh remains the site of its corporate headquarters, but most of its 2,500 employees are based at manufacturing facilities throughout the United States and Canada.

The company's original business was copper-clad steel wire and strand. Its patented molten weld process, Copperweld®, was made the company's name in 1924. Copperweld entered the steel tube business in 1952 with the acquisition of Ohio Seamless Tubing Company, now its Shelby Division, which manufactures mechanical tubing for hydraulic cylinders and mechanical parts for the automotive and other markets. The firm acquired the Regal Tube Company, now its Chicago Division, in 1972. The operation produces structural tubing for buildings, transport facilities, and other product applications.

In 1975, Copperweld opened a state-of-the-art bimetallic wire facility on a green field site in Fayetteville, Tennessee, and closed its obsolete wire facility in the Pittsburgh area in 1983. Today, its Fayetteville plant is the preeminent producer of this product worldwide, serving such markets as cable TV, telecommunications, electronics, and electric utilities.

Then, in 1995, Copperweld acquired Metallon Engineered Materials Company in Pawtucket, Rhode Island. The operation, now called Copperweld Metallon Division, produces clad metal strips for a number of markets.

A French company, IMETAL, purchased 65 percent of Copperweld's common stock in 1975, acquiring the remainder in 1990. Today IMETAL has interests in build-

ing materials, industrial minerals, and metals processing.

In 1990, the company opened a second structural tubing production facility in Birmingham, Alabama, to serve the fast-growing markets in the southern tier of the United States. And, in 1993, Copperweld increased its involvement in the markets for smaller, lighter-weight mechanical tubing by acquiring the Miami Industries Division of Armco, Inc., now its Miami Division.

Early in 1997, Copperweld took the largest growth step in its history, acquiring two respected Canadian tubing manufacturers—Sonco Steel Tube and Standard Tube Canada. These are now operating as divisions of Copperweld Canada. Also acquired at the same time were the assets of the Tube and Steel Company of America (TASCOA), which distributed certain of Sonco's and Standard Tube's products in the United States.

TODAY AND TOMORROW

As Copperweld prepares to enter the 21st century, the company is in the midst of expansion programs totaling more than $62 million; is forming a new Stainless Tubing

Division to tap the growing markets for that product; and has centralized its purchasing function to take advantage of the combined size of its operations.

"Some years ago," says President and CEO John D. Turner, "we adopted the phrase Leadership and Excellence as an expression of our standing in the markets we serve. We have every intention of maintaining our leadership in the steel tubing and bimetallics industries into the 21st century and beyond."

Copperweld Corporation's TuffDOM® line of cold-drawn, stress-relieved tubing is ideal for fluid power and other mechanical applications (top).

An operator performs crush testing of tube from Copperweld's Invader Plant, Sonco Steel Tube Division in Mississauga, Ontario (bottom).

FOUNDED IN 1918 AS HAGAN CORPORATION, CALGON CORPORATION is a recognized leader in developing and applying innovative water-treatment products and technologies for industrial and municipal plants in the United States and select locations worldwide. The company's specialty chemicals are also used

in papermaking, surface treatment, cosmetics, and specialty additives.

The company got its start as a developer of automatic combustion controls for industrial boiler systems, but its scientists quickly recognized a more urgent client need—preventing the costly boiler system failures that are caused when calcium scale is deposited on boiler tube surfaces. They discovered that sodium hexametaphosphate prevented scale in boilers and trademarked the chemical Calgon for "calcium gone." Quickly recognized as the standard treatment for preventing scale in boilers, Calgon is still widely used today.

DRIVING THE COMPANY

This versatile chemical, which was recognized as the Chemical of the Year at the British Industries Fair in 1935, became the raw material for a variety of water-treatment products. Its discovery also set the company's future direction and established its tradition of

science-based, results-oriented technologies designed to meet each customer's specific water system needs.

First, in the steel mills, power stations, and chemical plants that lined Pittsburgh's three rivers; then, across the country; and finally, wherever water was used around the globe, Calgon scientists analyzed

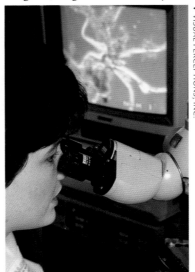

and solved water system problems. Although its controls business also flourished, it became clear that the company's brightest future was to be in water treatment. In 1963, the company sold its controls businesses and the Hagan name to Westinghouse Electric Corp. and adopted the name Calgon Corporation in deference to its most famous product.

Today, Calgon's primary business remains industrial water treatment. Each year, plants around the world require trillions of gallons of usable, trouble-free water to heat and cool, generate power, make paper, convey process materials, and carry away waste products. Thousands of these plants depend on Calgon's people and technology to prevent water from damaging equipment, impairing product quality, lowering productivity, or threatening the environment.

Calgon also finds itself in the rewarding position of servicing businesses driven by regulatory

State-of-the-art R&D and analytical capabilities have been trademarks of Calgon Corporation since its founding in 1918 (top).

Calgon's Robinson Township-based headquarters houses its main research center, where basic research, product development, and technical assistance are provided to a variety of industries (bottom).

pressures. Once water has served its essential role in manufacturing plants, it must be treated before it can be safely returned to rivers and lakes. As environmental concerns are addressed through such legislation as the U.S. Clean Air and Clean Water acts, manufacturing plants are saddled with increasingly stringent emission and discharge regulations from the Environmental Protection Agency. Plant personnel need even more help in developing and implementing sophisticated water treatment programs to meet those requirements. Calgon researchers are currently working on the treatment solutions to such future challenges.

Efficient water recycling also has become an urgent challenge. Increasing demands on limited supplies, coupled with years of abuse and neglect, already cause frequent shortages of usable water. To ensure that industries, farmers, utilities, and the public will always have the necessary quantity and quality of water, all users must squeeze more value from every drop. While many facilities already recycle much of their water, most will ultimately have to close their plantwide water loop entirely, thereby exacerbating the threat water problems pose to plant efficiency and reliability. Calgon scientists and engineers are working to develop the advanced technology that will make such zero-discharge operations practical.

OTHER MARKETS

In addition to water treatment, Calgon has found other markets where its proprietary technology can bring value. For example, Calgon products and services are used throughout the papermaking process to help enhance machine performance, maximize machine cleanliness, increase drying efficiency, decrease maintenance, simplify waste treatment, and optimize filler, fine, and fiber utilization. The company is also a leader in surface treatment, which involves the cleaning, protection, and preparation of metal or plastic surfaces prior to painting or coating.

For the past few decades, the personal-care industry has also benefited from Calgon's core competencies in water-soluble polymers that are used as functional ingredients in shampoos, conditioners, shower gels, and moisturizers. Calgon specialty additives are used throughout the world to preserve paints and coatings, adhesives, and latex emulsions, among other products.

LOOKING AHEAD

The key to Calgon's 80 years of leadership in the water-treatment industry is the company's unwavering dedication to delivering value to its customers—value that can make a significant contribution to each customer's bottom line.

As the business climate has shifted over the decades, Calgon has anticipated the demands of the marketplace, continuously adapting itself to profitably meet those needs.

Since 1993, Calgon has been owned by English China Clays, the world's leading supplier of minerals and pigments to the paper industry. English China Clays has positioned Calgon Corporation as its platform for growth within the specialty chemicals industry and has invested heavily in positioning the company for success. Together, English China Clays and Calgon will continue to explore new markets where their innovative mineral and specialty chemical technologies can deliver unequaled value to their customers.

**Clockwise from top left:
Through the expert application of world-class technology, Calgon Corporation helps its customers ensure their profitability through increased productivity, enhanced quality, and reduced operating costs.**

Calgon representatives work in partnership with customers to develop customized solutions to their water-related problems.

Municipalities throughout the nation depend on Calgon's pretreatment and wastewater-treatment expertise to provide a steady supply of safe, clean drinking water.

JOE JOY SPENT HIS TEENAGE YEARS DIGGING COAL, A JOB THAT required him to lie on his side in the wet mines while loosening the coal from the seam. He would then hand-load the coal into small, rail-mounted mine cars that were pulled up into the daylight by mules. During those long, laborious hours, Joy

would visualize ways to perform the same work mechanically, and by his 20th birthday in 1903, had sketched out his idea for a digging and loading device.

Joy eventually showed his device to John A. Donaldson, an officer of Pittsburgh Coal Co. Donaldson loved the idea, and Joy's first mechanical loader was shipped to Pittsburgh Coal in 1916. Since then, Joy Mining Machinery has continually brought machinery and technology to the mining industry, making coal mining more efficient, safe, and profitable.

Today, the Pittsburgh-based company, which employs more

than 5,300 people worldwide, is a subsidiary of Harnischfeger Industries, a Fortune 300 company with sales exceeding $3 billion. The company's global headquarters is located at Thorn Hill Industrial Park in Warrendale, approximately 15 miles north of downtown Pittsburgh. The company's global distribution center is located at Meadow Lands, Washington County, nearly 25 miles south of Pittsburgh.

MAKING MINING EFFICIENT

Joy Mining Machinery has logged more than 75 years' experience as a global leader in the development, manufacture, distribution, and service of underground min-

ing machinery for the extraction of coal and other embedded materials. Joy manufactures longwall shearers, roof supports, face conveyors, continuous miners, batch haulage (shuttle cars and articulated haulers), continuous haulage (chain haulage systems and flexible conveyor trains), entry drivers, drills, and loaders for use in longwall and room-and-pillar mining operations. Joy is the only manufacturer that offers a complete longwall system to the industry.

The company's role in modern society is crucial, since 55 percent of America's electricity and 25 percent of electricity worldwide is generated by coal-burning power-producing facilities. In 1997, the United States produced 1.094 billion tons of coal, the 11th consecutive year in which domestic production exceeded 900 million tons. At the present rate of recovery and usage, U.S. coal reserves will last at least another 250 years.

While coal production surges, safety in the industry has greatly improved, thanks, in part, to industry developments by Joy Mining Machinery. In 1930, more than 71,000 miners were injured and another 1,600 died for every 200,000 hours worked. By 1996, those numbers had dropped to 7,200 injuries and only 34 fatalities.

EFFICIENT UNDERGROUND MINING

Joy did not rest after developing that initial loading machine, and neither did the company that bears his name. By 1930, Joy Mining Machinery had developed a system of coal saws to undercut blocks of coal that were then drilled and blasted. In 1937, the company invented the first shuttle car. The following decade, Joy Mining Machinery introduced

In North America, most major mining operations use Joy Mining Machinery equipment to safely and efficiently mine coal via the longwall mining method. Coal industry insiders estimate that longwall mining has increased the coal recoverability rate in underground mining by as much as 80 percent since it was introduced in the market.

Continuous mining still accounts for more than 40 percent of coal taken from deep mines. In this process, the Joy continuous miner—first introduced in 1948—extracts the coal from the seam and automatically removes it from the area by conveyor.

Joy manufactures longwall shearers, roof supports, face conveyors, continuous miners, batch haulage (shuttle car shown at left), continuous haulage (chain haulage systems and flexible conveyor trains), entry drivers, drills, and loaders.

a continuous miner, a device that mechanically extracts coal from a seam.

In the underground coal mine of the 1990s, machines have largely replaced manual labor. As a result, the coal miner of today is far different from when Joy worked as a teenage laborer. Today's coal miner operates highly complex computers and machinery. And in North America, most major mining operations use Joy equipment to safely and efficiently mine coal via the longwall mining method.

In longwall mining, drums mounted on a shearing machine cut and load the coal onto a conveyor for removal from the mine. Longwall faces can be as long as 1,000 feet. Joy longwall systems have their own hydraulic roof supports that advance with the machine as the mining proceeds. The supports allow for high levels of production and recovery, but also increase miner safety. Once the seam has been adequately mined, the hydraulic supports automatically pull forward, allowing the ceiling to collapse behind the hydraulic supports. Meanwhile, the coal miners are safely covered, beginning to mine further into the seam. Coal industry insiders estimate that longwall mining has increased the coal recoverability rate in underground mining by

as much as 80 percent since it was introduced in the market.

To date, Joy has more than 120 longwall installations worldwide. Meanwhile, continuous mining still accounts for more than 40 percent of coal taken from deep mines. In this process, the Joy continuous miner—first introduced in 1948—extracts the coal from the seam and automatically removes it from the area by conveyor. Joy has added to the mix a flexible conveyor train, which has reduced workforce requirements while greatly increasing productivity. The coal is transported along the flexible conveyor train behind the continuous miner.

NEW AND AFTERMARKETS

Joy's role in the coal industry is that of a developer of new technology and equipment, as well as that of a service provider in the aftermarket. Joy operates aftermarket facilities throughout the United States, as well as in Australia, South Africa, Poland, India, and the United Kingdom. Mining operations throughout the world turn to Joy Mining Machinery to have their present equipment periodically serviced or refurbished.

At the same time, the company is constantly evaluating ways to improve its existing product line to increase efficiency and safety for end users. Joy Mining Machinery's vision is to be the preeminent supplier of underground mining equipment and services, allowing its customers to consistently produce at the lowest cost per ton over the lifecycle of the equipment.

THE WORK OF GRADUATES OF THE ART INSTITUTE OF PITTS-burgh can be seen everywhere (and in unexpected places). Astronomers preparing to face hostile temperatures in the Antarctic relied on Chris Cowen, a 1996 Industrial Design graduate, to create cold-weather gear for their trip. Remem-

ber the Elvis stamp? The U.S. Postal Service commissioned Mark Stutzman, a 1978 graduate, to illustrate it. And when people learn of world events through powerful photographs, they are often witnessing the unique vision of United Press International Vice President/General Manager Vince Mannino, a 1979 graduate.

From eye-catching illustrations to product designs that meet the real-world needs of scientists, The Art Institute of Pittsburgh's graduates make an impact in a variety of industries. Every year, hundreds of students from the Computer Animation, Graphic Design, Industrial Design Technology, Interior Design, Multimedia, Photography, Video Production, and Web Site Administration programs graduate and begin their professional careers not only in Pittsburgh, but across the country. Nationally known companies that employ graduates include Hallmark, American Greetings, Walt

Disney, Microsoft, and Industrial Light and Magic.

THE CREATIVE ARTS AT WORK

In 1996, The Art Institute of Pittsburgh marked its 75th anniversary. There was much to celebrate, including the school's national reputation as a leader in postsecondary education and the fact that more than 30,000 graduates have received practical, hands-on education.

At the heart of the school's commitment to excellence is the curriculum, developed and fine-tuned with help from industry professionals. The Art Institute of Pittsburgh faculty and staff keep abreast of industry trends so they can respond with programs that are tailored to the needs of the marketplace.

Another component in the school's commitment to student success is its investment in technology. Technology plays an integral role in many aspects of the creative arts, so the school responds by preparing students for the technological challenges they'll encounter once they begin their careers.

What brings it all together is the caliber of the faculty. Many instructors have professional experience in their fields of expertise. With each incoming class, instruc-

tors redefine strategies to strengthen students' skills and talents.

THE FLAGSHIP SCHOOL OF THE ART INSTITUTES INTERNATIONAL FAMILY

The Art Institute of Pittsburgh is the oldest and largest school within The Art Institutes International's (AII) network of professional schools in the United States. Associate degree programs are offered systemwide, while five locations offer bachelor's degree programs. Each Institute is accredited by federal and/or state agencies, including the Accrediting Commission of Career Schools and Colleges of Technology.

AII is owned and operated by Education Management Corporation, a leader in proprietary postsecondary education. Headquartered in Pittsburgh since 1961, Education Management Corporation has provided career-oriented education programs for more than 35 years. The corporation acquired The Art Institute of Pittsburgh in 1969.

In November 1996, Education Management Corporation's initial public offering (IPO) became effective. The company trades on the Nasdaq National Market under the symbol EDMC.

ROCK & ROLL SINGER, 1935-1977

1992 U.S. POSTAL SERVICE

The Elvis stamp, designed by The Art Institute of Pittsburgh graduate Mark Stutzman, was a huge hit with collectors and consumers alike.

The Art Institutes International's locations include Atlanta, Chicago, Dallas, Denver, Fort Lauderdale, Houston, Los Angeles, Minneapolis, Philadelphia, Phoenix, Pittsburgh, Schaumburg, and Seattle, and an affiliate, The New York Restaurant School. In addition to the programs offered by The Art Institute of Pittsburgh, The Art Institutes International also teaches Culinary Arts at nine locations, Fashion Merchandising at six locations, and Visual Merchandising at two locations.

MARK BOLSTER

WHEN THE TOP TWO INSURANCE BROKERAGE FIRMS IN Pittsburgh merged in 1997 to form J&H Marsh & McLennan, they created a company with more than 100 years of combined experience in the region. Johnson & Higgins and Marsh & McLennan, estab-

lished locally in 1946 and 1929, respectively, have long been mainstays of Pittsburgh business, but their presence in Pittsburgh dates back to 1901, when Henry W. Marsh himself hammered out the first risk management program for U.S. Steel.

"When these two intellectual powerhouses came together in Pittsburgh last year, it created tremendous synergy. Both firms had expertise in serving a variety of industries. The ideas that have come together complement each other perfectly," says Pittsburgh Branch Manager Norm Forrester.

J&H Marsh & McLennan is the largest publicly held insurance brokerage firm in the world. With offices around the globe, it draws on its worldwide resources to provide risk management expertise in such specialized industries as energy, transportation, aviation, construction, health care, government, space and telecommunications, and sports and entertainment.

Among the company's slate of risk management services are property and casualty loss prevention, property and casualty claims, and management information systems. The firm offers consulting and insurance products for companies wishing to make the leap to the ever expanding international marketplace. J&H Marsh & McLennan's financial and professional liability specialty group, FINPRO, is the largest network of financial and professional liability experts in the world, placing more than 40 percent of all premiums written in the global insurance market.

Serving big industries that flourished through the first half of this century, J&H Marsh & McLennan has grown and changed. As the shape of Pittsburgh business has evolved, the company's client list has become far more diverse,

Norbert D. Forrester is the Pittsburgh branch manager of J&H Marsh & McLennan, and Michael C. Barbarita is the head of the company's insurance operations in Pittsburgh.

with the firm serving midsize companies as well as large corporations. "Most Fortune 500 companies have on-staff professionals for risk management, while smaller companies typically do not have that capability. We can do for midsize companies what we've done for a long time for multinational corporations," says Mike Barbarita, head of insurance operations in Pittsburgh.

J&H Marsh & McLennan's size and access to global resources bring an added dimension to its midsize clients. "Our size and our expertise in the local and international markets," says Forrester, "give us more options to better

serve our clients and allow us to be a one-stop shop for all our clients. But it's not about being the biggest. It's about being the best."

This attitude extends to J&H Marsh & McLennan's role as an active corporate citizen in the Pittsburgh community. In addition to participating in the annual United Way Campaign, the company dedicates one day each year for all of its employees in Pittsburgh to perform volunteer work at local nonprofit facilities.

J&H Marsh & McLennan's dedication to giving its best—whether in business or in the community—assures the company's success, both now and in the future.

With offices around the globe, J&H Marsh & McLennan draws on its worldwide resources to provide risk management expertise in such specialized industries as energy, transportation, aviation, construction, health care, government, space and telecommunications, and sports and entertainment.

ARRY WERNER, DIRECTOR/PARTNER OF KETCHUM PUBLIC RELATIONS/ Pittsburgh, says, "A passion for excellence and results will take you a long way." For clients of the region's premier public relations firm, it's a service philosophy that helps them succeed across the country and around the world. The story

of Ketchum Public Relations (KPR) is a familiar one in Pittsburgh business: A pioneer in a fledgling profession grows into a respected leader in a dynamic industry. Now celebrating its 75th anniversary, KPR is the largest full-service public relations firm between New York and Chicago and an integral part of KPR Worldwide, a global agency that is ranked sixth largest in the world.

BEST TEAMS

The management and account staff at Ketchum provide support and leadership to clients worldwide as part of the agency's Best Teams approach to client service. Through Best Teams, Ketchum assembles the highest caliber of talent and experience available to serve the particular needs of clients around the world. Thirteen of KPR Worldwide's 15 largest accounts are global and are served by multiple Ketchum offices.

KPR's Pittsburgh office is a significant player in many of the

Best Teams, both contributing talent and drawing regularly upon the capabilities of offices in New York, San Francisco, Toronto, Mexico City, London, Paris, Milan, Munich, Tokyo, Sydney, and Hong Kong. In this respect, KPR/Pittsburgh provides a gateway to the world for Western Pennsylvania businesses seeking the best available communications services and counsel.

Known for its depth of talent, KPR's special practice fields are led by some of the most experienced and creative minds in the industry. Mike Kelly, associate director and senior vice president, leads the labor relations and workplace communications practice. Senior Vice President Kelley Murray Skoloda heads the consumer lifestyles marketing team, and Jerry Thompson, senior vice president and associate direc-

Show Me the Future was the theme of a virtual reality event planned by Ketchum to help Nationwide Insurance celebrate its newest investment product—America's FUTURE Annuity®. The event featured a multimedia presentation about the new product that was displayed on two video walls and more than 50 screens at XS New York, the nation's premier virtual reality playground (top).

Ketchum Public Relations celebrates 75 years of calling Pittsburgh home with advertising slated for 1998. The ads will highlight some of Ketchum's benchmark client achievements and strong partnerships with Pittsburgh's business community (bottom).

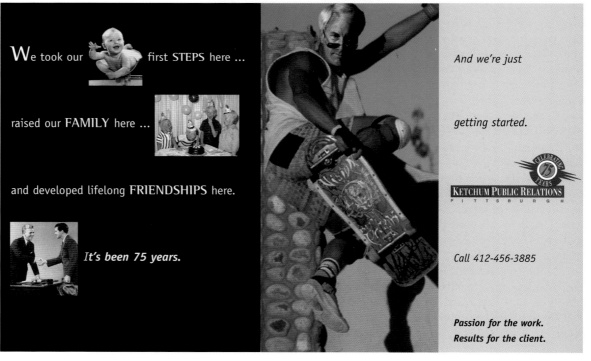

We took our first STEPS here ...

raised our FAMILY here ...

and developed lifelong FRIENDSHIPS here.

It's been 75 years.

And we're just

getting started.

CELEBRATING 75 YEARS
KETCHUM PUBLIC RELATIONS
PITTSBURGH

Call 412-456-3885

Passion for the work.
Results for the client.

tor, leads KPR's crisis communications, and business-to-business and corporate practice. The agency's health care and public affairs practices are growing as well.

A PR Pioneer

The ultimate Best Team is Ketchum Public Relations and its sister companies in the Omnicom Group, Inc., into which Ketchum merged in 1996. Omnicom is the largest communications holding company in the world, and Ketchum has become a key player in a powerful global network of advertising, marketing, public relations, and promotional firms. With Omnicom, Ketchum has access to greater resources and communications expertise than at any other time in its history.

Ketchum Public Relations was founded in 1923 as the vision of two brothers: George and Carlton Ketchum. The agency, known for much of its history as Ketchum MacLeod & Grove, had humble beginnings as what George called a "minnow among minnows" in Pittsburgh's—and America's—nascent communications industry.

Global Leadership

For any agency, true success is indicated by the quality of its clients. KPR's client roster includes a variety of regional and national blue-chip clients, such as H.J. Heinz Company, PPG Industries, General Nutrition Centers, Ormet, Mine Safety Appliances, the American Iron and Steel Institute, SmithKline

Beecham Consumer Healthcare, MCI, Nationwide Insurance, Del Monte, FORE Systems, Harris Semiconductor, Mylan Laboratories, Quaker State Corporation, and the Commonwealth of Pennsylvania. Many of these clients have long relationships with Ketchum.

Ketchum Public Relations Worldwide is now headquartered in New York and operates eight U.S. offices, with other affiliations and equity positions throughout the world. Its client roster includes numerous leading brands, such as FedEx, Visa, Miller Brewing, Delta Air Lines, the Aspirin Foundation, DuPont, Wendy's International, Pharmacia & Upjohn, Genentech, and Bristol-Myers.

Ketchum's commitment to client service has been recognized throughout the industry. In 1995, Ketchum Public Relations Worldwide was named Agency of the Year for the second time in five

years by *Inside PR*, a leading trade journal. In recent years, Ketchum Public Relations Worldwide has won more Silver Anvils—the most coveted award in the public relations profession—than any other agency. Ketchumites have also won numerous local and national Public Relations Society of America awards.

As part of this success, KPR is currently enjoying record-breaking performance. Since 1996, its annual billings have grown by 30 percent. The future continues to hold promise, as the agency grows in dynamic markets for communications services, including technology and health care. Ketchum Public Relations/Pittsburgh stands on the threshold of a new century, and Werner is confident in its prospects for growth and its ability to help the region's businesses reach out to the opportunities of the global marketplace. "At Ketchum PR, we have a passion for serving our clients, and our own people," he says.

Ketchum selected *Bon Appétit* columnist and cookbook author Melanie Barnhart (on right) to serve as spokesperson for the Steel Packaging Council. Barnhart joined Ketchum at the Food Marketing Institute Show in Chicago to spread the word that "What's in a Can Will Surprise You." Melissa Murphy (on left) and Jennifer Wylie, KPR account supervisors, also participated in the event (top left).

Supermodel Carol Alt (top right) and Ivana Trump (bottom right) joined Ketchum and the Steel Packaging Council for Fashionable Foods, a celebration of National Canned Food Month held at New York's Fashion Cafe.

Ketchum spotlighted Heinz's 50 years on the New York Stock Exchange with the help of Charlie the Tuna. Pictured from left are Jack Kennedy, KPR vice president; Charlie the Tuna; an NYSE representative; and Michael Mullen, KPR senior account executive (bottom left).

WITH A SIGNIFICANT PRESENCE IN NORTH AMERICA FOR more than 75 years, the name WESCO Distribution, Inc. is a familiar one. Today, the privately held electrical and industrial distribution company, headquartered in Pittsburgh, operates more than

320 full-service branches throughout North America, with more than 4,500 customer-focused employees responsible for generating and supporting annual product sales exceeding $2.6 billion. In all, WESCO distributes more than 130,000 different products from more than 5,000 manufacturers.

WESCO's product diversity is well illustrated by Roy Haley, WESCO's chief executive officer, who states, "Follow the wire. We handle everything from the power plant to the lamp inside the building." The major markets served by WESCO include industrial, construction, utility, manufactured structures, commercial, institutional, and governmental.

THEN AND NOW

WESCO was formed by Westinghouse Electric Corp. in 1922 to sell and distribute Westinghouse-manufactured products. Over the years, Westinghouse divested many of its industrial divisions, and in 1994, sold WESCO to the New York investment company Clayton, Dubilier & Rice.

Since 1994, the now-independent WESCO has added more than 70 new branches and completed more than a dozen strategic acquisitions of regional and industry-specific distribution companies, with Westinghouse-manufactured products now accounting for less than 2 percent of WESCO's sales. In fact, the only substantial remaining link to Westinghouse is the WESCO name, which once stood for Westinghouse Electric Supply Co. Today, WESCO sells products manufactured by such top-name suppliers as Asea Brown Boveri, Cutler-Hammer, Cooper Industries, and Hoffman Engineering. Customers include Ford Motor Company, USX, IBM, and Chevron.

CUSTOMER SERVICE

A key to WESCO's success during the 1990s has been its ability to help its customers operate with the lowest possible cost. Often, that means working closely with a client to unite all buying activities within a company as one process. For instance, WESCO client Foxboro Co., a Massachusetts-based maker of automated industrial control equipment, pooled its diverse commodity purchases across three divisions into one integrated supply system with WESCO. As a result, Foxboro realized overall cost sav-

Clockwise from top:
The order fulfillment desk at one of WESCO's five distribution centers utilizes the company's extensive computerized inventory tracking system.

This 250,000-square-foot distribution center maintains an inventory of more than 100,000 products to serve WESCO's customers and branches throughout the region.

WESCO maintains customer counter areas at its 320-plus branch operations located throughout North America.

VISUAL PERCEPTIONS, INC.

ings of 32 percent by streamlining the procurement process related to purchasing maintenance, repair, and operations supplies. Consequently, freight charges were reduced and productivity increased as employees spent less time on purchasing and more time on maintenance and repair.

On WESCO's end, the company worked with many of its existing suppliers, but also established relationships with some suppliers with whom Foxboro had an existing relationship. The difference was that the products from those suppliers now come through WESCO, which purchases from these suppliers at lower cost to Foxboro and with better service levels. Two WESCO account executives work on-site at Foxboro, using WESCO's computer system to send orders to the WESCO branch in Boston, where a "Foxboro war room" has dedicated phone, fax, and computer modem lines. WESCO delivers to Foxboro twice a day.

ORGANIZED FOR SUCCESS

The WESCO of today has a corporate environment in which management and employees are focused on the same set of growth objectives. To this end, every member of the WESCO team shares in the success of the business. That translates into better service for WESCO customers. Explains Haley: "We expect the branch managers to take responsibility, to be the frontline person, making decisions, keeping the operations going, and making sure customers are satisfied."

Each of WESCO's branch managers is a business manager and an entrepreneur, empowered through profit and loss responsibility to make decisions and commit resources that best serve the company's customers. For multilocation accounts, WESCO encourages creative and flexible thinking at the branch level, believing it key to customizing service relationships that meet the unique needs of each individual customer location. Equity in the company is distributed among a group of managers; staff, meanwhile, receives performance pay based upon the company's profitability and growth.

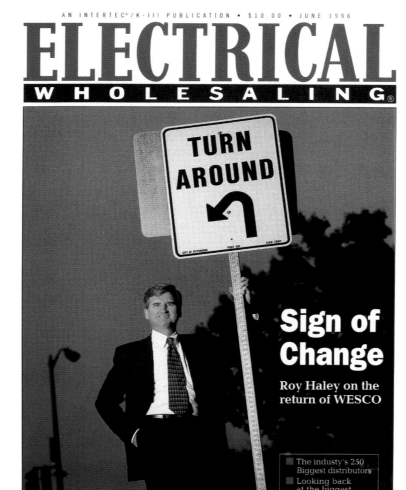

AN INTERTEC®/K-III PUBLICATION • $10.00 • JUNE 1996

ELECTRICAL
WHOLESALING®

TURN AROUND

Sign of Change

Roy Haley on the return of WESCO

■ The industy's 250 Biggest distributors
■ Looking back at the biggest

The June 1996 issue of *Electrical Wholesaling* magazine, a leading trade publication, featured WESCO Distribution, Inc. President and CEO Roy Haley.

THE STRATEGY PAYS OFF

Prior to being spun off from Westinghouse, the company's annual sales had fallen from about $1.8 billion in 1990 to less than $1.6 billion three years later. In fact, WESCO posted a $10 million loss in 1993, the year before the acquisition. This quickly changed to an $11 million profit for the first six months of 1994. Sales jumped to $1.87 billion by the end of 1995, and eclipsed $2.6 billion two years later. WESCO expects annual sales to surpass $4 billion within the next few years. And while revenues grow, expenses are declining. For instance, the sales growth has enabled WESCO to substantially reduce its bank debt, reducing annual interest payments by millions of dollars.

WESCO has also acquired a dozen small, strategic distribution companies and was ranked as the 54th-largest privately held company in the nation by *Forbes* magazine for 1996, rising from the 83rd largest in 1995. Most of the early progress was accomplished by simply returning WESCO to the core strategies followed during its best years as a Westinghouse subsidiary.

THE FUTURE

Many of WESCO's customers have enjoyed long-standing relationships with the company, and those relationships continue to grow and evolve. At many client sites, WESCO is the sole supplier for a broad range of electrical, safety, data communications, and industrial automation products. WESCO has proved that it is an organization that can see beyond the traditional methods of supply, and is a market leader with a demonstrated ability to innovate.

WESCO's headquarters is located at Station Square, and it has branches in New Brighton, Murrysville, and Lawrenceville, along with a distribution center in Warrendale. Firmly rooted in the Pittsburgh area, WESCO will remain a mainstay of the region, with many of its customers situated around the world.

WHEN WORKERS RAZED THE FORMER TERMINAL AT Pittsburgh International Airport during the summer of 1997, the pile of rubble looked nothing like a new car, a soda can, a refrigerator, or a bridge beam. But that's exactly where most of the debris from the

old terminal is ending up, thanks in part to Tube City, Inc., a privately held scrap processor and broker that has been serving the scrap requirements of the nation's steel and foundry industries for nearly 75 years.

"This is recycling at its best," says native Pittsburgher I Michael Coslov, who is chairman and chief executive officer of Tube City. "The material being generated at the airport terminal site is being processed in Pittsburgh and is very likely being melted and made into steel right here in the Pittsburgh metropolitan area. Steelmakers use old steel to make new steel. It's entirely possible that the steel beams that held up the old airport concourses could be recycled and end up in the new car you buy."

Tube City's core business is scrap management and steel mill services. The company's historic scrap business, which remains an integral part of its overall services today, involves purchasing obsolete steel, iron, and nonferrous metals from scrap dealers and industrial customers. Then, the scrap metal is prepared to conform with customers' specifications—usually defined by physical size and weight—and is shipped to the customer for remelting.

"Scrap management has evolved into a dynamic, cost-effective material control system," Coslov says. "By our actions, we have earned a place of prominence in the steel industry."

FULFILLING A VISION

Tube City was founded in 1925 by David Coslov, a young Lithuanian immigrant who first processed scrap iron and steel in McKeesport, just south of Pittsburgh along the Monongahela River. At that time, McKeesport was home to National Tube, the world's largest tube and pipe mill. McKeesport was thus nicknamed the Tube City, and Coslov named his company accordingly.

Current CEO Michael Coslov, David's grandson, has been with the company in a variety of positions since 1965. His modern-day vision for the company is to position it as a full-service company for the steel industry. In pursuit of that vision, Coslov has negotiated strategic alliances, such as the one with Krystal Bond, Inc. of Toronto. The resulting venture, known as SteelBond International, taps the expertise of both companies in recycling nonhazardous waste at large, integrated steel mills and minimills. For instance, SteelBond recycles a significant portion of the by-product waste generated at the Weirton Steel plant.

In 1995, a Tube City division was created that processes slag (another by-product of steel production) and recovers metal on-site at steel mills. Called Olympic Mill Services, it removes slag from the metal shop, cools it, and processes it. Once the slag is crushed and magnetically separated, the steel scrap is recovered and delivered back to the steel mill or sold into

Tube City, Inc. is a privately held scrap processor and broker that has been serving the scrap requirements of the nation's steel and foundry industries for nearly 75 years.

Current CEO Michael Coslov's modern-day vision for Tube City is to position it as a full-service company for the steel industry.

the scrap market. The nonmetallic slag, meanwhile, is sold commercially on the local construction and aggregate markets.

Tube City's operations in Pittsburgh, Philadelphia, Chicago, and Birmingham, Alabama, ship in excess of 250,000 tons of scrap each month. In order to achieve this high level of performance, the company must have the most modern equipment available. Says Coslov, "Whether the customers' needs call for baling, shearing, burning, breaking, or shredding, they can always be sure the proper equipment will be used to prepare the material effectively and efficiently."

PROTECTING THE ENVIRONMENT

Long before the groundswell of public support for resource conservation in the 1980s, Tube City was protecting the environment by recycling more than 4 million tons of scrap metal annually. Tube City operates recycling centers

that collect cans from the public, and, in partnership with major mills, supplies bundles of steel cans for remelting. The benefits for the environment include diverting materials from landfills, preserving natural resources for future generations, and cutting energy consumption required to manufacture new steel products.

"Each of our processing facilities has been designed to comply with environmental regulations that protect air, water, and soil quality," Coslov says. "We are constantly upgrading active and passive pollution control devices to ensure environmental protection. At the same time, all operating employees are trained in work practices that promote environmental awareness and conservation."

THE FUTURE

Tube City is planning for its future by implementing an award-winning quality assurance program and procedures to achieve regis-

tration under ISO 9000 international quality standards. One of the most sophisticated in the industry, Tube City's system is based on computerized statistical process control programs, technical training, and team-based problem-solving techniques that drive a continuous improvement initiative. In addition, quality control assures buyers that the material is consistent with their specifications.

The coming years at Tube City promise more innovation, both in processing products and in servicing customers. For instance, the company is synchronizing customer data entry and material definition auditing via an integrated data-video system. The system displays data, and gives traders and managers the ability to visually review an archive of material purchased. By using new technology to better serve the needs of its customers, Tube City will continue to lead its industry well into the future.

Tube City's core business is scrap management and steel mill services (left).

Tube City's operations in Pittsburgh, Philadelphia, Chicago, and Birmingham, Alabama, ship in excess of 250,000 tons of scrap each month (right).

Says Coslov, "Whether the customers' needs call for baling, shearing, burning, breaking, or shredding, they can always be sure the proper equipment will be used to prepare the material effectively and efficiently."

DURING ITS 55 YEARS IN PITTSBURGH, ICF KAISER HAS BECOME an internationally recognized company with a strong reputation globally, and in its own backyard. The company's strength and success are largely due to the two companies that came together to form ICF Kaiser International.

Kaiser Engineers, founded by colorful industrialist Henry J. Kaiser in 1914, has developed much of the infrastructure that propelled America to superpower status through the 20th century. In addition to building the Boulder Dam and locks at the Panama Canal, Kaiser constructed shipyards on both American coasts, battleships and airplanes that fought in World War II, rapid transit systems throughout the United States, and steel mills, aluminum smelters, and chemical plants around the world.

On the other hand, ICF began its corporate life in 1969 as Inner City Fund, an environmental consulting firm based in Washington, D.C. Having acquired Kaiser Engineers in 1988, ICF Kaiser International now offers engineering and construction services from feasibility and design studies through turnkey project management, as well as environmental and infrastructure engineering.

"We're a get-your-hands-dirty operation here," says Paul DeCoursey, vice president of marketing and sales. "We focus on heavy industrial design and construction, and environmental remediation, with a lot of work inside all kinds of plants."

From the Pittsburgh office, some 300 employees provide engineering and construction services for industrial projects around the globe, mainly for the iron and steel, aluminum, chemical, and heavy manufacturing industries. ICF Kaiser also manages and performs major environmental projects from Pittsburgh. All told, ICF Kaiser employs approximately 5,000 people in 70 offices worldwide.

SPECIAL EXPERTISE

If a steel mill is shut down for maintenance or modernization, it costs the plant dearly—in fact, only 10 days of that type of work requires months of planning. For those challenging situations, steelmakers have chosen ICF Kaiser to complete the project. The company's process and construction expertise and experience enable it to consistently bring outage projects in under budget and ahead of schedule.

ICF Kaiser recently completed four production outages for a major steel producer in Kentucky and Ohio. Every project was completed ahead of schedule—sometimes by as much as three days—while closing at or under budget. The company won safety awards for its performance, as well as an extended contract for additional services.

One tool that makes ICF Kaiser's projects work is the Kaiser Engineering Management System, or KEMS—a project management system that facilitates the rigorous tracking of every step of the engineering and construction process, from design to materials to cost and progress, generating performance reports along the way.

Another standout area for ICF Kaiser is its expertise in computer-aided design (CAD). The company has advanced three-dimensional CAD with years of experience and several proprietary methods, making virtual testing and analysis of intricate projects

ICF Kaiser is the turnkey contractor for the new Nova Hut hot strip mini-mill in Ostrava, Czech Republic.

a reality for clients. Automatic generation of material lists and piping isometrics is also available through this technology.

Protecting and restoring the environment is another priority at ICF Kaiser, which is why PPG chose ICF Kaiser for reclamation of lime lakes at its Barberton plant. Using an innovative approach, PPG and ICF Kaiser managed the mixing of lime slurry with sewage sludge to create an artificial soil, seeded it, and converted the area from a blight to a nature reserve. ICF Kaiser provided the consulting, engineering, project management, community relations, and ecological support. PPG has since won environmental awards for this ongoing program.

A GLOBAL COMPANY

The company's recent projects include a hot strip mini-mill for Nova Hut in Ostrava, for which ICF Kaiser is the turnkey contractor; an ammonia recovery plant for Baoshan Iron and Steel Corporation in Shanghai; and a mini strip mill for LPN Plate Mill Company in Bangkok. ICF Kaiser is also the turnkey contractor on a series of nitric acid plants throughout the southwestern United States and in Alberta. All of these projects were managed from Pittsburgh.

Locally, ICF Kaiser completed all engineering and contractor man-

agement for Herr's Island, during which it worked with the Pittsburgh Urban Renewal Authority to remediate and develop contaminated property into the mixed residential-office complex of Washington's Landing. That completed project has won many national awards for "brown field" reuse and development. ICF Kaiser has also done similar work at steel mill sites owned by U.S. Steel and LTV Steel in and around Pittsburgh. During 1997, Alcoa and ICF Kaiser became partners in a remediation subsidiary, where it will provide environmental

engineering, remediation, and construction management services at numerous Alcoa locations around the country.

"We tend to get called into very visible situations—places where real thought is required," says DeCoursey. "Some projects call for muscle—and we can provide that, too—but where we excel is when real insight, problem solving, and in-depth planning are called for. Value added on the front end of a project brings major efficiencies and savings throughout the rest of the job."

ICF Kaiser is the specialty subconsultant on the Port Authority of Allegheny County Phase I Airport Busway/Wabash HOV project. Shown here is the south portal building of the Berry Street Tunnel.

ICF Kaiser recently managed a remediation project for the Morgantown Ordnance Works in West Virginia, which included dewatering and sealing coke battery doorways.

T

HE PENNSYLVANIA STATE UNIVERSITY, A MAJOR MULTICAMPUS institution, was founded in 1855 as Pennsylvania's land-grant university. Since that time, its historic mission has remained unchanged: to improve the lives of people throughout Pennsylvania, the nation, and the world

About half of the university's approximately 80,000 undergraduate and graduate students attend the University Park campus. Located in State College, near Pennsylvania's geographic center, University Park is one of the nation's largest and most naturally beautiful campuses (left).

At Penn State McKeesport, a residential campus, the student body reflects the university's commitment to diversity and represents several countries, 16 states, and many communities throughout Pennsylvania (right).

through integrated programs in teaching, research, and public service. Today, Penn State offers more than 160 baccalaureate and 150 graduate programs at 24 locations across the state.

About half of the university's approximately 80,000 undergraduate and graduate students attend the University Park campus. Located in State College, near Pennsylvania's geographic center, University Park is one of the nation's largest and most naturally beautiful campuses.

The four Penn State campuses in Southwestern Pennsylvania—Beaver, Fayette, McKeesport, and New Kensington—are part of the university's Commonwealth College. More than 13,000 students

are enrolled in this academic unit, making it the largest in the university. The 12 campuses in the Commonwealth College offer baccalaureate and associate degrees, as well as certificate programs designed to meet students' needs.

PENN STATE BEAVER

Penn State Beaver is a 100-acre suburban campus located in Monaca, 30 miles north of Pittsburgh. The campus enrolls 850 students, 320 of whom live in two residence halls. Penn State Beaver is the only Western Pennsylvania campus to offer a two-year associate degree in hotel, restaurant, and institutional management, which prepares students for hospitality industry careers.

For 30 years, the Masquers student theater group at Penn State Beaver has introduced children's theater to thousands of preschool and elementary school students.

In 1997, the Penn State Beaver Blue Devils baseball team advanced to the World Series of the National Junior Collegiate Athletic Association.

The Brodhead Cultural Center has provided free or low-cost concerts and theatrical productions

each summer since 1977 in the J.P. Giusti Amphitheater on campus.

Adult Literacy Action of Penn State Beaver is recognized as a national resource for literacy research and education. Another outreach program, the Penn State Educational Partnership Program, was established in 1990 with the Aliquippa School District to enhance the lives of disadvantaged youths and their families by providing academic and life-skills support.

PENN STATE FAYETTE

Penn State Fayette is located on 160 acres of sprawling foothills in the Laurel Highlands of Southwestern Pennsylvania. The campus serves students in Fayette and Greene counties; parts of Somerset, Washington, and Westmoreland counties; and other in-state students, as well as those from neighboring states. Fayette campus offers the quality education of a major university with the friendliness of a small college within easy commuting distance.

Fayette campus confers four baccalaureate degrees, including administration of justice; nursing; letters, arts, and sciences; and gen-

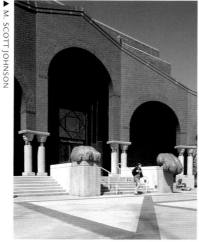

Clockwise from top left: Penn State New Kensington is located on a 75-acre site in Westmoreland County. The modern campus complex is in the heart of the Alle-Kiski Valley region, within easy commuting distance of Pittsburgh.

Since 1855, the university's historic mission has remained unchanged: to improve the lives of people throughout Pennsylvania, the nation, and the world through integrated programs in teaching, research, and public service.

Penn State Fayette is located on 160 acres of sprawling foothills in the Laurel Highlands of Southwestern Pennsylvania, and offers the quality education of a major university with the friendliness of a small college within easy commuting distance.

Penn State Beaver is a 100-acre suburban campus located in Monaca, 30 miles north of Pittsburgh.

eral business. Six programs offer two-year associate degrees: architectural engineering technology; electrical engineering technology; business administration; human development and family studies; letters, arts, and sciences; and nursing. The Continuing and Distance Education (CDE) Department offers a wide array of credit, noncredit, and management development courses on and off campus. CDE established a training and certificate program for emergency medical technicians and a Weekend College to serve adult students in the community. Construction on a new Biomedical Technology Center (nursing and natural science labs) began in late 1997.

PENN STATE MCKEESPORT

Just 15 miles southeast of Pittsburgh, Penn State McKeesport is nestled between the bustling community of White Oak and McKeesport's scenic Renziehausen Park. A residential campus, Penn State McKeesport's student body reflects the university's commitment to diversity and represents several countries, 16 states, and many communities throughout Pennsylvania. Nearly 200 of the 1,000 students are enrolled in graduate studies, including master's degree and certificate programs.

Penn State McKeesport is one of six designated science and engineering centers in the university's system. State-of-the-art engineering labs and classes taught by professors with research and industry experience help to prepare students for dynamic careers. The Women in Science, Engineering, and Technology (WISET) program gives women students the opportunity to explore options in these challenging fields.

With an 8-to-1 student-to-computer ratio, the McKeesport campus is a technology leader, and is the only Western Pennsylvania campus to offer Project Vision, a collaborative learning program. Students use their own laptop computers to learn on and off campus through Internet links and multimedia programs, always working together with their teammates and faculty. The campus' honors program provides students the opportunity to broaden their programs of study through specially designed curricula.

PENN STATE NEW KENSINGTON

Penn State New Kensington is located on a 75-acre site in Upper Burrell Township. The modern campus complex is in the heart of the Alle-Kiski Valley region, within easy commuting distance of Pittsburgh. The majority of students commute to campus from Allegheny, Butler, Armstrong, Indiana, and Westmoreland counties. Penn State New Kensington tailors programs and provides special services to meet the needs of its students, many of whom are returning adults. Some programs are offered part-time in the evening, as well as full-time days on campus. Customized on-site programs are available for companies interested in providing continuing education to their employees.

The New Kensington campus offers two baccalaureate and eight associate degree programs in the fields of engineering technology, allied health, and business. To help prepare graduates to compete in an increasingly high-tech world, the campus offers innovative classes that utilize state-of-the-art computer, engineering, robotics, and biomedical technologies. The campus' newest degree program, the bachelor of science degree in electro-mechanical engineering technology, was designed in partnership with manufacturing and technology industries to produce graduates with wide-ranging technical knowledge. Penn State's program is the only one of its kind in Southwestern Pennsylvania.

FOR MORE THAN A CENTURY, THE CHUBB GROUP OF INSURANCE Companies has been a leading provider of personal and commercial insurance. Over the years, Chubb has provided insurance protection for an array of assets, including air shipments from India of rhesus monkeys for the Salk anti-

polio program, a 48-foot replica of King Kong, French châteaus, antique cars, the Broadway hit *Phantom of the Opera*, computer chips, Thoroughbred horses, toy train collections, gold mines, and paintings by van Gogh. Around the world, Chubb has earned a reputation for understanding and managing the risks that people and businesses face.

Established in 1936, the Chubb office in Pittsburgh is proud to be part of this tradition. Working through a select group of independent insurance agents and brokers, Chubb provides insurance solutions throughout the region, from mining to metalworkers, broadcasters to banks. With more than $25 billion in assets, the Chubb Group today has a global network of 110 offices in 30 countries, and ranks among the top 15 property and casualty insurers in the world.

PROVIDING SOLUTIONS FOR BUSINESSES

Chubb insures many of the Pittsburgh region's largest corporations and is highly regarded for its specialized insurance programs. No matter what size the business, Chubb makes a point of understanding how a company works and what risks it faces day to day. By looking closely, for example, at how a manufacturing plant operates, Chubb can make specific recommendations designed to minimize workplace hazards, improve safety conditions, and ultimately reduce the likelihood

of accidents or downtime—all of which help the manufacturer protect the bottom line.

In providing insurance for a company's directors and officers, Chubb studies a company's management philosophy to gain insight into the risks its executives face. "We have to be able to anticipate how corporate officers will react in a crisis, and be confident in that assessment. That's very difficult unless you get to know an organization's values, business behavior, and the way they treat their employees, customers, and vendors," explains Linda Kortlandt, a Chubb vice president and Pittsburgh branch manager.

In addition to being the insurer of choice among many larger corporations, Chubb offers specialized programs for medium-sized businesses, a significant area of growth in Pittsburgh's economy. A new product that has been particularly well received is ForeFront by Chubb. Designed to protect a company and its directors and officers, the program is the first to combine

Linda Kortlandt is a Chubb Group of Insurance Companies vice president and the branch manager of the Pittsburgh office, which was established in 1936 (top).

For more than a century, the Chubb Group has been a leading provider of personal and commercial insurance (bottom).

The Power of

four key liability coverages for privately held companies into a single policy.

Chubb is also highly regarded for its industry-specific solutions. A leading provider of insurance for high-tech companies, Chubb has pioneered an array of insurance products ranging from multimedia liability to insurance for clinical trials. Similarly, Chubb is the only insurer with an underwriting group dedicated to serving the needs of financial institutions. Because of this expertise, Chubb insures some of the largest banks in Pittsburgh.

As an added benefit to all these companies, Chubb can help its customers grow within the changing world of commerce. As more and more local and regional businesses expand—whether they're working with a distributor in Seoul or importing parts from Stuttgart—they need to be able to count on a consistent level of coverage and service from anywhere they do business. With Chubb's international network, they can.

OFFERING A NEW APPROACH TO PERSONAL INSURANCE

When it comes to personal insurance, Chubb specializes in protecting individuals with substantial assets to protect. These assets may take the form of a large or architecturally distinguished home; a vacation property; a luxury car; or a collection of fine art, antiques, or jewelry. Discerning home owners and collectors, young and old, understand that insurance is an essential form of financial protection. They look to Chubb for financial strength, prompt and fair claim handling, broad coverage at a reasonable price, and excellent service.

By way of example, Chubb conducts appraisals on many of the homes it insures. Using its own staff of professionally trained appraisers, many of them knowledgeable about fine art or historic homes, Chubb relies on the appraisal to help determine the proper amount of insurance for a home. By providing this service early in the insurance relationship, both Chubb and the customer know up front what it will cost to repair or rebuild the home later if it is damaged, providing peace of mind.

REDEFINING SERVICE EXCELLENCE

In a world where many view insurance as a commodity, Chubb consistently demonstrates that there really is a difference between one insurance program and another. Often that difference lies in the level of service provided. As Kortlandt points out, "When corporate officers experience our commitment to quality and service after a home owner claim, they often tell their broker that they want the same kind of commitment for their business. It binds our relationship."

For all of its customers, Chubb's Pittsburgh team of 85 underwriters and claim and service staff set the highest standards for service. Relationships are also integral to the service equation. Because of that, Chubb is highly selective about the independent agents and brokers with whom it does business, working with those who share Chubb's service commitment. Chubb is equally selective in its choice of employees. "Lots of companies say this, but it really is our people and their strong relationships with agents and customers that have made Chubb a success in Pittsburgh," says Kortlandt. "Everyone here is really proud to be a part of this community."

JOE RENCKLY

JOE RENCKLY

Clockwise from top left:
Working through a select group of independent insurance agents and brokers, Chubb provides insurance solutions throughout the region, from mining to metalworkers, broadcasters to banks.

Chubb is highly regarded for its industry-specific solutions. A leading provider of insurance for high-tech companies, Chubb has pioneered an array of insurance products ranging from multimedia liability to insurance for clinical trials.

With more than $25 billion in assets, the Chubb Group today has a global network of 110 offices in 30 countries, and ranks among the top 15 property and casualty insurers in the world.

N DECEMBER 1996, BLUE CROSS OF WESTERN PENNSYLVANIA AND Pennsylvania Blue Shield celebrated the creation of Highmark Inc. by consolidating their operations. ■ With more than 60 years of serving the community as complementary but separate companies, the word Highmark was coined to represent Blue Cross of Western

Pennsylvania and Pennsylvania Blue Shield's continuing practice of setting standards for high-quality health care products and services.

The company conducts its health care business under the trade name of Highmark Blue Cross Blue Shield in the 29 counties of Western Pennsylvania. Elsewhere in the state, Highmark retains Pennsylvania Blue Shield as its trade name and continues to partner with freestanding Blue Cross companies.

As one of the nation's top 10 health insurers and the second-largest Blue Cross and Blue Shield company, Highmark provides coverage for more than 6.2 million Pennsylvanians. In addition to offering traditional health insurance coverage and managed care programs, Highmark also offers life and casualty insurance, and dental and vision programs.

Highmark continues to carry forward the mission the two organizations committed to 60 years ago.

FOCUSING ON THE FUTURE

In today's changing health care market, Highmark is in a sound position to help strengthen Pennsylvania's health care system. Through the integration of products and services, and the uniting of exceptional business practices, the consolidation presents excellent opportunities to stay competitive in the marketplace and achieve higher levels of service for Highmark customers. The consolidation also strengthens Highmark's support of community-based health education and wellness initiatives, reinforcing the long-standing mission to make quality health care affordable and accessible to all Pennsylvanians.

SOMETHING FOR EVERYONE

In competitive health care markets, Highmark has a very strong presence in Pennsylvania and throughout the country. Highmark continues to develop and create managed care plans that help contain health care costs and promote healthy lifestyles.

The strength of Highmark's managed care plans rests with its strong provider network of primary care physicians, specialists, and hospital and health care facilities. The company will continue to maintain a close working relationship with health care providers, promote the creation of regional health care systems, and improve customer service and benefit programs.

Highmark programs strive to deliver cost-effective, high-quality care to its members. KeystoneBlue, a health maintenance organization (HMO); SelectBlue, a point-of-service (POS) program; and PreferredBlue, a preferred provider organization (PPO), are Highmark Blue Cross Blue Shield's most popular managed care programs.

SecurityBlue, a Medicare HMO, is one of the fastest-growing programs of its kind in the nation,

Highmark Blue Cross Blue Shield's Pittsburgh headquarters includes Fifth Avenue Place in downtown Pittsburgh (left).

At Highmark, customer service is the most important job (right).

Highmark offers traditional and managed care coverage to all segments of the health insurance market, from large and small group customers to individuals of all ages.

and the largest Medicare HMO in in the region. SecurityBlue offers more extensive benefits with lower out-of-pocket expenses to seniors 65 or older.

Highmark also offers a number of supplemental programs to support its core health care business. United Concordia Companies, Inc. (UCCI) has rapidly moved from its Pennsylvania base to a national presence, and is one of the largest dental insurers in the nation. Clarity Vision Inc. offers group customers a complete package of quality vision products in Pennsylvania and nationally. More than 40 retail vision stores and four optical laboratories are administered by Davis Vision and owned by Clarity Vision Inc., making it the third-largest managed vision care company in the country. Trans-General Life and Casualty Group offers a wide range of employee benefit programs on a national scale including group term life insurance and disability coverage.

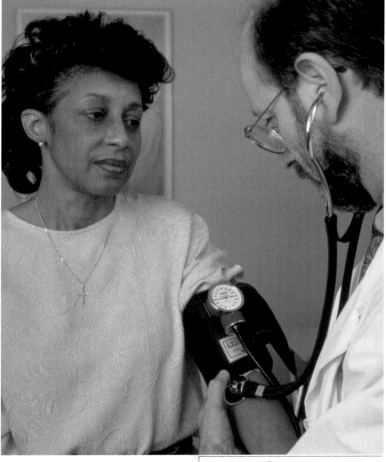

Highmark's high-quality health care services and strong provider network are valued by its customers.

BENCHMARKS

During 1997, Highmark received recognition and acclaim from several respected sources. Standard & Poor's affirmed an A+ rating for the company; AM Best affirmed an A rating; the National Committee for Quality Assurance (NCQA) gave Keystone Health Plan West accreditation; and accreditation was received by the Utilization Review Accreditation Committee. Additionally, KeystoneBlue HMO was rated number one in member satisfaction in 1997 by two independent surveys.

MAKING A DIFFERENCE

Highmark's community service mission is truly unique, and includes many programs and services. The company provides financial subsidies that enable the development and operation of programs that address the needs of the uninsured and underprivileged. Support is provided through direct corporate contributions for community-based health education and wellness programs. This process is enhanced by the many organizations that have benefited from Highmark Blue Cross Blue Shield's Matching Gifts program. Volunteers in Partnership and Project Connect are just two of the many internal programs that encourage employee volunteerism.

A 1997 study conducted by a national authority on employee benefit issues, the Employee Benefit Research Institute (EBRI), has shown that health insurance programs developed by Highmark for low-income and uninsured children and families have significantly contributed to Pennsylvania's fifth-place ranking among states with the lowest uninsured rate.

ENSURING A HEALTHY FUTURE

Living without adequate health insurance can be devastating, especially when children are involved. Nevertheless, in America, close to 10 million children are without health insurance.

In 1985, Blue Cross of Western Pennsylvania and Pennsylvania Blue Shield created the nation's first private-sector children's health care initiative—the Caring Program for Children. The program provides free (or low-cost) health care coverage to children falling through the cracks in the health care system because their families earn too much to qualify for medical assistance, but not enough to afford private insurance. More than 50,000 children have been enrolled in the program, which has become a model public/private partnership. Replicated in more than 20 states, the Caring Program for Children is funded by charitable contributions from the community. Highmark contributes matching funds and the program's administrative costs.

Modeled after the successful Caring Program for Children, the Children's Health Insurance Program of Pennsylvania (CHIP) was introduced in 1993, and offers expanded benefits that include dental care and hospitalization. Operating as BlueCHIP in the 29 counties of Western Pennsylvania, the program has benefited more than 100,000 children since its inception. BlueCHIP is funded by the state and administered by the Western Pennsylvania Caring Foundation.

HEALING HEARTS

Dedicated to children who are grieving the loss of a loved one, the Center for Grieving Children was established by Highmark Blue Cross Blue Shield in 1995. As a program of the Western Pennsylvania Caring Foundation, the center recognizes the need for children

The Caring Place provides a warm atmosphere, compassion, and support for grieving children and their families.

For communities where HealthPLACE is not accessible or available, the Health Education Center has hit the road with HealthPLACE on the Move.

to be able to express their feelings about the death of a loved one and begin the healing process. In December 1997, The Caring Place: A Center for Grieving Children opened. Staffed with volunteers and professionals trained in psychology, social work, and child development, the new Pittsburgh facility is designed to meet the unique needs of grieving families. The center's rooms and activities are designed to fit the needs and developmental stages of all children. Highmark has pledged a $500,000 grant to match contributions made by community organizations and individuals.

HELPING HANDS

SecurityBlue members in Western Pennsylvania who need assistance with daily routines can receive services from the Pals Program. In addition to providing health care services and benefits, SecurityBlue recruits and trains volunteers to provide nonmedical services, such as meal preparation and light housekeeping—a small effort toward making everyday living a little easier.

THE ROAD TO HEALTHY LIFESTYLES

A pioneer in health education and health promotion, the Health Education Center (HEC), a Highmark Blue Cross Blue Shield affiliate, established HealthPLACE in 1988.

HealthPLACE continues to serve the community with highly innovative wellness programs and healthy lifestyle classes, seminars, disease prevention screenings, and immunizations. In 1997, HealthPLACE's preventive health care programs were made available to the public. Previously available only to Highmark's managed care members, the programs are now accessible to Western Pennsylvania residents for a nominal fee.

HealthPLACE on the Move, HEC's specially equipped bus, travels throughout the state, providing the same healthy lifestyle classes, immunizations, and screening services as those offered at the HealthPLACE centers. HealthPLACE on the Move has traveled more than 60,000 miles and provided more

The Highmark Web site provides a wide range of up-to-date health care information and services.

than 250,000 services throughout the state.

In 1997, Highmark became the first health insurer in the United States to provide the Dr. Dean Ornish Program for Reversing Heart Disease. This innovative program is designed to supplement conventional treatments for heart disease and reduce the need for bypass surgery or angioplasty. The program is free to qualified members of Highmark Blue Cross Blue Shield's health insurance plans and is administered by HealthPLACE.

ALWAYS AT YOUR SERVICE

Highmark's Primary Care Centers in Western Pennsylvania are just what the patient ordered.

Designed to serve the entire community, the Primary Care Centers accept most major health insurance and provide patient-focused care with a staff of private-practice physicians and other health care professionals. Services include on-site specialists, laboratory, imaging, and pharmacy services. HealthPLACE libraries and classes are offered during patient-friendly

hours to meet people's real-life schedules and needs.

Access Health has been providing the Personal Health Advisor service to members since 1994. Members belonging to plans that subscribe to the service can call a toll-free number and speak with a specially trained, registered nurse for health care advice, home care measurements, and when necessary, referrals to the appropriate physician.

Highmark is committed to serving its members. A dedicated, comprehensive member service commitment that includes toll-free telephone service, regional member service representatives, interactive touch-screen service kiosks, and an exciting Internet Web site gives members information on their terms, at times and places convenient to them.

www.highmark.com
The Highmark Web site was inaugurated in 1996. It covers all Highmark core business and subsidiary companies, and provides a broad range of information to customers, health care professionals, and the public.

N 1931, FIVE PITTSBURGH FAMILIES WHO HAD BEEN IN THE GROCERY business in various capacities formed a partnership. Their respect for one another firmly cemented this partnership and established Giant Eagle's roots in Pittsburgh. From that time on, the men and women of Giant Eagle have taken risks, developed innovative methods to drive a

successful business, and helped the Pittsburgh communities in which they live and work.

Today, Giant Eagle, Inc. has grown from a small, neighborhood establishment to the region's leading supermarket retailer. The company has 61 corporate stores and 84 independent stores throughout Western Pennsylvania, Ohio, and West Virginia markets. Giant Eagle's mission is to offer the finest and most innovative products, departments, and services to make every customer's shopping experience rewarding.

And Giant Eagle doesn't stop there. The company recently acquired Cleveland-based Riser Foods Inc., which has wholesale and retail operations with 35 Stop N Shop corporate stores and 18 Stop N Shop independent stores. This acquisition provides Giant Eagle with an opportunity to expand its world-class service and one-stop shopping philosophy into another important market.

SUCCESS THROUGH THE YEARS
A look at the history of Giant Eagle reveals many reasons for its growth and success, and among them are determination and hard work. But the main ingredient for Giant

Eagle's success has always been, and will continue to be, its customers. Since 1932, Giant Eagle stores have been patronized by a loyal and supportive group of community members. These loyal customers are at the heart of Giant Eagle's success, and continue to make the company a leader in the community.

Giant Eagle's commitment to the people of Pittsburgh and the general community is its way of showing appreciation for the customers' patronage and loyalty through the years. The company

believes that by being an active, responsible member of each community it serves, it can help enrich the lives of customers and help ensure that they have every opportunity to achieve their goals and dreams.

Apples for the Students, United Way, Salvation Army Roundup for the Hungry, Race for the Cure, and Children's Hospital of Pittsburgh are just a few of the many community causes and events Giant Eagle is proud to support or sponsor. Since the late 1980s, Apples for the Students has enabled Giant Eagle to contribute more than $14 million in educational tools to area schools. Giant Eagle's employees take great pride in community involvement, and actively and willingly participate in these events at every level.

Giant Eagle's motto, It Takes A Giant To Make Life Simple, reflects the level of service each store and its employees strive to deliver. Through hard work and creativity, the company provides the products and services neighbors need, and continues to make the communities served better places to live and work. Giant Eagle is committed to growth and excellence . . . and to Pittsburgh.

Giant Eagle, Inc.'s mission is to offer the finest and most innovative products, departments, and services to make every customer's shopping experience rewarding.

Giant Eagle has grown from a small, neighborhood establishment to the region's leading supermarket retailer. The company has 61 corporate stores and 84 independent stores throughout Western Pennsylvania, Ohio, and West Virginia markets.

Michael Baker Corporation **1940**

Calgon Carbon Corporation **1942**

Schiffman Jewelers, Inc. **1942**

Meyer, Unkovic & Scott LLP **1943**

Three Rivers Aluminum Company (TRACO) **1943**

Kirkpatrick & Lockhart LLP **1946**

KDKA-TV2 **1948**

Oberg Industries **1948**

Ryan Homes **1948**

Eat'n Park **1949**

General Motors Metal Fabricating Division—

Pittsburgh Metal Center **1950**

The Soffer Organization **1950**

Central Blood Bank **1951**

The Galbreath Company **1952**

Bayer Corporation **1954**

Federated Investors **1955**

MARC **1955**

Allegheny County Sanitary Authority (ALCOSAN) **1959**

Dietrich Industries **1959**

Le Mont **1960**

Interstate Hotels **1961**

Prudential Preferred Realty **1962**

La Roche College **1963**

Management Science Associates, Inc. **1963**

ABB Extrel **1964**

Port Authority of Allegheny County **1964**

Frank B. Fuhrer Holdings, Inc. **1966**

Pittsburgh Penguins **1967**

Compunetics, Inc. **1968**

R. Davenport & Associates **1968**

Computerm Corporation **1969**

Microbac Laboratories, Inc. **1969**

Ampco-Pittsburgh Corporation **1970**

ANSYS, Inc. **1970**

FROM TOUCHDOWN AT PITTSBURGH INTERNATIONAL AIRPORT TO their destination in the Golden Triangle, travelers visiting Pittsburgh encounter some of Michael Baker Corporation's best work. From the new airport to many of the region's highways, bridges, and other infrastructure, Baker has helped

shape Pittsburgh's skyline. In the process, Baker has built a reputation as a leading engineering and construction firm in the United States and internationally.

Michael Baker Jr., the company's energetic founder, started the firm in 1940. By the 1950s, Baker was recognized as one of the country's top transportation design firms. In the 1980s, Baker became an employee-owned company and embarked on an aggressive plan for growth and diversification. During this period, Baker entered the construction and operations and maintenance fields. Baker now provides design-build-operate services for clients worldwide.

In 1994, Charles I. "Skip" Homan became Baker's president and chief executive officer. Homan reorganized the company into five market-focused business units: buildings, civil, energy, environmental, and transportation. The company has invested heavily in its people, processes, and systems, including project manager training, information technology, continuous improvement, and value management. Not coincidentally,

since 1994, Baker's financial results have climbed dramatically.

CORE COMPETENCIES, NEW DIRECTIONS

Transportation engineering has been a cornerstone of the company since its earliest days. Baker is consistently ranked in the top 20 design firms nationally and has plans in place to grow even more.

Baker's Buildings unit also offers design and construction capabilities. In 1990, Baker purchased Mellon Stuart Construction Co. and has since paired it with Baker and Associates, the company's architectural design group, to form Baker Buildings.

Baker Civil provides a broad range of services to a multitude of market segments including telecommunications, pipelines, government agencies, and a host of other private and public sector clients. Baker's civil skills include surveying and mapping, geographic information systems (GIS), military base operations, water and wastewater systems, and many more.

Baker Energy performs operations and training services for clients worldwide. Its primary offices are

in Houston and London. Baker Energy provides operations and technical services to large and small oil and gas producers.

Baker Environmental provides public and private sector clients with environmental investigation and remediation services. This unit provides environmental cleanup solutions to the U.S. Navy, other governmental agencies, and a number of Fortune 500 companies.

The expertise of each of Baker's divisions is facilitated by a tradition of utilizing cutting-edge technology. In the 1950s, Baker was one of the first engineering firms to purchase a computer strictly for design operations. Today, Baker continues to be a leader in the application of advanced technology. Baker is using GIS, for example, to save its clients both time and money in the management of their information systems.

Baker's expertise and role in the markets it serves continues to grow. The company and its people have been instrumental in shaping Pittsburgh's past, and are positioned and ready to play an active role in the renaissance of the city into the next century and beyond.

From the new airport to RPS' headquarters to many of the region's highways, bridges, and other infrastructure, Michael Baker Corporation has helped shape Pittsburgh's skyline.

TERRY CLARK

WILLIAM J. BOYD

WHEN PEOPLE THINK OF CALGON CARBON CORPORATION, chances are they think of activated carbon. That's because, since 1942, the company has led the world in the manufacture and supply of granular coal-based activated carbon. A product that removes

unwanted substances from gases and liquids, activated carbon does everything from purifying water to eliminating offensive odors, and from cleaning up environmental spills to protecting soldiers from chemical warfare agents. Activated carbon is used to remove the caffeine from coffee and whiten the sugar it is sweetened with, and is even used in the manufacture of medicines.

But today, Calgon Carbon's capabilities extend beyond activated carbon. The company's scientists and engineers are making advances in new technologies and products that safeguard the environment, keep companies competitive, and improve daily life in ways unimaginable just a few years ago. These ways include UV disinfection, a revolutionary technology that safely destroys the DNA of bacteria and viruses in municipal wastewater by exposing it to ultraviolet light. Contaminants are eliminated on-site, without any secondary handling liabilities or disposal concerns.

Calgon Carbon is also a leader in ion exchange, a cutting-edge technology that treats liquids and gases by replacing harmful ions with innocuous ones. Among other applications, Calgon Carbon's continuous ion exchange systems excel at purifying drinking water by removing nitrates—contaminants believed responsible for infant deaths. Chromatography is a similar methodology employed by Calgon Carbon that attacks hazardous chemicals on a molecular level. Again, the result is safe, effective treatment without creating hazardous by-products.

Another Calgon Carbon innovation is Centaur® catalytic carbon. Centaur is specially developed through a patented process to accelerate reaction rates—without adding chemicals—for odor control, chloramine removal from drinking water, phosphine abatement, and

other applications. Centaur can even be used to purify water for blood dialysis treatment, reducing the risks of hemolysis and anemia for patients.

Calgon Carbon literally leads the world—in more ways than consumers might think. It is the only company with a granular activated carbon production capacity of more than 85,000 metric tons. Headquartered in Pittsburgh, Calgon Carbon currently serves customers in 63 countries on six continents. It produces more than 40 specialized types and sizes of activated carbon—including carbon in cloth form—for more than 700 applications. Calgon Carbon is also the largest reactivation services supplier. It

is the only company in the world to have installed more than 250 advanced oxidation systems. Calgon Carbon supports the largest, most experienced technical and R&D staff in the carbon industry. Its scientists and engineers hold 70 patents in the United States and 98 patents from other countries.

Calgon Carbon's vision is to be the world's leading producer, supplier, and designer of innovative technologies, value-added products, and services specifically designed for the purification, separation, and concentration of liquids and gases. With its focus on activated carbon and related technologies, the company is on its way to achieving that goal.

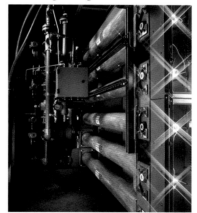

Clockwise from top left: Calgon Carbon's continuous ion exchange systems purify drinking water by removing nitrates—contaminants believed to cause infant deaths in agricultural communities.

Using the power of ultraviolet light, Calgon Carbon systems destroy the DNA of bacteria and viruses in municipal drinking water.

Since 1942, Calgon Carbon Corporation has led the world in the manufacture and supply of granular coal-based activated carbon.

WHEN IRVING SCHIFFMAN JEWELERS, INC. BEGAN IN the early 1940s, founder Irving Schiffman would neatly pack jewels into his leather carrying case and head out to meet with the power brokers and the captains of industry of his day. Crowded around a

lunch table, the group's conversation might bounce from business strategies to politics. Eventually, Schiffman would pull out a ring or bracelet, and the others would offer their compliments. Before the group dispersed, someone inevitably asked the question: "How much for that piece of jewelry?"

Today, the scenario doesn't play out so dramatically, but one thing has remained the same: jewelry connoisseurs from the mid-Atlantic states still turn to Schiffman Jewelers for top pieces of jewelry, whether it be gold or precious stones. Schiffman, who died in 1990, left the business to his two sons-in-law, Judah Samet and Ronald Barasch, who continue to operate the business from the third floor of the Clark Building in the heart of Pittsburgh's central business district. There, hidden from the street below, Samet, Barasch, and a staff of about eight others offer the finest gold and gems around.

"When you deal with the public from the third floor of a building for 55 years, you are doing something right," says Samet. "You can't fool the public. We have third-generation customers. Their grandparents purchased jewelry from us, then their parents purchased jewelry from us. Now, they are buying jewelry from us. That's three generations of satisfied customers. We know that if they buy from us once, they will buy from us again in the future."

TOP QUALITY, TOP SERVICE
In this age, jewelry admirers see gold and diamonds almost everywhere they turn, from department store chains to suburban shopping malls to the discount chain stores. But Schiffman sets itself apart by only offering top-quality products, and has maintained a steady clientele even during downturns in Pittsburgh's economy. Schiffman Jewelers deals only with New York firms when buying from wholesalers and gem cutters, some of whom have been supplying the firm for more than 40 years. New York is a global hub for diamond dealers, and many cutters there deal directly with the famous DeBeers cartel. Samet and Barasch have continued to upgrade their product lines, to the point where the firm is one of the few in the area to carry the biggest designer names in jewelry.

"Our reputation is really not the commercial, retail line of jewelry," Samet says. "About 85 percent of the jewelry sold today is commercial quality. Our customers want top quality. That's what we give

Schiffman Jewelers, Inc. was founded by Irving Schiffman in 1942, and is operated today by Ronald Barasch (left) and Judah Samet (right).

For more than half a century, Schiffman Jewelers has provided its customers with top pieces of jewelry, whether it be gold or precious stones.

The Power of

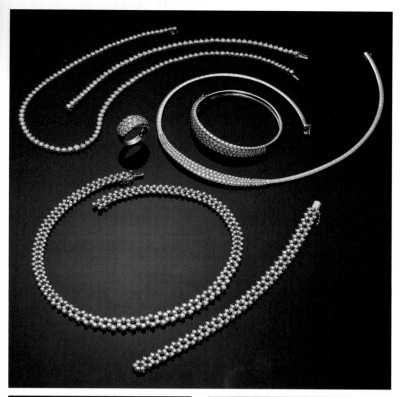

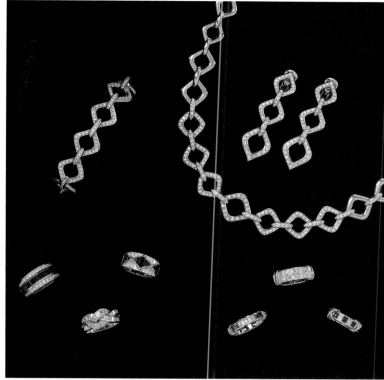

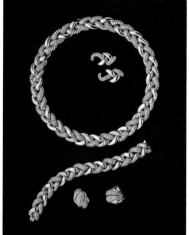

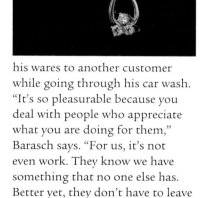

Samet and Barasch have continued to upgrade their product lines, and the firm carries the biggest designer names in jewelry.

them. We sell a lot of certificate diamonds and a lot of multicarat, investment diamonds. We still stick to quality."

Customers who demand top quality also demand top service, and Schiffman delivers. Each customer is paired with a salesperson, which allows the salesperson to develop a sense for the customer's personal taste. The salesperson is then able to suggest certain pieces or even call the customer when a shipment arrives that is consistent with that particular customer's needs.

"A relationship is forged with customers," Samet says. "When they call here, they don't just call the jewelry store. Instead, they are calling for me, or for Ron Barasch,

or for one of the other salespeople. They get to know us. We get to know them. It's a relationship built on trust. We know what they like, and we'll provide it with a personal touch."

And this quality service extends outside of the store as well. While Samet minds the day-to-day operations of the store, Barasch still visits customers personally, bringing the jewelry directly to them old-world style. Barasch has been visiting some of his customers for 38 years. They sit down in the customer's home and privately view the latest in precious jewelry. Barasch is more than willing to accommodate his clients, huddling with one customer in his meat locker for privacy, and showing

his wares to another customer while going through his car wash. "It's so pleasurable because you deal with people who appreciate what you are doing for them," Barasch says. "For us, it's not even work. They know we have something that no one else has. Better yet, they don't have to leave their home."

What began as one man selling watches out of his suitcase has now been a successful business for more than half a century. Schiffman and the captains of industry may be gone now, but Schiffman Jewelers in the Clark Building is still the jeweler with the top-quality gold and gems, accented by the personal service for which its founder was famous.

WELL-REASONED LEGAL COUNSEL, LONG-TERM STABILITY, and a philosophy of dedicated service have been the hallmarks of Meyer, Unkovic & Scott LLP since its founding in 1943. The firm's founders, A.E. Kountz, Clarence Fry, Austin L. Staley, and William A. Meyer,

established a culture for quality, stability, and growth by nurturing young professionals and staff with individualized, highly focused training. The result is a law firm that is traditional, yet progressive; steeped in the old-school philosophy of client and community service; and supported by the cutting-edge technology required to meet the needs of its clients and the region's community in the 21st century.

From the Oliver Building in the heart of downtown Pittsburgh's central business district, the firm counsels businesses and individuals across a broad spectrum of legal

matters, ranging from business law to real estate, and from litigation and employment law to estate and business succession planning.

FOSTERING PITTSBURGH'S ENTREPRENEURIAL SPIRIT
Meyer, Unkovic & Scott's business lawyers provide essential support to the entrepreneurial spirit of Pittsburgh's closely held and family-owned businesses. The firm helps its clients structure and restructure their regional businesses to meet the challenges of a highly competitive, and increasingly international, economy.

The result is that many of the firm's small and middle-market clients have thrived, and today play an increasingly important role regionally, nationally, and internationally.

HELPING PITTSBURGH GROW
The Pittsburgh community is eager to share in the growth and development enjoyed by other regions of the country. For decades, Meyer, Unkovic & Scott's real estate lawyers have played a prominent role in structuring and implementing the development and financing of business, commercial, and planned residential

Meyer Unkovic & Scott LLP counsels businesses and individuals across a broad spectrum of legal matters, including business law, real estate, litigation, employment law, and estate and business succession planning. The firm's offices are located in the Oliver Building in the heart of downtown Pittsburgh's central business district. (Painting by James P. Nelson)

properties in downtown Pittsburgh and throughout the entire region. Now, more than ever, their positive contribution can be seen in many of the Pittsburgh region's most exciting real estate development projects. The firm's lawyers share the creativity, energy, and thoroughness required to ensure successful real estate financing and development.

DISPUTE RESOLUTION

The firm's litigation attorneys have achieved widespread recognition throughout the business and legal communities, and bring to the litigation process a pragmatic and principled approach, recognizing that litigation's purpose is to resolve and conclude disputes, as quickly and as cost effectively as possible. From the very beginning, they establish business objectives for the litigation and chart a course of action for success. Throughout the legal process, litigation is a joint venture, requiring mutual communication and involvement between the firm's litigation attorneys and its clients.

A CHANGING LABOR ENVIRONMENT

Although organized labor's role in the workplace has diminished in recent years, the field of employment law continues to grow. The media is filled with countless stories of wrongful discharge or discrimination due to race, age, gender, or disability. The attorneys at Meyer, Unkovic & Scott assist employers in maintaining sound employee relations while minimizing confrontation. The firm counsels employers on a variety of issues, from establishing personnel policies for hiring, drug and alcohol testing, promotions, and discipline to employee benefits. Meyer, Unkovic & Scott believes that if its clients enjoy good, effective relations with their employees, they can be more competitive and successful.

THE SPIRIT OF PITTSBURGH'S FUTURE

Although a few Fortune 500 companies have departed from Pittsburgh, the region's many closely held and family-owned businesses continue to provide much-needed stability and growth. Meyer, Unkovic & Scott's lawyers are committed to helping closely held and family-owned businesses make the leap from this generation to the next. Big businesses cannot do it all. The firm's lawyers are doing their best to ensure that the region's small and midsize businesses continue to grow and prosper through timely and thoughtful business, succession, and estate planning.

SHARING AND GIVING

Meyer, Unkovic & Scott's founders contributed generously to the Pittsburgh community's civic and charitable endeavors. Now, with more than 50 years of dedicated service to the Pittsburgh community, today's professionals and staff at Meyer, Unkovic & Scott continue that rich tradition, generously sharing with their communities, schools, and regional charities their time, their money, their skills, and— most of all—their caring.

Meyer, Unkovic & Scott LLP, proud of its past and excited by the promise of its future, looks forward to its next 50 years of service to the region's community.

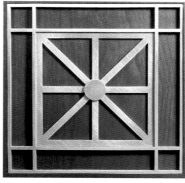

The law firm of Meyer, Unkovic & Scott LLP is traditional, yet progressive; steeped in the old-school philosophy of client and community service; and supported by the cutting-edge technology required to meet the needs of its clients and the region's community in the 21st century.

WHEN IT COMES TO PREMIUM DOORS AND WINDOWS, professionals across the nation have come to rely on one company: TRACO. But many of these professional builders may not know the name stands for Three Rivers Aluminum Company, based in Pittsburgh. Located in Cranberry Township, just 20 minutes north of downtown, the company has built a reputation over the past 55 years for superior-quality products and a commitment to customer service that surpasses all others in the business. Though TRACO today boasts thousands of satisfied customers and is recognized across the nation by builders, architects, and real estate developers, its beginnings were much more modest.

BORN OF NECESSITY

The company got its start in 1943, when founders Mae and E.R. Randall noticed a need for quality building materials due to Pittsburgh's flood of 1936. The flood had devastated thousands of homes in the Pittsburgh area, and the Great Depression and World War II had left many home owners financially strained and unable to undertake building new homes.

The Randalls, sensing that home owners were looking toward affordable remodeling instead of expensive rebuilding, set up a small manufacturing facility to house production of the first line of Three Rivers aluminum storm doors and storm windows. An immediate hit with consumers, sales continued to grow steadily over the next two decades into the mid-1960s, when the company expanded and introduced its original line of replacement windows.

In 1971, with son Robert Randall on board, the company began constructing what would eventually grow into TRACO's present headquarters and manufacturing site, a 950,000-square-foot complex. Today, what was once a two-person operation has grown into a company employing more than 1,100 team members, with four manufacturing facilities and numerous branch offices throughout the United States.

WINDOWS IN HIGH PLACES

TRACO's windows and doors, which are available in a full range of glass, screen, and muntin choices, grace everything from small businesses and homes to large apartment buildings, universities, hospitals, and national hotel chains. The company's custom windows, in fact, can be found in two of the world's most famous landmarks. TRACO artisans were responsible for handcrafting the 25 windows in the crown of the Statue of Liberty, as part of the $30 million torch-to-toe restoration project in the late 1980s. TRACO was also called upon to replace more than 6,000 windows in the 102-story Empire State Building during its recent renovation.

In other projects, TRACO provided more than 4,000 windows for the Olympic Village on the grounds of Georgia Tech University for the 1996 Summer Olympic Games in Atlanta, and 1,000 windows for the Maritime Academy in Vladivostok.

TRACO's custom windows can be found in two of the world's most famous landmarks. TRACO artisans were responsible for handcrafting the 25 windows in the crown of the Statue of Liberty, as part of the $30 million torch-to-toe restoration project in the late 1980s. The company was also called upon to replace more than 6,000 windows in the 102-story Empire State Building during its recent renovation.

The Power of

As the company heads into the next century, TRACO will continue to be on the cutting edge of technology with continued research and development, as well as an added focus on the residential arena.

HIGH-TECH WINDOWS

One reason TRACO continues to be an industry leader is its extensive testing of its products, both by the company's own testing facility and by an independent laboratory, to assure they meet or exceed the strict industry standards developed by the American Architectural Manufacturers' Association.

The company has also proved itself to be an innovator with such products as View-Safe® Tempered Safety Glass, which offers four times the strength of ordinary glass, and Low-E glass, which keeps heat from escaping from the home 30 percent more efficiently than regular glass. These innovations have been combined to produce the company's newest line, the Power Two family of windows. This product combines a strong, durable, aluminum exterior with a thermally efficient, beautiful, vinyl interior, offering the homeowner the best of both worlds in a single window.

TRACO's commitment to quality—and dedication to personal service—is also evident in the way the company fosters a relationship with its customers. Integrated Consultation By TRACO, or ICBT, enables staff to work hand in hand with clients, before a project even begins, to develop a thorough needs analysis, thus allowing TRACO to go beyond features and benefits, and focus on challenges and solutions. This results in the customers' finding the right product to fill their needs and, ultimately, in long-term customer satisfaction.

Located in Cranberry Township, just 20 minutes north of downtown, the company has built a reputation over the past 50 years for superior-quality products and a commitment to customer service that surpasses all others in the business.

CONTINUING GROWTH

As the home-improvement market continues to explode, TRACO is expanding right along with it, with distribution centers in Detroit, Denver, New York, Minneapolis, Chicago, Cincinnati, and Washington, D.C., and a sales force scattered throughout the United States. Recently, TRACO opened its first international venture, a manufacturing facility in Shanghai. TRACO CEO Robert Randall credits the company's continued success to its commitment to customer service, as well as its ability to offer true value for the dollar. "We've got such loyalty among our customers because they've discovered, through their own experiences, that our products prove themselves over time," Randall says. "Our track record tells our customers that we'll always be around to service our products and honor our warranties."

As the company heads into the next century, TRACO will continue to be on the cutting edge of technology with continued research and development. It will also focus more on the residential arena. To that end, in 1995, TRACO opened a new, 168,000-square-foot manufacturing facility in Red Oak, Iowa, dedicated solely to the residential market. TRACO also recently acquired Skytech Systems in Bloomsburg, Pennsylvania, a leading manufacturer of patio enclosures, sunrooms, greenhouses, skylights, and folding glass walls.

"We're planning to concentrate on the residential industry as we take TRACO to the next level," says Randall. "We have established a strong physical presence in the market, and now we want to service that market more effectively."

SINCE ITS FOUNDING IN PITTSBURGH IN 1946, KIRKPATRICK & Lockhart LLP has earned the distinction of being the largest law firm in the city and one of the 35 largest firms in the United States. A nationally recognized leader in the legal profession, the firm serves a diverse client base, with more than 400

attorneys practicing in offices in New York City, Washington, D.C., Boston, Miami, and Harrisburg, as well as in its principal Pittsburgh office.

The seven attorneys who founded Kirkpatrick & Lockhart shared the goal of helping clients develop practical and innovative solutions to challenging problems. As those challenges have been met by Western Pennsylvania businesses in the second half of the 20th century, Kirkpatrick & Lockhart has been integral to the region's economic development. The dramatic growth of the firm has not caused it to lose sight of each client's unique objectives, issues, and needs when legal services are provided.

"We work with each client to identify the best lawyer and team

for each engagement," says Donald E. Seymour, administrative partner in Kirkpatrick & Lockhart's Pittsburgh office. "We have professionals who listen, learn, and bring expertise and judgment to the assignment. This means that, when appropriate, we find the talent from throughout our six offices. Our lawyers maintain a commitment to excellence and to high-quality service in every geographic region and substantive area in which we practice."

HELPING SHAPE PITTSBURGH'S NEW ECONOMY

Kirkpatrick & Lockhart has been a key participant in the transformation of Pittsburgh's economy from a traditional manufacturing base to a technology- and service-based economy. The firm's attor-

neys have helped nurture the start-up technology companies that are driving the new economy by assisting with incorporation, venture financing, and the establishment of strategic partnerships. As these companies have matured, the firm has assisted with initial and secondary public offerings; structuring of licensing, manufacturing, and distribution arrangements in the United States and abroad; and protection of proprietary technology with patent applications, copyright and trademark registrations, invention assignments, and trade secret agreements.

Kirkpatrick & Lockhart has also acted as general corporate counsel to many companies, helping to structure stock options, assisting with employee issues like

Kirkpatrick & Lockhart LLP was founded in 1946 and is now the largest law firm in Pittsburgh.

CHUCK FUHRER

The Power of

employee incentive and noncompetition arrangements, and providing advice on exporting technology, negotiating government contracts, and preserving tax benefits. The firm also litigates disputes on issues ranging from intellectual property infringement and breach of commercial contracts to product liability claims and complex insurance coverage disputes. "We serve business enterprises that develop or utilize technology in advanced manufacturing and other operations, as well as business enterprises involved directly in technology industries, including computer software, networking equipment, health care, biotechnology, and telecommunications," Seymour says.

Kirkpatrick & Lockhart believes that it serves clients best by understanding the business and economic environment in which they function and by responding to their needs in the most efficient manner possible. The attorneys recognize that, when a client is purchasing time, nothing enhances value more than efficiency. To that end, the firm takes advantage of technological advances. Its lawyers are linked together into a single computerized national network that enables them to work concurrently across offices on engagements and to rapidly exchange questions, comments, and reflections.

Kirkpatrick & Lockhart's state-of-the-art communication capabilities explain why so many clients have replaced letters with electronic communications where appropriate. And the firm's heavy and prudent investment in litigation support resources has served to maximize the efficiency of litigation hours spent for its clientele.

A ROLE IN THE COMMUNITY

By serving the businesses that now form the economic infrastructure of Pittsburgh, Kirkpatrick & Lockhart has become deeply rooted in the community. The firm has a long tradition of donating resources, including the expertise of its lawyers, to the communities in which its offices are located. This dedication was recognized by the Pennsylvania Bar Foundation when it honored Kirkpatrick & Lockhart with the Louis J. Goffman Award, which recognizes significant contributions to pro bono representation in the commonwealth. In addition, attorneys in the Pittsburgh office are actively involved in more than 200 civic, educational, and charitable organizations, including leadership roles with the Allegheny Conference on Community Development, Greater Pittsburgh Chamber of Commerce, Carnegie Mellon University, and United Way.

Upon the celebration of the firm's 50th anniversary in 1996, Kirkpatrick & Lockhart returned to the community a gift of $250,000, earmarked to advance legal education, provide equal access to justice, and improve general community welfare within the region. "This was our way of saying thank-you to Pittsburgh for the support that we have received from the community throughout our history, enabling us to grow into the city's largest law firm," says Partner David Ehrenwerth. "This was our birthday present to the community—the best way we knew to share our success and start out our next 50 years together."

Kirkpatrick & Lockhart works with each client to identify the best team for each engagement.

WHEN NEWS REPORTERS ARE TRACKING A STORY, IT'S those who know the players and the territory who get the story first, and get it right. When Pittsburghers are looking for accurate, dependable news, they often turn to the local news team at KDKA-TV2.

KDKA-TV2 sent out its first signal on November 27, 1948, with the call letters WDTV, just in time to cover the inauguration of President Harry S Truman. The first television station to broadcast from Pittsburgh, WDTV originally broadcast on Channel 3 to black-and-white sets throughout the region, but switched over to Channel 2 in November 1952, where it remains today. The Westinghouse Broadcasting Co. purchased the station on January 31, 1955, and at noon that same day the call letters were officially changed to what they are today: KDKA-TV2.

The Truman inauguration would be the first of many significant news stories that KDKA-TV2 would cover through the years. Other firsts the station logged in Pittsburgh television history include the first to establish 24-hour programming, in 1952, and the first to broadcast noon news, in 1953.

KDKA-TV has always been best known for the accurate, groundbreaking reporting of its news team. The majority of its news team either grew up in the Pittsburgh region or has lived in the area for decades. For instance, KDKA-TV anchor Stacy Smith has lived in Pittsburgh since 1983, while his on-air partner, Patrice King Brown, joined the station in 1978 after growing up in the city's Sheraden neighborhood. Throughout the news team, there are roots reaching back to communities in Allegheny, Westmoreland, Beaver, Armstrong, and other counties. The station's hometown advantage is one of the main reasons that close to 1.3 million households tune to KDKA-TV in any given week.

HOMETOWN COVERAGE, HOMETOWN CONCERN

In addition to covering their hometowns, the members of KDKA-TV's news staff have a tradition of working to improve Pittsburgh. An example of this concern for the community is the annual Children's Hospital Free Care Fund drive, which since 1953 has raised millions of dollars to help provide health care for families that cannot afford it.

KDKA-TV has also taken steps to put food on the table of impoverished families at Thanksgiving. To do this, the station holds the KD Turkey Fund, a fund-raiser with the community food bank. Additionally, the station works with professional organizations comprised of pharmacists, physicians, and attorneys to bring advice on health care and legal matters to people who might not otherwise have access to it.

The goodwill has worked its way to the newsroom, where veteran reporter Brenda Waters in 1997 began nightly positive news reports about people who make a difference in the Pittsburgh region. The news segment, titled "On a Positive Note," was created in response to viewers' demands to balance hard news with good news. It was another first in Pittsburgh television news, and proof that KDKA-TV continues to be out front in modern-day Pittsburgh, reporting the news accurately and quickly, while working to improve the region.

KDKA-TV has always been known for the accurate, groundbreaking reporting of its news team, which includes (from left) Stacy Smith, Patrice King Brown, Jennifer Antkowiak, and Ken Rice.

The Power of

N THE YEARS AFTER WORLD WAR II, AS RESIDENTIAL DEVELOPERS RUSHED to meet the housing demands of the nation's burgeoning population, homes became increasingly harder to afford. It didn't take long for Edward Ryan, a Pittsburgh businessman, to decide that something had to change. He believed that a home was the American

dream, and established Ryan Homes in 1948 with the primary goal of offering families the chance to own their dreams at an affordable price.

A half-century later, Ryan Homes still follows that philosophy. With operations in Pennsylvania, New York, Delaware, New Jersey, Maryland, Ohio, Virginia, North Carolina, Tennessee, and South Carolina, the company today has delivered newly built homes for almost 200,000 families. In the Pittsburgh region, Ryan's operations cover most of Southwestern Pennsylvania and stretch as far north as New Castle.

DESIGN DIVERSITY

Prospective Ryan home owners can choose from a variety of exterior and interior designs. Ryan Homes conducts extensive consumer research to present designs reflecting what home owners are looking for. Today, that means a highly functional floor plan with comfortable, but practical, living spaces. For the construction of the home, Ryan procures top-of-the-line materials that it buys in volume, allowing it to pass on cost savings to the home owner.

"A home well built is a home built to last," says Tom DiOrio, vice president of Ryan Homes Mid-East Operations, located in Pittsburgh. "To guarantee quality homes, we ensure that our designs are built to stringent specifications. Only the highest-grade materials go into your new home. That's our guarantee—start to finish, top to bottom."

"We think we offer the best value," adds Grady Gaspar, Ryan Homes division manager in Pittsburgh. "Our value combines price, financing, location, and our warranties, including 10 years on structural issues. That's peace of mind. That's outstanding service."

J.S. DOWNS & ASSOCIATES

NVR INC.

In 1987, McLean, Virginia-based NVHomes Inc. acquired Ryan Homes, and changed its name to NVR Inc. Since then, the company has been traded on the American Stock Exchange under the symbol NVR. NVR Inc. also enables Ryan Homes to offer prospective home owners financing through an affiliated mortgage company called NVR Mortgage. The mortgage company maintains more than 40 branch offices nationwide, giving Ryan customers complete service from application and appraisal to rate lock-in and final settlement. NVR Settlement Services Inc., another affiliate, is a full-service residential title and settlement agency that provides everything needed to close on the purchase of a home.

Assisted by NVR's well-rounded services, Ryan Homes is continuing its tradition of offering value and service, as well as diversity and flexibility, to families looking for

J.S. DOWNS & ASSOCIATES

newly built homes. In 1998, the company introduced six new home designs, each of which had options built into the interior design, and introduced to the market a new, three-level town house design with an integrated, two-car garage. These are the features that home buyers are looking for today. As DiOrio says: "A Ryan home is like a home of your own creation. Each detail, each feature, is as if you had designed it yourself."

Prospective Ryan home owners can choose from a variety of exterior and interior designs. Ryan Homes conducts extensive consumer research to present designs reflecting what home owners are looking for.

BERG INDUSTRIES WAS FOUNDED IN 1948 BY DONALD E. Oberg, who pioneered using tungsten carbide components in the manufacture of high-speed stamping dies. The use of carbide revolutionized the tool and die industry because carbide offered an advantage of having approximately 10 times the wear resistance of high-carbon, high-chrome tool steels. Producers of laminations soon learned that Oberg dies made parts of consistent quality while sustaining long production runs before die servicing was required.

From laminations, the use of tungsten carbide tooling spread to the producers of both flat and formed parts. Whenever millions of parts requiring critical tolerances were needed, more and more customers looked to Oberg for dies of unmatched quality.

Oberg's dedication to quality and precision led the company to establish its own apprentice program during the 1950s to ensure future generations of skilled craftsmen. That dedication has established Oberg Industries as the benchmark of quality in precision manufacturing throughout the world. In 1985, Oberg was named Man of the Year by *American Machinist* magazine. After Oberg's death in 1992, his son, Eric, and daughter, Karen, assumed leadership of the company, and continue the tradition of quality and excellence in his name.

During its 50-year history, Oberg Industries has extended its dedication to precision and quality into other successful products and markets. Many of the world's most demanding manufacturers have used and continue to use dies and other manufacturing solutions provided by Oberg as part of their own quest for quality. Today, Oberg Industries is a company of more than 700 employees, spread among seven divisions located in Pennsylvania and Arizona, with gross revenues of more than $80 million in 1997. Oberg serves customers in more than 40 countries, spread over five continents. The company has sales and service offices in Europe and Asia, staffed with Oberg-trained personnel, and is tied to a global network of distributors and manufacturers' agents.

SUCCESS IN MANY AREAS

Oberg is a source for replacement carbide die components and stocks thousands of standard, semifinished forms to provide customers with finished die components in the shortest amount of time. Every component is precision made to ensure complete interchangeability and is guaranteed to fit exactly the same as the original. Oberg also offers customers a complete range of services from engineering and prototyping to

Clockwise from top:
Employees at the first Oberg manufacturing facility in Tarentum, Pennsylvania, used their talents and skills to help Donald Oberg pioneer the use of tungsten carbide in high-speed stamping dies that literally gave birth to the carbide die industry throughout the world.

Manufacturers requiring electrical laminations use Oberg precision tooling to produce high-quality stacks in the die, eliminating secondary stacking operations and, in many cases, significantly reducing time and cost of balancing operations.

This precision carbide stamping die, which is manufactured by Oberg Industries, is used for the production of grid straps that locate the fuel rods in nuclear fuel assemblies.

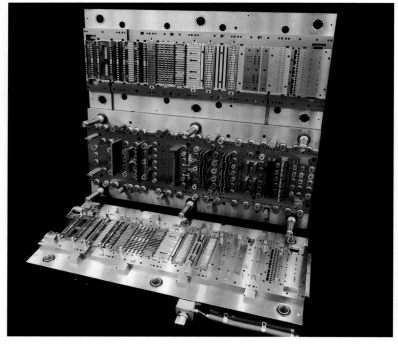

secondary operations such as assembly, deburring, and plating.

Over the years, Oberg's success in tungsten carbide die making, coupled with its dedication to solving customer problems, has led to competitive advantages in many other manufacturing processes. The company is involved in precision grinding, with the capability of machining and grinding components to within 0.00002 inch, or 1/150th the diameter of a human hair. This level of expertise has enabled Oberg to expand into grinding and polishing tungsten carbide and hardened steel into specialized components that are highly resistant to wear. In addition, Oberg has a comprehensive array of automated equipment used for contract metal parts stamping, prototype metal stamping, and precision machining.

In order to remain a front-runner in the industry, Oberg also recognized the need for and developed electronic automation systems to enhance manufacturing processes. Oberg now designs and produces sophisticated in-die electronics that permit customers to monitor die performance, misfeeds, and other variables throughout the manufacturing process.

Further expansion into tooling for the container industry has also met with great success. Oberg's precision container tooling is used in the manufacture of two- and three-piece food and beverage cans all over the world.

The demand for precision-engineered plastic parts prompted Oberg to apply its expertise in die design and manufacturing to plastic injection molds and plastic part production. Combining its manufacturing capabilities for metal and plastic parts with its experience in die and mold design, the company also has the capability to fabricate integrated metal and plastic assemblies.

"Oberg is market- and customer-focused," says Ralph Hardt, president and CEO of Oberg Industries. "In rapidly changing markets, speed, precision, and versatility are essential to the manufacturer—and these are exactly the advantages that Oberg offers its customers," Hardt adds. "Oberg has always maintained an unparalleled reputation for excellence, not simply by meeting the needs of customers today, but by anticipating and preparing to meet the manufacturing needs of tomorrow's markets. At Oberg, we've always strived to be one step ahead in terms of the available technologies and expertise that we offer, and to create truly Innovative Manufacturing Solutions for our customers."

TRAINING AND DEDICATION

Oberg takes no shortcuts with quality. For example, the company supplies its professionally trained and highly dedicated employees involved in manufacturing with the finest grinding and EDM equipment and machine tools available. Prospective employees undergo a rigorous selection process. Those chosen for employment enter Oberg's world-renowned apprenticeship program that requires up to four years and 9,000 hours of classroom and on-the-job skills training to complete. These skilled craftsmen are an important part of the company's success, and the quality of Oberg's personnel is reflected in the quality of the products they produce.

Oberg Industries earns accolades from the communities surrounding its facilities as well. The company supports local civic and charitable organizations such as the YMCA and YWCA; the Pittsburgh Zoo; Pittsburgh's prestigious Children's Hospital; area food banks; and the United Way. Further, Oberg's success has spurred other industries in Pennsylvania's Allegheny River Valley, where entrepreneurs have started their own businesses to fill niche areas in the tool and die industry.

From innovative tool design and manufacturing to working closely with customers to develop products that improve the quality of our lives, Oberg Industries has been a vital industrial resource not only for the Pittsburgh area and Western Pennsylvania, but for the world. Oberg stamping dies and injection molds are used to make a variety of parts for customers who make automobiles, computers, electronics, consumer products, health care items, appliances, and many other products.

Moving into the next century, Oberg Industries will continue to provide innovative products and manufacturing solutions, developed and produced with the same dedication, precision, and quality customers have come to know and expect.

Clockwise from top:
Oberg craftsmen work routinely in tolerances of millionths of an inch.

High-precision, injection-molded plastic parts are manufactured at Oberg's ISO 9002 certified production facility.

An example, shown actual size, of a precision-made Oberg plastic part

Oberg provides a reel-to-reel plating process that applies nickel, copper, or tin/lead plating to stamped parts after they are formed.

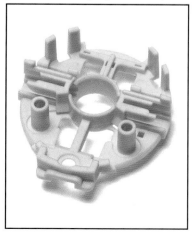

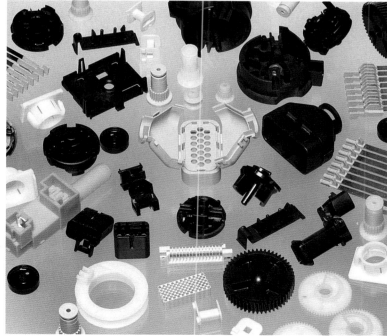

N 1949, AMERICA HAD ITS FIRST TASTE OF PREPARED CAKE MIXES, ITS first tug at Silly Putty, and its first chance to visit Eat'n Park. Back then, the tiny, two-toned, yellow restaurant had just 13 seats inside. But outside, there was a narrow parking area where 10 bustling carhops served customers in their Ramblers and Studebakers.

Ever since its grand opening caused a traffic jam that blocked Saw Mill Run Boulevard for six hours, Eat'n Park has been a local favorite, specializing in giving its customers exactly what they want. As customer tastes change, the restaurant menu changes to suit them. And as new trends in customer preferences prompt shifts in dining style and building designs, Eat'n Park responds accordingly.

It's a recipe for success that translates into growth for the chain and accolades from industry leaders as well. In fact, for three consecutive years, the National Restaurant Association named Eat'n Park's menu one of the best in the country. As a testament to this accolade, *Consumer Reports* recently rated the restaurant chain third for overall family dining experience, based on a national survey. Eat'n Park's willingness to adapt, perhaps more than any other feature, has helped propel this local Pittsburgh favorite to top-performing status in family dining all across the tristate area.

In 1949, America had its first chance to visit Eat'n Park. Back then, the tiny, two-toned, yellow restaurant had just 13 seats inside. But outside, there was a narrow parking area where 10 bustling carhops served customers in their Ramblers, Packards, and Studebakers (top).

The Smiley™ Cookie has come to embody the spirit of Eat'n Park, and serves as a reminder that the restaurant has maintained its place in the hearts of Pittsburghers as the Place for Smiles (bottom).

Innovation, affordability, friendly customer service, and the Eat'n Park Superburger® have become trademarks of the restaurant chain. Eat'n Park is also continually upgrading its existing dishes—all except the Superburger. Although the days of carhops are long gone, the double-decker burger with melted cheese, pickle, lettuce, and sauce supreme on a sesame seed bun remains to this day an Eat'n Park tradition.

A PITTSBURGH FAVORITE

One recent addition that has enjoyed much success is the Bakery'n Pie Shop at Eat'n Park. Every restaurant built since 1986 has been equipped with these in-store bakeries, which symbolize Eat'n Park's commitment to fresh, homemade goodness, as well as the fact that the Pittsburgh restaurant chain is a dynamic company seeking to deliver the highest-quality customer service.

Eat'n Park's most successful bakery item has become a modern-day Pittsburgh icon. The Smiley™ Cookie—a round, white-icing-coated cookie painted with a colorful smiling face—is free to children 10 and under after any meal. Smiley has come to embody the spirit of Eat'n Park, and serves as a reminder that the restaurant has maintained its place in the hearts of Pittsburghers as The Place for Smiles™. Each year, the company sells more than 3 million Smiley Cookies and gives away nearly 3 million more to kids of all ages.

BRANCHING OUT

Another Eat'n Park success story has been the establishment of Parkhurst Dining Services. Created to meet the dining service needs of colleges, corporations, and institutions, Parkhurst already serves Carnegie Mellon University, Highmark Blue Cross Blue Shield, Saint Vincent College, Robert Morris College, FORE Systems, Elliott Company, and Carnegie Museums of Pittsburgh in Oakland. Parkhurst has created a variety of corporate brands and dining areas that have the appearance of individual storefronts, providing a retail environment and a greater selection of food choices. Some popular Parkhurst brands include Pepperazzi™, a line of fresh-dough pizzas and pastas; East Street

Deli™, a New York-style deli; and Parkside Diner™, offering traditional American entrées and comfort foods.

OVER THE YEARS

As Eat'n Park has grown through the years, so has the number of its employees. In 1949, the first two restaurants employed only 40 workers. Today, this number has increased to more than 7,500, making Eat'n Park one of the top 20 employers in the tristate area. The restaurant chain even awards scholarships to employees pursuing post-high-school restaurant, hospitality management, business, or liberal arts studies. Additionally, Eat'n Park has created the STAR awards for employees who refer other successful employees.

One of the best ways Eat'n Park serves its customers is by benefiting the communities in which they work and live. By giving its time, money, skills, and resources, the restaurant chain has had a remarkable impact on the communities where it does business. On an annual basis, Eat'n Park employees raise more than $500,000 for institutions such as United Way and children's hospitals in each of the markets they serve.

Over the years, the restaurant chain has earned quite a reputation for lending a helping hand through its Corporate Giving Program, Employee Volunteer Program, and Community Relations Department. In addition, Eat'n Park is proud to sponsor a wide variety of events, groups, and organizations— more than 130 in all. From neighborhood organizations to schools and churches to large-scale events, some of the beneficiaries include the Pittsburgh Great Race, Harmarville Hoops, Junior Achievement, Scouting for Food, and local food banks. In addition, Eat'n Park contributes to programs with the Carnegie Science Center, Phipps Conservatory, and the Pittsburgh Steelers, Pirates, and Penguins

sports teams. The family restaurant chain also has been a long-time supporter of *Mister Rogers' Neighborhood*, the widely acclaimed children's television program filmed in Pittsburgh.

For half a century, Eat'n Park has defined success in two ways. The first is to serve an ever increasing number of satisfied customers by providing quality food at a reasonable price; the second is to help employees realize their individual goals. It is because of this unique combination that Eat'n Park has grown into the regional family restaurant chain it is today: a remarkable success that, in 50 years and through more than 70 restaurants, has become a Pittsburgh family tradition.

Clockwise from top left:
Consumer Reports recently rated the restaurant chain third for overall family dining experience, based on a national survey.

As Eat'n Park has grown through the years, so has the number of its employees; today, the number has increased to more than 7,500, making Eat'n Park one of the top 20 employers in the tristate area.

For three consecutive years, the National Restaurant Association named Eat'n Park's menu one of the best in the country. From the Superburger® and a shake to home-style dinners, Eat'n Park has something for everyone.

P ITTSBURGH HAS ALWAYS BEEN KNOWN FOR ITS STEEL PRODUCTION, so it's logical that companies relying heavily on the use of steel would also maintain a significant presence in the region. Such is the case with automotive giant General Motors (GM), which operates its Pittsburgh Metal Center 11 miles south of downtown in West Mifflin. There, approximately 900 men and women, including some 775 hourly employees represented by the United Automobile Workers, cover three shifts at the 880,000-square-foot facility.

The 72.3-acre plant compound includes 18 enclosed acres that are dedicated to the production of automotive body components for cars driven daily around North America. Operating at full capacity, the plant processes approximately 100 tons of steel each day through its production equipment, which includes seven major press lines, six metal assembly processes, 8,000 service dies, and 44 major presses.

Nearly 2 million cubic yards of earth were carved out of a West Mifflin hillside to build the only General Motors production facility in Pennsylvania.

▲ W. BRADLEY BARNES

FIVE DECADES IN PITTSBURGH

The West Mifflin plant opened in 1950 as part of the Fisher Body Division of General Motors Corp. For nearly four decades, the plant fabricated sheet metal body parts for current model GM cars and trucks. In 1989, the plant's role changed to that of a niche supplier of the GM Service Parts Operations, fabricating parts for past vehicle models.

The plant stamps sheet metal into panels, which are then welded into assembled panels. The finished product is then shipped to various GM Service Parts Processing and Distribution centers around the country. Each year, in excess of 42 million pounds of steel coil are formed into more than 7 million sheet blanks covering 530-plus General Motors part numbers. The plant's six assembly areas ship more than 1 million door, hood, and fender assemblies for more than 375 styles annually. Each year, 2,500-plus trucks and some 2,400 railcars ship the parts to 18 locations. The plant has a railroad connection to all major railroads throughout the United States, Canada, and Mexico, and has a mile of track on-site, allowing it to spot fifteen 60-foot railcars inside the plant.

A MON VALLEY INSTITUTION

Just like the steel plants that dot the Monongahela River Valley south of Pittsburgh, the GM Pittsburgh Metal Center is an institution in the Mon Valley. Through its five decades of existence, the Pittsburgh plant has developed a reputation for good union and management relations, evidenced by minimal work stoppages at the West Mifflin facility. The plant is known throughout the industry for its commitment to employee training and continuous improvement.

In addition, workers function in teams to continually improve production to keep the GM Pittsburgh Metal Center competitive within its markets. The plant's quality council actively works on implementing quality network strategies.

The GM Pittsburgh Metal Center's excellent care of its employees and its importance in the automotive market position the facility as a significant contributor to the Pittsburgh economy.

▲ JAMES F. CAPP

Press technicians remove hood inners stamped in presses that utilize computer-controlled automation and robotics.

The Power of

SINCE ITS FOUNDING AS SOFFER REALTY IN 1950, THE SOFFER Organization has been creating solutions to office, commercial, and residential development challenges. Applying an integrated team approach to the analysis and execution of every new development, the Soffer Organization utilizes

its experts in planning, programming, project design, construction, marketing, and property management to ensure that its high-quality projects are completed on time and within budget.

The Soffer Organization has developed property throughout the Pittsburgh area, including shopping centers like Norwin Towne Square, a retail complex in Wilkins Township that includes Sears, National City Bank, CompUSA, and The Shops at Penn Center; and Shadow Wood, which features 114 town house units in Pittsburgh's eastern suburbs. Other Soffer developments include Carolina Corporate Centre, a 400,000-square-foot office park in Raleigh, North Carolina, and Plaza Office Building in Pensacola, Florida.

PREMIER MIXED DEVELOPMENTS

The Soffer Organization pioneered the building of mixed-use developments when it created Penn Center East in 1964, the first suburban complex in the Pittsburgh area to combine high-rise commercial office buildings, upscale retail shops, restaurants, and service facilities in one location. Penn Towers Apartments, a 241-unit, luxury high-rise, is home to many local professionals. Penn Center

East provides more than 160 corporations, small businesses, and professionals with an address of distinction. The center brings together a total of more than 1,172,531 square feet of commercial and residential space to meet the tastes of the discriminating tenant.

Another Soffer Organization development, Penn Center West, is the hallmark of distinction in the airport corridor. It was designed and developed in 1981 by R. Damian Soffer, president of the company and the son of Joseph Soffer, founder, who believed that future growth in Pittsburgh would take place between the downtown area and the airport. Today, the 90-acre site, 10 minutes from the airport and downtown, is Pittsburgh's premier office park,

with four buildings of contemporary design. Penn Center West features an on-site conference center and beautiful landscaping that includes a waterfall along the entrance drive. The Soffer Organization is currently developing 60 additional acres at Penn Center West for a new technology park. It will feature three state-of-the-art buildings, four additional class A office buildings, and a 120-room hotel.

SERVICE

The Soffer Organization operates on the belief that on-site tenant services are key to its leasing success. This philosophy includes providing complete build-out services, excellent maintenance, and highly responsive security for its tenants. The company also pays close attention to what it calls "outdoor space for indoor people," providing extensive landscaping, walking paths, and outdoor eating environments at each of its developments.

The company's attention to detail, wide range of services, and diversified portfolio of real estate developments have ensured its success in the last half century. It is a tradition that the Soffer Organization will continue to build on, as it makes a lasting contribution to the communities that it serves now and into the next century.

Clockwise from top:
Visitors are always impressed with the landscaped atriums, paintings, and sculptures that embellish each of the lobbies at Penn Center West.

Penn Center West is the hallmark of distinction in the airport corridor, featuring four buildings of contemporary design, an on-site conference center, and beautiful landscaping.

The Soffer Organization pioneered the building of mixed-use developments when it created Penn Center East, the first suburban complex in the Pittsburgh area to combine high-rise commercial office buildings, upscale retail shops, restaurants, and service facilities in one location.

M. HARITAN

ENTRAL BLOOD BANK HAS A CHALLENGING MISSION—TO PROVIDE a consistently safe and adequate blood supply for the residents of Pittsburgh and the surrounding region. With a demand that's nearly twice the national average, Central Blood Bank must collect 180,000 units of blood annually in order to

meet the needs of the local health care community.

Central Blood Bank was founded in 1951 by the Pittsburgh Jaycees and a group of physicians who were committed to unifying the area's blood supply. Today, Central Blood Bank is the Pittsburgh community's nonprofit blood center, providing blood products and transfusion services to more than 40 hospitals in Western Pennsylvania and northern West Virginia.

Serving as the bridge between healthy donors and patients in need, Central Blood Bank's role is multifaceted. Central Blood Bank is responsible for collecting, processing, screening, and storing the community's blood supply. In addition, Central Blood Bank offers apheresis

collection programs that enable donors to give plasma or platelets, blood products used by patients with cancer, leukemia, sickle-cell anemia, and other illnesses. Central Blood Bank is also the regional link to the National Marrow Donor Program, typing donors to be matched with patients from all over the country who are in need of bone marrow transplants.

MEETING THE DEMAND

Despite miraculous advancements in medicine, there is no substitute for human blood. In Pittsburgh, patients in need of blood are dependent on the generosity of volunteer blood donors and the ability of Central Blood Bank to maintain an adequate blood supply. Over the

years, the number of blood donors in the Pittsburgh region has decreased, while the need for blood products has increased. An aging population and advanced trauma and transplant centers place heavy demands on the local blood supply.

To adequately supply area hospitals, Central Blood Bank must recruit an average of 700 donors every 24 hours. Local residents may donate at one of Central Blood Bank's 20 community donor centers, located throughout the region. Central Blood Bank also operates seven mobile teams and two self-contained donor coaches that travel to businesses, churches, schools, and other locations to set up on-site blood drives.

Special programs are critical to Central Blood Bank meeting its goals. Central Blood Bank works with the area's larger corporate and community groups to organize comprehensive blood programs. Small and midsize businesses and organizations without the space or staff for an on-site blood drive can contribute to the community blood supply through a Community Care Club. Gift of Life Donor (GOLD) Clubs encourage donors to commit to giving frequently throughout the year, especially at times when donations are typically at their lowest. The high school scholarship program helps to educate and recruit young people to become blood donors, and gives scholarships to the schools on the basis of percentage of participation and number of donations.

Central Blood Bank plays a crucial role in the Pittsburgh community. By consolidating donor recruitment, blood collection, testing, and distribution for the region, Central Blood Bank puts each donor's precious gift to best use. Through these efforts, the lives of thousands of area citizens are improved every day.

Serving as the bridge between healthy donors and patients in need, Central Blood Bank is responsible for collecting, processing, screening, and storing the community's blood supply. Central Blood Bank has 20 community donor centers, and also operates seven mobile teams and two self-contained donor coaches that travel to businesses, churches, schools, and other locations to set up on-site blood drives.

DANIEL LEVIN PHOTOGRAPHY

SINCE KENNETH P. DIETRICH FOUNDED THE COMPANY IN 1959 in Blairsville, approximately 50 miles east of Pittsburgh, Dietrich Industries, Inc. has become the nation's largest producer of metal framing products serving the construction industry. These products are used to frame interior walls,

exterior walls, floor joists, and roof trusses in schools, hospitals, and office buildings, as well as in multifamily and single-family homes.

Eighteen plants employing some 1,500 people make Dietrich Industries the only national manufacturer of its product line. Dietrich Industries distinguishes itself by developing state-of-the-art manufacturing and design innovations that continually improve customer service and satisfaction. Says William S. Dietrich II, company president, "We at Dietrich pride ourselves on quality products, extensive service that assists in design applications, and dependable deliveries. Our framing products provide designers, contractors, and suppliers with a vast array of product alternatives at a single source."

While possessing the broadest product line in the industry, Dietrich also offers the services of the nation's largest group of design engineers dedicated to metal framing. These in-house engineers field thousands of calls each year to assist the industry with design calculations and solutions in these products' applications in construction. Although more than 90 percent of the product is used in commercial construction, the company is developing new products and software to impact the residential framing market. Steel, unlike lumber, does not warp; is recyclable; is lightweight but strong; is vermin-resistant; increases design flexibility in framing and applying synthetic textured wall finishes; and is less price volatile.

A WORTHINGTON SUBSIDIARY

In February 1996, Dietrich Industries was acquired by Columbus, Ohio-based Worthington Industries, a leading manufacturer of metal and plastic products that tallies annual sales of nearly $2

billion; employs more than 9,700 people; and operates 53 facilities in 21 states, Canada, France, and Mexico. The deal was a logical move for Worthington since Dietrich commands more than 35 percent of the domestic market for metal framing. The synergy of the two steel-related companies has contributed to the strength of

Worthington's core business and philosophies.

Still active in the steel industry, Dietrich remains president of the company and has a seat on the board of Worthington Industries. Both Dietrich and the directors at Worthington expect solid growth for the One Mellon Center, Pittsburgh-based company.

Since its founding in 1959, Dietrich Industries, Inc. has become the nation's largest producer of metal framing products serving the construction industry (top).

Steel, unlike lumber, does not warp; is recyclable; is lightweight but strong; is vermin-resistant; increases design flexibility in framing and applying synthetic textured wall finishes; and is less price volatile (bottom).

WHEN IT COMES TO PITTSBURGH'S FINEST BUSINESS addresses—USX Tower, Fifth Avenue Place, and CNG Tower, to name a few—only one commercial real estate firm comes to mind: The Galbreath Company. Responsible for the leasing and manage-

ment of more than 6.4 million square feet of office and industrial properties, The Galbreath Company offers services including property management, leasing, tenant representation, investment sales, consulting, construction services, development, and redevelopment. And in Pittsburgh, the company is known for placing businesses in some of the city's most prestigious addresses.

The Galbreath Company offers services including property management, leasing, tenant representation, investment sales, consulting, construction services, development, and redevelopment. Perhaps the best-known business address managed by The Galbreath Company is the USX Tower at 600 Grant Street, a 64-story, 2.5 million-square-foot steel structure and a Pittsburgh landmark since it opened in 1970.

Perhaps the best-known business address is the USX Tower at 600 Grant Street, a 64-story, 2.5 million-square-foot steel structure that is home to steel and energy conglomerate USX; PNC Bank, one of the fastest-growing financial institutions in the country; food giant H.J. Heinz Company; and many other companies both large and small. The Galbreath Company manages the building, a Pittsburgh landmark since it opened in 1970, and serves as the leasing agent. The building sits within walking distance of all major downtown hotels and entertainment and meeting facilities.

A History of Success

John W. Galbreath established the company that bears his name in Columbus, Ohio, in 1921. The company first came to Pittsburgh in 1952 and developed the original U.S. Steel headquarters. The building opened in 1954 and is known today as Three Mellon Bank Center. In 1970, The Galbreath Company completed the new USX Headquarters Building, known today as USX Tower.

John Galbreath and his son, Daniel M. Galbreath, built the family business into the 15th-largest property management services company in the nation, with a management portfolio of approximately 270 properties in 33 U.S. cities by the mid-1990s. At that time, it operated domestically in Columbus, Cincinnati, Cleveland, Chicago, Denver, Fort Lauderdale, New York City, Orlando, Philadelphia, Pittsburgh, San Francisco, Stamford, and Washington, D.C.

In 1997, the Galbreath family entered into plans to merge with LaSalle Partners, a Chicago-based real estate services and investment firm. In Pittsburgh, however, local owners Jack R. Norris and E. Gerry Dudley moved to exclude the Galbreaths' Mid-Atlantic Region

office from the merger. The result was the continued presence of the Galbreath name in Pittsburgh, independent of its former parent company.

Local Facilities

Galbreath manages and leases Pittsburgh's top properties because it has an unparalleled track record of retaining and adding asset value to its properties. Galbreath works to maximize value as well as investment returns over the long term, utilizing proactive management proprietary techniques that reduce operating costs.

In addition to USX Tower, Galbreath's portfolio includes Fifth Avenue Place, a 31-story, 736,000-square-foot office building at 120 Fifth Avenue, whose chiseled steeple dominates the Pittsburgh skyline day and night. The building, for which Galbreath is the office rental agent, is home to Highmark and Chubb Insurance, and offers retail shops and restaurants on its first two floors. Centrally located, Fifth Avenue Place is bounded by Pittsburgh's main arteries—including Stanwix Street and Fifth, Liberty, and Penn Avenues—and public transportation stops dot each corner of the building.

In the heart of the Cultural District at 625 Liberty Avenue is the CNG Tower, for which Galbreath is both the managing agent and rental agent. The 32-story, 623,000-square-foot facility features a Dakota mahogany and Texas rose granite facade, and its lobby and common areas are adorned with polished marble, mahogany, and brass. Its tenants include Consolidated Natural Gas, Rockwell International, and Mortons of Chicago. The building is only a few steps from such Cultural District staples as Heinz Hall and the Benedum Center for the Performing Arts.

Back on Grant Street, a few

The Power of

steps from USX Tower, Galbreath is the leasing and managing agent for 437 Grant Street, known as the Frick Building. This 20-story, 341,000-square-foot building opened in 1902 and was renovated in 1989. Its tenants include the Court of Common Pleas of Allegheny County, several midsize law firms, and major title insurance companies. A few blocks down Grant Street is 601 Grant Street, known as the Home Loan Bank Building. This 18-story building sits directly across from USX Tower and is Pittsburgh's newest Class A office building.

THE SUBURBS

Galbreath's presence in the Pittsburgh region as a commercial real estate broker extends well beyond the central business district. Approximately 10 miles east of downtown, in Monroeville, Galbreath is the managing and leasing agent at the IT Building, a nine-floor, 130,000-square-foot facility whose primary tenant is International

Technology Corporation. Other tenants include the Monroeville Area Chamber of Commerce and United General Title Insurance Company. The facility is literally seconds away from the Pennsylvania Turnpike and Interstate 376.

Approximately 15 miles north of the city, Galbreath is jointly developing and leasing Cranberry Business Park, future home to six multi-use buildings totaling 400,000 square feet. The location in Cranberry Township boasts abundant free parking. The park, a joint venture between Galbreath and Douglas Elliman Realty, also has excellent access to Interstate 79 and the Pennsylvania Turnpike, and is approximately 30 minutes by car from the Pittsburgh International Airport.

With such prestigious facilities in and out of the city, it's no wonder that the Galbreath name has become so deeply entrenched in Pittsburgh. With its history of growth and success, the company

is sure to be an important part of the Pittsburgh community for many more years to come.

CORPORATE FACILITIES

In addition to its investment property portfolio, Galbreath manages approximately 1 million square feet of owner-occupied, corporate headquarters facilities in the Pittsburgh market. Stemming from its roots in development and service to Corporate America, Galbreath has a long tradition of servicing the unique requirements and challenges of corporate facilities. Galbreath's first facility management assignment began right here in Pittsburgh after completing the development of U.S. Steel Corporation's original headquarters at 525 William Penn Place, now called Three Mellon Bank Center.

Galbreath's distinguished list of corporate clients includes Alcoa, Calgon Corporation, PSI, RPS, and Solid State Measurements, Inc.

In the heart of the Cultural District at 625 Liberty Avenue is the CNG Tower, for which Galbreath is both the managing agent and rental agent. The 32-story, 623,000-square-foot facility features a Dakota mahogany and Texas rose granite facade (left).

Galbreath's portfolio includes Fifth Avenue Place, a 31-story, 736,000-square-foot office building at 120 Fifth Avenue, whose chiseled steeple dominates the Pittsburgh skyline day and night (right).

ONE OF PITTSBURGH'S MOST RECOGNIZABLE LANDMARKS IS the Bayer Corporation sign on Mount Washington, within clear sight of downtown Pittsburgh. Illuminated after dark, the mile of neon tubing is seen by an estimated quarter million people every day. ■ Pittsburgh-

Helge H. Wehmeier, president and CEO of Bayer Corporation (top)

One of Pittsburgh's most recognizable landmarks is the Bayer Corporation sign on Mount Washington. It is seen by an estimated quarter million people every day (bottom).

based Bayer Corporation is the largest subsidiary of the multinational chemical and pharmaceutical company Bayer AG. Founded more than 130 years ago in a small town in Germany, Bayer AG established its first American presence with a coal tar dye factory in Albany, New York. The company first arrived in Pittsburgh in the 1950s under the name of Mobay Corporation, which was then a joint venture with the chemical giant Monsanto. In 1967, Bayer bought out Monsanto, and Bayer's U.S. chemical operations have been headquartered in Pittsburgh ever since.

Bayer has grown in the United States through a series of acquisitions and mergers, including one involving Miles Laboratories in 1978, which marked Bayer's entry into the U.S. health care arena. In 1992, the company consolidated its U.S. operations under the name of Miles Inc. and made Pittsburgh the corporate headquarters. Three years later, the company reacquired the rights to the Bayer name and the Bayer Cross logo in North America (which had been lost during World War I), and Bayer's U.S. operations were renamed Bayer Corporation. Today, the company has businesses in health care and life sciences, chemicals, and imaging technologies.

THE BUSINESS OF BAYER

A group of 16 buildings comprises Bayer's corporate headquarters in the suburban Pittsburgh community of Robinson Township. The facilities provide some 800,000 square feet of working space for 1,800 Bayer employees. In addition to serving as U.S. corporate headquarters, the campus houses the headquarters of Bayer's four U.S. chemical divisions: Polymers; Fibers, Additives, and Rubber; Industrial Chemicals; and Performance Products. There are also numerous application development laboratories at the site.

At the Pittsburgh locale, Bayer's diverse staff manages the development of new technologies and applications for Bayer products in a wide range of areas—from the materials used to make computer housings to plastics used in automotive components. The company produces plastics; pigments; spandex fibers; Agfa film; Advantage flea control products for dogs and cats; Cipro, an antimicrobial; Glucometer blood glucose testing products; Alka-Seltzer antacid; and its flagship product, Bayer aspirin. In 1997, Bayer invested $657 million in research and development in the United States. The company's commitment to research and development accounts for much of its past success and forms the foundation of its future.

BAYER IN THE COMMUNITY

Bayer not only calls the Pittsburgh region its American home, but also makes a conscious effort to invest in the city and surrounding area. "Pittsburgh is a fine city in which to live and work, and we're proud to call it our home," says Bayer Corporation President and Chief Executive Officer Helge H. Wehmeier. "We benefit greatly from being here, and for that reason, we are more than pleased to reinvest in the outstanding quality of life that we have all come to enjoy."

Bayer's community involvement is also implemented through the Bayer Foundation, which has invested considerable resources in dozens of civic and charitable organizations in the Greater Pittsburgh area. To name a few, support has been directed to the Pittsburgh Cultural Trust, the Carnegie Insti-

The   Power   of

tute, the Pittsburgh Zoo, and the Pittsburgh Symphony, where the novel Audience of the Future and Science Students at the Symphony series seek to attract young people to the symphony.

The company has also distinguished itself in the promotion of science education—not only in Pittsburgh, but nationwide. Bayer's Making Science Make Sense program includes enormously successful hands-on, inquiry-based science education programs in the Pittsburgh region and other Bayer communities.

In addition, the company supports a national public education campaign promoting science literacy. To implement the program in Greater Pittsburgh, Bayer created Allegheny Schools Science Education and Technology (ASSET) Inc. in 1992. ASSET has received additional support from the National Science Foundation and many other area foundations and businesses. Currently, 25 of the 43 school districts in Greater Pittsburgh are involved with the ASSET program.

Bayer's commitment also extends to higher education. In 1995, Bayer endowed Duquesne University with a $2 million grant

to establish a department that would further the growth of environmental science. The Bayer School of Natural and Environmental Sciences was the company's first academic partnership with a university. "We believe strongly that products need to be manufactured, distributed, used, and disposed of in an environmentally responsible manner," Wehmeier says. "This investment underscores our reliance on science for the development of products, as well as the proper disposal of them."

INVOLVED EMPLOYEES

Bayer's corporate philosophy of supporting the community also manifests itself through the com-

pany's employees. The personal commitment of Bayer's staff to the community can be easily seen in the extensive work they have done for the United Way. Through the late 1990s, Bayer has teamed up with its employees to raise more than $1 million for the organization.

At the same time, Bayer employees remain serious about what they do. The company has a firm commitment to safety and quality. In addition, the company's statement of vision, values, and beliefs encourages employees to participate in all communities where they live and work. Bayer's employees take this commitment seriously, helping to make Bayer a valuable asset to the Pittsburgh area and beyond.

A Bayer scientist performs a hands-on science show at the Carnegie Science Center as part of Bayer Corporation's Making Science Make Sense program. This interactive show was written and designed by the volunteer group Bayer Association for Science in Communities, or BASIC, and has been adopted by the Science Center as part of its regular programming.

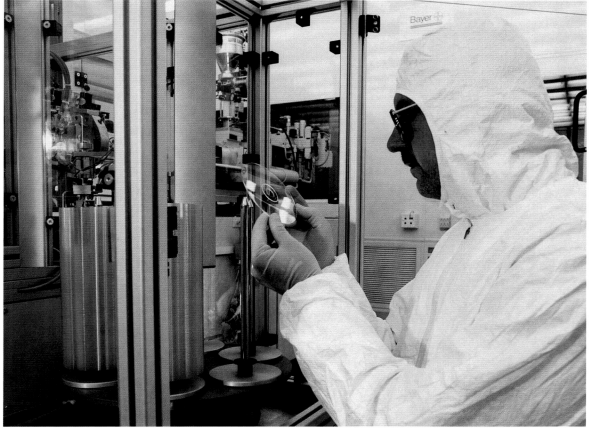

With upgrades to its Optical Media Lab, Bayer Corporation's Polymers Division will remain on the leading edge of technology as it develops and optimizes polycarbonate resins for compact discs (CDs) and digital versatile discs (DVDs). The state-of-the-art lab now features an 80-ton Krauss Maffei injection-molding machine with special processing features for the DVD market.

W

HEN MOST PEOPLE THINK OF THE INVESTMENT WORLD, an image of the New York Stock Exchange's frenzied trading floor comes to mind. A more realistic view, however, can be found at the corner of Liberty Avenue and Grant Street in Pittsburgh, where

Federated Investors maintains the headquarters of a global corporation that is a leader in today's competitive investment management business.

"People think of New York or Charlotte as the hubs of the financial services industry," says J. Christopher Donahue, president and chief operating officer at Federated. "They are surprised to find a world-class investment management firm in their own backyard."

In addition to Pittsburgh, Federated operates satellite offices in New York City; Dublin, Ireland; and Boston, where the company's transfer agency function is located. More than 2,000 dedicated individuals and experts work at these offices, and a large network of marketing and sales representatives, who serve as the front line of every client relationship, is scattered throughout the United States.

PERSONAL SERVICE AND INNOVATIVE PRODUCTS

Since its earliest days, Federated has striven to provide products and services that meet the needs of its investors. Founders John F. Donahue and Richard B. Fisher started out in 1955 by explaining the concept of mutual fund investing to Pittsburghers across their kitchen tables. Nearly 50 years later, the company still emphasizes that type of personal service.

Today, Federated establishes relationships with financial organizations, and provides them with mutual funds and other investment products designed especially to meet the needs of its clients, whether they be individuals or multinational corporations. Federated maintains relationships with more than 100,000 investment professionals, including bank trust officers, broker/dealers, bank broker/dealers, registered investment advisers, and others. Through these financial intermediaries, more than 1 million consumers nationwide invest in Federated products.

Although it has grown to become one of the nation's largest and most respected investment management and financial services companies, Federated is known for much more than its size. The company's reputation stems from a consistent approach to investing, development of timely and innovative investment products, and an attention to detail that ranks among the best in the business.

"The investment reputation of this company was established with a strong foundation in money market funds," Donahue says. "But this is a dynamic industry, and as the needs of our customers have changed over the years, we have responded with a variety of investment products and services that can help them meet their financial goals."

In 1995, Federated expanded its investment operations in the domestic and international equity arenas by launching its Global Investment Unit. Located in New York City, the unit has the expertise to manage any type of international equity or fixed-income

Federated Investors, one of the nation's top investment management firms, has its headquarters at the corner of Liberty Avenue and Grant Street in Pittsburgh.

"Federated's history in the business has been a distinguished one," says J. Christopher Donahue, president and chief operating officer at Federated. "We have a strong foundation of dedicated employees and quality products that position us as a world-class money manager right here in Pittsburgh."

Federated has nearly 1,800 employees and offices in New York City; Dublin, Ireland; Boston; and Pittsburgh, where the company was founded in 1955.

product. Assets in these areas already exceed $11 billion.

Today, Federated offers a complete range of investment choices that cross all market sectors: global, equity, bond, and money markets. And the company's highly skilled and experienced portfolio managers and analysts manage the funds to pursue performance over the long term, and avoid investment gimmicks and surprises.

Federated's investment style has helped grow its assets—ranked in the top 1 percent of all money market managers, the top 5 percent in bond funds, and the top 7 percent in equity funds. Currently, Federated manages or administers more than $130 billion in assets in more than 300 mutual funds, and these numbers are growing every day.

Such success has not gone unnoticed. Federated has consistently earned three-, four-, or five-star fund rankings from industry watchdog Morningstar. In addition, it has received a number of honors from Boston-based DALBAR, Inc., with special distinction given to Federated's Bank Proprietary Services, Bank Retail Services, and trust area. The company frequently comes out on top of DALBAR polls, which asks

banks nationwide to rank fund companies based on several criteria, including overall impression, organizational service and support, products, and sales/marketing.

MUTUAL FUND PIONEER

Federated's commitment to providing the best possible products and services to its customers has kept it on the cutting edge of the ever changing mutual fund industry. In the mid-1970s, the company created the first money market fund for institutional investment. Simultaneously, Federated pioneered the use of the amortized cost method of accounting, which is now the industry standard for pricing money market fund shares

at $1. Federated was also the first firm to offer private label mutual funds to affinity groups.

Federated's municipal group developed the first tax-free income fund and the first tax-free money market fund specifically for financial institutions. In addition, the company's data processing experts designed the industry's first on-line system for purchasing and redeeming money market shares.

"Federated's history in the business has been a distinguished one," says Donahue. "We have a strong foundation of dedicated employees and quality products that position us as a world-class money manager right here in Pittsburgh."

OUNDED IN 1955, MARC IS THE LARGEST FULL-SERVICE marketing communications agency in Pennsylvania, with 245 employees and annualized billings of $245 million. While based in Pittsburgh, MARC is a national agency that also operates offices in Miami, Indianapolis, Tulsa, Orlando, and

Dallas. From these locations, MARC offers the full scope of advertising, promotions, direct marketing, and public relations, with experience concentrated primarily in the areas of retail and consumer brand goods and services.

Over the years, the agency has created many memorable ad campaigns and garnered scores of the industry's top national awards. The agency's current client list includes Rite Aid, the nation's largest drugstore chain; TruServ, a 10,500-member hardware store cooperative

formed by the merger of True Value and SERVISTAR COAST TO COAST; PPG Industries; Bryant Heating and Cooling; the Eat'n Park restaurant chain; Dick's sporting goods chain; Simon DeBartolo Group shopping malls; Schwebel Baking Company; Pittsburgh Zoo; and Carnegie Museum of Natural History.

Reengineering the Company
In addition to supplying cutting-edge creative products, MARC has been an industry groundbreaker

Michele Fabrizi, MARC advertising president and chief operating officer (top)

MARC is team oriented, with teams comprised of people from all agency disciplines—media, creative, production, public relations, account service, and business management (bottom).

with respect to corporate structure. Late in 1992, under the direction of its chairman and CEO, Anthony L. Bucci, MARC became the first advertising agency in the nation to undergo a complete, top-to-bottom restructuring of the company.

MARC completely restructured its staff, physical plant, and financial organization, eliminating all departments. Since then, the company's model of reorganization has been imitated by agencies around the world. "Reengineering MARC meant totally dismantling the agency, both physically and philosophically," says Bucci. "We tore down the walls—literally and figuratively."

MARC's traditional hierarchical and departmental structure was replaced with a horizontal structure of client-focused teams. Clients love the structure, primarily because they are the focus of a team, and have direct and immediate access to art directors, media buyers, and production people alike. Under the old system, a client had to work through a single point of entry—the account service person. That method sometimes resulted in miscommunication and a slower than necessary response time to the client.

A Unique Use of Space
An important element of MARC's egalitarian structure is the way office space is allocated. There are no executives in big corner offices at MARC; even the CEO has a small, interior work space. Instead of large, individual offices, the agency has been reconfigured to create smaller, personal work spaces for everyone and much larger interactive areas.

In essence, each team has its neighborhood with its own personality, and when members of a team need to put their heads together, they have plenty of space

in which to interact. For larger meetings, they can go to the Towne Center, where the entire agency gathers regularly to hear the latest news, to share successes and challenges, to recognize the achievements of team members, or to hold a party.

MARC staffers like the team approach, which eliminates communication gaps and misinterpretation. In turn, there is a massive reduction in the duplication of efforts, and, since a team doesn't have to reinvent the wheel time and time again, the end result is cost savings for the client and a much stronger creative product.

The team structure brings out the best in everyone, since team members share responsibility and credit. All team members are empowered to make decisions that impact the client and, in the end, benefit themselves through the company's profit-sharing program.

LEAVING A MARC ON THE COMMUNITY

MARC is widely recognized for its commitment to the Pittsburgh community. The agency does more pro bono work than all the other advertising agencies in Pittsburgh combined. When MARC staffers work on a project for a nonprofit group, they approach it with the same creative intensity they exert for the paying clients. In fact, many of MARC's campaigns for non-profits have won industry awards.

Meanwhile, both individually and as a team, MARC employees have donated thousands of hours and given generous financial support to a wide range of charities, including the Pittsburgh Public

Theater; Make-a-Wish Foundation; March of Dimes; Three Rivers Center for Independent Living; Pittsburgh Hearing, Speech, and Deaf Services; Junior Achievement; Family Health Council; Pittsburgh AIDS Task Force; Salvation Army; Visiting Nurse Association Foundation; and Pittsburgh Opera.

Most important, MARC's commitment to community permeates the organization. In 1997, Bucci was honored as Outstanding Volunteer Fund-Raiser of the Year by the National Society of Fund-Raising Executives' Western Pennsylvania Chapter.

Through MARC's admirable efforts to serve the local community and its outstanding achievements on behalf of its clients, this full-service agency is indeed leaving its indelible mark on Pittsburgh and the advertising industry.

UP UNTIL 1959, ALL WASTEWATER AND RAW SEWAGE FROM HOMES and businesses in the Pittsburgh region flowed directly into the waterways untreated. Recognizing that the rivers were Pittsburgh's greatest resource, and with growing concerns about public health, Allegheny County Sanitary Authority

(ALCOSAN) began operations. Today, aquatic life, riverfront development, and recreational use of the three rivers and their tributaries are all thriving.

Incorporated under the Pennsylvania Municipal Authorities Act in 1946, ALCOSAN is governed by a seven-member board of directors—three appointed by the mayor of Pittsburgh, three appointed by the Allegheny County Commissioners, and one joint city-county appointee —with each serving a five-year term. An executive director appointed by the board oversees daily operations. ALCOSAN is a nonprofit organization financed by user charges, not taxes, with capital projects funded through the sale of bonds.

ALCOSAN processes an average of 200 million gallons of wastewater each day, and services almost 320,000 residential, commercial, and industrial accounts across 83 communities, including the City of Pittsburgh. ALCOSAN serves a population of 896,500 and operates 24 hours a day, 365 days a year.

TOP FACILITIES, INEXPENSIVE SERVICE

ALCOSAN's wastewater treatment plant—located along the Ohio River just downstream from the city of Pittsburgh—provides complete sewage treatment for the area at a cost to consumers of about $13 per month, which is significantly less than consumers pay in other major cities. The 56-acre plant is currently undergoing a major renovation that will improve the quality of life for nearby residents and position plant operations comfortably into the next century.

Under the capital improvement plan, many of the facilities are being covered for odor control, and enhancements will allow ALCOSAN to better handle combined sewer overflows (CSOs) during storms. The region is currently attempting to find ways to deal with a combined sewer system, where sewage and storm drains flow together; prolonged or heavy rains or snowmelt fill the lines up quickly, and the diluted wastewater overflows into streams and rivers untreated. Municipalities in the area are currently working with ALCOSAN and the county health department to find viable, cost-efficient solutions to reduce CSOs to meet federal regulations. As part of this action, ALCOSAN is upgrading its capacity from 200 million to 250 million gallons of wastewater treated daily.

The sewage treatment process is a two-step procedure. In primary treatment, which ALCOSAN first adopted in 1959, trash is separated from liquid waste. Then, the wastewater is pumped through a grit

All wastewater enters ALCOSAN'S main pump station to begin the treatment process. Odorous air is drawn off the wet well and transported to the incinerators via piping to be used as combustion air.

The Power of

chamber into a primary sedimentation tank, where solids are allowed to settle to the bottom for collection, and floating waste is skimmed from the top. Primary treatment removes only 40 to 50 percent of solids in the wastewater. Through secondary treatment, which ALCOSAN began implementing in 1972, air is pumped through the water to help grow microorganisms that consume harmful organic material. The water is then sent to a second sedimentation tank, where activated sludge settles out, leaving water that, when treated with a disinfectant, can be safely returned to the Ohio River.

ALCOSAN's commitment to recycling extends beyond water reclamation. The effluent (treated water) is utilized for in-plant needs, and steam from the sludge (biosolids) incineration process provides heat to in-plant buildings, as well as generating electricity on-site to provide a portion of the plant's operating needs. In addition, studies are being finalized to determine the viability of utilizing ash from the incineration process in building products.

Almost 450 wet tons of biosolids are produced daily at ALCOSAN. Two-thirds of the biosolids are recycled to energy, while the remaining third is processed with lime to produce a product known as ALCOSOIL. ALCOSOIL has been used to reclaim more than 5,000 acres of abandoned strip mines and farmland into rich growth areas. ALCOSOIL provides benefits over conventional fertilizers in that its nutrients are released slowly over time, and therefore do not contribute to runoff pollution. These are just a few steps in ALCOSAN's efforts to turn what others think of as waste by-products into materials to enrich the community while containing customer rates.

SERVICING INDUSTRY

ALCOSAN operates an extensive pretreatment program to regulate industrial customers and ensure the safety of the air, water, and biosolids that ultimately leave the plant. Local industries that fall into one of 46 Environmental Protection Agency (EPA) categories are issued discharge permits. ALCOSAN is then in a better position to monitor industrial use of the sewer system and to enforce regulations where necessary. ALCOSAN also operates a surcharge program in which almost 1,500 customers with high-strength wastes—small businesses such as supermarkets, restaurants, and food processing companies—pay add-on charges, if appropriate, and are subject to required monitoring.

In addition, ALCOSAN carries out an impressive effort to educate individuals, businesses, and communities on pollution prevention. Local residents can call a hot line to learn about proper disposal of common household products that might contain hazardous waste, such as insecticides, paint, varnish, and automobile oil. The hot line also provides information about environmentally safe substitutes that can be purchased or made at home.

ALCOSAN has moved well beyond its original mandate, which focused only on basic wastewater treatment principles. Today, area residents enjoy Pittsburgh's new reputation as a clean and livable city, and ALCOSAN is a major part of that achievement.

The distributed control system is the central operating system for the main pump station, grit and screening, headworks odor control equipment, and other related processes. Through remote control, staff can immediately identify and correct potential problems. Incineration operations also have a similar system (top).

ALCOSAN's wastewater treatment plant—located along the Ohio River just downstream from the city of Pittsburgh—provides complete sewage treatment for the area, at a cost significantly less than consumers pay in other major cities (bottom).

PERCHED ON A CLIFF ATOP MOUNT WASHINGTON, LE MONT IS ONE of Pittsburgh's ultimate dining experiences. In addition to gourmet cuisine, Le Mont features a dining room sumptuously decorated in deep hunter green and rich burgundy, accented by weeping willow trees adorned with Spanish

moss. Tuxedoed waiters serve award-winning dishes—many prepared at the table—to diners who enjoy a spectacular view of downtown Pittsburgh from every table in the house. Over the restaurant's 37 years, diners at Le Mont have included Presidents Kennedy, Ford, Carter, and Reagan, and many other world-renown celebrities and dignitaries. Like its fine vintage wine collection, Le Mont has aged to perfection over nearly four decades, most recently receiving the esteemed DiRoNA Award from Distinguished Restaurants of North America.

"There are only 500 restaurants nationwide that have received this award, and it's truly an honor to be among the best in the world," says James A. Blandi Jr., son and namesake of the restaurant's founder. Le Mont has also received *Travel Holiday*'s Fine Dining Award for 30 consecutive years and has been named Pittsburgh's Finest Restaurant by *Esquire*. Addition-

ally, Le Mont was chosen as the Most Romantic Restaurant by *Pittsburgh Magazine*, the *Pittsburgh Post-Gazette*, the *Tribune Review,* and the *City Paper*. Other honors include the *Wine Spectator*'s Award of Excellence and the American Automobile Association's Four Diamond Award. Le Mont is the only Four Diamond independently owned restaurant within 200 miles of Pittsburgh.

OFFERING THE FINEST

A few of Le Mont's best-known dishes are raspberry duck, steak Diane, and rack of lamb persillade. Le Mont's wine cellar, meanwhile, is one of the city's finest in the volume and breadth of its collection of both domestic and European wines.

For wine and cigar aficionados, Le Mont offers custom-designed wine and cigar tasting dinners. Le Mont Cigar and Spirit Society is one of the most enviable societies

in Pittsburgh, with members treated to the fine art of cigar dinners: gourmet dining, vintage wines, and the finest cigars served with single malt scotches and cognacs. Le Mont is famous for its corporate entertaining, and can accommodate banquets for up to 500 guests. The restaurant is one of the city's top places to entertain on the corporate level, and is considered one of the finest assets of the city of Pittsburgh.

Le Mont creates happy memories for very special occasions, including weddings, anniversaries, bar and bat mitzvahs, retirement dinners, and birthdays.

A complete dining experience caters to all the senses, and Le Mont fulfills this requirement with ease. Excellence in food preparation and presentation, impeccable yet warm service from the full staff, and an excellent view of Pittsburgh's skyline are the winning attributes of Le Mont.

Excellence in food preparation and presentation, impeccable yet warm service from the full staff, and an excellent view of Pittsburgh's skyline are the winning attributes of Le Mont (right).

James A. Blandi Jr. is the son and namesake of Le Mont's founder (left).

O VER THE YEARS, PRUDENTIAL PREFERRED REALTY HAS experienced considerable change in Pittsburgh, but one thing has remained constant: top-notch service. The company got its start in 1962 as Hammill-Quinlan Realtors, which consisted of one sales office and a

first-year sales volume of $1.5 million. By 1978, sales volume had climbed to $123 million and, by 1979, Hammill-Quinlan had become the second real estate firm nationwide to be purchased by Merrill Lynch Realty Inc.

In 1989, Merrill Lynch sold its national real estate operation to the Prudential Insurance Company of America. Two years later, the Pittsburgh franchise was purchased by Ron Croushore and Helen Sosso, who had worked for the company for several years. Croushore, president, and Sosso, executive vice president, quickly embarked on a series of acquisitions that allowed the franchise to expand into new markets and add experienced agents. As a result, the agency now operates 23 residential sales offices covering eight counties and, in 1997, had a sales volume exceeding $780 million that was generated by more than 550 residential sales associates.

THE RELOCATION PROCESS
Prudential Preferred Realty handles a large percentage of Pittsburgh's residential sales—in fact, the second-largest share in a very competitive marketplace. The company assists a number of local corporations, including Bayer, PPG Industries, IBM, US Airways, Mellon Bank, and Alcoa, in relocating employees to the region.

A key part of the relocation process is selling an employee or prospect on the Pittsburgh region. Trained employees in Prudential Preferred Realty's Relocation and Counseling Center provide information on the area and address any concerns without pressuring the individual or family to buy a home. At the client's request, a Prudential agent will also take him or her on a tour of the area.

Only when a client is ready to begin the home search will Prudential assign a top agent who is experienced in handling the needs of

transferees. If the client has a home to sell, Prudential will provide solid marketing advice so the client is relieved of that burden as quickly as possible. And if necessary, Prudential will offer an objective market analysis to ensure that the property is properly priced so it will sell in a shorter time.

BEYOND RELOCATION
In addition to specializing in marketing and selling new construction, Prudential Preferred Realty operates ancillary businesses in mortgage financing, title services, home owner's insurance, referrals, and buyer's services. One of the company's most successful programs is Value Range Marketing,

which allows sellers to list their home at a set price and market it within a price range, rather than at a single price. The program has reduced the average number of days a home stays on the market from 106 to 38.

Croushore and Sosso expect computer technology to play an increasingly larger role in home sales, with homes being bought and sold on the Internet.

Regardless of what the future brings, says Sosso, "Our philosophy is to remain in touch with what Pittsburgh's home buyers and sellers are looking for, and to selectively hire and train only the finest agents to provide those services to our customers."

Clockwise from top:
The Pittsburgh Prudential Preferred Realty agency now operates 23 residential sales offices covering eight counties.

In addition to specializing in marketing and selling new construction, Prudential Preferred Realty operates ancillary businesses in mortgage financing, title services, home owner's insurance, referrals, and buyer's services.

The Pittsburgh franchise was purchased in 1991 by Ron Croushore and Helen Sosso.

WHEN MILTON FINE AND HIS LAW PARTNER ED PERLOW entered the hotel business back in 1961, they were in search of investment opportunities for their clients. They found an opportunity in Erie—the small Capri Motel. What Fine and Perlow would soon discover,

Clockwise from top left: Milton Fine (seated) founded Interstate Hotels with Ed Perlow in 1961 and is now chairman of the company; Tom Parrington (standing) serves as president and CEO.

In Pittsburgh, the company owns the Pittsburgh Airport Marriott, manages the Pittsburgh Green Tree Marriott, and manages and is a minority owner of the Pittsburgh Marriott City Center.

however, was that the Capri would become more than just an investment. Rather, it would be the start of a remarkable success story.

Shortly after they had purchased the property from the owner, who had agreed to stay on to manage the motel, the man passed away—and Fine and Perlow instantly became hotel managers. While they became hotel managers unexpectedly, Fine and Perlow made the most of that unexpected turn of events, forming a company that would become one of the major players in the hotel industry.

Today, Interstate Hotels, the business Fine and Perlow founded, is widely recognized as the largest independent hotel management company in the United States. Interstate Hotels owns, manages, leases, or performs related services for more than 220 hotels, with a total of more than 45,000 guest rooms. In Pittsburgh alone, Interstate Hotels manages and owns the Pittsburgh Airport Marriott, manages the Pittsburgh Green Tree Marriott, manages and is a minority owner of the Pittsburgh Marriott City Center, and manages and

owns the new Residence Inn by Marriott near the airport.

Perlow died in 1989, and, says Fine, "it was a difficult time for the company and me personally because of my longtime partnership with Ed, and more importantly, my longtime friendship with him." Still, Fine continued to lead the company to greater success, eventually taking it public in 1996.

The secret to Interstate Hotels' long-term success in the hotel industry can be traced back to its roots in the early 1960s when Fine and Perlow began developing Howard Johnson Motor Lodges along Pennsylvania interstate highways. When Fine and Perlow were successful with their Howard Johnson properties, they decided to turn their attention to another and newer hotel brand for a property that they wanted to develop on a site between downtown Pittsburgh and the airport. The brand was Marriott, and, after convincing the Marriott organization to give them a franchise, Fine and Perlow built the Pittsburgh Green Tree Marriott, which opened in November 1972.

Interstate Hotels is now the largest Marriott franchisee by far,

JEFF GREENBERG

The Power of

Interstate Hotels is now the largest Marriott franchisee by far, but it also manages hotels under most of the major hotel brands, including Hilton, Westin, Sheraton, Radisson, Double-Tree, Embassy Suites, and Crowne Plaza. Shown from left are Chicago Embassy Suites and the Westin Washington D.C. City Center.

In addition to its properties in the United States, Interstate manages hotels in Russia, the Caribbean, and Canada. Pictured is the Hotel Tverskaya in Moscow.

but it also manages hotels under most of the major hotel brands, including Hilton, Westin, Sheraton, Radisson, DoubleTree, Embassy Suites, and Crowne Plaza. In addition, it manages one of the largest portfolios of luxury independent hotels in the industry, such as the beautiful Don CeSar Beach Resort & Spa in St. Petersburg Beach, Florida, and the prestigious Charles Hotel in Cambridge, Massachusetts.

SHREWD BUSINESS PHILOSOPHY

The hotel business is one of cycles, which Fine recognized shortly after he and Perlow entered the industry. The company's success today is directly related to getting the most out of the cycles, whether they are downturns or upturns. That is how Interstate Hotels became known first as a successful hotel owner and developer, and then as the largest independent hotel management company in the United States.

In the late 1980s, Fine recognized that there would soon be a downturn in the industry and so Interstate stopped developing hotels; instead, the company turned its attention to managing properties for third-party owners, such as financial institutions that became saddled with hotels they had received through foreclosures. Soon, Interstate Hotels became known as a hotel management company that could quickly turn around distressed properties.

"One of the reasons we are successful is that we do something different in every cycle," Fine ex-

plains. "Instead of fighting the currents, we try to see which way the currents are going and take advantage of them."

Fine points out that the company recognized in the early 1990s that real estate values were going to increase. "We knew this better than anyone because we could see demand increasing in the hotels that we managed," says Fine. "We could see rates starting to creep up, so we started to buy hotels. That's been tremendously successful: it has enhanced our growth, and it has permitted us to make money in real estate as well as in hotel management. When it made sense to build hotels, we did that. When it made sense to pull back from that, we shifted our strategy to concentrate on third-party management. Now, we are back into building and developing hotels."

Interstate completed its initial public offering in June 1996; at the same time, Interstate Hotels acquired a portfolio of 14 upscale, full-service hotels and has continued to acquire upscale properties in growing markets.

THE MANAGEMENT BUSINESS

When travelers choose a hotel, they usually make a decision based on brand names they know and trust. What most guests do not realize is that it's the management company that often dictates the level of quality at a specific hotel. Interstate Hotels is known for the high level of quality it instills at the upscale, full-service properties

it manages, as well as for running profitable hotels for its owners. Meanwhile, Crossroads Hospitality Company, a division of Interstate Hotels, provides the same services for mid-market hotels, such as Hampton Inn and Courtyard by Marriott.

Over the past four decades, Interstate Hotels has grown into a company that employs some 24,000 people worldwide, with about 1,500 in Pittsburgh alone. In addition to its properties in the United States, Interstate manages hotels in Russia, the Caribbean, and Canada.

Interstate Hotels will continue to monitor the industry's changing cycles, and find ways to grow from them and to maximize shareholder value. Interstate Hotels' successful history of adapting to change has secured the company's role as a true leader. As Fine says, "We always seem to be one step ahead of everyone else."

AT LA ROCHE COLLEGE, JUST MINUTES NORTH OF DOWNTOWN Pittsburgh, education is more than just the time spent in classrooms. The private Catholic college offers a values-based liberal arts education with professional preparation that provides students with the solid foundation they

will need to succeed in the 21st century.

"Academics in the form of high-quality, stimulating instruction and innovative, challenging major programs of study are very important at La Roche," says Monsignor William A. Kerr, Ph.D., president of La Roche. "Recognizing, however, that students spend 75 percent of their college careers out of the classroom, the student life staff and a number of other college offices are in place to meet the needs of the highly diverse group of students who enroll here each year, and they add tremendous vitality to the La Roche educational experience."

The college's facilities also provide a valuable complement to students' academic and extracurricular experiences. For example, the Kerr Fitness and Sports Center is a state-of-the-art recreational facility equipped with racquetball courts, an indoor jogging track, weight room, dance/karate studio, and basketball courts. The college's apartment-style residence halls are

newly renovated, and include all new furniture and carpeting. Two new computer labs recently opened, featuring brand-new computers, which give students instant access to the Internet.

La Roche was founded by the Sisters of Divine Providence in 1963. Built on the foundation of the Catholic tradition in education, the college encourages the spiritual as well as the intellectual

development of its students. Today, La Roche welcomes students, faculty, and staff from all religious, cultural, national, and racial backgrounds.

The academic programs offered by La Roche range from graphics, design, and communications to the business-focused administration and management programs. Nationally accredited as a baccalaureate-degree-granting business division by the Association of Collegiate Business Schools and Programs, the administration and management division offers accounting, finance, management, and computer information systems majors. Other areas of study cover education, the humanities, natural and mathematical sciences, and nursing.

POSITIONED FOR THE FUTURE

La Roche's academic programs strongly mirror the feedback provided by employers in the Pittsburgh region. This flexibility and cooperation within the academic program keep instruction up to date, while keeping La Roche graduates in demand.

"Dynamic change is an important component of La Roche 2000, the college's strategic planning blueprint for the future," says Kerr. "The single most important defining element of the La Roche tradition, however, will never change. Students are the center of all that we do here at the college. La Roche is strongly committed to preparing students to become contributing members of our ever changing global society."

Armed with an education rich in the Catholic tradition, career-focused professional experience in the form of internships, and a liberal arts foundation, graduates of La Roche College are well prepared for today's changing marketplace.

Monsignor William A. Kerr, Ph.D., serves as president of La Roche College (top).

Interacting with members of the student government, Kerr remarks, "Students are the center of all that we do here at the college. La Roche is strongly committed to preparing students to become contributing members of our ever changing global society" (bottom).

THREE DECADES AGO, WHEN A CONSUMER MADE A PURCHASE, the retailer logged the sale in the ledger while the consumer went on his or her way. But to Dr. Alfred Kuehn, the purchase was only the beginning of a process. Kuehn's Pittsburgh-based company, Management Science

Associates, Inc. (MSA), would compile information from every transaction, then analyze the data so its client could use the information to make future business decisions.

Today, MSA is a leader in developing information-based solutions for companies around the world. In addition to its headquarters in Pittsburgh, MSA has six branch offices in North America, along with offices in the United Kingdom and Malaysia, from where MSA develops knowledge databases for a broad range of industries. Its client base has expanded from consumer-packaged-goods manufacturers to include the top 35 cable television networks, advertising agencies, and financial institutions, among others.

"With an explosion in the amount of data available to us, we are faced with the need to synthesize this information," says Kuehn, who continues to serve as chairman of MSA and has coauthored three books on marketing research. "The rate of technological innovation will continue to increase exponentially, creating a world of instant, multidimensional information. Real-time information will fuel the global economy in which opportunities are many, but short-lived, and competition has no boundaries, " Kuehn says.

MANAGING INFORMATION FOR SUCCESS

Today's businesses are more sophisticated than when MSA first began harnessing data for companies in 1963. Scanners at checkout counters track information, while many manufacturers of consumer goods run promotional contests that generate extensive data about their consumers. To keep up with these new technologies, MSA's Business Analysis and Consulting division uses analytical software and information-based systems to help companies manage and analyze their

data. This new knowledge can then be used by the clients to implement strategies to build customer loyalty while keeping prices competitive and increasing profitability.

MSA's Information Management Solutions division, meanwhile, designs, develops, and maintains large data warehouses and is the acknowledged leader in the implementation of supply chain management systems. MSA is one of the world's largest processors of diverse marketing, sales, financial, media, and other client information, integrating and maintaining more than four terabytes of client data for Fortune 100 clients.

Some companies want to manage data themselves, so MSA's KnowledgeWare division develops state-of-the-art data access and analysis tools, and offers consulting, software integration, and hardware

implementation services. One of MSA's largest business segments consists of customers related to or in the media, and these companies rely heavily on MSA's Media division. For these customers—from large advertising agencies and cable networks to local television stations—MSA provides business process automation and electronic commerce solutions, which allow them to be more responsive to an ever changing marketplace.

MSA has been a leader in the information-based solutions field since its inception. Says Kuehn, "Our track record speaks for itself. We have over three decades of continuous growth and more than 500 employees serving hundreds of clients. The essence of MSA is creativity and innovation. We are committed to discovering new frontiers in information-based solutions."

Management Science Associates is a leader in developing information-based solutions for companies around the world.

VER ITS 35-YEAR HISTORY OF PRODUCING MASS SPEC-
trometers—which use an analytical technique that
utilizes the unique molecular structure of substances to
identify and quantitate them—ABB Extrel has developed
into a highly efficient, customer-focused organization.

ABB Extrel, recognized worldwide as the foremost producer of mass spectrometry components and as the world leader in process mass spectrometers used in on-line analysis, is the mass spectrometry arm of ABB Process Analytics, located in Lewisburg, West Virginia. ABB Process Analytics, the premier supplier of on-line analytical instrumentation, including process gas chromatographs and spectrophotometers, is in turn a division of $40 billion ABB Inc.

In Pittsburgh, ABB Extrel operates out of the RIDC Park in O'Hara Township, where it employs approximately 70 people. The company's roots in Pittsburgh date back to 1964, when Wade L. Fite and Richard T. Brackman, who at the time were members of the physics faculty at the University of Pittsburgh, established Extranuclear Laboratories. The company's name changed in 1985 to Extrel Corp. to conform with the company's expanding scope, and

the ABB tag was added in 1995, when Extrel was acquired by ABB Inc.

Today, ABB Extrel's products are used in a wide variety of markets, and in applications that impact many aspects of day-to-day life. Components and systems are sold via the Quadrupole Mass Spectrometry (QMS) group to government and commercial research facilities to do an incredible variety of research including new semiconductor improvements and development of cutting-edge materials. Products are also sold to other manufacturers as key components in their products.

The Industrial Mass Spectrometer group markets systems designed for continuous analysis in an industrial setting, with major markets including hydrocarbon processing, environment, pharmaceuticals/biotechnology, and metals production. All of ABB Extrel's products are developed and manufactured in Pittsburgh.

QUADRUPOLE MASS SPECTROMETRY

The QMS products are descendants of an innovative RF power supply design Brackman and Fite developed for their own research at the University of Pittsburgh. As demand for their electronics grew, they added additional components to their product line, starting with quadrupole mass filter assemblies and ultimately including complete turnkey systems, including vacuum chambers and pumps.

The research components business that evolved from this pioneering innovation has grown to include the solutions to problems of an incredibly diverse nature. Through continuous innovation and vacuum component design improvements, along with updated electronics assemblies, the QMS business has grown to become the premier supplier of research grade quadrupole mass spectrometer components to the worldwide research community in areas of

In Pittsburgh, ABB Extrel operates out of the RIDC Park in O'Hara Township, where it employs approximately 70 people.

atomic and molecular physics, physical and physical organic chemistry, semiconductor process development, and atmospheric research, as well as OEM systems for inductively coupled plasma mass spectrometry and secondary ion mass spectrometry.

Many of the world's top scientists use ABB Extrel products. For instance, Mario Molina, who was the 1995 Nobel Prize winner in chemistry, used ABB Extrel products to confirm the possibility that chlorofluorocarbons have the potential to deplete the ozone layer in the earth's upper atmosphere. Two other researchers, Dudley R. Herschbach and Yuan T. Lee, who received the 1986 Nobel Prize in chemistry, used ABB Extrel products to probe the dynamics of chemical reactions. And researchers in the laboratory of Swedish 1981 Nobel laureate Kai Siegbahn used ABB Extrel products to characterize the physical properties of buckminsterfullerenes, or buckyballs—an elegant, newly discovered form of carbon wherein 60 carbon atoms form a soccer-ball-shaped sphere with intriguing characteristics that have captured the imagination of scientists and scholars around the world.

The 1995 introduction of the Merlin data acquisition and control system opened up an even wider array of opportunities for solving problems with ABB Extrel quadrupole components. The current product offering in ABB Extrel quadrupole research components includes systems with the highest sensitivity in the market, the highest attainable quadrupole resolution, the highest available quadrupole mass range, and the greatest flexibility for integrating ABB Extrel components into larger systems, including systems containing multiple quadrupoles.

INDUSTRIAL MASS SPECTROMETRY

ABB Extrel was one of the original pioneers in process mass spectrometry, with its first product, the PROMASS, being introduced in 1976. More than 20 years of experience, coupled with ABB Extrel's reputation for working closely with customers to understand and solve their problems, have made ABB Extrel the world's leading supplier of process mass spectrometers.

The Questor™ Process Mass Spectrometer product series, introduced in 1994, is ABB Extrel's latest line of real-time analyzers. Questor was developed uniquely through ABB Extrel's close relationship with a customer advisory board formed specifically for the purpose of developing a new process mass spectrometer platform.

Since its introduction in 1995, ABB Extrel's Questor series of process mass spectrometers has grown at twice the market growth rate and exceeded all other competitors' platforms. ABB Extrel customers note the Questor's speed, ease of use, and low maintenance requirements as the leading attributes for the rapid growth of the business. Key markets served by ABB Extrel's process mass spectrometer business include hydrocarbon processing, biotechnology, steel processing, and environmental monitoring.

CUSTOM MASS SPECTROMETRY

By combining the technical expertise of the Research Components' business unit with the real-time mass spectrometry capabilities of its Industrial Mass Spectrometry group, ABB Extrel has developed the ability to solve technically complex problems that are very customer specific. The resulting customer-driven products have provided the ability to analyze such widely diverse things as the tiny gas bubbles contained in the glass used for television picture tubes and the almost nonmeasurably low level of organic hydrocarbon waste in a river providing cooling for a major gasoline refinery.

The 1995 introduction of the Merlin data acquisition and control system opened up an even wider array of opportunities for solving problems with ABB Extrel quadrupole components.

Customer Service and Support is a key selling point for ABB Extrel, which provides customers with unsurpassed technical support. To support its customers for the life of the instrument, the group has a team of application scientists, engineers, and service specialists, backed by more than 30 years of experience (top).

The Questor™ Process Mass Spectrometer product series, introduced in 1994, is ABB Extrel's latest line of real-time analyzers. Questor was developed uniquely through ABB Extrel's close relationship with a customer advisory board formed specifically for the purpose of developing a new process mass spectrometer platform. Since its introduction in 1995, ABB Extrel's Questor series of process mass spectrometers has grown at twice the market growth rate and exceeded all other competitors' platforms (bottom left and right).

ABB Extrel has found the key to this business to be the focusing of a group of technically diverse people on a very specific problem. This ability to solve tremendously complex problems has resulted in some of the largest names in the industry approaching ABB Extrel to help solve analytical problems that previously were thought to be unsolvable.

Customer Service and Support is a key selling point for ABB Extrel, which provides customers with unsurpassed technical support. To support its customers for the life of the instrument, the group has a team of application scientists, engineers, and service specialists, backed by more than 30 years of experience.

This support is critical because ABB Extrel research components

are designed to last for decades, and can be modified and updated to work in a wide range of applications. ABB Extrel research components are world renowned for their durability, with many systems delivered to customers more than 25 years ago still actively used in research. With their diverse array of high-performance technology, ABB Extrel research components offer one-stop shopping for the discriminating researcher.

With ABB Extrel's strong technology, the company has built a world-class customer service organization. After reliability, customer service and response time are the most important needs of the customer. Recognizing this, Extrel set about to build the best and largest global service network in the marketplace. This strategy involved hir-

ing degreed professionals as service engineers, installing field service offices around the globe, developing advanced troubleshooting software and hardware, and quickly delivering spare parts. Today, the company can service its products around the world through modem links, respond within hours to field service requirements, and deliver spare parts anywhere in the world faster than any competitor. ABB Extrel's eminent reputation is due primarily to its commitment to customer service and support.

Integrated with ABB Process Analytics, Extrel's service organization provides local support in a global environment. Products are distributed and supported internationally through ABB's corporate structure, which is well known as a model for international business activities. Every activity from new product development to service support structures is developed in order to provide customers with tools that allow them in turn to be more productive.

This focus on the customer and on understanding and meeting the customer's needs is present in every function of the company. It has allowed ABB Extrel to become the world leader in sales and technology for its products, and has given its support organization an unsurpassed reputation for true customer service.

O N OCTOBER II, 1967, THE PITTSBURGH PENGUINS PLAYED their very first game in the National Hockey League (NHL)—against the venerable Montreal Canadiens at Pittsburgh's Civic Arena. The Canadiens won that game 2-1, but, since then, the Penguins have proved that they

belong among the NHL's elite teams. In fact, in the 1990s, the Penguins have qualified for the play-offs in seven straight seasons, and in 1991 and 1992, the team won two Stanley Cups in a row.

Much of the Penguins' success during the 1990s can be attributed to Hall of Famer Mario Lemieux, who retired after the 1996-1997 season. Arguably the greatest goal scorer in the history of the NHL, Lemieux won the Art Ross Trophy, given to the league's top scorer, six times. And in both of the team's Stanley Cup years, he was awarded the Conn Smythe Trophy as the most valuable player of the play-offs.

TODAY'S PENGUINS

Despite Lemieux's departure, the Penguins' future looks bright. The team is beginning a new era under coach Kevin Constantine, who accepted the job less than

two months after Lemieux played his final game. Constantine inherited a solid nucleus of veterans, including center Ron Francis and perennial all-star right wing Jaromir Jagr. Constantine truly embodies the spirit of the Penguins, believing in hard practices and making known his strong distaste for losing.

"We are very excited about the direction of the franchise," says co-owner Howard Baldwin. "We all are looking forward to working with our new head coach, Kevin Constantine. He is a bright, young, enthusiastic coach—exactly the kind of guy we need to lead us into this new era."

Adds Roger Marino, co-owner since summer 1997, "I am excited by the opportunity here. Under Howard's ownership group, this has been one of the most successful franchises in the National Hockey

League. Stability is going to be there. We are going to have a quality team, because I am a fan."

ON THE ICE

Hockey games in Pittsburgh are more than just sporting contests— they're also social events. Fans often make a night of it, starting with dinner at a nearby restaurant before heading to the Civic Arena, which is located in the heart of Pittsburgh's central business district. Affectionately called the Igloo, the Civic Arena has hosted an average of nearly 16,000 fans at home games throughout the 1990s.

The Penguins' training facility, Iceoplex at Southpointe, is also a fan favorite. Part-owned by Lemieux and the current team owners, the venue contains a sports-themed restaurant and public meeting rooms, not to mention an NHL ice surface that is used by youth and adult hockey leagues, high schools, figure skaters, and learn-to-skate programs.

With its top-notch facilities and programs, Iceoplex helps develop the talents of young skaters, and at the same time creates new fans for the Penguins—a team that has made Pittsburgh proud for three decades.

In the 1990s, the Pittsburgh Penguins have qualified for the play-offs in seven straight seasons, and in 1991 and 1992, the team won two Stanley Cups in a row. The Penguins' Joe Mullen is shown here after the 1991 Cup presentation (right).

Much of the Penguins' success during the 1990s can be attributed to Hall of Famer Mario Lemieux, arguably the greatest goal scorer in the history of the NHL, who retired after the 1996-1997 season (left).

P

PORT AUTHORITY OF ALLEGHENY COUNTY PROVIDES A NETWORK of public transportation services to those traveling within a 730-square-mile area, which includes the city of Pittsburgh and all of Allegheny County. Port Authority (PAT) is one of the largest and most diversified public transit agencies in

the United States. A fleet of more than 900 buses and 60 light rail vehicles and rehabilitated trolleys run daily throughout the area carrying people to and from work, shops, doctor's appointments, and many other destinations.

Port Authority is Allegheny County's largest public service provider, with 10 to 15 percent of Allegheny County's population using its services daily. Port Authority's nearly 225 routes include more than 15,000 bus stops and nearly 5,000 Park and Ride parking spaces that are available for commuters. PAT also sponsors ACCESS, the nation's largest paratransit program for senior citizens and persons with disabilities.

Port Authority began operations in March 1964 after Pennsylvania's legislature approved the consolidation of 33 private transit carriers, including the Pittsburgh Railways Co. and 32 bus and inclined-

plane companies. The consortium combined fare structures and centralized operations, resulting in a unified transit system in Allegheny County.

Today, Port Authority's 2,900 employees provide public transportation services to approximately 250,000 riders daily and 72 million riders annually. Port Authority's board of directors also authorizes the operation of many other carriers, such as hospital shuttles, which add an additional four million rides per year and push the annual ridership total within PAT's family of services beyond 76 million.

CONNECTING TO THE SUBURBS

Among Port Authority's facilities is a 25-mile, light rail transit system known as the T. Commuters from the South Hills of Pittsburgh can board the system at various stops, some of which are only a few steps from their homes. The

climate-controlled cars operate above ground primarily in the South Hills, and then via subway in the heart of downtown Pittsburgh. Port Authority is currently renovating an additional 12 miles of trolley lines in other parts of the South Hills.

Riders who live south of downtown Pittsburgh also have the luxury of the South Busway, a roadway limited strictly to bus traffic that enables riders to quickly travel to and from downtown. For riders who live east of downtown Pittsburgh, the Martin Luther King Jr. East Busway provides similar quick access. Riders can board a bus right outside their homes and travel to downtown in minutes.

In 1996, Federal Transit Administrator Gordon Linton awarded Port Authority $59.1 million for its Busway System Expansion Program. By 2001, riders from the western suburbs will see their commutes

A fleet of more than 900 buses and 60 light rail vehicles and rehabilitated trolleys run daily throughout the area carrying people to and from work, shops, doctor's appointments, and many other destinations. Port Authority is Allegheny County's largest public service provider, with 10 to 15 percent of Allegheny County's population using its services daily.

The Power of

improve when Phase I of Port Authority's Airport Busway/Wabash HOV Facility opens, linking Carnegie to downtown Pittsburgh. The busway is expected to provide transportation for an estimated 50,000 riders daily, substantially reducing travel time to and from downtown. Additionally, the project is expected to provide thousands of future job opportunities in the airport corridor.

In the meantime, Port Authority continues regularly scheduled routes from Oakland and downtown with its 28X Airport Flyer. Utilizing small transit vehicles (STVs), PAT began offering the regular airport service for the first time in November 1996, and ridership quickly topped initial projections.

While modernization continues, a bit of the past remains via the Duquesne and Monongahela inclines, both of which ascend and descend the jagged face of Mount Washington on a daily basis. They are among the few remaining inclines in the country, and have become tourist favorites. Beyond providing a unique public transportation option to area residents, the inclines provide one of the best views of Pittsburgh's unique downtown skyline.

PAT IN THE COMMUNITY

For many years, the Pittsburgh community has recognized Port Authority as a leader in community-based programs. PAT employees are active in community causes, including the United Way, Boy Scouts of America, and Central Blood Bank. Over the years, PAT has also been a leader in helping the community deal with weather-related emergencies. It has altered routes to maintain transportation needs of riders in its service area, as it did during the blizzard that crippled the Northeast in 1993.

Facility improvements, service enhancements, and community support have all contributed to PAT's success. Whether its riders choose public transportation out of necessity or out of benefit to the environment, PAT plays a key role in the economic growth and vitality of Allegheny County.

DIANE DABALDO/FRED P. KENDERSON PHOTOGRAPHY

While modernization continues, a bit of the past remains via the Duquesne and Monongahela inclines, both of which ascend and descend the jagged face of Mount Washington on a daily basis. Beyond providing a unique public transportation option to area residents, the inclines provide one of the best views of Pittsburgh's downtown skyline.

FRED P. KENDERSON PHOTOGRAPHY

Among Port Authority's facilities is a 25-mile light rail transit system known as the T, operating above ground primarily in the South Hills, and then via subway into the heart of downtown Pittsburgh.

WHEN FRANK FUHRER WENT OUT ON HIS OWN IN 1966 to start Frank B. Fuhrer and Associates, he had no idea his company would be where it is today— the exclusive regional distributor for Anheuser-Busch and Coors, as well as a number of smaller

brewing companies. But during the past three highly successful decades of growth and change, one key element of the company has remained the same: Fuhrer is still the sole shareholder.

One other enduring characteristic of the company, now called Frank B. Fuhrer Holdings, Inc., is that the company, its employees, and the communities where it does business all profit. "I'm like the Smith Barney ad," says Fuhrer. "I do things the old-fashioned way— I earn it."

HUMBLE BEGINNINGS

Fuhrer's roots are in East Brady, about 60 miles north of Pittsburgh, where his father ran a men's clothing store. After graduating from Allegheny College and the University of Pittsburgh's MBA program, Fuhrer remained in Pittsburgh to work for Northwestern Mutual Life Insurance Company. When his father died in 1956, he returned home to help his mother sell his father's business. "I couldn't sell it—$5,000 was the best offer, and there was $25,000 worth of inventory in it," recalls Fuhrer. "I had to go up there and take over. I borrowed money and expanded the store and it went great for a while, until USX closed their limestone plant. Then I ended up with a store in a ghost town." It took Fuhrer until 1964 to recover. "I learned so much. I think that was the foundation that enabled me to be successful. I finally got the debt paid off, but I had nothing but the experience to stand me in good stead," says Fuhrer.

He returned to Pittsburgh and the insurance business, forming a partnership with his brother. "We were making a good living, but we weren't going to get rich," says Fuhrer. "I had that entrepreneurial spirit—I wasn't satisfied." In 1966, he went out on his own to sell credit insurance. "I had $8,000 in the bank, four kids, and I said, 'I'm going out to do this on my own,'" recalls Fuhrer. "It took four months to get an account, and from there on the business grew. By 1973, I was doing more than $30 million in premiums and grossing more than $3 million a year."

DIVERSIFICATION

Frank B. Fuhrer and Associates was on its way. In the mid-1970s, Fuhrer added another company to sell warranty insurance. In 1977, he bought a life insurance company. The insurance business generated the cash flow for Fuhrer to diversify into other industries. And diversify he did. In 1981, Fuhrer bought Ridgeway Chemical Co. in Charlotte, which manufactured

Frank B. Fuhrer, who serves as chairman of Frank B. Fuhrer Holdings, Inc., says the future direction of the company will be decided by his sons (left).

David Fuhrer serves as president of the company (right).

paint sealants. In 1982, he purchased the Anheuser-Busch distributorship for Western Pennsylvania. In 1984, Fuhrer acquired a Lincoln Mercury dealership in Columbia, South Carolina, and Roffler, a Pittsburgh-based hair care products company. Since he had a small conglomerate going at the time, the name of the company was changed to Frank B. Fuhrer Holdings.

Today, Frank B. Fuhrer Holdings is solely a beer distributorship, and the largest wholesaler in the Pittsburgh area. Fuhrer sold off the other companies during the 1980s; both he and his sons, David and Frank, preferred to focus on the distributing business. They are the exclusive distributors for Anheuser Busch in Allegheny County and, in 1988, began distributing Coors products as well. The company distributes Coors throughout nine counties in Western Pennsylvania, including Washington, Fayette, Butler, Westmoreland, and Lawrence. Fuhrer also distributes Corona, Moosehead, Foster's Lager, Beck's, and St. Pauli Girl.

"I wanted to get into a consumer-oriented business," says Fuhrer. "I'd had enough with the intangibles. My philosophy of running any business is the same: I don't know anything about any of them; I just have a good strategy. Hire good people who understand that strategy and accept it, and if you do that, you can make any business work. Be honest and fair and serve your customers."

COMMUNITY SERVICE
Fuhrer's goals for the company haven't changed, either. Some of his tenets: Grow the business by investing capital in it; pay your employees well; and give back to the community. On the latter point, Fuhrer is unfailingly generous, spending an estimated $1 million in community giving annually. He's funded a wing at Shadyside Hospital, and lends continuing support to the Family House in Oakland, raising about $3 million with a golf tournament featuring top PGA touring pros. Fuhrer supports Pittsburgh's firemen and police, the Pittsburgh

Today, Frank B. Fuhrer Holdings is solely a beer distributorship, and the largest wholesaler in the Pittsburgh area (top).

Frank B. Fuhrer Jr. acts as operations vice president and manager of the company (bottom).

Zoo, and the Pittsburgh Regional History Center, as well.

Fuhrer, who serves as chairman of the company and makes financial decisions, says the direction in which the company will go is now up to his sons, David, the president, and Frank, who's operations vice president and manager. With such a firm foundation, Frank B. Fuhrer Holdings, Inc. will surely continue to be a success.

OT TOO MANY COMPANIES CAN SAY THEY'VE HELPED astronauts in space communicate with people on Earth. Or that they've had a hand in defeating a world chess champion. But Compunetics, a privately held company located east of Pittsburgh in Monroeville, boasts both

accomplishments, along with a three-decade history of developing top-notch printed circuit boards and telecommunications equipment.

Employing some 240 people, Compunetics and its subsidiaries, Compunetix, Inc. and Chorus Call, Inc., generated consolidated revenues of $35 million in 1997. Their customers include NASA Goddard Space Flight Center, which uses Compunetix voice- and data-switching technology for space shuttle support and other missions. Compunetics also designed and built circuit boards for Deep Blue, the IBM computer that beat chess whiz Gary Kasparov in 1997.

In 1997, the Pittsburgh High Technology Council honored Compunetics as one of the 50 fastest-growing technology-oriented companies in Southwestern Pennsylvania. Compunetics experienced 50 percent growth, placing it among the top 10 companies in the region with gross revenues of $25 million to $100 million.

QUALITY AND CUSTOMER SERVICE

Compunetix, Inc. specializes in state-of-the-art telecommunications technology, namely large-scale multimedia, multipoint teleconferencing systems, both in the commercial and government markets. Compunetix is committed to active research and development in the fields of advanced interconnection networks and complex information processing systems. A standard line of commercial products provides reliable teleconferencing to telephone companies, PTTs, private service bureaus, distance learning organizations, and corporations. Teleconferencing systems range in size from large-scale service bureau systems to small-scale corporate systems. Compunetix products are modular, allowing simple transi-

tions when expanding the number of ports in a system. Patented space division switching architecture allows customers to easily migrate between audio and multimedia MCUs.

Compunetix provides mission-oriented teleconferencing systems under the product names of CONTEX 500T, 1000T, and 2000T. This CONTEX series was designed to meet the extremely demanding requirements of the military and aerospace industries, and is built to operate in crisis management- and mission-oriented situations in which reliability is not an option, but a critical requirement. Systems have been provided for launch control centers, launch support facilities, satellite control centers, air traffic control, emergency access centers, command and control facilities, and vessel traffic control.

Compunetix has developed the latest skills and technologies needed to establish and maintain

Compunetics, Inc. is headquartered just east of Pittsburgh in Monroeville, in a 103,000-square-foot facility that houses Compunetix and Chorus Call.

leadership in the production from conception to completion of highly sophisticated electronic systems. Compunetix is a vertically integrated organization that stands firm in its belief that when all levels of electronic design and manufacture are available internally, the quality of the product can be strictly controlled. The Instrumentation Systems Division of Compunetix is a sophisticated electronics manufacturer that serves a comprehensive list of external customers, as well as internal manufacturing needs. Versatility in manufacturing extends from simple board-level production to complex system-level integration.

Chorus Call, Inc., a subsidiary of Compunetics, provides both audio and video teleconferencing services primarily in the U.S. market. Chorus Call, Inc. has a wholly owned subsidiary, Chorus Call, SA, which serves the European market from its offices in Lugano, Switzerland. Applications for conference calls are as far reaching as the imagination, and users receive friendly, professional assistance with conferencing quality unsurpassed in the industry.

In addition to Compunetix and Chorus Call, Compunetics has operating activities through its Printed Circuit Boards Division, which has always maintained a

position at the forefront of the design and manufacture of high-tech printed circuits. Specialties include fine line circuitry and controlled impedance manufacturing of prototypes and low- to medium-volume production.

Compunetics' dedication to high-quality products and well-rounded customer service, along with its significant advances in telecommunications technology, ensures that the company will add to its already long list of accomplishments—whether it be in space, on Earth, or in the rarefied atmosphere of international chess championships.

THE TYPICAL FORTUNE 500 COMPANY RECEIVES UP TO 7 million employment inquiries in one year, and potential employers spend seven to 10 seconds reading each of those résumés. If a job seeker actually makes it in the door, employers in most cases will make a hiring decision within

the first four to seven minutes of the interview. The message? Job searching is a difficult process, and it's no wonder that as many as 30 million Americans suffer long-term unemployment annually. But one Pittsburgh company, R. Davenport & Associates, has established a track record of helping job seekers land quality positions—often much more quickly than they would in a typical search.

"The average person changes jobs about every eight to nine years. That's only four or five times in a lifetime that they are trying to secure a new job," says Robert C. Davenport, who founded the company in 1968. "We do this every day. We know what needs to be on a candidate's resumé. We know how they should present themselves

during an interview. Most important, we know about many jobs before they are even advertised."

A Teaching Process

Job seekers, many of whom are referrals from former clients, work with Davenport project managers and learn how to secure the position they truly want. What sets the company apart from the legions of headhunters and outplacement firms is that Davenport is actually contracted by the job seekers, who view the fee as an investment in their own future. In contrast, headhunters are paid by companies working to fill positions, while outplacement firms are paid by employers that have recently terminated staff and are helping them secure other employment.

At Davenport, the focus is on the job seeker, beginning with a thorough evaluation of each client. Candidates first undergo several written tests. Shortly afterwards, their oral presentation skills are evaluated and honed to ensure that they present themselves in the best manner possible during an interview. Some candidates receive helpful suggestions regarding their appearance—from hairstyles to clothing choice. Clients also learn how to effectively negotiate in an interview setting, so they are better prepared to secure the salary and benefits they deserve when a job is offered.

Covering the Spectrum

Davenport clients range from young professionals leaving their first postcollege position to seasoned executives, and salaries can range from $18,000 to $300,000. After signing a contract and paying the firm's fee up front, clients enjoy a lifetime commitment from Davenport. Although most of the company's matches are successful and long-lived, anyone who subsequently loses a job can return to Davenport for additional assistance. The firm often taps into its vast network of former clients, many of whom have become decision makers within the ranks of successful companies, to offer leads for current candidates.

According to Davenport, it is this tried-and-true networking approach that really pays off: "I tell all our clients that they have two choices: to network or not work." It's all part of R. Davenport & Associates' service, which has successfully counseled job candidates for three decades.

R. Davenport & Associates' dedicated staff has successfully counseled job candidates for three decades. (From left, back row) David J. Donohue, Karen H. Welsh, Patricia Barrett, Ginny Litzel, Dorothy T. Bannow, Joan C. Trombetta, Linda Buick Campbell; (front row) Charles H. Logue Jr., Robert C. Davenport, Donald Rice

WHEN A. WARNE BOYCE TOOK OVER A SMALL FOOD- and water-testing business in 1969, he had lofty aspirations for its future success. Calling the new venture Microbac Laboratories, Inc., Boyce and his wife, Dr. Doreen E. Boyce, slowly started to shape

the company into one of the nation's leading analytical laboratory groups. Today, the group includes 20 labs nationwide, employs some 250 people, and earned revenues of $16 million in 1997.

Headquartered in the Regional Industrial Development Corporation park properties at Thorn Hill, just north of Pittsburgh, Microbac offers a wide array of testing services on hazardous waste, drinking water, air emissions, wastewater, and food chemistry, as well as microbiology testing. The latter two are performed in the laboratory on McKnight Road.

In its first 20 years, Microbac could attribute much of its growth to the regulatory development of the Environmental Protection Agency, the Department of Agriculture, and the Food and Drug Administration. The lab performed the environmental tests necessary for industrial companies to conform to federal regulations. Then, when a gradual decline in regulations began, Microbac worked to help its customers achieve National Pollutant Discharge Elimination System (NPDES) permit conformance and began many other customer-oriented programs.

Recently, the government has required new standards for meat testing. Due primarily to *E. coli* and salmonella scares, meat and poultry processors and packers

must now perform tests to detect the presence of lethal bacteria strains. Microbac is there to perform such tests. Not only has its microbiological strength been advanced by the knowledge and direction of its chief microbiologist, Mark A. Matrozza, but its increasingly sophisticated food chemistry section under Vice President David J. Danis is developing advanced procedures of international importance.

STEADY GROWTH

The key to the growth of Microbac has been the strategic planning of the Boyces, along with the more recent leadership of their son J. Trevor Boyce, president and chief operating officer. Moreover, despite a difficult economic climate in the industry, the company has been able to provide steady pricing nationwide, allowing for local trends when necessary. The group's policy

has kept it comparatively out of the commodity pricing wars that have characterized the environmental testing industry of the 1990s. The result has been a stable, yet growing, operation in an industry that has experienced severe setbacks.

In the future, Microbac, currently the foremost authority on extraneous substances in fruit juices in the country, plans to continue expanding in the United States and abroad. In addition to acquiring new labs, the company will explore some new areas, such as nuclear magnetic resonance analytical work. In 1997, Microbac was rated the 14th-largest lab in the United States; by combining its environmental interests with food quality and nutritional analytical work, the company is sure to remain within the ranks of the top U.S. testing laboratories for many years to come.

Clockwise from top left: Microbac Laboratories, Inc. Chairman and CEO Warne Boyce beside a digesting apparatus

Robert W. Morgan acts as senior vice president of Microbac.

One of the nation's leading analytical laboratory groups, Microbac includes 20 labs nationwide, employs some 250 people, and earned revenues of $16 million in 1997.

J. Trevor Boyce serves as president and chief operating officer of Microbac.

ONE MIGHT EXPECT TO FIND A HIGH-TECH COMPUTER COMPANY in a futuristic building in the middle of a suburban research park. But Computerm Corporation, which manufactures channel extension products for mainframe computers, has chosen instead to make its home in a

restored historic structure in downtown Pittsburgh. From the outside, the building looks like a turn-of-the-century law office or trading house. Yet inside, engineers are helping to move vast amounts of data over great distances. And just as it has done with its choice of locations, Computerm has succeeded in business for the past three decades by going against industry expectations.

"Just a few years ago, when personal computers were really taking off, news reports predicted that the mainframe era was over, and that networked PCs would take over the market," says Computerm President Ed Nash. However, many experts failed to note that some businesses—particularly those that have traditionally relied upon mainframe computers for a decade or more—would be somewhat reluctant to make a switch. Many such companies have spent enormous amounts of money developing the software and systems to run on mainframes. Still, while mainframes are very good at running several large computing jobs at one time, they are expensive to purchase and operate, and many companies, when expanding to different

cities or countries, may look for less-expensive alternatives to installing an additional mainframe.

Computerm developed the Virtual Mainframe Channel™ (VMC) system to provide an effective means to use a single mainframe at more than one location. With one VMC unit connected to a channel on the central mainframe computer and another connected to a peripheral device in another city, users in a remote location are able to access the mainframe as if they were on-site. It's all done via software technology that emulates the mainframe. The data is sent over analog, digital, or even satellite communica-

tion. The system, in essence, fools the mainframe into thinking that the peripherals—be they printers, tape drives, or check sorters—are only 400 feet away instead of across the nation or globe.

AN ENTREPRENEURIAL START

Computerm first got its start in 1969, when two Westinghouse employees, Regis Herbst and Richard Madden, developed the channel extension idea for internal use as an experiment. After their suggestion that Westinghouse develop and market the technology was met with a lukewarm response, the pair decided to strike out on

Clockwise from top:
Computerm Corporation has grown from a two-man operation in 1969 to a company that employs more than 100 people supporting 1,500 systems for approximately 300 companies in more than 25 countries around the world.

For more than 29 years, Computerm has continued to develop advanced technologies to serve large corporate data centers.

Looks can be deceiving. Behind the historic facade of Computerm's headquarters, a high-technology company produces mainframe connectivity products.

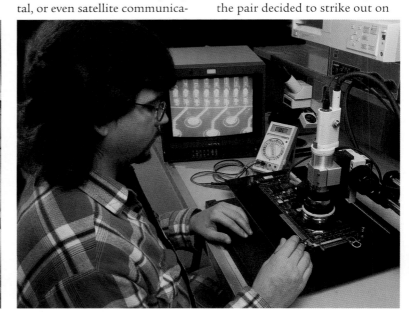

their own, working to develop and improve the technology out of a basement.

Before too long, Madden and Herbst had installed a prototype at the University of Pittsburgh, and with that, the company was on its way. Today, the two-man operation has grown to employ a staff of more than 100, and to serve a client base exceeding 300 companies in more than 25 countries around the world. To date, more than 1,500 systems have been installed.

Part of the company's success can be attributed to the fact that many of today's businesses are still better suited to mainframes, which excel at large jobs such as manipulating and storing databases that can't fit on a PC. Mainframe manufacturers, such as IBM, consequently are shipping more mainframes now than in past years.

SPEED, POWER, AND RELIABILITY

Computerm currently offers three systems—the VMC 8100, 8200, and the new 8250—that provide different levels of speed and power. The company has earned the loyalty of many of its customers through its products' reliability, as well as its unsurpassed customer service and support, which is offered 24 hours a day, 365 days a year. Computerm almost exclusively serves data centers at large Fortune 500 firms, which have a need to manipulate large amounts of data, as well as unique equipment specifications for reliability, service, and support.

Though its largest customers are banks, Nash points to outsourcing of computing centers as a strong market for Computerm's channel extension products, noting that, "Large corporations, in order to save money, are beginning to contract service providers to run the mainframe operations." And with Computerm products, a computer outsourcer can manage a number of mainframes, each for a different corporate customer, with no disruption to the customer's remote processing center.

"Regis and Dick's strategy was that we'd rather be the best, and not just the biggest, company in our market," Nash adds. "We

Computerm's products can be found in Fortune 500 data centers helping companies connect mainframes and devices across the globe (top).

Computerm offers a variety of systems to meet customers' networking requirements (bottom).

want to grow, but not at the expense of being able to fully support existing customers." Computerm does not plan on straying from the strategy that has proved successful for almost three decades. The company continues to develop advanced technologies to serve large corporate data centers. And although sales continue to increase by upwards of 30 percent a year, Computerm plans on expanding only in carefully chosen markets, including those overseas.

In addition, the company remains committed to its com-

munity and to the idea of remaining in Pittsburgh, to the point of including that goal in its vision statement. "So many times, businesses get successful, and then they leave Pittsburgh," says Nash. "But we want it to be known that we're going to stay here." All but two of its 115 employees—including those in sales, technology development, and customer support—operate out of Computerm's Wood Street headquarters. "We like our employees," says Nash, "and our employees like Pittsburgh. It's home for us."

AMPCO-PITTSBURGH CORPORATION—THE CORPORATE PARENT of six separate businesses, each of which manufactures and markets engineered equipment—was formed in 1970 by the merger of Screw and Bolt Corporation of America and Ampco Metal Company. ■ Listed on the New York and

Philadelphia stock exchanges, Ampco-Pittsburgh employs approximately 1,300 people. Its operations include Buffalo Air Handling Company, Aerofin Corporation, Buffalo Pumps, Inc., New Castle Industries, Inc., Union Electric Steel Corporation, and F.R. Gross Company. The corporation's products serve both national and international markets.

BUFFALO AIR HANDLING COMPANY

Ampco-Pittsburgh acquired Buffalo Air Handling in May 1995. Located in central Virginia near the town of Amherst, it is one of the leading manufacturers of large standard and custom air handling systems for a wide range of industrial and commercial customers.

Products from Buffalo Air Handling Company control the indoor environment of some of the most prominent buildings in North America. These include many hospital, university, government, and institutional buildings. A wide range of industrial custom-

ers, including many Fortune 500 companies, also purchase Buffalo equipment for use in chemical, pharmaceutical, microelectronic, automotive, and transportation manufacturing facilities.

AEROFIN CORPORATION

Aerofin, located in Lynchburg, Virginia, has manufactured the industry's most extensive line of heat exchange coils since 1923. Uniquely designed surfaces consist of smooth, tapered fins helically wound on tubes, providing maximum heat transfer with minimum air friction. The coils come in a wide range of fin spacing, and are fabricated from aluminum, copper, and other special materials. Plate fin coils are also offered.

Aerofin manufactures equipment for a wide array of users including nuclear and conventional power plants, pulp and paper mills, and chemical processing plants, and provides coils for use in heating, ventilating, and air-conditioning systems. In addition to its manufacturing leadership, Aerofin also provides customers with consulting and engineering services in heat transfer.

BUFFALO PUMPS, INC.

Located in North Tonawanda, New York, Buffalo Pumps has been producing centrifugal pumps for customers in the power generation, refrigeration, marine defense, pulp and paper, and lube oil markets since 1887. Buffalo Pumps has long been recognized for its pioneering efforts in canned seal-less pump technology, and its products meet the requirements of ISO 9001 registration.

The company has its own research and development labora-

A vertical lube oil pump for a major turbine manufacturer is being fabricated at Buffalo Pumps, Inc.

New Castle Industries, Inc. supplies customers with screw and bimetallic barrel combinations for use in the plastics processing industry.

tory on-site, and pumps are thoroughly tested before leaving the plant. In recent years, the company has been growing as an international supplier, serving customers in Latin America and Asia.

NEW CASTLE INDUSTRIES, INC.

New Castle Industries has been engineering and manufacturing extrusion and injection feed screws for the plastics processing industry from its Feed Screws Division plant near New Castle, Pennsylvania, since 1966. With the 1995 addition of Bimex, the company can supply customers with screws and bimetallic barrel combinations that have maximum compatibility and peak performance capabilities. In 1997, New Castle acquired satellite screw manufacturing facilities in New Hampshire and South Carolina, making it one of the largest screw manufacturers in North America.

In addition, the company manufactures hard chrome chill rolls in a wide range of finishes for the paper, film, glass, and plastics industries. New Castle also engineers, builds, and retrofits extrusion processing machinery.

UNION ELECTRIC STEEL CORPORATION

Union Electric Steel is the world's leading manufacturer of forged, hardened steel rolls for the ferrous and nonferrous material finishing industries. The company, founded in 1923, has melting, forging, and machining operations at its Harmon Creek facility in Burgettstown, Pennsylvania, and has finishing plants in Carnegie, Pennsylvania; Valparaiso, Indiana; and Tessenderlo, Belgium. It also operates an electroslag remelt facility in Erie, Pennsylvania.

Union Electric Steel is also an industry leader in the development of ultra-deep, hardened work rolls, which have superior microstructure and resultant longer service life. Rolls are custom-made to strict customer specifications, and meet the requirements of ISO 9001, to which the company has been registered since 1993.

The company is a major participant in global markets, not only in Europe, where it has production facilities, but in the Pacific Rim, India, and South America. Markets served by sheet and strip materials produced with Union Electric Steel rolls include the automotive, appliance, aircraft, packaging, and construction industries.

F.R. GROSS COMPANY

This Stow, Ohio, company was acquired by Ampco-Pittsburgh in 1997. Its principal business is in the design and manufacture of heat transfer rolls used in the plastics, packaging, printing, and associated industries. The company also has a steel fabricating operation in Warren, Pennsylvania, where it specializes in the custom fabrication of carbon steel, aluminum, and stainless steel.

**Clockwise from top right:
Buffalo Air Handling Company made this air handling unit—the largest ever manufactured by the company—for a Boston hospital.**

A large return-bend cooling coil manufactured by Aerofin Corporation awaits shipment to a pulp and paper mill after testing.

Workers inspect cold mill work rolls from Union Electric Steel Corporation prior to shipment.

E ACH YEAR, PHYSICIANS ARE CONFRONTED WITH SOME 10,000 NEW patients with spinal cord injuries, and are challenged with the task of trying to limit the damage stemming from these injuries. When Memphis-based Sofamor Danek Group Inc., known internationally as the "spine specialists," wanted to develop a new

computer model of the human spine, it looked to ANSYS, Inc., a software development company that was founded just south of Pittsburgh in 1970.

ANSYS, Inc., formerly known as Swanson Analysis Systems Inc., develops finite element analysis software, which design engineers use to stress-test products and bring them to market more quickly and efficiently. Sofamor Danek used ANSYS software to develop a computer-based, finite element model of the spine. This model now helps doctors across the country evaluate the effects of different methods of using implants to stabilize an injured spine.

But ANSYS' software products improve productivity in other industries as well. Heavy equipment manufacturer Eaton Corp. used ANSYS software to develop and test a new steer axle for heavy trucks. Another company used ANSYS

software to improve actuators in wing flaps of commuter planes.

"Part of providing our customers with the right tools is to consistently develop state-of-the-art technology," says Peter J. Smith, chairman and CEO of ANSYS, Inc. "We remain focused on our strong foundation and leadership in this area. As a strategic software provider, we are sensitive and responsive to customer demands."

THE FOUNDER

Dr. John A. Swanson founded ANSYS, Inc. and remains the company's chief technologist today. ANSYS, Inc., headquartered at the Southpointe business park in Washington County, was acquired in 1994 and underwent a management restructuring. The company name was then changed to ANSYS, Inc. to reflect its new and broader scope.

Swanson, an internationally recognized authority and innova-

tor in the application of finite element methods to engineering, continues to provide a guiding hand in the company's product development efforts. In 1994, he was named an American Society of Mechanical Engineers Fellow. The same year, *Industry Week* named him among the top five in its listing of 50 Research & Development Stars in the United States. In 1996, Washington and Jefferson College named Swanson Entrepreneur of the Year.

ANSYS TODAY

The ANSYS program, the industry's leading broad-based multiphysics finite element analysis package, remains essential to the company's continued growth and success. Additionally, ANSYS, Inc. aggressively pursues development of products integrated within popular computer-aided design packages. These software applications allow customers to access design data directly, which eliminates duplica-

ANSYS, Inc., a software development company founded just south of Pittsburgh in 1970, is headquartered at the Southpointe business park in Washington County.

tion of efforts and facilitates reuse of data and collaboration among engineers.

Since its founding, ANSYS, Inc. has grown to more than 200 employees, and established long-term relationships with customers in a range of industries, including transportation, electronics packaging, biomedical, industrial equipment, and consumer goods. Throughout the world, ANSYS products are used by thousands of companies, including 68 of the Global Fortune Industrial 100 companies. ANSYS, Inc. markets its products principally through a network of more than 40 independent distributors who maintain more than 70 offices in 34 countries. ANSYS, Inc. was the first finite element analysis software developer to obtain ISO 9001 certification, the internationally accepted quality standard for the software industry.

"We have learned by working closely with companies that a major concern today is to find effective, affordable ways to improve upon the product development process, building better products faster and less expensively," says Smith. "To be competitive, manufacturers in the forefront of their industries are combining best-in-class technology with the most efficient product development methods."

Effective communication with the customer is one key element to developing long-term relationships. Another is providing support for the product after the sale. ANSYS Technical Enhancements and Cus-

tomer Support (ANSYS TECS) keeps customers up to date on advancements in ANSYS software. The company also offers training that enables customers to gain a measurable return from its ANSYS software shortly after bringing it on-line. Additionally, ANSYS offers consulting services that help customers increase productivity by maximizing the return on their investment in ANSYS software.

ANSYS TOMORROW

The days of manually conducting destructive testing on new products are long over. Also gone are the extremely high costs traditionally associated with research and development. As Smith explains, "Engineering software technology is constantly evolving—driving the marketplace and allowing companies to bring better products to market faster and at lower cost. Each new software release provides breakthroughs that allow compa-

nies to rely more on virtual product development and less on hours of laboratory, build-and-break studies. What used to take companies months or even years, costing a lot to design and build, now can be done in just weeks without great expense. This evolution is a direct result of the changing role of design analysis and optimization software.

"It was once thought of as an extra step, but today this software is used throughout the product development process," Smith adds. "At ANSYS, we develop the software tools that allow companies to bring the full power of analysis and simulation to the mainstream of engineering."

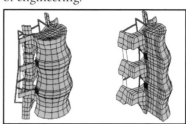

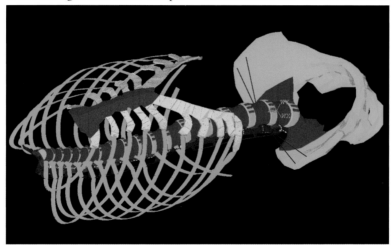

Sofamor Danek used ANSYS software to develop a computer-based, finite element model of the spine. This model now helps doctors across the country evaluate the effects of different methods of using implants to stabilize an injured spine (top and middle).

ANSYS' software products improve productivity in other industries as well. Heavy equipment manufacturer Eaton Corp. used ANSYS software to develop and test a new steer axle for heavy trucks (bottom left and right).

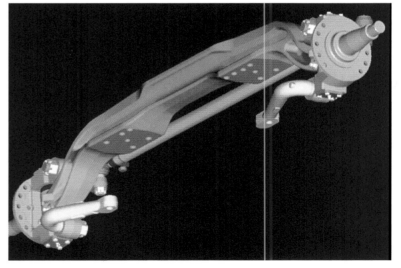

L.D. Astorino & Associates, Ltd.	1972
Bohlin Cywinski Jackson	1972
MCI Telecommunications Corporation	1973
Chelsea Building Products, Inc.	1975
Coldwell Banker	1975
Ramada Plaza Suites & Conference Center	1975
Allegheny Financial Group, Ltd./Allegheny Investments, Ltd.	1976
Industrial Scientific Corporation	1976
OMEGA SYSTEMS Inc.	1976
Respironics	1976
Center for Organ Recovery and Education (CORE)	1977
Sumitomo Corporation of America	1977
Zink Partners/Dorchester Towers Apartments	1977
First Western Bancorp, Inc.	1980
David L. Lawrence Convention Center	1981
Metplas Inc.	1981
Mannesmann Demag Corporation	1982
Pittsburgh Business Consultants Inc.	1982
Carnegie Group, Inc.	1984
Grantmakers of Western Pennsylvania	1984
International Technology Corporation	1984
RPS, Inc.	1985
Aristech Chemical Corporation	1986
Powerex, Inc.	1986
Corporate Accommodations, Inc.	1987
Koppers Industries, Inc.	1988
The Minority Enterprise Corporation	1989
Sony Technology Center-Pittsburgh	1990
Carnegie Science Center	1991
Getting to the Point, Inc.	1991
Armco Inc.	1993
Fiserv	1993
MotivePower Industries, Inc.	1993
The Andy Warhol Museum	1994
Aerial Communications, Inc.	1997

WITH MORE THAN 25 YEARS OF HISTORY AND TRA-dition, L.D. Astorino & Associates, Ltd. (LDA), a 130-person, Pittsburgh-based architecture, engineering, and environmental (AEE) firm, prides itself on innovative design technique and a complete continuum-of-service business approach.

Known for quality service, the firm serves a broad base of clients in a variety of industries. "We're not dominated by any single client or industry; we provide the same high quality of service to clients with projects of all sizes. Solving problems and leaving behind a better place for our clients and their communities has always been a primary focus," says Louis D. Astorino, FAIA, founder and chairman of the firm.

As one of the largest AEE firms in Pittsburgh, LDA completes projects both nationally and internationally. It prides itself on being a generalist firm, but with technical expertise in each industry served. LDA successfully supports the sports and entertainment, health care, commercial, retail, education, liturgical, and criminal justice industries. Some of the firm's work well known in the Pittsburgh metropolitan area includes the Trimont, University of Pittsburgh Stadium improvements and locker room renovations, Municipal Courts facility, PNC Bank Operations Center, Blue Cross Primary Care Centers, Passavant Hospital's master site plan and hospital expansion, Bethel Medical Center, and UPMC Moon Medical Center.

CONTINUUM OF SERVICES

Every project LDA undertakes is managed by a team approach. Foremost on that team is the client, who is a partner throughout the entire process. Through the firm's continuum of services, each project flawlessly transitions from phase to phase of development. "We don't design in a vacuum. We diligently work with each client to meet their needs," says Astorino. LDA's cohesive, full-service team approach ensures quality results.

There are numerous reasons for a continuum-of-service philosophy, but ultimately the main reason is cost control. For example, LDA's in-house construction management department conducts cost comparison studies, which reveal to clients options for achieving the highest value per budget. The result: lower construction costs, improved design efficiency, and accelerated progress, all while meeting—if not exceeding—project objectives.

"We do not achieve our goals at the expense of our clients, but rather with them," Astorino says. "That philosophy has been rewarded by the community. We've successfully designed and supervised the construction of sports facilities; commercial and industrial developments; prisons; medical centers; public and private housing; government facilities; and mixed-use projects, including offices, banks, shopping centers, restaurants, and warehouse distribution facilities. Each year, our project list continues to grow."

L.D. Astorino & Associates, Ltd. (LDA), an architecture, engineering, and environmental firm, designed the local Masonic Temple (bottom) and also worked on the Pennsylvania State University library (top). LDA prides itself on being a generalist firm, but with technical expertise in each industry served.

ED MASSERY, MASSERY PHOTOGRAPHY

ED MASSERY, MASSERY PHOTOGRAPHY

The Power of

Adds Dennis Astorino, AIA, president of LDA's architectural division, "An integral part of the AEE business is the development of relationships. A lot of our work is repeat business from our clients, indicating not only our depth and breadth, but more important, the trust our clients place on us."

DIVERSIFIED TALENTS

Trust isn't the only reason clients return to LDA for professional service. They also return for the firm's diverse capabilities. LDA has trained architectural specialists who possess numerous years of experience creating designs for their specific industry specialty. "We have expert engineers to handle building system issues as well as environmental concerns. Our specialists know what works and what doesn't. They are experts at creating designs that are functional and effective for the particular application," says Patrick Branch, PE, president of LDA's engineering division.

Clients appreciate the continuum-of-services approach because it provides them with the benefit of one-stop shopping for all of their professional service needs. LDA offers real estate service to help clients select and analyze a site, conduct feasibility studies, and even finance a project. The firm's engineering services, meanwhile, provide expertise in civil, electrical, structural, and mechanical engineering. Interior design specialists provide space planning and programming, furniture selection, and manufacturing resources for furniture, lighting, fabrics, carpeting, and accessories.

The environmental engineers and consultants provide extensive health and safety, indoor air quality, and asbestos management, as well as the traditional environmental services. "As part of the design team, our environmental specialists identify potential problems with a site and work through the issue to resolution. In-depth knowledge of the metals and chemical industries as well as the health care sector allows for practical, cost-effective solutions for our clients," says Bernard Quinn, CIH, president of LDA's environmental division. And finally,

construction management services are offered to assist clients throughout the construction process.

What began as one man's vision has become a multifaceted, world-renowned company known for its innovation and style. LDA has built a reputation for quality designs and consulting services in a wide variety of fields. Above all else, the company has remained dedicated to putting the client first. "The result," Louis Astorino says, "is top-quality service—the best in design performed cost effectively and, above all, exceeding the client's expectations."

Clockwise from top left:
LDA prides itself on innovative design technique and a complete continuum-of-service business approach, evident in the Pittsburgh Municipal Courts facility.

The Blue Cross primary care facility is one of many examples of the firm's work in the Pittsburgh metropolitan area.

LDA, known for quality service to a broad base of clients in a variety of industries, stretches its services southward to Bradenton's McKechnie Field, the Pittsburgh Pirates' spring training facility.

A LONG PITTSBURGH'S FIFTH AVENUE, AMID VENERABLE St. Paul's Cathedral and Mellon Institute, stands a modern building that personifies Pittsburgh's melding of yesteryear's manufacturing-based economy with the modern-day, technology-based infrastructure. Called the

Software Engineering Institute at Carnegie Mellon University, the building blends nicely with the older structures of its neighbors, while providing an interior workplace that facilitates the development of rapidly advancing software technology.

Such architectural mastery is the work of Bohlin Cywinski Jackson, one of the leading design firms in Greater Pittsburgh. The national firm has also completed projects in Pennsylvania, Maryland, New York, New Jersey, and Washington.

Bohlin Cywinski Jackson was founded as Bohlin and Powell in 1965 in Wilkes-Barre, and opened an office in Pittsburgh in 1977. The firm adopted its present name in 1991, recognizing the inclusion of Jon Jackson, who manages the firm's Pittsburgh office. In addition to offices in Pittsburgh and Wilkes-Barre, the firm also maintains offices in Philadelphia and Seattle.

KARL A. BACKUS

Bohlin Cywinski Jackson has many well-known projects in Pittsburgh, including the University of Pittsburgh Biotechnology and Bioengineering Center (top) and the Senator John Heinz Pittsburgh Regional History Center (bottom).

BEST-KNOWN PROJECTS

Perhaps Bohlin Cywinski Jackson's best-known project in the Pittsburgh region is the Software Engineering Institute at Carnegie Mellon University, a joint venture with Burt Hill Kosar Rittelmann Associates. The building was chosen for an American Institute of Architects (AIA) national award.

A few miles down the road, Bohlin Cywinski Jackson also designed the University of Pittsburgh Biotechnology and Bioengineering Center, the first new construction at the Pittsburgh Technology Center, which is built on an old steel mill site along the Monongahela River. The facility is a state-of-the-art research building for biological sciences that also features magnificent views of the river and the distant city skyline.

Bohlin Cywinski Jackson subsequently designed the Carnegie Mellon Research Institute and the Aristech Polypropylene Center at the Pittsburgh Technology Center. Together with the Biotechnology Center, this group of buildings illustrates Bohlin Cywinski Jackson's abilities in creating distinguished architecture while meeting the demands of diverse technological programs. Other well-known projects in and around Pittsburgh include the Senator John Heinz Pittsburgh Regional History Center, the renovation of the Harris Theater for the Pittsburgh Cultural Trust, and the Winchester

Thurston School's North Campus. The firm has also provided design services to a number of the Pittsburgh region's corporations, including Westinghouse, Rochester and Pittsburgh Coal Company, WESCO, Computerm, and Aristech Chemical.

Among the firm's most well-known commissions nationally is the 47,000-square-foot, residential compound for Microsoft chairman William Gates III. Designed in collaboration with architect James Cutler, the Gates compound blends the architectural traditions of the Northwest with the accommodation of intensive, state-of-the-art technology.

Bohlin Cywinski Jackson's spectacular designs have garnered the firm a number of industry awards. The pinnacle came in 1994, when the AIA awarded Bohlin Cywinski Jackson the Architecture Firm Award, presented annually to the company that has produced distinguished architecture consistently for at least 10 years. It is the highest honor the AIA can bestow on a firm. Bohlin Cywinski Jackson continues to live up to the award by designing impressive structures for both the local and national landscapes.

KARL A. BACKUS

The Power of

WITH AN ANNUAL REVENUE OF MORE THAN $18.5 BILLION, MCI Telecommunications Corporation is one of the world's largest and fastest-growing telecommunications companies. MCI offers a full range of integrated communications services to more than

20 million customers, including long distance, local access, wireless, paging, Internet access and software, on-line services, business software, network management, and systems integration.

MCI, credited with opening up the nation's long-distance market in 1984, helped customers save money after rates fell by 70 percent. Today, MCI is doing the same for local callers in 25 cities across the country, including Pittsburgh, where it provides facilities-based service for business customers. For the first time, businesses in Pittsburgh and surrounding areas have the freedom to choose their local carrier.

MCI is committed to offering unequivocal services and products that provide such features as call forwarding, call waiting, speed calling, and conference calling. MCI Local Service also offers full-service features such as operator and directory service, emergency 911, service success codes, universal calling, IntraLATA toll calling, and voice messaging services.

CUTTING EDGE

MCI's local service initiative offers Pittsburgh-area mid- and large-sized business customers state-of-the-art switch technology with networkMCI One, which can inte-

grate local, domestic and international long distance, toll-free, private line, data, wireless, Internet access, videoconferencing, paging, and conferencing, all on a single bill. MCI is the only company, in Pittsburgh and throughout the nation, with this comprehensive offering.

By providing discounts on bundled communications services, MCI helps business customers benefit from fully integrated products and services at lower costs, with the convenience of one-stop shopping.

HELPING PITTSBURGH COMMUNICATE

With local offices in Pittsburgh and Carnegie, MCI and MCI Direct employ approximately 150 area

residents. However, as an active and committed corporate citizen, MCI affects the lives of many more people in the Pittsburgh area. By sharing its Internet expertise, MCI is committed to improving technical literacy and to enhancing academics. Through the efforts of the MCI Foundation, MCI has brought Internet access to neighborhood libraries and schools. For example, in early 1997, the MCI Foundation awarded the West Allegheny school district a $20,000 grant for hardware, software, and access to provide dedicated Internet connectivity.

Additionally, MCI helps provide and enhance a number of Pittsburgh community programs such as Marine Corps Toys for Tots and the Southwestern Pennsylvania Junior Achievement Club, and MCI executives donated their time and business acumen to teach local area junior high and high school students real-world business classes, such as applied economics.

At the forefront of the communications technology revolution for three decades, MCI has provided Pittsburgh residents and businesses with telecommunications service for a quarter of a century. As a full-service telecommunications provider and as a local business, MCI looks forward to maintaining its tradition of excellence and commitment to the community.

At the forefront of the communications technology revolution for three decades, MCI Telecommunications Corporation has provided Pittsburgh residents and businesses with telecommunications service for more than 25 years.

With an annual revenue of more than $18.5 billion, MCI is one of the world's largest and fastest-growing telecommunications companies.

N RECENT DECADES, PERHAPS ONE OF THE MOST IMPORTANT INNOVATIONS in home and office design and construction has been the vinyl window. Because they provide better insulation and require less maintenance than traditional wood or metal framed windows, vinyl windows and doors actually increase energy efficiency and contribute

to the value of a building. Chelsea Building Products, Inc. was one of the pioneering companies in the U.S. vinyl window industry. Chelsea made a good idea even better, when it introduced the first all-vinyl, double-hung tilt window system to the U.S. market shortly after the company's window extrusion operation was founded in Pittsburgh in 1975.

For more than two decades, Chelsea has continued to improve upon its original window designs, contributing many innovations to the window and door industry. The company was the first U.S. extruder to offer vinyl windows in a variety of colors, giving designers and contractors more choices to offer home buyers. Chelsea also was the first manufacturer to offer a warranty on its products to the end user—the consumer investing in a new home or improving an existing home with vinyl windows.

Chelsea Building Products' headquarters is part of a modern, 500,000-square-foot complex that includes production and distribution facilities and is based in Oakmont, an Allegheny Valley community about 11 miles east of Pittsburgh.

Chelsea has more than 300 employees who design, develop, and extrude vinyl and composite window and door systems destined for installation in homes and office buildings around the world.

CHELSEA GROWTH

Begun as Maynard Plastics in the late 1940s, the company began ridged plastic extrusions in the mid-1960s. In 1975, the company's first window extrusion operation was started on Frankstown Avenue in the Pittsburgh suburb of Homewood. It began with one extrusion machine in a small warehouse facility. By 1980, the company, now with five extruders, moved to larger quarters on Braddock Avenue near Wilkinsburg. By 1985, the company had grown to 15 extrusion machines and moved to its present location in Oakmont, an eastern suburb. In 1989, the company had grown to more than 24 extrusion lines and, officially, became Chelsea Building Products, as it began expanding its product development beyond windows and doors.

Chelsea has added to its Oakmont facility several times, and has grown to more than 45 extrusion lines that run 24 hours a day, seven days a week and produce in excess of 120 million feet of extrusions per year.

Today, Chelsea remains a leading designer and extruder of rigid vinyl and composite extrusions for window and door systems, as well as other building products.

THE BENEFITS OF VINYL

By the late 1990s, about 20 million vinyl windows were being installed annually in new construction and remodeling projects across the United States, according to research sponsored by the American Architectural Manufacturers Association. That's an increase of nearly 300 percent from 1989, when slightly more than 7 million vinyl windows were sold. Enhanced energy performance is a main reason for the increase in demand. Vinyl windows reduce heating and cooling costs, and allow builders to meet stringent energy codes across the country. Vinyl windows actually pay for themselves over time through lower heating and cooling bills, as well as reduced maintenance costs. Vinyl windows are also stronger and more stable, resulting in product longevity. In contrast, traditional wood window frames can split, rot, or become infested with insects, thus requiring more maintenance and oftentimes full replacement.

An International Reach

In December 1996, the Belgian firm Tessenderlo Chemie purchased Chelsea Building Products, which, prior to the sale, had been held and managed privately. Based in Brussels, Tessenderlo is a diversified chemical company traded on the Brussels Stock Exchange, with annual sales of approximately $2 billion. Chelsea became part of

the company's Plastics Processing Division, which operates profile and pipe extrusion plants in Belgium and France, and employs about 1,300 people. Tessenderlo has more than 6,000 employees and operates more than 50 plants worldwide.

A Quality Company

Chelsea's headquarters is part of a modern, 500,000-square-foot complex that includes production and distribution facilities and is based in Oakmont, an Allegheny Valley community about 11 miles east of Pittsburgh. There, more than 300 employees design, develop, and

extrude vinyl and composite window and door systems destined for installation in homes and office buildings around the world.

Research indicates that the number of vinyl windows installed by the beginning of the 21st century will be close to 22 million annually, as the popularity of vinyl window and door systems continues to grow with consumer demand for products that are both durable and cost efficient. With Chelsea Building Products' history of innovation, quality, and service, the company is sure to remain a key part of the continuing growth in the industry.

Vinyl building components are gaining in popularity today as the vinyl industry produces more styles, shapes, sizes, and options. Chelsea offers a vinyl product that is right for virtually any window and door need.

As Pittsburgh attracts new businesses and their employees, Coldwell Banker is there to help them get settled. Coldwell Banker offers newcomers to the region expertise in Buyer Agency, where the main priority is to represent the best interests of the home buyer. That means analyzing the market, including listed and unlisted properties; negotiating the lowest price possible; and helping structure the purchase transaction so it benefits the buyer. That's in stark contrast to most brokerage firms, whose agents represent the seller and therefore structure the transaction to the seller's advantage.

"Nine out of 10 people who have worked with Coldwell Banker would recommend Coldwell Banker to someone else," says George A. Hackett, president of the Pittsburgh region. "If you're moving to Pittsburgh, most important to you is our expertise in relocation. We offer personalized relocation kits, customized reports from the National School Reporting Services, sales associates who are trained and certified as relocation specialists, and an unparalleled level of customer service."

PITTSBURGH'S LARGEST REALTOR

Coldwell Banker has 17 residential real estate offices in Pittsburgh, along with separate divisions for corporate relocation services, property management, commercial real estate, new construction, and mortgage and title services, in addition to more than 800 sales associates. Coldwell Banker Residential Brokerage is the nation's largest real estate brokerage firm, with more than 300 offices and 13,000 sales associates. Coldwell Banker can be found on the Internet at www.coldwellbanker.com.

In 1996, Coldwell Banker Residential Brokerage did more business across the country than any other real estate brokerage, with more than 173,000 transactions. When Coldwell Banker is chosen, a company with the experience and expertise to meet the clients' needs is chosen. Much of that experience is due to Coldwell Banker's extensive relocation services, which are provided around the world. The company's Relocation Division—HFS Mobility Services—manages employee relocations for more than 1,800 corporations and works with more than 82,000 transferees annually.

At Coldwell Banker, more than 800 sales associates—more than any other local company—are the most productive agents in the Pittsburgh area. The company does more business per office than any other area company, which means the agents are exposed to more listings and sales than anyone else. All that activity ensures that Coldwell Banker can definitely find the home that's right for the client.

In the end, Coldwell Banker's larger presence in the Pittsburgh region benefits its clients. With all of Pittsburgh's neighborhoods covered, Coldwell Banker offers a wide selection of properties for incoming families. Says Hackett: "Living in Pittsburgh is about energy, culture, discovering a neighborhood, family life, recreation, sports, and business. And nobody knows Pittsburgh better than Coldwell Banker."

Services such as customized marketing plans, an Internet Web site, and expertise in luxury home sales make Coldwell Banker a leader in real estate.

NDUSTRIAL SCIENTIFIC CORPORATION IS A LEADING DEVELOPER AND manufacturer of gas monitoring solutions, offering a comprehensive line of products and services worldwide. In virtually every industry and in a host of diverse applications, products from Industrial Scientific protect people and property from harmful

exposure to a wide variety of gases.

Headquartered in an advanced ISO 9001-certified facility near the Pittsburgh International Airport, Industrial Scientific provides equipment for detecting, measuring, and monitoring a broad spectrum of toxic and combustible gases, as well as oxygen. Working with customers to provide sustainable, effective solutions to potential gas hazards has always been an integral, core strength of Industrial Scientific. The company was founded in 1976 as the Industrial Safety Division of National Mine Service Company to help coal mine operators comply with new regulations imposed by the Federal Coal Mine Health and Safety Act. In 1985, the division was sold and began independent operations as Industrial Scientific Corporation. Expansion into other industries followed quickly.

CORPORATE MISSION

The corporation's culture is centered around its mission: To design, manufacture, and sell the highest-quality products for the preservation of life and property, and to provide the best customer service available. In order to provide an environment where this mission can be pursued with genuine intent, the organization structure and management philosophy emphasizes employees, customers, and shareholders—in that order. Industrial Scientific believes its best growth potential will result from talented employees working in a supportive, challenging, and flexible environment, responding enthusiastically to the changing needs of customers.

The mission that began with 30 dedicated employees and an uncompromising commitment to quality has grown to be the definitive standard in the gas monitoring industry. As an active member

in the worldwide marketplace, Industrial Scientific is consistently in the forefront, meeting and exceeding the toughest demands and standards. The company was the first gas detection manufacturer in North America to be independently certified to the ISO 9001 quality standard, and continues to supply customers with reliable, durable products of the highest quality, backed by the most rigorous performance testing in the industry.

DIVERSIFYING PRODUCTS

Satisfying customer needs is still Industrial Scientific's central purpose. The product base that began as a single product specific for the mining industry has grown to a full line, ranging from portable instruments to complex gas monitoring systems and networks. Every day, millions of men and women in a variety of settings risk exposure to potentially explosive or lethal doses of harmful gases. Industrial Scientific products and services provide reliable protection for them as well as their property.

Because of the life-preserving nature of the products, the high-

est quality and the best customer service are the most critical distinguishing characteristics of Industrial Scientific. All employees are continuously challenged to achieve the highest possible product and service standards. Aggressive investment in research and development is a key strategy for maintaining and enhancing the company's leadership position. The future of gas monitoring is being developed at Industrial Scientific today through its commitment to exploring and developing the most promising technologies.

With a devotion to preserving human life through sound scientific principles, Industrial Scientific Corporation is proud to contribute to the integrity and success of the Pittsburgh region.

Clockwise from top:
Industrial Scientific Corporation is headquarted in an advanced ISO 9001-certified facility.

The company provides equipment for detecting, measuring, and monitoring a broad spectrum of toxic and combustible gases.

Industrial Scientific products and services provide reliable protection against exposure to potentially explosive or lethal doses of harmful gases.

LOCATION, LOCATION, LOCATION. ANYONE IN BUSINESS KNOWS ALL too well it can make or break even the most solid of endeavors. Placed right in the heart of Pittsburgh, the Ramada Plaza Suites & Conference Center reaps all of the benefits a prime location can offer. Guests are in walking distance of all major city office buildings, the Convention Center, Civic Arena, and Cultural District.

But at the Ramada, location is only the beginning. Guests from all over the world are also drawn to the Ramada for its luxurious space, generous amenities, and affordable prices. Regional residents are lured to its state-of-the-art, expanded conference center during the workday, and its fine cuisine during the evenings.

The Elmhurst Group, owned by the Hunt family, is well known around Pittsburgh. Captain Alfred E. Hunt was one of the founders of the Aluminum Co. of America, better known as Alcoa. Today, the Elmhurst Group holds extensive real estate investments and controls a number of operating companies, which include the Ramada Plaza Suites & Conference Center.

The Elmhurst Group bought the 20-story hotel and upgraded the facility to an overnight, professional executives' lodging facility used by PNC Financial Corp., Mellon Bank, USX Corp., PPG Industries, and Alcoa. It acquired a Ramada franchise in 1988.

During the past 10 years, the Elmhurst Group invested an additional $4 million in room upgrades and an 18,000-square-foot expansion of the hotel's meeting and conference center.

GETTING DOWN TO BUSINESS

The Elmhurst Group has created an unparalleled resource for the Pittsburgh region's business and convention communities. The newly constructed conference facility is second to none for everything from the smallest business gatherings to grand-scale conferences.

Seven spacious meeting rooms occupy the 11,000-square-foot facility, which gives the Ramada conference center space for up to 600 people. The designers paid special attention to communications wir-

Ramada Plaza Suites & Conference Center is downtown Pittsburgh's only all-suite hotel. Every guest has spacious, modern accommodations, designed to maximize comfort for both short and extended stays.

Ramada's new, 11,000-square-foot Conference Center's seven rooms can accommodate up to 600 people. From high-tech presentations to the very last detail of a grand wedding, Ramada's new conference and banquet rooms can handle it all with skill and style.

Each hotel guest is invited to take advantage of the on-site, 10,000-square-foot athletic club, which includes exercise machines, a track, sauna, steam room, and indoor pool. A full range of weight-lifting and cardiovascular exercises make a dip in the pool a sweet reward for a first-class workout.

The Ruddy Duck Restaurant & Lounge serves breakfast, lunch, and dinner—and even late night snacks.

ED MASSERY

ing, acoustics, and lighting, which are crucial in this age of high-tech communications. Planners studied the needs of business guests in years past, and planned for the latest technological equipment. The result is that even the most technologically advanced companies are right at home staging a meeting at the Ramada. For instance, an international company hosting an international meeting at the Ramada can link the attendees via teleconference with other employees in other parts of the world. All can interact as though they were in the same room, rather than thousands of miles apart. Additionally, the conference center is equipped with ergonomic chairs, fiber-optic wiring, sound-proof rooms, and adjustable lighting.

The Ramada also has trained its staff to be able to help with set-up needs of clients, and to respond if they need assistance during their presentations. These enhancements have earned the hotel Ramada's distinguished Plaza Suites designation, which stands for the highest quality and finest hospitality the nationwide group has to offer.

The Grand Scheme of Things

But the Ramada has much more to offer than state-of-the-art conference rooms. The Ramada is the only downtown hotel in which all rooms are suites, and all are furnished with kitchen appliances, comfortable bedrooms, and living areas. Additionally, each kitchen is equipped with a microwave, refrigerator, and coffeemaker. The living rooms have large, comfortable recliners.

After a day full of meetings or sight-seeing in downtown Pittsburgh, guests have plenty of room to either spread out and relax or prepare for the next day. The Ramada knows that what is outside the suites needs to be just as impressive. With this in mind, the hotel features a wide variety of services for its guests. A florist, dry cleaner, travel agency, and convenience store are all under one roof, and the 10,000-square-foot health club with an indoor pool is unmatched in Pittsburgh. The club is so impressive, in fact,

that many locals purchase private memberships to take advantage of its padded running track, aerobic studio, aquatics classes, and modern Nautilus equipment. One of Pittsburgh's well-known restaurants, the Ruddy Duck Restaurant & Lounge, is also located in the Ramada, along with a grand ballroom that can host events ranging from weddings to retirements.

Even with all the room to move, there's one thing at the Ramada that isn't big: the price. Despite its luxury accommodations, high-tech conference center, fine restaurant, sophisticated ballroom, modern health club, and host of other luxuries, the Ramada Plaza Suites is known for its reasonable, affordable prices, making the Ramada one of the biggest assets of a growing downtown Pittsburgh.

NDEPENDENT, PERSONALIZED FINANCIAL PLANNING ADVICE IS A RARE commodity, but it is one that Allegheny Financial Group, Ltd./ Allegheny Investments, Ltd. has been supplying to clients in Southwestern Pennsylvania for more than 20 years. Located in Pittsburgh's North Hills area, the firm has dedicated itself to providing

financial planning advice based solely on the client's particular needs and goals.

Because Allegheny Financial does not rely exclusively on commissions—instead charging a mix of flat fees and percentages of assets—it is able to recommend only those financial investments the client really wants or requires. The firm's fee structure allows its representatives to concentrate on the client's particular needs at all times, whether that client is just beginning to invest or is preparing for retirement.

IN THE BEGINNING

Allegheny Financial Group, Ltd. was formed in 1976 by James D. Hohman and James J. Browne, financial professionals who wanted to counsel clients on an independent and personal basis, free from the pressures of commissioned

sales. The company has continued to offer financial planning services on a fee-only basis.

In 1978, in order to meet client demand, the two men founded Allegheny Investments, Ltd. The brokerage, which is licensed to conduct business in more than 30 states, is a NASD-registered investment banker.

"We wanted to help people build wealth, as well as provide those services necessary to be able to stay with them over the long haul," says Hohman, who has been recognized as one of the 200 Best Financial Planners in the Country in *Money* magazine's 15th-anniversary issue and was named one of the best financial advisers in the country by *Worth* magazine in 1996 and 1997.

This recipe for success has worked well. While Allegheny Financial Group started with

only 20 clients, it has grown to approximately 1,200 financial planning clients. Allegheny Investments' nearly 200 associates place millions of dollars each week on behalf of their clients. Nearly 50,000 such accounts have been opened over the years. All the while, the company has maintained a pristine record with organizations like the Better Business Bureau and the industry's many regulatory agencies. The company, too, is well regarded by other professionals in the financial arena, including attorneys, accountants, and competitors.

WORKING FOR THE CLIENT

One of the reasons the company has flourished is because of its philosophy that, in order to fully serve a client, a financial planner must thoroughly understand, and plan for, all aspects of the customer's needs. "We do not try to sell sizzle and take shortcuts," says N. John Marinack, senior vice president of Allegheny Investments. "We work to make sure our customers get the kind of service we, ourselves, expect as consumers. Our clients' satisfaction is more important than the size of our profits."

Allegheny is not merely about making money or forging relationships with would-be clients. The firm is also committed to educating the general public about the financial planning and investment process. For several years, representatives have gone into local businesses and produced seminars to explain the employees' benefit packages—training that goes beyond a mere sales pitch for their company's services. "We want workers to be able to understand their benefits, as well as general financial concepts, in a nonproprietary way," says Hohman.

Allegheny's money manage-

Allegheny Financial Group, Ltd./ Allegheny Investments, Ltd. is among the largest independently owned financial firms in the Northeast. Pictured at Allegheny's headquarters are some of the company's nearly 200 associates.

BLACKMAN AND BELL

Leadership is provided by the firm's partners: (on stairs, from left) James J. Browne, James D. Hohman, (balcony, from left) N. John Marinack, Joseph M. DiCarlo, Karl G. Smrekar Jr., and Philip M. Gallagher.

ment process involves virtually all aspects of a client's financial well-being, including asset allocation, income tax planning, education funding, retirement planning, and estate planning. The group currently employs more than a dozen financial advisers, who have accumulated more than 200 years of financial planning experience. In addition, all six of Allegheny's principals are Certified Financial Planners. The planners and staff also have each earned several advanced degrees and credentials, including MBAs, CFAs, and law degrees.

TOP-OF-THE-LINE SERVICE

The firm helps its clients to focus on three areas. The first, portfolio design, is where Allegheny Financial representatives gain a full understanding of the clients' needs and goals, their requirements for liquid capital, and the time period for investment. Representatives then draft a plan that will allow the client to maximize returns.

Second, Allegheny Financial implements the agreed-upon strategy, with assets being deployed by carefully selected money-manage-

ment organizations. Assets are invested only with the top money managers for each area of the capital market, rather than simply with one organization, thereby ensuring maximum results. Allegheny Financial also ensures that the client is given realistic expectations regarding the return on an investment.

Finally, the investment strategy is reviewed and compared against Allegheny Financial's proprietary research. Adjustments are then made as necessary.

Having made a commitment to provide independent, professional advice, Hohman insists that all his principals be professionally

trained and certified. That independence—and integrity—is also evident within Allegheny Investments' corps of registered representatives.

"We do not sell proprietary products, so we have no ax to grind," notes Marinack, who points to the company's low turnover rate, among both employees and clients, as a measure of the company's commitment to top-of-the-line service.

"We're deeply aware that our clients' money was earned by them and belongs to them," adds Hohman. "Accordingly, we make sure that the clients are making the decisions along with us, rather than our making them on their behalf."

Thorough reviews are conducted to ensure full client awareness of critical issues (right).

Allegheny staffers assist clients utilizing state-of-the-art software as well as hardware; a company intranet eases communication across departments (left).

OMEGA SYSTEMS INC., A PITTSBURGH-BASED INFORMATION management consulting firm, has been helping Western Pennsylvania organizations solve business and operating problems with technology since 1976. And in doing so, the firm has played a significant role in the region's

transformation from an industrial to an information-based economy.

Reflecting the area's employer diversity, OMEGA's clients range from Fortune 500 companies to nonprofit organizations, and include local, national, and international firms, government agencies, financial institutions, health care services, and universities. The company customizes information technology (IT) solutions for each client's unique operating environment, regardless of the type of hardware or software used by the client.

PITTSBURGH'S PIONEER IN TECHNOLOGY

Early in the information revolution, Dr. Neal Grunstra and William D. Mariotti identified a need for adjunct expertise at Western Pennsylvania firms that were developing information systems on large mainframes. Although few organizations were using third-party consultants at the time, Grunstra and Mariotti incorporated OMEGA SYSTEMS Inc. and began recruiting top-notch computer professionals who were interested in full-time consulting careers. OMEGA grew steadily and earned a reputation for quality services, including project management, systems analysis, and programming expertise. By 1984, the firm's employment total had risen to 45, and

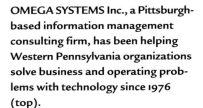

OMEGA SYSTEMS Inc., a Pittsburgh-based information management consulting firm, has been helping Western Pennsylvania organizations solve business and operating problems with technology since 1976 (top).

All consultants are specially trained by OMEGA to examine and manage the human and operating factors in applying technology, because OMEGA measures success by how well technology empowers users and how economically automation raises an organization's efficiency (bottom).

Grunstra had sold his equity portion to Mariotti and other investors.

As daily information management activities moved from the mainframe to the personal computer, OMEGA management anticipated a shift in demand for contract programming, the company's mainstay, and refined its project management methodology. In the 1990s, under the direction of Vice President Kathy Detar Gennuso, OMEGA turned its focus to strategic information priorities, including project management, applications design/implementation, electronic commerce, database development, and Internet/intranet technology.

Today, OMEGA is indebted to Pittsburgh's internationally recognized high-tech training grounds and universities for nurturing its professional team, which now numbers some 100 strong. All consultants are specially trained by OMEGA to examine and manage the human and operating factors in applying technology, because OMEGA measures success by how well technology empowers users and how economically automation raises an organization's efficiency.

ΩINSIGHT™

Much of OMEGA's success is due to ΩINSIGHT™, a proprietary

methodology for designing and implementing projects, which enables OMEGA to outperform industry norms and consistently deliver projects on-time, on-budget, and on-specification. ΩINSIGHT was viewed as an innovative, prudent approach to managing IT outsourcing risks when presented at the international convention of the Software Engineering Processing Group in San Jose. In addition to this revolutionary methodology, OMEGA has formed partnerships with local universities and national industry leaders to assess emerging technologies and products. This forethought will help OMEGA to remain on the leading edge of this dynamic industry.

On the threshold of a new era in information management, few IT shops have the internal manpower, resources, or expertise to meet challenges on their own. Even fewer are poised to evaluate and capitalize on new technologies. OMEGA has all these qualities. With all these strengths and a reputation for quality, OMEGA SYSTEMS will continue to serve as Western Pennsylvania's strategic partner—providing intelligent, cost-effective IT solutions powered by people.

THE ELEGANT APARTMENTS OF THE DORCHESTER TOWERS are secluded, yet remain convenient and affordable. That's one reason residents of the luxurious apartment community are proud to invite their friends and relatives to their homes at the beautifully landscaped property in the heart of Pittsburgh's South Hills.

At Dorchester Towers, residents find what they expect from an upscale apartment community, and more: spacious rooms, large closets, wall-to-wall carpeting, central heat and air-conditioning, ceramic tile baths, electric ranges, dishwashers, garbage disposals, balconies, and laundry facilities on every floor. Additional amenities include a large swimming pool, community rooms, social activities, storage lockers, refuse chutes on each floor, garages, and a generous amount of free parking.

TOP SERVICE

Despite the facility's features, the main attraction to this complex is service. Dorchester Towers, managed by Zink Partners, Inc., is serviced by a professional staff 24 hours a day. "When we started this company, one of our major goals was to ensure good relations with our residents, and that's the basis for all our policies," says Daphne Walls, Zink Partners' director of property operations. "We've focused our attention on achieving that goal. So at our properties, 24-hour service means two things. First, if you have a service need of an emergency nature, at any time, day or night, we have maintenance personnel ready to respond promptly to that need. Second, if you call or visit our office to report a problem in your apartment, that problem will be fixed within 24 hours, or we'll let you know why there's a delay and when the job will be completed."

Zink is able to keep its 24-hour promise at Dorchester Towers by maintaining a 30-day inventory of all the parts that are routinely used for property repairs. Since everything is kept in stock, there are no runs to the hardware store. Zink also takes steps to limit the number of problem calls by exercising preventive maintenance.

LOCATION, LOCATION, LOCATION

Perhaps one of the best features of Dorchester Towers is the location. Professionals have quick and easy access to both the local shopping mall and their downtown office. The South Hills location is just a short walk away from two major shopping malls, theaters, restaurants, and health care facilities. What's more, a light rail transit station is nearby, providing quick and inexpensive transportation to Station Square and the Pittsburgh central business district. Access to the major highways is simple, too, with Parkway West and Interstate 79 just minutes away.

With first-rate facilities, an ideal location, and service that is second to none, Dorchester Towers has become one of the area's premier addresses. Add to this mix a professional, caring staff, and Dorchester Towers becomes an excellent choice for apartment living in Pittsburgh.

With first-rate facilities, an ideal location, and service that is second to none, Dorchester Towers has become one of the area's premier addresses (right).

At Dorchester Towers, residents find what they expect from an upscale apartment community, and more: spacious rooms, large closets, wall-to-wall carpeting, central heat and air-conditioning, ceramic tile baths, electric ranges, dishwashers, garbage disposals, balconies, and laundry facilities on every floor (left).

RESPIRONICS DESIGNS, DEVELOPS, MANUFACTURES, AND MARKETS respiratory therapy products used in hospitals, diagnostic clinics, and patients' homes, and in emergency care situations. The company has experienced rapid growth in the past decade, with net sales totaling $23 million in

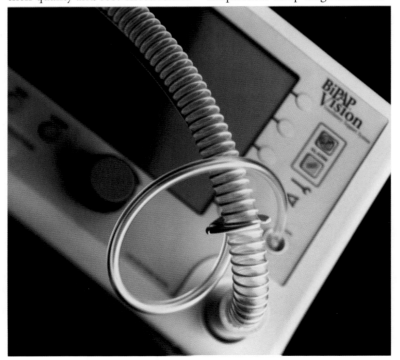

fiscal 1990, nearly $100 million in 1995, and exceeding $175 million in 1997. Following its acquisition of similar-sized Healthdyne Technologies, Inc. in February 1998, Respironics is poised to enter the new century as a $500 million enterprise.

Respironics' performance ascent is linked directly to a determined pursuit of its core objective to be first and to remain the best in each of its product and market realms. Consequently, with only minor exceptions, the development, introduction, and refinement of Respironics' products have been in close accord with a comprehensive, four-stage strategy. Specifically, the company has succeeded in identifying the pulmonary physician's needs for devices not yet available. It designs those products to function reliably in a highly regulated environment, produces them in sufficient volume to satisfy rapidly rising user demand, and increases their quality and cost-effectiveness

to maintain competitive advantage over suppliers subsequently attracted to the marketplace by the results of Respironics' pioneer efforts.

The company's position in several key markets attests to the soundness of its business approach. Respironics' sleep diagnostic and

therapy devices, noninvasive ventilatory systems, portable volume ventilators, and asthma management products are worldwide leaders in their respective treatment areas. And recent advances in the company's line of patient interface equipment—masks, therapy control, and readout mechanisms—have established new performance standards for products of their type.

Given the considerable size of the respiratory market segments Respironics serves, the impact of the strong share positions it enjoys is significant. In the treatment of obstructive sleep apnea (OSA)—easily the most prevalent of known sleep disorders—the 1998 market is estimated at $300 million with future growth projected at 25 percent annually. Having pioneered the commercial application of OSA devices, the company's current product range accommodates customer preference for mode of therapy delivery—continuous versus bi-level pressure—while offering a broad array of operational features at corresponding points all along the OSA pricing chain. Respironics has con-

A market-leading line of portable ventilators, obtained in the 1997 acquisition of Lifecare International, Inc., complemented Respironics' long-standing position as the global leader in noninvasive ventilation therapy.

The BiPAP® series of noninvasive ventilatory support systems was developed for the treatment of acute and chronic respiratory failure and respiratory insufficiency.

sistently maintained its market lead in this core business through the timely introduction of next-generation or breakthrough products at all treatment levels.

The company's early success in the OSA field served as the strategic model for subsequent new product initiatives. Most notably, perhaps, was the development of the BiPAP® series of noninvasive ventilatory support systems for the treatment of acute and chronic respiratory failure and respiratory insufficiency. Strengthened by additional patent protection in 1995, BiPAP's proprietary technology enables the company to lead its competitors in noninvasive ventilation. The fiscal 1997 acquisition of a leading portable ventilator line, moreover, together with the integration of Healthdyne Technologies a year later, materially broadened Respironics' position in the $500 million ventilation market. The addition of Healthdyne-developed asthma management products, meanwhile, immediately established the company as a competitive force in a large and rapidly growing business sector.

With three production locations in the Far East, a fourth in Germany, and far-reaching sales and distribution capabilities, Respironics is thoroughly global in character. Its products are especially well established in Europe and Australia, and in several Asian and Latin American markets, and sales have increased

steadily throughout the 1990s—both in real terms and as a share of the growing corporate total. Entering fiscal 1998, nearly one-half of the company's workforce was based outside the United States. It is not unrealistic to project that, by the close of the decade, non-U.S. business volume could well approach one-half of overall sales as well.

No profile of Respironics' business would be complete without appropriate reference to the more than 2,000 people who currently address the company's opportunities and meet its obligations. The broad employee group is strongly attuned to the corporatewide objective of customer satisfaction, and is given incentives by a compensation structure that recognizes teamwork, self-development, and

duration of quality service. And the board of directors benefits by the presence of the two individuals whose vision formed the foundations of Respironics and Healthdyne Technologies initially. By virtually any measure, these key elements of Respironics' organizational structure have demonstrated the ability to continue the company's progress through to the close of the century and beyond.

The design and superior function of all Respironics products result from the company's acute awareness of the role of pulmonary physicians and its ability to meet their needs.

IMAGINE THAT THE HEART FROM A YOUNG BOY KILLED IN A TRAFFIC accident may extend the life of another child whose heart was damaged irreversibly by a virus. Imagine that a new cornea can restore sight so that a young mother may see her newborn's first smile. Imagine that a small bone segment may be used to reinforce an injured spine.

"Let the leaves symbolize the donors; like softly fallen petals that nourish the earth, they have touched the lives of others." This inscription greets visitors to *A Special Place*, the garden dedicated to donors and their families by the Center for Organ Recovery & Education (CORE) (top).

Once organs are recovered, timing is crucial in keeping them viable for transplantation. CORE often will transport the organs and the recovery team by a chartered jet (bottom).

Imagine that you are among the thousands of people who each year await an organ, tissue, or corneal transplant to save your life or greatly improve the quality of it. There is, however, no need to imagine that an organization called the Center for Organ Recovery & Education (CORE) is dedicated around the clock to helping to provide these organs, tissues, and corneas for transplantation.

CORE is one of 63 federally designated entities in the United States known as a not-for-profit organ procurement organization (OPO). CORE plays a pivotal role as an intermediary between potential donors and patients awaiting transplantation. In addition to offering families the opportunity to donate, CORE coordinates the physical recovery of organs, tissues, and corneas, as well as the placement of donated organs and corneas.

Founded in 1977 as the Transplant Organ Procurement Foun-

dation of Western Pennsylvania, and later known as the Pittsburgh Transplant Foundation, CORE changed to its existing name in 1992 to reflect its expanding role in the procurement field. CORE's assigned region encompasses almost 6 million people throughout western and central Pennsylvania, West Virginia, and a small portion of New York.

ALEX BELLOTTI

Each of the 160 hospitals within CORE's designated region serves as a referral site for potential donors. Six of the hospitals also perform lifesaving organ transplants, and a host of others use tissues and corneas for transplantation. While corneas are used to give the precious gift of sight, tissues—such as bone, skin, ligaments, and tendons—are used in a variety of orthopedic and orthodontic reconstructive procedures. Heart valves also my be used for transplantation.

RECOVERY EFFORTS
Each of the hospitals within CORE's service area operates a routine referral program. Introduced by CORE in 1989, the routine referral program has become a model for OPOs throughout the country. Under the program, hospitals notify CORE of every death. CORE then conducts a medical assessment to determine donor suitability. If the individual is suitable for donation, CORE will inquire about a donor designation or a signed donor card. In the absence of a donor card or designation, CORE will present the family with an opportunity to donate.

Once the decision to donate has been made, organs and tissues are recovered in a surgical procedure that will not disfigure the body. The donor's height, weight, and blood type will be entered into a computer at the CORE office. The computer then generates a list of people awaiting an organ transplant who most closely match the donor's height, weight, and blood type. At the six CORE-affiliated organ transplant hospitals, 1,600 people at any given time are awaiting an organ transplant. Many transplant candidates will be a match; therefore, those who are most urgently in need of the organ will receive priority, followed by those with the most time accumulated on the waiting list.

The Power of

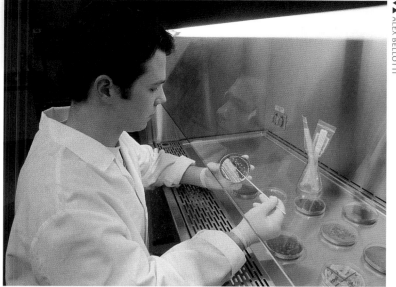

ALEX BELLOTTI

ALEX BELLOTTI

Clockwise from top left:
The internal laboratory strengthens CORE's ability to perform testing on donated organs, tissues, and eyes in an efficient and timely manner.

The addition of the Eye Bank unit propelled CORE into the full-service arena for procurement agencies. CORE is one of only a handful of organ procurement organizations throughout the country that offer organ, tissue, and eye banking services under one entity.

Caring for the donor family is paramount to CORE's mission. In addition to booklets that explain the donation and grieving processes, CORE also offers support groups and personal counseling for donor families.

CORE offers a variety of brochures and informational materials as part of its active educational efforts to build awareness and understanding about donation.

LEADING THE WAY

Since its inception 20 years ago, CORE has helped to provide more than 250,000 organs, tissues, and corneas for transplantation. The gifts of life provided through CORE would not be possible without the individuals who chose to volunteer for life through donation.

To honor the donors, CORE in 1993 created *A Special Place*, a parklike area outside the CORE office in RIDC Park, O'Hara Township. On the graduated, granite walls forming *A Special Place*, a leaf has been engraved for every CORE donor. More than 3,500 leaves adorn the walls of *A Special Place*.

The organization's dedication to donor families, recipients, and the communities it serves is matched only by its commitment to achieving advances in the procurement field. In 1990, CORE established the first in-house specialist position to accept the growing number of

referrals from hospitals. Additionally, CORE created in 1995 the first donor database in Pennsylvania accessible 24 hours a day.

CORE has continued its efforts to lead the procurement field by becoming a full-service OPO. In 1996, the organization added tissue recovery and eye banking services to its organ recovery component. It enhanced its line of services by opening an internal laboratory in 1997, where CORE performs the necessary tests to help ensure viable organs, tissues, and corneas for transplantation.

EDUCATING THE PUBLIC

CORE devotes a significant portion of time to heightening awareness about organ donation. An integrated media and public educational initiative has created a variety of programs targeted toward increasing understanding about such donations. The organi-

zation annually delivers hundreds of presentations to schools, and to business, professional, civic, and church organizations.

Strengthening these public educational endeavors is an extensive media component. In addition to working closely with Pittsburgh-area media, CORE has participated in several national and international media segments. In 1996, CORE became the first OPO to deliver on *Nick News* a segment about organ donation tailored to children.

The strong presence CORE retains in the procurement field and in local communities is designed to fulfill one mission: To increase the number of organs, tissues, and corneas available for transplantation. The organization's responsive, multifaceted efforts have created a strong foundation on which CORE can build the future of procurement, not only for Pittsburgh, but for CORE's entire region.

SUMITOMO CORPORATION OF AMERICA (SCOA) IS PLAYING A significant role in the revitalization of America's iron and steel business by trading steel and ferrous raw materials with suppliers and manufacturers located around the world. In fact, it was the steel industry that brought this diverse American

company to Pittsburgh, where it does business from its office high atop USX Tower.

"Sumitomo Corporation of America, one of the largest dealers in both carbon and specialty steel, handles millions of tons of rolled steel products on a regular basis," says Masahiko "Mark" Nakagawa, senior vice president and general manager at SCOA's Pittsburgh office. "The Rolled Steel Department imports and exports a wide spectrum of steel products, such as sheets, plates, bars, and shapes. Sumitomo Corporation of America is also a leading importer and supplier of tin products, used for specialty applications like cable wrap in the U.S. market."

SCOA is also a key supplier of the American railroad industry, having provided U.S. railroads with rail, track work, and accessories for more than 20 years. In 1989, Sumitomo established Arkansas Steel Associates, a joint venture with Yamato Kogyo of Japan, to manufacture steel tie plates. The company has since become the leading supplier of this product in North America.

CPS PHOTOGRAPHY, INC. CARL STILLITANO

ORIGINS IN THE ORIENT

While Sumitomo is very much an American company, its roots are with its Japanese parent company, Sumitomo Corp. The company's personality has been shaped by a history dating back to the early 17th century, when Masatomo Sumitomo opened a book and medicine shop in Kyoto. Later in life, Sumitomo created his Founder's Precepts, which laid out his business philosophy. The Sumitomo Business Principles,

stressing integrity and sound management, were originally based on the Precepts and have been a central force shaping the spirit of each Sumitomo company for more than 350 years.

Sumitomo Corp.'s initial mainstay business was copper mining. The company later diversified into a variety of fields, including finance, insurance, iron and steel, and real estate. The current Sumitomo Group traces its roots to 1919, when Osaka Hokko Kaisha Ltd. was established to undertake a land reclamation project in Osaka Bay. In 1945, the company decided to enter the trading business, and in 1950, set up its first overseas office in Bombay. The following year, Sumitomo stationed a representative in the United States, marking its incarnation as the trading arm of the Sumitomo Group.

The 1960s and 1970s saw tremendous expansion and internationalization of the Japanese economy, spurred by heavy industry, such as the steel and chemical sectors. Accordingly, Sumitomo Corp. evolved into an integrated trading company, and diversified its product range to include iron and steel, nonferrous metals, electrical and electronics products,

Clockwise from top:
Adopting new electronic technologies in the workplace, such as videoconferencing, has helped the Sumitomo Corporation of America (SCOA) Pittsburgh office improve efficiency by staying in constant "face-to-face" touch with the rest of the company's network.

The company's vision of becoming an integrated business enterprise encourages staff to brainstorm and aggressively pursue new investment opportunities in such fields as multimedia.

The USX Tower at 600 Grant Street has been the home of SCOA's Pittsburgh office since it opened in December 1976.

CPS PHOTOGRAPHY, INC. CARL STILLITANO

The Power of

machinery, agricultural and marine products, chemicals, textiles, natural resources, and real estate. In addition, the company expanded its business to cover such sophisticated areas as resource development, plant construction, joint venture formation, financing, and investment.

In 1988, the corporation set forth its vision of becoming an integrated business enterprise. This initiative has two focuses: one is to strengthen existing trading operations; the other is to aggressively pursue new investment opportunities in such fields as multimedia and downstream activities, notably retailing.

A Successful Mix

Today, Sumitomo Corp. of America maintains offices in several major U.S. cities, including New York, Chicago, Detroit, Houston, and San Francisco. The mix of U.S. and Japanese customs is one factor that makes SCOA successful. "As an American company with roots in Japan, we continually demonstrate our ability to draw from the well of our American and Japanese heritage, and bring forth fresh commitments to success," says Nakagawa.

Out of the Pittsburgh office, SCOA works closely with U.S. Steel and several other well-known steelmakers in a variety of roles. For instance, Sumitomo trades numerous ferrous raw materials and is involved in financing U.S. coking coal exports for Brazilian Steel

Industries. Recently, the company made an equity investment in Steel Dynamics Inc. for the joint development of a new virgin iron project.

SCOA's supply base also extends to aluminized products as well, and the company is the leading distributor of aluminized products for one of the largest U.S. aluminized steel mills, Wheeling-Nisshin.

"We provide customers with just-in-time delivery services, guaranteed supply, and monitoring systems to ensure the highest-quality products," Nakagawa says. "We are absolutely committed to consistently offering our customers an extensive, high-quality

supply source for rolled steel and ferrous raw material products."

SCOA has adopted as the company emblem the *igeta*, a frame placed around wells in old Japan. The igeta emblem represents the fresh water that gushes from a fountainhead, which forms a mighty river and finally flows into the ocean. As Nakagawa explains, "The igeta is symbolic of the freshness in spirit and substance, like the never ending flow of a spring, that we at Sumitomo Corporation of America bring to our clients' businesses."

In order to provide customers with more information about the company, SCOA has a Web site at www.sumitomocorp.com.

Clockwise from top left: Mark Nakagawa (left), general manager of SCOA's Pittsburgh office, and his staff frequently find humor that can help to bridge cultures.

Vicksmetal Corporation, a SCOA subsidiary, manufactures electrical silicon steel.

Recognizing the demand for specialized, cost-saving processed steel products, SCOA has invested in a number of North American steel service centers, like Michigan Steel Processing, located in the south Detroit region.

P I T T S B U R G H

485

DURING THE MID-1990S, AS TRENDS IN THE BANKING INDUSTRY pushed many financial institutions toward technology-based services and away from personal services, First Western Bancorp, Inc. turned a deaf ear to the rest of the industry. Instead, the bank listened to a different group

of people: its customers. "As more banks close offices and add fees for teller assistance, you have to wonder whether they're aware of what's important to customers," says Thomas J. O'Shane, First Western's president and chief executive officer. "Millions of people still feel the most comfortable when they're banking with a friendly face at their branch office. Bankers need to keep that in mind."

It's that same customer focus that has enabled First Western to maintain steady growth during a turbulent period in the banking industry. While many midsize banks were being acquired by large regional banks during the mid-1990s, First Western remained independent, and was ranked among the 10 fastest-growing public companies in Western Pennsylvania for four straight years by Pittsburgh's *Executive Report* magazine. No other bank made the list as often.

REMAINING INDEPENDENT

First Western Bancorp, with roots in community banking, is head-

quartered in the quiet town of New Castle, about 50 miles northwest of Pittsburgh. The bank has assets of more than $1.7 billion and is the parent of First Western Bank, N.A., a full-service bank. In all, First Western employs more than 650 people and operates 39 financial stores in the six Western Pennsylvania counties of Lawrence,

Mercer, Beaver, Butler, Erie, and Allegheny, and in the Eastern Ohio county of Ashtabula.

The total number of banks nationwide fell from 14,450 at the end of 1982 to fewer than 10,000 by the end of 1997. To survive the decline, banks had to develop defined business plans. First Western's business strategies have focused on boosting customer satisfaction levels while limiting expenses. An example is the bank's move in the summer of 1997 to merge its thrift and trust subsidiaries into its largest subsidiary, First Western Bank, N.A. The consolidation, accomplished without layoffs, reduced the number of organizations regulating First Western from three to two, cutting the costs associated with examinations and other regulatory compliance activities. Meanwhile, advertising, forms processing, payroll management, contracting, and other administrative costs associated with maintaining separate organizations also dropped.

"The best antitakeover device or poison pill I know is strong performance," O'Shane says. "An increase in shareholder value is the

"Despite the moves by some institutions to centralize banking services, we believe that our customers want to do their banking in their neighborhoods and with institutions who can make decisions at the community office level," says Thomas J. O'Shane, president and CEO of First Western Bancorp, Inc. Below, bank associates celebrate the opening of First Western's Chicora financial store.

direct result of solid and core earnings growth.

"Successful banks have developed a proactive sales culture that eliminates excess layers of management throughout the organization," he adds. "Responsiveness must be accomplished in a cost-efficient manner through direct customer solicitation, alternative delivery systems, and cross-selling throughout the branch network."

FOCUSING ON RETAIL

A big part of First Western's focus on the customer is its commitment to retail banking. To improve banking convenience, First Western has opened in-store locations in the Wal-Mart Super Center in New Castle, the Giant Eagle in Chippewa, the Clearview Mall Giant Eagle in Butler, and the Cranberry Mall Shop 'N Save in Cranberry. The in-store locations, which are open seven days per week, enable customers to bank while they shop. These in-store locations provide shoppers all of the services available at First Western's other full-service offices, but with longer hours.

With a focus on quality service and a commitment to community loyalty, First Western recently reorganized its retail banking division. "As we grow, the realignment enables us to increase our emphasis on the delivery of banking products and services at the community office level," O'Shane says. "Despite the moves by some institutions to centralize banking services, we believe that our customers want to do their banking in their neighborhoods and with institutions who can make decisions at the community office level. We have a system in place to make sure First Western continues to excel in this area."

While personal service remains a key part of First Western's business strategy, the bank has remained on the leading edge of technological advancements within the financial services industry. For instance, First Western enables customers to handle banking transactions securely from their home computers. The bank's Info-Voice service enables customers to access account information and transfer funds via personal computer. The bank also offers Presto-Pay, which en-

ables customers to pay bills by telephone or personal computer.

Cutting-edge technology is also helping the bank to process loan applications faster and to seize cross-selling opportunities with current customers. The new technology helps to control costs, while better positioning the bank to manage its own growth in the years to come. Nevertheless, focus still remains on the bank's commitment to personal customer service.

"As exciting as technology is, I believe it has to be managed carefully," O'Shane says. "The most effective bank managers tread carefully, with one foot leading off to the technological future and the other planted safely in the traditional past."

THERE IS A SAYING THAT THE SUCCESS OF A MEETING OR convention can be determined not only by what happens during the meeting, but what happens before it begins. The staff at the David L. Lawrence Convention Center agrees—and strives to provide everything needed to ensure the

success of each event it hosts. "We work with the customer on all phases of planning and execution, from beginning to end," says James Kiesel, executive director of the Center. "When an event is in progress, we're always close by to provide for any last-minute details." That detailed service and professionalism are why the David L. Lawrence Convention Center is where Pittsburgh meets. The Convention Center's distinctive personal touch and attention to detail keep guests coming back. "The event is the focus of our attention," says Kiesel. "Guests have my personal guarantee that every single member of our team—from the catering and kitchen staff, to the labor force, from our maintenance and security personnel right to the meeting specialist in charge of the event—will do his or her very best to ensure its success. That's what we're all about."

SET FOR SUCCESS
The Convention Center opened in 1981 as part of Pittsburgh Renaissance II, the rebuilding process that transformed the city from a smoky steel town to one of the most striking cities in the country today. The Center sits along the Allegheny River, within walking distance of first-rate hotels, restaurants, entertainment spots, parks, and major shopping centers. Pittsburgh's Cultural District, where world-class symphony, ballet, and theater performances can be found year-round, is also nearby. Professional sports are a hugely popular attraction in Pittsburgh, and the Convention Center is convenient to both Three Rivers Stadium, home of the Steelers and the Pirates, and the Civic Arena, home of the Penguins.

The Convention Center's efficient, professional staff is a key element in producing top-notch events. Meeting specialists arrange

all aspects of an event, including special parking and security requests, in-house catering, audiovisual support or videoconferencing, Internet gateway, and computer planning. The Center has a wide selection of meeting rooms of varying capacities, shapes, and styles from which to choose.

Conventions, exhibitions, and trade shows are staged in a 131,000-square-foot, column-free exhibition area. Regional leaders approved a plan in 1996 that will triple the size of the current Convention Center, while increasing the number of hotel rooms immediately adjacent to the facility. The existing center pumps more than $60 million annually into the regional economy, and the expanded center should bring in more than $70 million of additional spending to the region by convention delegates and exhibitors.

The Convention Center has hosted many high-profile events—from speeches by President Bill Clinton to gatherings for the United Steelworkers of America and the NAACP—and its expansion will enable the Center to host even larger groups. But it will be the professionalism and personal service of the staff of the Convention Center that will keep them coming back.

Clockwise from top:
The detailed service and professionalism of the David L. Lawrence Convention Center attract a variety of organizations, such as the Mary Kay Cosmetics Inc. career conference.

Conventions, exhibitions, and trade shows, such as the All-Star Fanfest, are staged in a 131,000-square-foot, column-free exhibition area.

The Convention Center's meeting specialists arrange all aspects of an event, including special parking and security requests, in-house catering, audiovisual support or videoconferencing, Internet gateway, and computer planning.

N 1981, WHEN RUSSELL E. FINSNESS FOUNDED METPLAS INC., A company specializing in machining metal and plastic components for use by original equipment manufacturers, the computer was just beginning to be used in the manufacturing arena. Finsness immediately invested in computer numerical control machining,

totally automating his fledgling business. In the process of integrating technology into his manufacturing business, Finsness also implemented a philosophy that continues to serve the company today, by helping it to increase productivity and quality while simultaneously reducing costs.

"It is really a matter of survival," Finsness says. "Like other manufacturers, we are continually being squeezed by global competition and lower pricing. Cutting our manufacturing costs is essential to maintaining our profitability."

GROWTH AND SUCCESS

Today, the company employs 47 people at its manufacturing facility in Natrona Heights, about 15 miles northeast of Pittsburgh, and continues to invest in automation and technology. As a result, Metplas is capable of both long- and short-run production, manufacturing prototypes, mechanical assembly, silk screening, and painting of all NEMA (National Electrical Manufacturers' Association) grades of plastic and nonferrous metals, including aluminum and brass

castings, as well as precision secondary machining of custom-molded parts.

The biggest demand for Metplas' components comes from the medical, transportation, and electrical industries, from clients like Westinghouse Air Brake (WABCO), General Electric, and ADtranz. Metplas' total quality process includes computerized order entry and inventory control, coupled with electronic data interchange to provide timely delivery. These and other improvements—implemented by Metplas' World-Class Manufacturing/ISO 9002 teams, which have met weekly since 1995 to discuss quality—have resulted in continuous growth in the company. Sales exceeded $4 million by 1997, with the company growing 10 to 15 percent annually through the mid- to late 1990s.

CUSTOMER SATISFACTION

Finsness says the company's new quality policy statement, written by a Metplas machinist and selected in a competition among employees, best sums up his corporate philosophy: "Our quality products and services are the foundation for customer satisfaction."

That the company follows this philosophy is evident; some of Metplas' biggest proponents are its customers. In 1996 and 1997, for instance, four customers initiated quality audits at Metplas facilities. When the audits were complete, all the clients included Metplas on their approved vendor lists. Two of the larger clients conferred a rating of elite on Metplas, and included the company on their certified vendor lists. The elite rating permits warehouses to accept shipments of Metplas products without inspection. WABCO gave Metplas a perfect, 100 percent quality rating and a 93 percent delivery rating for the year ending July 1997. ADtranz, a manufacturer of transportation cars that names six Valued Suppliers out of 600 suppliers each year, included Metplas among its honorees six times during an eight-year period in the 1990s.

Customer satisfaction, quality products and services, and continuous improvement in technology and manufacturing processes ensure that Metplas will continue to serve its Pittsburgh and regional clients for many years to come.

Laser technology for precision cutting and forming keeps Metplas on the cutting edge of the industry (right).

Metplas' commitment to ISO 9002 certification has led to the use of employee teams dedicated to improving quality while reducing production times and costs (left).

T STARTED WITH A STEAM ENGINE INVENTED TWO CENTURIES AGO IN Germany. Developed by Mechanische Werkstatte Harkort & Co. (MWH), a Berlin company founded in 1885 by brothers Rheinhardt and Max Mannesmann, the engine drove the burgeoning mining and metallurgical industries. Soon, MWH became one of the most

important suppliers of machinery for the construction of blast furnaces, steelworks, and rolling mills.

Meanwhile, another German firm, Demag Engineering AG, pioneered the development of thin slab casting technology. This process greatly reduced steelmakers' capital investment and operating costs, while making the steelmaking process more efficient. Demag AG entered the North American steel industry in the mid-1960s in New York. In 1972, Mannesmann AG acquired Demag AG and its entire U.S. operations, creating the Mannesmann Demag Corporation.

Today in Pittsburgh, Mannesmann Demag Corporation has evolved into an international company, playing as large a role in the modern metals industry as did its forebears in Germany.

MANNESMANN DEMAG IN NORTH AMERICA

Within 10 years after the acquisition of Demag AG, Mannesmann Demag established an engineering office in Pittsburgh, the longtime heart of the American steel industry. Initially, the Pittsburgh location employed only eight people, but the company grew rapidly as Mannesmann Demag sold its large

Clockwise from top:
The North American office of Mannesmann Demag, employing nearly 300 persons, is located in Pittsburgh. As one of the world's leaders in supplying the latest in process technologies, through computer-aided design, solutions are offered to the North American metals industries for supply of metallurgical plants and equipment.

A continuous steel casting equipment order for a Warren, Ohio-based steel producer consists of a single-strand continuous slab caster. Completely designed and manufactured by Mannesmann Demag, this caster produces approximately 1 million tons of steel annually.

As the turnkey supplier of the Greenfield project, located in Montpelier, Iowa, Mannesmann Demag's responsibility encompasses the overall plan, design, manufacture, and supply of the equipment and technology, and supervision of the construction and erection, as well as the start-up of the complete steelmaking plant.

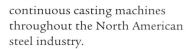

continuous casting machines throughout the North American steel industry.

Today, Mannesmann Demag employs about 250 people in Pittsburgh, all of whom are proficient in the complete steelmaking, casting, and rolling mill process, as well as metals-finishing technology for the nonferrous industry. The Pittsburgh office services more than 285 steel-producing facilities and more than 25 aluminum-producing facilities in the United States and Canada. These facilities collectively produce in excess of 115 million

tons of steel and 20 million tons of aluminum annually.

To maintain its edge in the metals markets, Mannesmann Demag is developing new technology that will make steel production a more environmentally friendly process. That is especially critical for industry in Western Pennsylvania and other cities in North America, which are subject to stringent federal Clean Air Act requirements. The emerging technology will enable large steel producers to shut down coking operations at their blast furnaces, greatly reduc-

ing the amount of volatile emissions currently being released into the atmosphere. As a result, their environmental compliance costs will drop dramatically and manufacturers will recognize significant cost savings.

MULTIPLE MARKETS

Mannesmann Demag consists of four product divisions: Ironmaking and Steelmaking; Continuous Casting and Hot Rolling Mill; Cold Rolling and Processing Line (all of which are directly involved with the steel and metals industries); and the Tube and Pipe division.

Mannesmann Demag workers in the Ironmaking and Steelmaking division develop technology that helps manufacturers convert raw materials and scrap metals into pure, liquid steel. Mannesmann Demag also creates the technology that allows specialty steelmakers to enhance the pure liquid steel for the production of stainless steel, titanium, and other high-quality alloys. This is the first step in the production of steel for use in automobiles, homes, bridges, and high-rise office buildings.

The Continuous Casting and Hot Rolling division develops technology that is used to form pure, liquid steel into usable shapes. Liquid steel is poured into a continuous caster, emerging as a solid slab measuring as large as 75 feet long, 10 feet wide, and six inches thick, and weighing 90 tons. From there, the slab enters a hot mill, which reduces the thickness to 1/16 of an inch and rolls the steel into a coil. These coils are destined for use in automotive frames or as steel bridge decking.

The Cold Rolling and Processing Line division develops technology for finishing steel for end use in products such as filing cabinets, household appliances, or automobile doors. Mannesmann Demag's technology allows manufacturers to clean and galvanize the steel.

BUILDING A REPUTATION

Mannesmann Demag provides technology as well as production machinery to steel and metals pro-

ducers in Pittsburgh and other North American cities. In 1992, WCI Steel commissioned a twin-strand slab casting machine for their production facility in Warren, Ohio. The complete continuous casting facility was provided on a turnkey basis by Mannesmann Demag, and included a ladle metallurgical furnace, vacuum degassing facility, and twin-strand slab casting machine. Mannesmann also provided other associated equipment and a water treatment plant.

In 1993, Pittsburgh-based Allegheny Teledyne put Mannesmann Demag to work on a new annealing and pickling line for its stainless steel finishing plant in Vandergrift, just outside of Pittsburgh. In 1996, Cleveland-based Qualitech Steel Corp. contracted with Mannesmann Demag for a complete supply of melting, refining, and casting equipment for its Greenfield Special Bar Quality plant in Pittsboro, Indiana.

Other major projects include a new plate facility for IPSCO, and an annealing and pickling facility for AK Steel. When these facilities

are completed and operational, they will produce in excess of 4 million tons of new product annually.

From the early 1800s in Germany, to the late 1990s in North America, Mannesmann Demag has consistently been a major source of cutting-edge technology for heavy industry. In the United States today, as it was across Europe almost two centuries ago, there are hardly any steel or rolling mills not equipped with technology produced by Mannesmann Demag.

This in-line strip production facility was designed and manufactured by Mannesmann Demag. With an annual production capacity of 750,000 tons, hot strip steel is reduced to one-millimeter thickness through implementation of the continuous cast and hot rolling process (top).

Modern steelmaking incorporates the latest design in slag-free tapping of an EBT (eccentric bottom tapping) electric arc furnace (bottom).

WHEN TOM FALLAT RETIRED TO PITTSBURGH AFTER 20 years as a Washington, D.C., police detective, he presumed his next career would consist of security work. While searching the help wanted ads, Fallat noticed one for a company that provided résumé

Pittsburgh Business Consultants, Inc. (PBC) helps companies harness technology to achieve business objectives. The company's specialties include contract programming, analysis and design of computer systems, development and support of software, and technical writing, along with many other services. Additional information on PBC's services may be found at the company's Internet Web site, located at www.cotl.com.

assistance. Since he was in need of a well-written résumé, Fallat called the company and met with the owner—and ended up leaving the meeting hired as a recruiter. After working as a recruiter in the permanent placement industry for several months, Fallat discovered a tremendous need in Pittsburgh for contracting services in addition to permanent placement services. After gaining technical recruiting knowledge, he was ready to offer similar placement services. Instead of solving crimes, he'd help companies solve technology and employee problems through contract placement.

Today, Fallat's idea—Pittsburgh Business Consultants, Inc. (PBC)—has grown from a modest, three-person operation in 1982 into a company that employs nearly 500 people at five offices nationally, including its headquarters in downtown Pittsburgh. PBC's niche is helping companies harness technology to achieve business objectives. The company's specialties include contract programming, analysis and design of computer systems, development and support of software, and technical writing, along with many other services.

"No matter what hardware, software, operating environments, databases, or languages a business is utilizing, PBC is able to provide

carefully screened, interviewed, and tested contract consultants who possess the knowledge that a business needs today to get ahead tomorrow," Fallat says. "We help businesses get the most out of technology and people."

Pittsburgh Business Consultants' clients include some of the country's largest companies, such as Mellon Bank and telecommunications giant MCI. Whether large or small, these companies are looking for top performers, many of whom make the transition from PBC consultant to full-time employment with the client. Many others remain as full-time, permanent consultants for PBC and receive ongoing professional development opportunities, along with a competitive salary and benefits package. PBC attracts experienced

consultants by maintaining large recruiting staffs at offices in Pittsburgh, San Diego, Cedar Rapids, Denver, and Colorado Springs.

STRONG CORPORATE PARENT

While Fallat remains involved in the business today, Pittsburgh Business Consultants is now part of Cotelligent Inc., a publicly held, San Francisco-based provider of information technology consulting and staffing services, traded on the Nasdaq exchange under COTL. Cotelligent, which acquired PBC by a pooling of interests in 1996, is an aggressive acquisition company, currently consisting of more than 17 operating groups with offices in 25 metropolitan areas.

The new millennium will bring many challenges to businesses that must rely daily on the proper functioning and performance of technology. To meet these challenges, Pittsburgh Business Consultants will continue its mission of providing quality-driven, competitively priced, value-added services to improve each client's information systems technology. Fallat recognized the need for high-quality information systems contract placement 16 years ago, and today PBC continues to fullfill his vision with tremendous success both in Pittsburgh and on a national level.

Says Tom Fallat, founder of PBC, "No matter what hardware, software, operating environments, databases, or languages a business is utilizing, PBC is able to provide carefully screened, interviewed, and tested contract consultants who possess the knowledge that a business needs today to get ahead tomorrow."

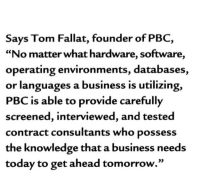

PITTSBURGH-BASED SOFTWARE DEVELOPER CARNEGIE GROUP, Inc. is a thriving example of the emerging high-technology economy in Pittsburgh. ■ Carnegie Group, Inc. provides business and technical consulting, custom software development, and systems integration services to improve clients'

productivity and market position. Carnegie Group focuses on two robust niches in the information technology professional services market: customer interaction; and logistics, planning, and scheduling. Within these areas, the company targets its services to clients in the financial services, government, manufacturing, and telecommunications industries.

LARRY RIPPEL

THE COMPETITIVE EDGE

Carnegie Group's competitive edge is to leverage reusable software templates to accelerate the development of custom software solutions. Reusable templates provide a prebuilt foundation for developing new solutions. Equally critical to Carnegie Group's formula for success is the flexibility to integrate these new solutions into a broad range of existing computing environments. As a result, Carnegie Group's solutions renew and revitalize clients' existing technology investments.

Carnegie Group technology is at work in an integrated, intelligent call handling and routing system for U S WEST; a medical evacuation planning and scheduling system for the U.S. Transportation Command; a laptop-based intelligent diagnostic application for Philips Medical Systems' field service operation; scheduling for the hot end of Bethlehem Steel's flagship steel plant; and a BellSouth Web site that enables small-business customers to receive customized, individualized recommendations for telecommunications solutions.

Dennis Yablonsky is chief executive officer for Carnegie Group, which was founded in 1984. The company's founders, Drs. Jaime Carbonell, Mark Fox, John McDermott, and Raj Reddy, continue to provide technical guidance to the company and link Carnegie Group's research and

development efforts with the groundbreaking research at Pittsburgh's Carnegie Mellon University.

Based in downtown Pittsburgh, Carnegie Group employs 200 in its Pittsburgh headquarters and has regional offices in Atlanta; Denver; Fairview Heights, Illinois; Arlington, Virginia; and Oakland, California.

Carnegie Group clients include BellSouth Telecommunications, Inc.; Highmark Blue Cross Blue Shield; Caterpillar, Inc.; First USA Bank; Gulf States Steel, Inc.; IBM Printing Systems Company; Philips Medical Systems; Reuters America Inc.; U S WEST Communications, Inc.; the U.S. Army; and the U.S. Transportation Command.

Carnegie Group, Inc. is listed on Nasdaq under CGIX, and also maintains a site on the World Wide

MARK PERROTT

Web at www.cgi.com. With a full array of services to improve clients' productivity and market position, Carnegie Group will be an important part of Pittsburgh's emerging high-technology industry for many years to come.

Carnegie Group's headquarters is located at Five PPG Place in downtown Pittsburgh (top).

Dennis Yablonsky is president and chief executive officer of Carnegie Group, which was founded in 1984 (bottom).

WHEN RESEARCHERS AT THE UNIVERSITY OF PITTSBURGH studied their city's social problems during the mid-1990s, they concluded that Allegheny County spent about $120 million per year on child welfare, juvenile detention, juvenile probation, and related

Created in 1984, Grantmakers of Western Pennsylvania's mission is to improve, through education, the effectiveness of philanthropy in meeting the needs of the people, organizations, and communities of Western Pennsylvania. The Early Childhood Initiative is just one of many examples where the foundations and corporations in Pittsburgh have teamed up to improve the quality of life in the region by creating and funding a program that reaches children at a young age and points them in the right direction.

programs. That's a lot of money, money that members of Pittsburgh's philanthropic community felt could be better spent in other ways. So the foundations and corporations in Pittsburgh teamed up to improve the quality of life in the region by creating and funding a program that reaches children at a young age and points them in the right direction.

The Early Childhood Initiative (ECI), as it became known, is just one of many examples of Pittsburgh's rich philanthropic tradition, which dates back to the days of generous industrialists Andrew Carnegie and Henry Clay Frick, and continues in modern-day Pittsburgh. During the mid-1990s, a study of per capita giving in the United States' 50 largest cities ranked Pittsburgh eighth. And today, members of the corporate and foundation community continue to address community issues.

"We have great philanthropic resources here and it is something we are very proud of," says Alcoa Foundation Vice President Kathleen W. Buechel, who is president of Grantmakers of Western Pennsylvania, a group consisting of more than 60 philanthropic corporations and charitable trusts. "These philanthropic resources work hard, collectively and individually, to solve community problems—through prevention, as well as intervention," says Buechel.

Created in 1984, Grantmakers' mission is to improve, through education, the effectiveness of philanthropy in meeting the needs of the people, organizations, and communities of Western Pennsylvania. The group encourages the active participation of all grant-making organizations throughout the region, so it can maximize the opportunity for exchange of information and collaboration on common interests such as community development, the arts, education, health care, and human services.

HELPING CHILDREN

ECI is just one of the many examples of Pittsburgh's philanthropic community at work. ECI is based on four simple premises: First, that children who start behind, stay behind. Second, that early childhood experiences that are high quality can make a difference in the lives of children even if they continue to live in poverty. Third, that children who perform well in school are more likely to avoid problems later. And, lastly, that if the ECI reaches enough children, it can make an impact on the quality of life for the entire community over the next 10 to 20 years.

In the first year, about $26 million of the five-year goal of $59 million was pledged by foundations and corporations. Major gifts included a $12 million commitment from the Heinz Endowments and a $10 million pledge from the Richard King Mellon Foundation. Other commitments were made by the Eden Hall Foundation, the Grable Foundation, the Hillman Foundation, the Jewish Healthcare Foundation, the Pittsburgh Foundation, and the Staunton Farm Foundation. In addition, the Alcoa Foundation, PNC Bank Foundation, PPG Industries Foundation, and Westinghouse Foundation all made significant pledges from the corporate community.

BUILDING AN ECONOMY

Another way Pittsburgh's philanthropic community helps improve the Pittsburgh region is by providing seed money that is being invested to build the region's technology-based economy of the 21st century. In 1996, a $40 million private investment fund was established to encour-

age economic development in Southwestern Pennsylvania. The Strategic Investment Fund provides creative financing arrangements needed to attract private capital into young, growing companies. More than 30 corporations, foundations, and individuals in Southwestern Pennsylvania helped to capitalize the fund.

The use of program-related investments to help capitalize the Strategic Investment Fund was not only a first for many foundations in Pittsburgh, but the joint participation of several foundations in the fund was a national innovation, as well. Recognizing that the long-term solution to many problems in the region would come from creating new jobs for unemployed and low-income individuals, the philanthropic community developed the fund's regional investment strategies to encourage and assist this kind of job creation.

PROMOTING QUALITY OF LIFE

One of the more attractive parts of downtown Pittsburgh is the Cultural District, where Heinz Hall, Benedum Center for the Performing Arts, and Byham Theater form a triangle of top venues for the Pittsburgh Symphony, Pittsburgh Ballet Theater, Civic Light Opera, and many other performing arts organizations. In the early 1980s, the Pittsburgh Cultural Trust bought the old Stanley Theater and, with $43 million in public and private funds, transformed it into the Benedum Center. The Cultural Trust receives funds from the Heinz Endowments, as well as many other private and corporate foundations in the region. The philanthropic community values a rich cultural life in the region as critical to the quality of life and

as an economic enhancement to the area's momentum.

A UNITED EFFORT

All communities have problems and goals. In some regions, philanthropic groups address problems and pursue goals individually. While their efforts are worthwhile, frequently this results in efforts being duplicated and money being spent that could be directed toward other goals. In Pittsburgh, members of the philanthropic community identify regional needs, then often address them with a united front.

By identifying community needs at an early stage, and disseminating information about those needs to those with the ability and resources to respond, Grantmakers is working to create a new and better world for the citizens of Pittsburgh, Allegheny County, and all of Western Pennsylvania.

Many arts and cultural programs are supported by grants from private and corporate foundations in the region (left).

Programs that support education and economic opportunity are an important part of the mission of the philanthropic foundations and organizations in Western Pennsylvania (right).

WHEN THE U.S. GOVERNMENT SEEKS A CONTRACTOR TO augment its environmental mission, it consistently turns to industry leader International Technology Corporation (IT). From the cleanup of the nation's largest and most complex Superfund sites to

remediation of numerous military installations, IT provides a full range of cost-effective environmental services utilizing a turnkey approach that includes problem definition, remedial design, and solution implementation.

With its largest office based in Pittsburgh since 1984, IT moved its corporate headquarters to the city in June 1997 in a strategic move to integrate and consolidate key corporate functions, and to be closer to its major shareholder, lender, investment, and client communities. IT has more than 50 offices in the United States and select locations throughout the world, including Mexico and the Pacific Rim.

To strengthen its leadership role in the $11.5 billion U.S. environmental consulting and remediation industry, IT signed a definitive agreement on January 15, 1998, to merge with OHM Corporation of Findlay, Ohio. The merger will create a firm with projected 1998 revenues of $1 billion and a backlog of $3 billion. Says Anthony J. DeLuca, IT's chief executive officer and president, "The merger represents a continuation of IT's strategy to strengthen its core remediation business while providing resources to allow continued diversification into complementary businesses and new markets. In addition to becoming a leader in remediation, we will also become a stronger low-cost competitor."

A HISTORY OF ENVIRONMENTAL ACCOMPLISHMENTS

IT was founded in 1926 as the California Ship Service. Established by William H. Hutchison in Wilmington, California, the company originally provided marine cleaning services for ocean vessels, ship tanks, and machinery. Early on, it became a recognized leader in marine and oil spill cleanups on the West Coast, and obtained patents for the first marine vacuum system,

Clockwise from top:
International Technology Corporation (IT) provides a full range of consulting services to issues concerning risk management, life-cycle analysis, environmental health and safety, air quality, environmental planning, and pollution prevention/ waste minimization.

IT has successfully remediated many of the nation's largest and most complex hazardous waste sites.

IT utilizes a value engineering approach to evaluate and design solutions that provide optimum performance at the lowest possible cost.

as well as several other innovative cleanup techniques.

IT's current name was adopted in 1977, ushering in a period of rapid growth and significant milestones that continue today. IT has had many firsts, including its first major project outside California in 1979 to study Louisiana's hazardous waste problems and the first-ever Superfund cleanup in 1981.

Throughout the 1980s, the company realized rapid expansion in its technical capabilities through the acquisition of several leading engineering firms and laboratories. And throughout the 1990s, IT has been recognized as the number one hazardous waste design firm for seven consecutive years by *Engineering News-Record*.

A PROMISING FUTURE

While approximately two-thirds of IT's work is realized through

government-related contracts, the company also serves numerous private entities, where contract values range from as little as $1,000 to projects in the millions. IT remains committed to its diversification plans in the areas of operation and maintenance, nuclear facility decontamination and decommissioning, high-end environmental consulting, water and wastewater, and other projects related to infrastructure. The majority of its new business will focus on engineering and infrastructure development, and involve value-added services such as risk assessment, information and natural resource management, and land redevelopment.

Through its solid foundation and strategic plan, IT is positioning itself as the premier provider of turnkey environmental infrastructure solutions.

N 1985, RPS SET OUT TO BECOME THE BEST BUSINESS-TO-BUSINESS, small-package ground carrier in the transportation industry. To accomplish its goal, the fledgling firm had to compete where many others had tried and failed. Yet only nine years after delivering its first package, RPS recorded the fastest growth in

transportation history, exceeding $1 billion in revenue in 1993.

Founders Daniel J. Sullivan and Stephen Handy—then executives of Ohio-based Roadway Express—plotted the course in a Pittsburgh hotel room for what would become RPS. The door to that rented suite now stands on display in RPS' 350,000-square-foot headquarters in Moon Township—a fitting reminder of the company's modest beginnings. RPS chose Pittsburgh as its home because of its skilled and committed workforce, central geographic location, and healthy business environment.

When RPS opened for business, it served 33 percent of the United States with 36 terminals situated east of the Mississippi River. By 1996, it served 100 percent of North America and 28 countries in Europe.

Headquartered in Pittsburgh, RPS, Inc. is the fastest-growing, small-package ground carrier in transportation history.

INDUSTRY FIRSTS

RPS transformed the shipping industry forever by treating small-package shipping like the important business function that it is. The company not only introduced competitive pricing to small-package shippers, but also gave them such process improvements as en route tracing, itemized invoicing, and a COLLECT program for large retail consignees.

Such industry firsts were made possible by RPS' revolutionary use of bar coding. The first small-package ground carrier to use a bar code on every package in its delivery network, RPS literally changed the way small packages are processed and delivered. The company boasts the most sophisticated package-sorting technology in the industry, installed in all of its U.S. hubs. This, coupled with cellular on-van communications equipment used by its contractors, has earned RPS its reputation as a true industry innovator.

Another RPS first is its entrepreneurial workforce of independent contractors, who own their tractors or vans and are paid by the packages they pick up and deliver. Today, more than 9,000 independent contractors comprise the RPS driver team.

A COMMITMENT TO SAFETY

As a service provider, RPS has remained committed to the needs of its customers. As a transportation company, a natural extension of that commitment has been RPS' efforts to promote safety on the road. In 1996, the company garnered top honors for its corporate safety program by winning the American Trucking Associations' prestigious President's Trophy in the Over 20 Million Miles category. RPS is the first company to win this award with a driving team comprised entirely of independent contractors.

RPS takes its safety message to the general public through its support of Mothers Against Drunk Driving (MADD). A corporate sponsor of the Western Pennsylvania Chapter of MADD, RPS regularly sponsors red-ribbon campaigns in and around the Pittsburgh area.

FUTURE GROWTH

Formerly an operating unit of Caliber System, Inc., RPS became

an operating company of FDX Corporation after the acquisition of Caliber System by Federal Express in January 1998. The merging of RPS with Federal Express has created a $15 billion powerhouse in global transportation and logistics, in which RPS is sure to play a significant role.

RPS transformed the shipping industry forever by treating small-package shipping like the important business function that it is.

A

RISTECH CHEMICAL CORPORATION HAS THE DISTINCTION OF being both a modern, technologically advanced, growing enterprise and a business with its roots deep in America's industrial past. A world-class producer of chemicals and polymers, Aristech traces its beginnings to the early years

of this century as the chemical division of Pittsburgh's U.S. Steel Corporation.

The chemical division of U.S. Steel evolved from its historic base in coal chemicals, which were made from by-products of the coking process in Clairton, Pennsylvania. Over the years, the division shifted its focus toward the faster-growing petrochemical market, and grew through acquisitions.

In 1986, the steel company, then known as USX Corporation, intended to concentrate on its core businesses of steel and energy. As a result, it spun off the chemicals division into an independent company, and offered its common stock on the New York Stock Exchange. On its own, the new company needed a name, and it drew on the Greek words *aristos*, meaning excellence, and *techne*, meaning craft.

In 1990, facing a hostile take-over attempt, Aristech was taken private through a management-led leveraged buyout. The transaction was financially supported by Mitsubishi Corporation and several other Mitsubishi group com-

Members of Aristech Chemical Corporation's senior management group include Charles W. Hamilton, president and COO; Masatake Bando, former chairman and COO; and Jiro Kamimura, chairman.

panies. Today, Aristech is owned principally by Mitsubishi Corporation. And throughout the course of the past decade, Aristech has remained true to its name. Aristech is committed to excellence in craft, and dedicated to the pursuit of new horizons of excellence in all of its endeavors.

A BROAD PRESENCE

Headquartered in Pittsburgh, Aristech operates five strategically located manufacturing facilities

in four states. The company also has one advanced research and development center in Monroeville and a newly opened polypropylene technical center on Second Avenue in Pittsburgh. Aristech maintains a strong and focused position in its core business markets—chemicals and polymers—each of which has a wide variety of end uses in products that help to improve the lives of countless consumers.

Aristech's chemicals business produces both industrial and intermediate chemical products. The company's industrial chemicals are key ingredients in the manufacture of many products used in everyday life. These include plywood adhesives, pharmaceuticals, plastics, coatings, appliance parts, compact discs, dyes, and photographic chemicals. Aristech's industrial chemicals are made at the company's plant in Haverhill, Ohio, located along the Ohio River.

Intermediate chemicals—made at Aristech facilities on Neville Island, Pennsylvania, and in Pasadena, Texas—are vital to the manufacture of many items, ranging from vinyl plastics and food wrap to flooring and medical applications.

Bisphenol-A, manufactured at Aristech's Haverhill, Ohio, plant, is a key ingredient in compact discs.

The company's primary polymer product—polypropylene—is a plastic used in the manufacture of synthetic fibers for carpet, upholstery fabrics, and disposable diapers. Polypropylene is also used to make automotive battery cases and interior trim, medical syringes and vials, and packaging film for food and many other consumer products. Aristech produces polypropylene at plants in Neal, West Virginia, and La Porte, Texas.

The company also maintains an interest in the acrylic sheet and decorative surface material businesses. In partnership with Mitsubishi Rayon Company, Ltd., Aristech has a presence in the acrylic sheet business through a joint venture called Aristech Acrylics LLC. Located in Florence, Kentucky, the jointly owned company manufactures materials used in bathtubs, outdoor signs, countertops, spas, and other products. Aristech also holds a controlling interest in Avonite, which produces surface material for countertops, walls, and other decorative and architectural applications at its Belen, New Mexico, plant.

As an integral part of all its operations, Aristech is committed to continuously improving its environmental, health, and safety performance. Through the collective efforts of employees, Aristech's facilities are continually being made safer and more environmentally sound. The company holds a strong commitment to protect the environment to make its plant communities safe. In addition, Aristech maintains community advisory panels at each of its locations to inform the public about plant activities, and environmental and safety programs. The company's efforts in these areas have been widely recognized by industry and government organizations.

THE FUTURE

Aristech has prepared a solid foundation for growth in its businesses by leveraging its core capabilities and positioning itself to meet the challenges of competition in the global marketplace. The company's growth strategy is

based on expanding its presence in the markets it serves, and forming solid business alliances to even further enhance the company's competitiveness. Aristech is realizing its potential through initiatives to drive continuous improvement in technology and processes, customer focus, and employee development.

All the while, Aristech maintains its time-honored tradition of making excellence in craft a guiding principle, and is setting a course for the next century that will serve all of its stakeholders

well. As former chairman Jiro Kamimura says, "At this stage in our growth, Aristech must look toward its future. We will continue our commitment to quality, safety, and the environment. We will continue to seek growth in our core businesses. And with the vast, global resources of our Mitsubishi shareholders supporting us, we will grow. And, as has always been the case, it will be the knowledge, experience, and loyalty of our employees that will provide the foundation for Aristech's success."

Aristech has five manufacturing sites in four states: Neville Island, Pennsylvania (top right); Haverhill, Ohio; Neal, West Virginia; La Porte, Texas; and Pasadena, Texas (top left).

Aristech's plasticizers are used to make flexible vinyl plastic products, such as a child's raincoat (bottom right).

Aristech's polypropylene technical center on Second Avenue includes the latest equipment for polymerization, analysis, compounding, and applications development (bottom left).

F OR YEARS, ELECTRONICS GIANTS WESTINGHOUSE ELECTRIC CORP. and General Electric Co. (GE) competed for shares of the semiconductor market. But the fierce competition ended in 1985. On January 1, 1986, GE, Westinghouse, and Mitsubishi Electric America joined together to form Powerex, Inc. to jointly

produce and sell power semiconductor devices, which are used with circuitry that controls and conditions power. Choosing to be located just outside of Pittsburgh in Youngwood, where Westinghouse had maintained its semiconductor operation, the joint venture today employs more than 300 people in Youngwood and operates offices throughout the world.

"Powerex evolved from the power semiconductor divisions of Westinghouse and General Electric, and there's no doubt that they pioneered the power semiconductor industry," says President and Chief Executive Officer Stanley Hunt. "Some 40 years ago, Westinghouse led the development of power diodes and transistors, and GE developed the first silicon controlled rectifier. Both companies were part of the birth of the integrated circuit business. In fact, it started right here in Youngwood."

SEMICONDUCTORS AND MORE
Powerex produces a broad range of related products, including transistors, rectifiers, silicon controlled rectifiers, and assemblies of those products. Most of the

Powerex products end up connected to a motor in one form or another. For instance, transportation systems like the high-speed trains in Europe are full of semiconductors that control the motors on their axles. In the United States, most of the diesel locomotives in the railroad industry use Powerex semiconductors. And in the typical American residence of the future, a Powerex semiconductor will control the flow of power through the motor that drives the dishwasher or washing machine.

Powerex commands a substantial share of the high-power semiconductor market in the United States, larger than that of any of its competitors, and boasts a significant piece of the markets in Europe and Asia. With the sale of Westinghouse Electric shares in 1994, General Electric and Mitsubishi Electric became equal majority shareholders of the company.

As it has moved toward the 21st century, Powerex has seen more demand for semiconductors that can handle larger amounts of power. To that end, Powerex and Mitsubishi Electric engineers developed a broad family of high-power devices that

enable equipment makers to meet high-power, high-current requirements by combining multiple power components into one package. Powerex introduced the Insulated Gate Bipolar Transistor, the forerunner of a family of intelligent power modules that feature integrated control and protection logic. To address the need for application-specific custom power modules, Powerex has a Custom Power Products Department, dedicated specifically to providing cost-effective solutions to complex semiconductor applications.

"Our future in the industry will be driven by our ability to provide key leading-edge technology and quality service," says Hunt. "We make it our business to listen closely to customers—and respond with products and services shaped by what customers need and expect from Powerex."

CUSTOMER SATISFACTION
At Powerex, keeping customers satisfied goes beyond quality control within the production process. The company also takes seriously its system of delivering semiconductors to the manufacturers who use them in their products. In an era when late deliveries mean lost customers, Powerex has developed a reputation of having customers who keep coming back for more.

During 1996 and 1997, Powerex underwent a companywide redesign of business processes that streamlined production and reduced manufacturing cycle time. At the same time, Powerex consolidated its administrative offices and installed a powerful management information system that provided more efficient order entry, a broad database for more effective technical sales and marketing, and fully networked communications.

Powerex has also been a leader in developing partnerships with

"Powerex evolved from the power semiconductor divisions of Westinghouse and General Electric, and there's no doubt that they pioneered the power semiconductor industry," says President and Chief Executive Officer Stanley Hunt (left).

Headquartered in Youngwood (right), Powerex today has offices all over the world.

The Power of

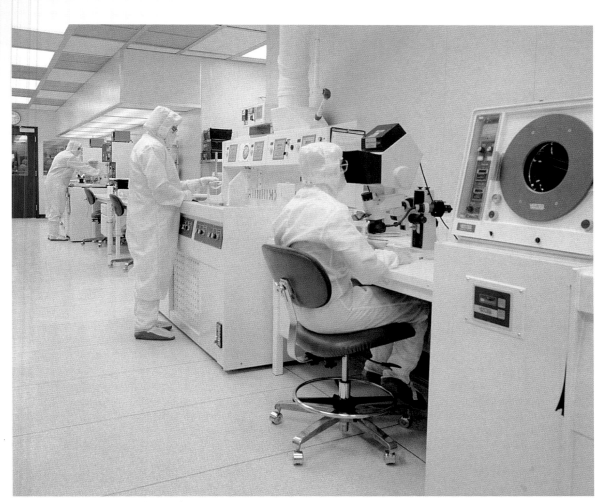

At Powerex, keeping customers satisfied goes beyond quality control within the production process. During 1996 and 1997, Powerex underwent a companywide redesign of business processes that streamlined production and reduced manufacturing cycle time; consolidated its administrative offices; and installed a powerful management information system that provided more efficient order entry, a broad database for more effective technical sales and marketing, and fully networked communications.

customers that base product delivery entirely upon the customer's immediate needs. For instance, the company kicked off a Supplier Pull Program early in 1997, under which the customer provides Powerex with weekly forecasts of inventory needs and generates pull orders based upon consumption and desired stock levels. Armed with that information, Powerex ships products to the customer in a five-day, order-to-delivery cycle. "By providing products only as needed, we're helping our customers improve their material input flow and reduce inventory levels," says Hunt. "The program is a true service success story and is the cornerstone of a sound business partnership."

Powerex is also adept at customer support, utilizing special in-house-designed test equipment to help customers identify and solve problems in the field. Powerex engineers can recommend circuit modifications or design changes that will eliminate field problems before they start. Test conditions are structured to simulate product environments.

JM PAPARIELLO STUDIO

LOOKING FORWARD

The business partnership at Powerex has been the genesis of a myriad of technological breakthroughs with power semiconductors that allow customers to produce better products in the end market. And Hunt expects the innovations to continue: "Our high profile in technology and strategic initiatives are the result of years of hard work on the part of the entire Powerex team. From our design, process, and applications engineers in Youngwood to our technical sales representatives and distributors around the world, the shared vision is to anticipate the ever changing needs of our customers and markets. We want to deliver the highest-quality products, then surround those products with services that speak volumes about our integrity and commitment to our customers. That's the future of Powerex."

Powerex and Mitsubishi Electric engineers have developed a broad family of high-power devices that enable equipment makers to meet high-power, high-current requirements by combining multiple power components into one package.

CORPORATE ACCOMMODATIONS, INC. PROVIDES HIGH-QUALITY interim housing in comfortable, fully furnished apartments, town homes, and condominiums that are available on a daily, weekly, or monthly basis. With locations in Pittsburgh's central business district and in the suburbs, Corporate

Accommodations gives visiting businesspeople quick access to their place of business from a convenient, clean apartment.

"It's like a home away from home," says Paul Bates, president of Corporate Accommodations. "For some guests, just being able to cook their own meals is a real plus. Many guests also comment on the amount of space they get for their money, much more than in a conventional hotel or a suite hotel. They can spread their work out on the dining room table. There is real separation, and they have more room to get their work done.

"We have a large amount of return customers, so we know the guests are satisfied with their temporary living arrangements," Bates adds. "Many who experience this type of lodging never return to a hotel. You can't beat the home-like atmosphere."

THE SHORT-TERM BENEFIT

The short-term apartment business is the fastest-growing segment of the lodging industry. More and more businesspeople choose this alternative to hotels because they know staying in a short-term apartment makes sense both economically and in terms of personal comfort—they get more benefits for less money than a hotel room.

Whether the stay is for only a few days or as long as a few months, staying in a fully furnished Corporate Accommodations apartment will save guests anywhere from 20 to 40 percent over the cost of an average hotel room, while providing at least three times the space. The kitchen is loaded with the conveniences of home: coffeemaker, microwave oven, and pots and pans, and the list goes on. The arrangement allows for a fresh cup of coffee in the morning, a home-cooked meal, or a late night snack without having to leave the premises.

And even though the living quarters amount to the size of an apartment, there is no lease to sign, nor is there a deposit. That means guests have complete flexibility. When permanent housing is established or when the business project is wrapped up, the client simply checks out and leaves.

"We are totally flexible," Bates says. "We don't book anyone behind a guest until we have a firm departure date. Some of our competitors require a two-week notice before checkout. With us, when you're ready to go, you go, and we'll see you the next time you're in town."

Clockwise from top:
The hotel alternative—three times the space, with a full houseware package, at a considerable cost savings.

Corporate Accommodations guests have full use of all amenities provided by apartment communities.

"Home away from home"—that's the feeling guests have in a fully stocked, well-appointed Corporate Accommodations apartment.

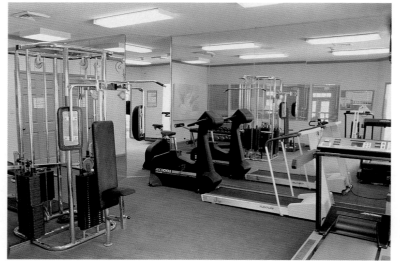

N THE 1980S, THE ALLEGHENY CONFERENCE ON COMMUNITY Development and the Pittsburgh Urban League sponsored a study of the issues impacting the economic development of the region. This study recognized that growing business opportunities in the minority community would help that population in the long run,

and, as a result, the Minority Enterprise Corporation (MEC) was formed in 1989 to nurture minority entrepreneurs. The corporation is founded on the philosophy that teaching people to help themselves is more sustainable than public welfare.

"It follows that if we can start enough businesses, we can advance the opportunities for economic stability within the African-American community. If you want to improve economic growth, turn the entrepreneurial spirit loose in those communities that have been a drain on the region. Employing the unemployed is a double dip—put them on the tax roll and take them off the welfare roll," says Earl Hord, who founded MEC under the auspices of The Enterprise Corporation, a local entrepreneurial development agency.

TIERED EDUCATIONAL STRUCTURE

To succeed, MEC had to take the nurturing methods already being used at The Enterprise Corporation, which generally serves graduates of the University of Pittsburgh and Carnegie Mellon University, and tailor them for a population with less business savvy. MEC's program is successful today because of the tiered

education structure it offers to minorities with all levels of business knowledge—from entrepreneurs with dreams of successful businesses to professionals looking for more advanced systems in bookkeeping or inventory management.

MEC's Micro Business Advisory (MBA) program is a 10-week course taught by business-qualified professionals at three levels. The program has graduated more than 500 since its inception.

"Not all of those 500 individuals have gone into business, but of those who have, 90 percent are still in business," says Sharon K. Williams, president and CEO of the corporation. MEC also helps graduates to identify opportuni-

ties and funding sources, as well as ways to structure a business for success. Williams is also working with local corporations and government entities to open opportunities for minority businesses.

One of the funding sources available to minority entrepreneurs is the Keystone Minority Capital Fund, which Hord started in 1996 after seven years at the helm of MEC. Education is necessary for entrepreneurs to get underway, but Hord saw that capital is needed for them to stay afloat.

"The plan for the equity fund is to demonstrate that there is a large underserved market of entrepreneurs who, except for lack of capital, are capable of growing strong, profitable firms," says Hord.

To date, the fund has made several investments. Antaire, a small, Pittsburgh-based service company developing scheduling software for rest homes, was initially capitalized with $400,000, and an additional investment is currently under way.

"Our focus is on QMBE—quality minority business enterprise. We're not looking for set-asides; we're looking for an opportunity to compete just like everyone else and provide a quality product," concludes Williams.

Sharon K. Williams, Minority Enterprise Corporation president and CEO, says, "It follows that if we can start enough businesses, we can advance the opportunities for economic stability within the African-American community."

Assisted by the Minority Enterprise Corporation, Kevin Butler now owns a Subway restaurant.

TRUE TO ITS PITTSBURGH ROOTS, KOPPERS INDUSTRIES, INC. IS a company characterized by a strong renaissance. Headquartered in the historic art deco building that bears its name, the company has strong leadership positions in basic industries serving U.S. and international markets. ■ Evolving from the original Koppers Company that was founded in 1912 to pioneer the modern coking process, the new Koppers Industries began in 1988 as a management-led buyout in such businesses as the processing of coal tar, chemicals, roofing, and treated wood cross-ties and poles.

Today, Koppers is the nation's largest coal tar distiller and supplier of railroad cross-ties and utility poles. The diversified industrial organization is a market leader in the production of creosote for wood treating, pitch for the aluminum carbon electrode and roofing markets, and a number of related chemical products that have valued use in the plastics and resins industries.

OTHER BUSINESS UNITS

A contemporary research and development operation is operated by Koppers Industries in Harmarville, about 10 miles northeast of Pittsburgh, and the company has overseas affiliations in Australia, Denmark, and Great Britain. Technology and development are characterized by advances in energy utilization, environmental improvement, and total quality, through such developments as cogeneration to create energy from discarded cross-ties, chemicals with higher purity levels, low-emission aluminum pitches, and preassembled railroad track panels.

The company has an open management style that is made even more effective by the participation of employees in the ownership of the company. This culture of ownership enables Koppers people to embrace the contemporary concepts of total quality and open communications with a high degree of involvement. As employees benefit from increased responsibilities within the organization, customers realize better levels of service and quicker response to requirements.

In recent years, as aluminum, chemical, railroad, and steel markets have grown, Koppers Industries has met new demands and opportunities with a combination of acquisitions and plant improvement programs aimed at enhancing quality and environmental

The Pittsburgh skyline has an impressive array of architectural design, and the Koppers Building achieves prominence as the city's premier example of art deco style. Headquarters for Koppers Industries, the 31-story building is a crown jewel in the evening Pittsburgh skyline (left).

The Koppers Clairton plant distills carbon pitch, creosote, and naphthalene oils from crude tar produced by USX Corporation (right).

The Power of

compatibility. In the 1990s, more than $75 million in acquisitions has included a tar distillation facility in Clairton and a coke oven battery in Monessen—both communities that are south of Pittsburgh. Additionally, Koppers has added a wood treatment plant in Somerville, Texas.

KOPPERS IN PITTSBURGH

Koppers Industries has a sizable presence in Western Pennsylvania with 400 employees. In addition to the recently acquired plants, the company also operates a tar processing plant in Follansbee, West Virginia. Local customers include such well-known corporations as USX, Alcoa, and PPG Industries.

Strength in operations, coupled with the advantages of spirited employee ownership, gives Koppers Industries an optimistic vantage point for future opportunities. The company maintains market leadership in most of its businesses, and has kept pace or surpassed customer demands for higher quality and efficiency. Much of Koppers business is concentrated in several distinct markets, such as industrial production, transportation, and durable goods. This business mix, along with growing international diversification, positions the company to grow meaningfully in the 21st century.

Indeed, as a Pittsburgh business leader, Koppers Industries is well poised to participate in the nation's industrial renaissance.

The nation's needs for electric power are met by a sophisticated Koppers Industries distribution system for treated wood utility poles. The company is the leader in wood treating (left).

Coke is a vital raw material for the metals industries, and Koppers Industries supplies this material from a modern production base. The company's Monessen coke plant utilizes extensive environmental controls and a number of technological advances for efficiency (right).

Railroad track maintenance is a top infrastructure priority for the U.S. economy. Preassembled track panels, developed by Koppers Industries, provide labor savings and faster installation for the nation's railroads.

FOR THIS HIGH-TECH COMPANY, THE STEEL CITY REGION PROVIDES the perfect location. Sony Technology Center-Pittsburgh's 800-acre Mount Pleasant site holds Sony Electronics Inc., Sony Chemicals Corporation of America, and the American Video Glass Company. Sony selected the Pittsburgh area after a long

At Sony Technology Center-Pittsburgh the American Video Glass Company's state-of-the-art manufacturing facility is located across the street from one of its largest customers, Sony Electronics (top).

The Sony building in Mount Pleasant is home to Sony Electronics Inc. and Sony Chemicals Corporation of America (bottom).

U.S. search because it provides easy access to national transportation and a highly skilled workforce with a long history of manufacturing. Among the three facilities, Sony has invested more than $550 million throughout the late 1990s. The site uses more than 800 local suppliers and currently has more than 2,300 employees, with plans for further expansion.

Sony Electronics Inc. was the first to take advantage of the location, beginning operations in 1992. Sony's popular 35-inch Trinitron® is manufactured only at this site, which also produces 41-, 48-, 53-, and 61-inch rear projection Videoscope® sets.

In 1995, the Sony Chemicals Corporation of America established its headquarters for the Americas on the site. Sony Chemicals coats and slits thermal transfer ribbon used for bar coding goods to assist in inventory control and materials tracking. As a totally integrated manufacturing site, the facility also houses sales and market development functions, as well as comprehensive research and development, applications engineering, and quality laboratories.

In November 1995, ground was broken to add the American Video Glass Company to the site. This company represents a unique partnership between Sony Electronics Inc., Corning Inc., and Asahi Glass America, Inc. The companies joined forces to produce the high-quality glass used for television picture tube manufacturing. When the plant began operations in spring 1997, the Sony Technology Center-Pittsburgh became the only vertically integrated TV manufacturing facility in the world. The process

begins at American Video, where the sand comes in and is converted to television glass. It ends at Sony Electronics, where the television set is finished and shipped.

The site's continuous expansion, along with Sony's innovative team-approach management style, earned the Sony Technology Center-Pittsburgh recognition by Arthur D. Little, Inc.'s Best of the Best program as one of America's top 20 companies in manufacturing management. Sony's sense of teamwork also extends into the community. The site-based business groups have adopted two local schools, take part in the Adopt-a-Highway program through the Pennsylvania Department of Transportation, and participate in the Educator in the Workplace program, which allows area educators to spend a week gaining real-life experience to share with students. Additionally, employees of all three companies, ranging from manufacturing staff to key executives, are active in many nonprofit organizations in the community.

SONY ELECTRONICS INC.

Sony Electronics Inc. continues the Sony tradition of being consistently first. In 1990, Sony Electronics became the first company to locate at the Sony Technology Center-Pittsburgh, investing nearly $100 million in the operation. In 1991, *Executive Report* magazine named Sony as the first recipient of its Best Deal Award for best corporate impact on the Pittsburgh region. Since that time, Sony Electronics has had an even larger effect on the local economy by employing more than 1,600 people and contracting with more than 800 local suppliers.

The Mount Pleasant location does more than just make televisions. It is the world engineering headquarters for Sony's rear pro-

The Power of

jection television division, and is responsible for designing new models. The plant is also the first, and only, to make Sony's 35-inch Trinitron model. Working toward complete vertical integration, Sony began manufacturing aperture grilles in Mount Pleasant. It was the first, and to date the only, in-house maker of this key component for Sony's Trinitron televisions.

Sony's worldwide reputation for quality products extends to concern for the quality of the environment. For example, when Sony Electronics' Aperture Grille (AG) division first began production, Company Members worked to find the best way to handle the iron chloride waste that resulted from the manufacturing process. They discovered that the chemical could be used to control pollutants in wastewater by removing harmful sediments. As a result, the iron chloride generated at the plant is safely managed and sold to a local community treatment plant for purifying wastewater. The AG division was rewarded for this effort by being selected to receive the 1997 Sony Environmental Award, one of only two to be awarded in the United States. In 1998, Sony Electronics completed its ISO 14001 (Environmental Management System) certification.

There are more firsts ahead for Sony Electronics. The company constantly looks for new ways to make Sony Technology Center-

Pittsburgh the world's first completely vertically integrated television manufacturing site. This integration benefits both the company and the local economy. Sony saves on shipping costs, and can produce more televisions, resulting in more local employment and purchasing.

AMERICAN VIDEO GLASS COMPANY

For the American Video Glass Company, the decision to locate in the Pittsburgh region was an excellent choice. The rich glass-making history of the region delivered the added benefit of prior glass manufacturing experience to a significant portion of American Video's new workforce. Additionally, the site provides excellent proximity to the various suppliers of the bulk raw materials. Utility costs, which are a large component in the cost of making glass, are

among the lowest in the industry. Another benefit is the neighbors. American Video has the veteran Corning Asahi sister TV glass facility a mere 120 miles away in State College, Pennsylvania, and the Sony cathode ray tube facility, an American Video customer, is located on the same site. The highly skilled workforce available in the area and the top-rated universities round out the location picture.

As a partnership, American Video gains strength from both its parents. The Corning Asahi Corporation and its parents—Corning Inc. and Asahi Glass Co.—have more than 80 years of TV glassmaking experience accumulated between them. This has been passed down to American Video in the form of refined plant, process, and equipment designs, as well as in knowledgeable veteran

Clockwise from top:
A Sony Company Member inspects a Videoscope® rear projection television as it is assembled.

A Sony Electronics robot mates a 35-inch panel and funnel to form a cathode-ray tube (CRT) for a Sony Trinitron®. Each CRT weighs more than 150 pounds.

Company Members work in teams to assemble Trinitron television sets. The mirrors are used for inspection throughout the assembly process.

employees. Sony adds world-class manufacturing automation systems developed over 30 years in its picture tube facilities around the globe and a deep understanding of product requirements. The resulting combination makes American Video the world's most technologically advanced TV glass plant.

American Video Glass is housed in a state-of-the-art, 500,000-square-foot facility. It employs approximately 550 team members, who are dedicated to manufacturing the highest-quality glass components for use in the production of Sony's 27-inch and larger Trinitron picture tubes. The current facility is capable of delivering more than 4 million pieces of these large-size glass parts per year. To do this, American Video melts nearly 500 tons of raw material each day. Once melted, "gobs" of molten glass are dropped into molds and pressed into the desired shape. After the glass cools, it is polished to make an optically flawless viewing surface. Finally, the glass is packed and shipped to the customer.

SONY CHEMICALS CORPORATION OF AMERICA

Sony Chemicals Corporation of America (SCCA) has emerged as a global leader in thermal transfer ribbon technology used for bar coding goods to assist in inventory control and materials tracking. Sony Chemicals offers superior-performing ribbon products and services that keep its customers a step ahead of their competition. In addition, customers with difficult bonding or protective coating applications look to Sony Chemicals for solutions. Sony's innovative liquid adhesives and tapes are used for demanding applications in consumer electronics, communications, automotive, and aeronautics industries. Specialty UV-curable coatings provide high-performance benefits to customers with demanding computer, television, and CD/DVD manufacturing challenges.

Sony Chemicals' commitment to value and excellence sparks the ongoing work with customers to develop an ever expanding range

Clockwise from top left:
American Video robots automatically unload funnels from the annealing lehr (oven).

Everyday, American Video feeds nearly 20,000 gobs of molten glass, as seen here, into its panel and funnel forming processes.

Company Members individually inspect each panel as the final step in American Video's vigorous quality control procedure.

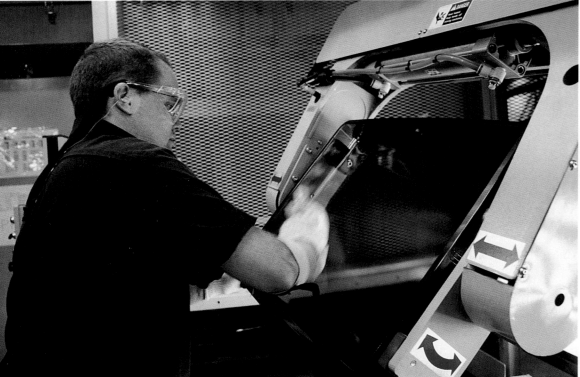

The   Power   of

of products that optimize performance and deliver the highest-possible quality. It is also why Sony Chemicals constantly strives to improve the innovative mixing, coating, and finishing technologies that are the cornerstone of Sony Chemicals' overall performance, quality, and cost advantage. By bringing together advanced mixing, coating, and slitting technologies and methodologies developed for two of its most notable areas of expertise—chemicals and electronics—Sony Chemicals is poised to anticipate manufacturers' needs to continuously create more innovative, high-performance, high-quality products.

For Sony Chemicals Corporation of America, being on the forefront of developmental technology is only half of the equation. That's why it backs commitment to product quality and value with an equally strong commitment to service excellence. An integral part of Sony's vision is to work with customers to clarify and define product and market problems, and offer innovative solutions that afford everyone it comes in contact with the opportunity to achieve excellence. Sony Chemicals' dedication to market leadership and technical superiority is guided by integrity and respect for the individual.

Sony Chemicals also understands the need to safeguard the health and well-being of its employees and customers, while preserving the environment. Sony has received an award for a recyclable packaging design and is instituting measures that reduce waste by following ISO 14001 protocol. In 1998, Sony Chemicals attained registration for ISO 9001 (Quality Management System) and 14001.

The Pittsburgh-area facility is at the center of a plan to expand the scope of business geographically by targeting the unique needs of evolving worldwide markets, including North America. Sony Chemicals Corporation, Tokyo has established a network of manufacturing and distribution affiliates in Europe, Asia, and the United States to supply products quickly and efficiently to users worldwide.

Clockwise from top left:
Sony Chemicals is recognized around the world for superior thermal transfer ribbons that deliver performance and total cost advantages.

Sony Chemicals is the leader in delivering solventless, environmentally friendly adhesives and specialty coatings for demanding applications such as CD and DVD production.

Sony Chemicals' technical services laboratory is available for problem solving and product testing.

CARNEGIE SCIENCE CENTER IS A PARENT'S DREAM, WITH MORE than 250 hands-on exhibits, a planetarium, an Omnimax Theater, and a WWII submarine. Everything is designed to engage children and their parents in an atmosphere of discovery and fun. Beyond mere fun, however, the Science

Center is on the leading edge of science education and economic development, introducing children in the Pittsburgh region to the ever changing technologies that drive the area's economy.

"We have two main priorities," says Seddon Bennington, director of the Science Center. "First, we want to be a leader in science education, strengthening math, science, and technology in the region's schools. Secondly, we see ourselves at the forefront of introducing technology and careers to young people. For many, the Science Center is the first encounter with technology in a way that speaks to their own lives." The educational role is accomplished by working with educators through professional development, student field trips to the Science Center, and community outreach programs.

Carnegie Science Center has also introduced the future to both young and old with the creation of its popular *Robotics*™ exhibit, now on nationwide tour. *Robotics* features a seven-foot basketball-shooting robot that makes 99 percent of its shots and can be operated by visitors. Another robot featured in the exhibit, Terregator, is a six-wheel, self-driven buggy similar to a robot that journeyed from Los

Carnegie Science Center is located along the Ohio River on Pittsburgh's North Side.

Angeles to Pittsburgh without a driver.

Robotics is the result of a partnership between the Science Center, Carnegie Mellon University's Robotics Institute, the National Robotics Engineering Consortium, and industry partners. This unique exhibit provides visitors with a glimpse at the role robots will play in the future, while marking Pittsburgh as an international leader in the field.

The Science Center also highlights Pittsburgh's heritage with the 2,300-square-foot Miniature Railroad Village and The Works Theater, which features a working foundry. Another exciting feature at the Science Center is The Rangos Omnimax Theater, featuring a

four-story, domed screen and a 54-speaker surround-sound system. The Creative Technology Center integrates technology with the classroom, and gives the general public a chance to explore the latest in hardware and software.

Although Carnegie Science Center was opened in 1991, its history can be traced back to the original Buhl Planetarium and Institute for Popular Science, founded in 1939. The Buhl was one of the first planetariums in the country and was at the forefront of entertaining, educational technology. Today, the Science Center continues this ambitious tradition with the state-of-the-art Henry Buhl, Jr. Planetarium & Observatory. Carnegie Science Center productions, including Journey into the Living Cell, a unique interactive biology show using Digistar technology, have been sold to planetariums worldwide.

Carnegie Science Center is one of the Carnegie Museums of Pittsburgh, and is a dynamic facility that continues to grow to meet the needs of the region and provides leadership in both formal and informal science education. "People who visit have fun," says Bennington. "The bonus is that they also learn and become prepared to be active participants in today's increasingly technological world."

Visitors to the *SciQuest* exhibit can touch a tornado (left).

Volunteer Joe Bosco explores cryogenics with a young visitor (right).

RELOCATION TO THE GREATER PITTSBURGH REGION IS AN unexpected pleasure. The hills and valleys are cloaked with clean air. The region's cultural activities, endowed by the wealth of a manufacturing past, now support the education and entertainment of a high-technology future. The intrinsic

values of the population have been built upon a heritage of hard work and neighborliness. Newcomers are welcomed, and enjoy an excellent quality of life.

Getting to the Point, Inc., a premier independent relocation consulting firm, provides services that enhance the newcomer's relocation experience. Getting to the Point, Inc. assists major corporations and new high-technology companies in the Pittsburgh area in recruiting and relocating their senior personnel. The services provided by the company are tailored to meet the unique needs of each individual and family. "We show each candidate that the life he or she wants to lead is available in Pittsburgh," says Ellen A. Roth, Ph.D., president. "This approach, combined with a desirable job offer, proves to be effective in bringing the best talent to our area."

FOCUS ON THE TRAILING SPOUSE

Getting to the Point is a powerful recruiting partner, both for the hiring corporation and for fami-

lies relocating to the region. The firm's special strength is addressing the needs of the potential recruit's "trailing spouse," who most often is a woman. By making the spouse feel comfortable with a move, Getting to the Point increases the probability that the family will relocate. In fact, it was the focus on the trailing spouse that was the basis for the business when Roth and coprincipal Jacqui Fiske Lazo, Esq., founded it in 1991. "We wanted to provide a service for other women that was not available to us when we moved here," says Lazo.

To that end, the company offers career assistance for spouses who wish to work, which is often a very important incentive for families considering relocation. Getting to the Point's consultants also stay in touch with each family for six months after relocation, in order to facilitate a smooth transition.

FEELING AT HOME

Getting to the Point's additional major services include customized, in-depth tours of Pittsburgh, sur-

rounding suburbs, and the region. It also provides clients with information about the region's schools, networking introductions, and emotional support. Upon request, the firm also furnishes a choice of referrals for specialized services ranging from doctors and hair stylists to veterinarians and health clubs.

Among the most appreciated services offered by Getting to the Point is a comprehensive orientation tour of the city and surrounding areas. This tour provides objective, baseline information on neighborhoods, while also telling the story of Pittsburgh's economic transformation from a smoky steel town to one that is driven by education, health care, and high technology. The introduction tour gives potential newcomers an overview of the region's growth and development.

In addition to families, companies exploring the Greater Pittsburgh region as a potential site for establishing their businesses have also found Getting to the Point, Inc. to be helpful in learning about the area and its competitive advantages.

The former Jones & Laughlin Steel Mill (right) is now the site of the University of Pittsburgh Center for Biotechnology and Bioengineering (left). Ellen A. Roth, Ph.D., president of Getting to the Point, Inc., with Jacqui Fiske Lazo, cofounder, explains Pittsburgh's economic transformation to newcomers James C. Diggs, senior vice president and general counsel of PPG Industries, Inc., and Philip Lebowitz, M.D., chief anesthesiologist of UPMC Health System/ Presbyterian University Hospital.

STARTING A BRAND-NEW STEEL COMPANY FROM SCRATCH, EVEN in 1900, required more than just the enormous amount of faith in people and vision that George Verity brought to the beginnings of his business. To compete with big, established steel companies called for an entirely new

approach, and Verity selected specialty steels as the focus of his venture, which has evolved into the modern Armco® Inc.

Formed in Middletown, Ohio, Armco has operated a plant in Butler, Pennsylvania, since 1927. In December 1993, the company moved its headquarters from Parsippany, New Jersey, to Pittsburgh, which is now home to 100 of its 6,000 employees nationwide.

Well known as a center of specialty steelmaking, Pittsburgh makes an ideal site for Armco headquarters. The Steel City is not only located near Armco's customer base,

it is close to the steelmaker's largest specialty mills, including the world-class Butler facility.

A Company of Firsts

From the beginning, Armco has been driven by research and development efforts derived directly from customer needs and goals; one of the company's early moves was to institute the first research center in the American steel industry in 1910. Impressive results included developing the first electrical steels made specifically for magnetic applications like generators, motors, and transformers. Today,

Armco is the only full-line producer of electrical steels, and uses the same forward-looking approach in the development of electrical steels for tomorrow's applications, including electric cars and high-frequency motors.

Armco has also been a company of firsts in workplace management. It was Armco that bought the first steel industry group life insurance policy for employees in 1918, and several years later instigated the eight-hour workday.

From the earliest years, Armco inventions and product developments, including Ingot iron, continu-

An early Armco innovation replaced the hand rolling of steel sheets shown below. The development of continuous rolling of steel cut sheet costs in half, and made possible the mass production of consumer goods fabricated from steel.

The Power of

ous rolling of steel, PH® stainless steels, and Nitronic® steels, have been introduced to the marketplace on a regular basis. In all, the company holds nearly 600 patents in the area of specialty steels technology.

Such customer-driven technical advances continue as the hallmark of Armco operations. Recent years have seen the company divest most of its ancillary businesses, generating operating cash to be invested in the core business of technology-oriented specialty steels.

Facility upgrades have given Armco two of the most formidable and flexible specialty steel melt shops in the world. Ongoing modernization allows the plants to produce an impressive mix of stainless and electrical products geared to the demands of the market. As a result, Armco holds a significant market share of flat-rolled specialty steels, and is the largest tonnage producer of specialty steels in the country.

Armco uses a quality management process in the production of specialty steels that has earned ISO 9002 certification, recognized worldwide as the quality designation earned only by organizations dedicated to continuous improvement. Keeping such certification means steel producers must undergo a semiannual, on-site audit of the process by an independent registrar. This reassures customers that Armco is committed to attaining the highest levels of quality and delivery performance of its specialty steel products.

SPECIALTY STEELS

Stainless steel offers a number of advantages over other steel products, as well as products made from aluminum or plastic. For example, stainless steel provides an extremely high strength-to-weight ratio, and is naturally corrosion resistant in even the fiercest environments. It is readily formable, castable, and weldable by well-established methods.

Such advantages make it easy to see why Armco stainless is used in everything from aerospace parts

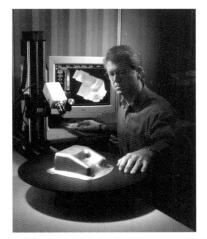

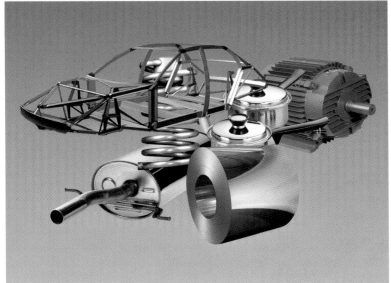

to automobile air bags to specialty cutlery to dishwashers and even the kitchen sink. Stainless steels used in automotive exhausts comprise the largest part of Armco's business: The majority of all American cars and light trucks produced since 1996 contain Armco stainless steel in their exhaust systems.

Coupled with Armco development of steel chemistries and grades, the decision to make exhaust components from stainless steels has resulted in exhaust systems with increased corrosion resistance and improved durability. Today's stainless steel exhaust systems are designed to meet service life mandates of eight years or 80,000 miles.

Looking ahead, Armco is moving to meet the increasing demand for stainless steel in functional applications, such as fuel systems, safety systems, hose clamps, windshield wipers, bumpers, and more. The company is also working with

an engineering design firm to develop a stainless steel modular automotive frame for the car of tomorrow. This frame affords a new look at the advantages of stainless steel in functional applications. The lightweight stainless frame is evidence of Armco's focus on increasing awareness of stainless steel's strength-to-weight ratio, as well as the advantages to be had from designing with stainless. The stainless steel automotive frame represents a new approach to traditional applications that could prove very beneficial to manufacturers and consumers alike.

A major player in the specialty steel industry for most of this century, Armco's philosophy of developing and implementing new technologies and new products to meet customer demand has the company well positioned for continued success.

W ITH KEEN MARKET AWARENESS AND A LEGACY of innovation, Fiserv Pittsburgh is leading financial institutions safely through the explosion of technological and behavioral changes influencing the financial services industry today.

The financial services industry is experiencing rapid change. Consumer demand for access to financial services is the driving force behind the deployment of new technologies that provide convenient banking services. To survive and remain competitive, financial institutions must deliver new products and services quickly, through new delivery channels. Many turn to Fiserv Pittsburgh for the technology they need to get ahead today, and to stay ahead tomorrow.

RECENT PITTSBURGH ARRIVAL, LONG PITTSBURGH HISTORY

Fiserv Pittsburgh helps financial institutions provide attractive products, develop convenient channels, and operate more efficiently.

Occupying offices since 1993 in a contemporary building on the edge of the Allegheny River, Fiserv Pittsburgh now employs more than 600 highly skilled banking analysts, systems engineers, and technology experts who focus on the data processing and information management needs of large commercial banks. Fiserv Pittsburgh is a business unit of Milwaukee-based Fiserv, the country's leading provider of systems and services to banks, credit unions, savings

JEFF COMELLA

institutions, regional banks, and mortgage companies. Fiserv serves more than 5,000 financial institutions worldwide.

How can a relatively recent Pittsburgh arrival claim a 35-year history in the city? Fiserv Pittsburgh was established in 1993 when Fiserv acquired an established Pittsburgh organization that had been providing financial data processing services for more than 30 years. Since then, Fiserv Pittsburgh has expanded staff, products, and its customer base, contributing significantly to Fiserv's double-digit growth through the 1990s.

SPOTLIGHT ON INFORMATION TECHNOLOGY

The secret of Fiserv's success lies in the wide range of technology-based products and services that it offers. From back-office automation and call centers to Internet-based financial services, Fiserv provides a variety of leading-edge information technologies designed specifically to help financial institutions keep pace with the demands of their markets.

The country's most innovative mid- to large-size financial institutions turn to Fiserv Pittsburgh to help them deliver a diverse set of retail and commercial services. By outsourcing account processing to Fiserv, these institutions offer more sophisticated account features and financial services than they could if they were running their own data processing operations. Through the shared use of the Fiserv accounting systems, banks eliminate the hardware, operating systems, and application software normally required to process and account for thousands of daily customer transactions. With Fiserv systems, banks streamline operations, increase efficiency, and free their personnel to focus on service, sales, and the business of banking.

INNOVATION SETS THE COMPANY APART

In addition to account processing, Fiserv provides powerful, integrated technologies that arm a financial institution with the information and tools needed to ensure positive customer interaction.

JEFF COMELLA

Fiserv Pittsburgh occupies a contemporary facility on the edge of the Allegheny River.

Fiserv InformEnt®, a complete data warehouse solution developed specifically for the financial services industry, collects and transforms data from diverse systems into a single source for comprehensive, timely, accurate, and easy-to-use information on customers, products, and services. InformEnt consolidates a financial institution's raw data at various levels to deliver management information needed to understand customer behavior, improve marketing effectiveness, and produce accurate and timely financial and regulatory reports. With demand for consolidated information increasing here and abroad, Fiserv Pittsburgh has expanded its markets for InformEnt in Canada, the United Kingdom, Western Europe, and South America.

The Fiserv Customer Service and Call-center Solution (CSCS®) takes advantage of computer/telephony integration and knowledge base automation to help financial institutions create and foster customer-focused sales and service cultures. CSCS brings information and technology together at the workstation to help bank agents provide personalized service and target cross-sale opportunities quickly and accurately.

The Fiserv Account Sales and Teller System (FAST) is a set of interactive tools that allow bank representatives to tailor sales efforts based on customer needs and profiles. FAST speeds the processing of new accounts and helps ensure peak performance on the teller line.

The Fiserv line of client/server-based Backroom Systems' products is designed to identify untapped revenue sources and dra-matically streamline back-office operations such as correcting erroneous transactions and returning checks. The systems help banks maximize productivity by eliminating keystrokes, and reducing the time and labor normally required to respond to customer inquiries.

A GLOBAL PARTNER WITH A LOCAL FOCUS

Fiserv is dedicated to developing dynamic, long-term strategic partnerships with financial institutions around the world. With a proven track record of putting its clients' interests first and delivering powerful solutions, Fiserv rates among the highest in the industry for client retention and new sales. Fiserv Pittsburgh is an ISO 9001-certified company, using established processes for the consistent delivery of high-quality products and services that address client needs.

Augmenting a substantial range of products and services is Fiserv's most important resource: its people. Knowledgeable individuals develop close working relationships with each client that help them anticipate and respond to new opportunities and changes affecting the financial services industry. These relationships, based on performance and the mutual goal of service quality, make Fiserv the partner of choice for financial institutions worldwide.

"These are exciting times to be in the financial services industry," says James C. Puzniak, president of the Fiserv Pittsburgh business unit. "When the changing market demands advanced products and services, the prospects for forward-thinking providers are quite exciting. Fiserv is positioned to address rapid changes in consumer behavior with technologies our customers need to remain competitive in the financial services arena."

▶ JEFF COMELLA

▲▼ JEFF COMELLA

Clockwise from top: Fiserv Pittsburgh's president, James C. Puzniak

Fiserv Pittsburgh's highly skilled banking analysts, systems engineers, and technology experts work together to develop effective information technologies.

As part of the company's commitment to effective partnerships, Fiserv Pittsburgh associates regularly review client needs.

ORE THAN 40 PERCENT OF THE NATION'S VITAL FREIGHT— products ranging from coal and food to chemicals and vehicles—moves along America's rail system. In fact, through the mid-1990s, the amount of freight carried by rail increased annually by 4.1 percent. As America's

manufacturers have increased their usage of railroads for transporting goods, the demand also has increased for locomotives that can pull the freight. To help meet the challenges of this increased demand, Pittsburgh-based Motive-Power Industries, Inc. manufactures and distributes locomotive components, provides locomotive fleet maintenance and overhauls, and manufactures midrange locomotives with engines having up to 4,000 horsepower.

MotivePower Industries services every Class 1 railroad in the United States, including Burlington Northern Santa Fe,

Union Pacific, and CSX, and is making substantial inroads with regional railroads and short lines. The company's stock is traded publicly on the New York Stock Exchange under the symbol MPO. Headquartered in Pittsburgh, MotivePower Industries employs more than 2,100 people in the United States and Mexico. Its products and services supply the power that pulls tons of freight every day.

SIX COMPANIES AS ONE
MotivePower Industries consists of six companies, all of which are leading suppliers in the railroad industry. Boise Locomotive Co. manufactures custom-designed, low- and midrange horsepower locomotives that are used for commuter trains and switching yard service. The company also rebuilds locomotives and provides fleet maintenance for railroads all over the United States.

Since MotivePower Industries is a vertically integrated company, Boise has access to the competitively priced locomotive parts supplied by other MotivePower

Industries companies that produce these parts. One is Power Parts Company, one of the nation's most comprehensive distributors of locomotive and railcar parts, from power assemblies to brake rigging to sanitation and waste retention systems. Power Parts supplies parts for Class 1, regional, and short line railroads throughout North America and 25 countries around the world. The company's "fire wagon service" reputation stems from its ability to deliver a variety of needed parts at competitive prices, within 48 hours.

Pittsburgh-based Motor Coils Manufacturing Co. is the primary supplier of traction motors and related components to virtually every railroad and independent repairer and rebuilder of locomotives in the United States. The company's popular unit exchange program delivers a completely remanufactured motor in exchange for a failed unit.

Another MotivePower Industries company, MPI de Mexico, is Mexico's leading overhauler and remanufacturer of locomotives. Railroads in Mexico also outsource

MotivePower Industries' Boise Locomotive subsidiary builds new, high-technology switcher locomotives (left).

In Pittsburgh, the Motor Coils Manufacturing subsidiary rebuilds traction motors and ships them around the world to countries such as Egypt and Australia (right).

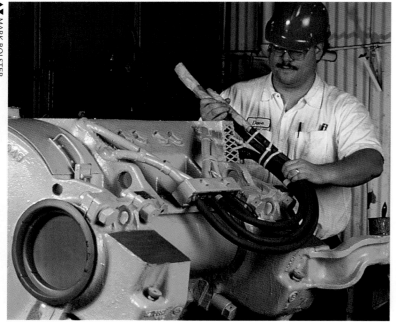

MARK BOLSTER

The Power of

fleet maintenance duties to this company, which helps Motive-Power Industries reach markets in Mexico and Central and South America.

Engine Systems Co. concentrates on manufacturing and rebuilding turbochargers that drive engines used not only in railroads, but also on ships and in manufacturing facilities around the world.

Touchstone Company is the nation's leading producer of radiators, proprietary oil coolers, and custom heat transfer systems for Class I, regional, and short line railroads. The company's products also reach into nonrail markets, including off-road construction and marine. Touchstone's strengths lie in its deep technical acumen, its advanced production facilities, and its experienced engineering and workforce.

Once known as MK Rail, the company took the name Motive-Power Industries in 1997, which was a key year for the firm. It was the first full year of operation for MotivePower Industries' new management team that included Chair-

man John C. "Jack" Pope, the former president of United Airlines, and Michael A. Wolf, president and chief executive officer, who had previously served as CEO of Pandrol Jackson Inc. The year also saw MotivePower Industries post record net income of $20 million on sales of $306 million, after the company slashed debt from $128 million to $50 million during the prior year. The company decentralized several corporate functions, unleashing the earning power of its subsidiaries by returning performance responsibility to each of them.

In the Future

The railroad industry continues to be on an upswing. In recent years, the U.S. rail industry has recaptured traffic once lost to trucks and barges. Internationally, MotivePower Industries has targeted at least 15 countries that have large fleets of U.S.-made locomotives. In 1996, it won a contract to provide $4 million worth of traction motors and related components to railroads in Egypt. The company later won orders in China,

Venezuela, and Croatia. By 1997, MotivePower Industries had signed a Pacific Rim distribution agreement with ANI Railway Transportation Group, the leading rail freight company in Australia. ANI is purchasing components from MotivePower Industries that it will distribute to customers in Australia, New Zealand, Malaysia, Indonesia, and Thailand, where more than 3,000 locomotives operate.

MotivePower Industries' business strategy for the future is to continue growing its core businesses through the millennium. "Throughout North America, railroads have an immediate need for additional locomotive power due to high demand and congestion in the system," says Wolf. "Their need for more reliable and available power continues to translate into higher overall demand for our products and services. At the same time that we are meeting those short-term needs, we are continuing to make excellent progress on strategic initiatives that are positioning the company for sustained, long-term growth and profitability."

MotivePower Industries' employee-associates ensure that the company maintains precision and quality at every step of the manufacturing process (left).

Rebuilding locomotive engines has been one of the company's core competencies for more than two decades (right).

**ERIAL COMMUNICATIONS, INC. IS A YOUNG HIGH-TECH COMPANY** with regional headquarters for the Pittsburgh and Columbus areas in Pittsburgh. Aerial entered the Pittsburgh market just as the region's economy was moving away from being the manufacturing powerhouse of decades ago, and into the

leadership position it currently holds in today's global information society.

Aerial Communications is a majority-owned subsidiary of Telephone and Data Systems, Inc., a multibillion-dollar telecommunications firm based in Chicago. As part of an aggressive nationwide rollout for Aerial that included markets in Columbus, Minneapolis, Kansas City, Tampa, and Houston, the company began offering wireless telecommunications services to Pittsburgh in June 1997. During its first 38 days of the rollout, Aerial added 28,000 customers—an average of 730 customers per day. Today, the client list continues to grow.

Aerial provides personal communications services (PCS)—a new telecommunications service that transmits information at a higher frequency than cellular—in regions covering 27.6 million people. PCS is 100 percent digital, which means clearer signals and static-free conversation. PCS technology is especially important in Pittsburgh, where it can service the difficult terrain, with its many hills and tunnels. Digital also means no cross talking, no number cloning, and the ability to encrypt transmission so it is absolutely secure. PCS has the ability to provide paging, text messaging, caller ID, conference calls, enhanced fax, and even E-mail, all on one phone without needing a land line. It's a communications service that can create the virtual office.

WIRELESS EVOLUTION AND AERIAL

Competition was the idea behind the creation of the new wireless standard, as well as the ability to support more customers with a greater offering of services. Demand for wireless services is expected to more than double in the next 10 years—reaching nearly 105 million subscribers worldwide—thus creating a burden the current cellular analog technology could not hope to accommodate.

Aerial CEO Don Warkentin is no stranger to the telecommunications industry. In addition to serving as vice president of US WEST's Multimedia Marketing, Warkentin also directed the marketing efforts of the United Kingdom's One-2-One, the first commercial PCS network in the world. Warkentin brings unique expertise and experience to his role at Aerial, leading the company's effort to create one of the nation's largest wireless networks.

Believing that there are tremendous opportunities for growth in the communications marketplace,

Aerial Communications, Inc. provides personal communications services (PCS)—a new telecommunications service that transmits information at a higher frequency than cellular—in regions covering 27.6 million people.

Aerial's focus is to provide what the customer needs and wants by offering certain advantages over other wireless providers. For instance, Aerial uses the Global Systems for Mobile Communications (GSM) standard, which has been used by more than 50 million subscribers in more than 100 countries around the world since 1992.

The GSM Alliance, created in August 1997, brings together the seven leading GSM PCS carriers to form the world's first PCS network throughout the United States and Canada. The agreement will integrate networks and streamline international roaming agreements, as well as offer opportunities to improve retail distribution and pool certain purchasing. This alliance promises to make GSM the strongest communications solution yet for business customers.

Warkentin, who serves as chairman of the GSM Alliance, says, "GSM Alliance members and affiliates will benefit by gaining the ability to offer stronger product propositions, better serve national customers, strengthen their product distribution networks, and achieve economies of scale."

Customers of Alliance companies will now enjoy the same PCS services throughout North America as they do at home. Warkentin and the Alliance are also working to expand the agreement worldwide in the near future.

Adds Warkentin, "The GSM Alliance is providing the best wireless solution for customers, more so than any other U.S. or Canadian competitor. The GSM Alliance will remove the fear factor from using wireless services when roaming. Customers will have no more personal identification numbers or unknown roaming rates. And with GSM's multilevel security, cloning is a nonissue."

Other advantages Aerial provides include the Smart Card, a unique chip that stores a customer's calling plan information and old phone numbers. In the near future, removable Smart Cards will allow use of different phones, as the chip can be placed in any GSM unit and can carry all of a customer's phone numbers and billing information. Aerial focuses on customer needs with services such as the Aerial Value Check^{SM}, which provides an assessment that indicates if a customer could be saving more

money by using a different calling plan.

Perhaps the greatest differences between Aerial and its competitors are noticed by customers when they receive their monthly bills. Aerial is the only company that offers true per-second billing rather than rounding up to the next minute. The company never charges an activation fee and doesn't require long-term contracts.

Aerial works to keep its customers' business month after month and strives to make life easier for each customer. By doing so, Aerial will continue to be a preferred service provider for wireless communications into the new millennium.

PCS is 100 percent digital, which means clearer signals and static-free conversation. Digital also means no cross talking, no number cloning, and the ability to encrypt transmission so it is absolutely secure.

Aerial established its regional headquarters for Pittsburgh and Columbus in Pittsburgh in 1997.

THE ANDY WARHOL MUSEUM RECOUNTS THE STORY OF modern America, as seen from the perspective of one of the most celebrated personalities and artists of our time. "His work is a template through which we can see contemporary life," says Museum Director Thomas Sokolowski.

"Warhol chronicled the modern age with reverence and a wry wit that lets you see both the good side and bad side of life."

The Andy Warhol Museum, which opened its doors in 1994, is located on Pittsburgh's North Side, only a few miles from where the artist was born Andrew Warhola in 1928. After graduating from Carnegie Tech, now Carnegie Mellon University, Warhol moved to New York City, where, dropping an *a* from his last name, he amassed a following that still lines up today to view his art, films, published writings, and personal effects.

The seven levels of The Andy Warhol Museum house more than 900 paintings, 77 sculptures, 1,500 drawings, and 400 black-and-white photographs, and an on-going film program featuring daily screenings of Warhol's large film and video output. The Archives Study Center on the third floor contains a variety of materials relating to Warhol's life and times. A voracious collector, Warhol began packing thousands of items—among them personal effects, souvenirs, clothing, correspondence, recordings, films, and source material for his art—into cardboard boxes in 1974. Today, these Time Capsules, as he called them, provide an intimate look into four decades of his personality.

The museum also features The Warhol Café, and a plethora of books and Warhol-related items in the Museum Store. The Mellon Bank Education Resource Center is located on the museum's underground floor, where the ongoing education programs and weekly hands-on art activities such as the Weekend Factory are based. The museum has a lively series of changing exhibitions devoted to work by Warhol and other artists.

The Andy Warhol Museum is one of the four Carnegie Museums of Pittsburgh, and is a collaborative project of the Carnegie Institute, the Dia Center for the Arts, and the Andy Warhol Foundation for Visual Arts, Inc. A favorite for after-hours functions hosted by businesses and nonprofit organizations, the Entrance Gallery in the museum is also a top meeting place for Pittsburghers, and is free to the public during museum hours.

The museum's collection of Warhol's work spans four decades. In the 1950s his work mostly consisted of illustrations and sketchbooks, but by the mid-1960s, Warhol was lauded for his trademark pop culture paintings, such as the Campbell's soup cans, and of celebrities, such as Elvis Presley and Marilyn Monroe. During the 1970s, Warhol produced portraits, many on commission, including his famous work of Chinese leader Mao Tse-tung. In the years just prior to his death in 1987, Warhol produced some of his finest works, including *The Last Supper*.

"The museum is the largest repository of art from a single artist in the world, and includes not only Warhol's fine art works, but also personal material," says Sokolowski. "As a result, it is as much a library as it is a museum." The museum's vast collection of personal archives makes it one of the primary resources for the study of the Pop Art movement, as well as being the definitive source of research material and information on Andy Warhol and his work.

The Entrance Gallery in The Andy Warhol Museum is a top meeting place for Pittsburghers, and is free to the public during museum hours (left).

Visitors enjoy the Portraits Gallery, which houses only a sampling of the museum's collection of more than 900 paintings, 77 sculptures, 1,500 drawings, and 400 black-and-white photographs (right).

John Beale, a Pittsburgh photojournalist, has received more than 100 awards for his work. In 1997, he was named the National Press Photographers Association's Region 3 Photographer of the Year, and the News Photographers Association of Greater Pittsburgh has named him Photographer of the Year four times.

Greg Blackman, originally from western New York, is a freelance photographer and a partner of Blackman and Bell Architectural and Industrial Photography. A former student at Allegheny College and the Brooks Institute of Photography in Santa Barbara, Blackman has taught photography classes at the Art Institute of Pittsburgh, Point Park College, and La Roche College. In addition, he has worked with such companies as Alcoa, JCPenney, Bayer, Pittsburgh Public Theater, Servistart, American Federation of Teachers, St. Clair Hospital, and Carlow College, and his images have appeared in trade journals, corporate publications, newspapers, and magazines.

Roger A. Bonifield, a native of Columbus, Ohio, specializes in corporate and industrial photography. A graduate of Ohio University, he works out of his Pittsburgh studio—R.A. Bonifield, Photography—and enjoys outdoor, animal, and people photography.

Herb Ferguson, who hails from the Pittsburgh area, studied photography at the Rochester Institute of Technology and received a master of education from the University of Pittsburgh. In addition to attending many photography workshops and seminars, he taught motion picture production and still photography for 10 years. Currently the owner/president of Ferguson Photographic Enterprises, which specializes in commercial and industrial photography, he enjoys architectural, travel, nature, and wildlife photography. Among Ferguson's clients are Alcoa, Mellon Bank, United Way, University of Pittsburgh, and USX. Ferguson also has illustrated children's books, scientific publications, and numerous brochures.

Denis J. Helms, a collector and restorer of antique cameras, enjoys taking pictures of the countryside at dawn. Currently living in Monaca, Pennsylvania, he works for Denis Helms Photography and Sukolsky-Brunelle Photographics. Helms specializes in night shots, portraits, and wildlife.

The Image Finders, founded by Jim Baron in 1986, is a stock photography company located in Cleveland, Ohio. Its files cover a broad range of subjects, including agriculture, animals, butterflies, families, food, sports, travel, transportation, trees, and western states.

John D. Ivanko, an award-winning photographer and writer, resides in Browntown, Wisconsin, on a turn-of-the-century organic-farm-turned-bed-and-breakfast. Ivanko's images have been published in *Fodor's* guidebooks, *Wisconsin Trails*, and Delta Air Lines' *Sky* magazine. His work is also featured in *Children from Australia to Zimbabwe: A Photographic Journey around the World*, a book sponsored by SHAKTI for Children, a nonprofit group dedicated to helping develop children's understanding of and respect for the diversity of cultures. Ivanko's clients include United Parcel Service, Red Wing Shoe Company, Wilderness Travel, and Johnnie Walker brands from Schieffelin & Somerset. He is represented by the 11th Hour Stock Photography Agency in Chicago.

Richard D. Kelly, a native of Beaver Falls, Pennsylvania, is a Pittsburgh- and New York City-based photographer. Having taken pictures since he was 12, Kelly has shot portraits of many Pittsburgh and national celebrities. Most recently, his work has been published in *Swing Magazine*, *USA Weekend*, *Mirabella*, *Parenting*, and *Pittsburgh Magazine*.

Carol Kitman worked as staff psychologist for five years at the Smithers Alcoholism Rehabilitation Unit of St. Luke's/Roosevelt Hospital in New York City. She still considers herself an observer but in another mode: Her psychological training has made insightful portraits a specialty, and she has worked for many hospitals and health care services. A native of New York City, Kitman received a bachelor of arts from Brooklyn College and a master's degree from City College of New York. Recently, her work has been featured in *Sky*, *Mature Outlook*, *Odyssey*, and *Travel & Leisure* magazines, as well as in Towery Publishing's *New Orleans: Rollin' on the River*.

Dan Levine, a contract photographer, received a bachelor of fine arts in visual communication from Ohio University. A former staff photographer for the *Dallas Times Herald* and the *National Sports Daily*, Levine currently specializes in editorial and location photography, and resides in his home state of Washington with his wife and their two children, Meredith and Ethan.

Joel B. Levinson, a lifelong resident of Pittsburgh, specializes in capturing his hometown on film and paper. His stock photography is used by many local and national companies, including Microsoft, Coors, and Lenzner Transportation. Currently working at J.B. Jeffers Ltd., he has served as editor of *Carnegie Technical*, published a photography book, and written two novels. Married for more than 40 years, Levinson has four sons and four grandchildren.

Edward R. Massery is a native of the Pittsburgh area who graduated from Penn State University with a bachelor of science in mechanical engineering. Now self-employed at Massery Photography, he specializes in architecture, interior, landscape, and aviation photography. Massery has also published two books, *The Art and Architecture of St. Bernard Church* and *The Architecture of Benno Janssen*.

Joanna Michaelides, a first-generation American of Cypriot descent, is a self-taught photographer who specializes in fashion photography. Her clients include Paul Mitchell Systems, the University of

Pittsburgh, Carlow College, and Little Earth Productions. Michaelides was named one of *Pittsburgh Magazine*'s 50 Finest in 1997, and she was a Pittsburgh Cultural Trust nominee for the Emerging Artist Grant the same year.

Venetia L. Palm, a photo editor for the *New Pittsburgh Courier*, also maintains her own

photography business. Specializing in black-and-white photography, environmental portraiture, and photojournalism, Palm's work has been exhibited at the University of Pittsburgh. Among her clients are Exxon, Minority Enterprise Corp., Healthy Starts, Columbia Gas, Intersound Records, and Olivetree Gift Shop.

Photophile, established in San Diego in 1967, has more than 1 million color images on file culled from more than 85 contributing local and international photographers. Subjects range from images of Southern California to adventure sports, wildlife/underwater scenes, business, industry, people, science and research, health and medicine, and travel. Included

on Photophile's client list are American Express, *Guest Informant*, Franklin Stoorza, and Princess Cruises.

Jonathan Postal, born in New York City, lived and worked in London, Sydney, Milan, and New Orleans before settling in Memphis. The creative director of *Eye* magazine, his work has

been featured in *Rolling Stone*, *Vanity Fair*, and numerous other publications. Postal's images have appeared in many of Towery Publishing's books, including *Memphis: New Visions, New Horizons*; *Minneapolis-St. Paul: Linked to the Future*; *New Orleans: Rollin' on the River*; *Nashville: City of Note*; *The Image Is Rochester*; and *Toronto Tapestry*.

TOM BELL

Robert P. Ruschak, a member of the Associated Artists of Pittsburgh and president of the Photoimagers Guild, graduated from Point Park College with a bachelor's degree in photography. Self-employed, he specializes in architectural and editorial photography, public relations, and annual reports. His work

The Power of

was recently published in *Fallingwater: Frank Lloyd Wright's Romance with Nature* and *Designing for Alzheimer's Disease*. Among Ruschak's clients are Perkins Eastman Architects, Miller Melone, Duquesne University, and Slippery Rock University.

John Sanderson is a self-employed photographer based in

of corporate and architectural clients, and his work has appeared in *Pittsburgh Magazine, Field & Stream, Scientific American, Today's Homeowner, Woman's Day, Architecture,* and *Architectural Record*. He has two books to his credit, *The Allegheny River* and *Lehigh Reflections,* and his aerial photos appear in *Over America: 30 Photographers View America from Above.*

tagging black bears and helping to open up several newly discovered caverns.

Ron Volpe is an avid backpacker and hiker whose love of the outdoors has led him to a career in nature photography. Originally from Beaver County, Pennsylvania, Volpe hiked the entire Appalachian Trail, from Maine to Georgia,

John Wee studied photography and biology at Central Michigan University. After graduating, he worked for the U.S. Forest Service and as a medical photographer, earning his Registered Biological Photography board certification. Moving to Pittsburgh in 1982, Wee taught evening classes at the Art Institute of Pittsburgh while building his commercial photography business. His assignments have included photographing people, industry, technology, and architecture around the world, as well as creating a wide range of adventure and travel stock images. Wee's photographs are used in corporate brochures, magazines, annual reports, and advertising.

Jack A. Wolf received a bachelor's degree from the School of Journalism at West Virginia University. A native Pittsburgher, he is self-employed at Wolf Photography and specializes in editorial photography.

▶ HERB FERGUSON

Other photographers and organizations that contributed to *The Power of Pittsburgh* include Blackman and Bell Architectural and Industrial Photography, Aubrey Gibson, Mark Gibson, Dave Grib, the Historical Society of Western Pennsylvania, Roger Holden, Image Finders, mayor's office, William B. McCullough, the *New Pittsburgh Courier*, the Pittsburgh Pirates, Pittsburghscape, the River City Brass Band, WTAE TV/Radio, and Drew Yenchak.

Pittsburgh. A graduate of the Art Institute of Pittsburgh, he owns and operates John Sanderson Photography Inc.

Jim Schafer, a freelance commercial photographer, specializes in editorial, architectural, and corporate/industrial work. His assignments cover a variety

Tony Tye, originally from the United Kingdom, moved to the Pittsburgh area more than 20 years ago. Employed by the *Pittsburgh Post-Gazette*, Tye enjoys all types of photography and has received numerous awards for his work, including the Golden Quill. His most memorable experiences include

in 1978. In addition, in one 12-month period, he hiked the Grand Canyon, Yellowstone National Park, and Glacier National Park. Currently, Volpe is an interim teacher with Davidson County School District and operates a small business, marketing his photographs to corporate clients.